Get the eBook FREE!
(PDF, ePub, Kindle, and liveBook all included)

We believe that once you buy a book from us, you should be able to read it in any format we have available. To get electronic versions of this book at no additional cost to you, purchase and then register this book at the Manning website.

Go to https://www.manning.com/freebook and follow the instructions to complete your pBook registration.

That's it!
Thanks from Manning!

Spring Start Here

LEARN WHAT YOU NEED AND LEARN IT WELL

LAURENŢIU SPILCĂ

FOREWORD BY VICTOR RENTEA

MANNING

SHELTER ISLAND

For online information and ordering of this and other Manning books, please visit
www.manning.com. The publisher offers discounts on this book when ordered in quantity.
For more information, please contact

> Special Sales Department
> Manning Publications Co.
> 20 Baldwin Road
> PO Box 761
> Shelter Island, NY 11964
> Email: orders@manning.com

Manning Publications Co.
20 Baldwin Road
PO Box 761
Shelter Island, NY 11964

Development editor:	Marina Michaels
Technical development editor:	Al Scherer
Review editor:	Mihaela Batinić
Production editor:	Andy Marinkovich
Copy editor:	Michele Mitchell
Proofreader:	Keri Hales
Technical proofreader:	Jean-François Morin
Typesetter:	Gordan Salinovic
Cover designer:	Marija Tudor

ISBN 9781617298691

Printed in the United States of America

brief contents

contents

foreword

Born as an alternative to EJBs in the early 2000s, the Spring framework quickly overtook its opponent with the simplicity of its programming model, the variety of its features, and its third-party library integrations. The Spring ecosystem grew over the years into the broadest and most mature development framework available in any programming language. Its main competitor quit the race when Oracle stopped the evolution of Java EE 8, and the community took over its maintenance via Jakarta EE.

According to recent surveys (http://mng.bz/l9VB and http://mng.bz/B1Ar), Spring is the framework underlying more than half of the Java applications. This fact builds up an enormous codebase that makes it critical for any Java developer to learn Spring, as it's inevitable you'll encounter this technology in your career. I've been developing applications with Spring for 15 years, and today the teams that I train in hundreds of companies are almost all using Spring.

The reality is that despite being so popular, it's pretty hard to find quality introductory material. The reference documentation is thousands of pages long, describing all the subtleties and details that could be helpful in very specific scenarios, so it's not an option for a newcomer. While online videos and tutorials typically fail to engage the student, very few books capture the essence of Spring framework, often spending long pages debating topics that prove to be irrelevant to the problems faced in modern application development. With this book, however, it's very hard to find anything to remove; all the concepts covered are recurring topics in the development of any Spring application.

The reader is gently brought to a level sufficient to become rapidly productive in a project based on the Spring framework. My own experience training thousands of employees showed me that the vast majority of developers working with Spring today don't see the ideas as clearly as this book paints them. Furthermore, developers are unaware of the many pitfalls about which this book warns its readers. In my opinion, this book is a must-read for any developer starting on their first Spring project.

The attention with which Laurențiu anticipates the typical questions occurring in the reader's mind proves his extensive experience teaching Spring in class. This teaching fluency allows the author to adopt a personal, warm tone that makes this book an effortless and pleasant read. The book has a clear, sharp structure, and I really loved how complex topics were progressively revealed and explained and reiterated in subsequent chapters.

This book shines in that the reader is also introduced to fundamental concerns regarding a legacy project using the Spring framework. In an ecosystem dominated by Spring Boot, I find it very useful to sneak a peek under the hood. On the other end, the book also gently introduces the reader to last-generation technologies, like Feign clients and even reactive programming.

I wish you a pleasant reading, and never hesitate to get your hands dirty with some code whenever you think things get complicated.

—VICTOR RENTEA

JAVA CHAMPION, TRAINER, AND CONSULTANT

preface

Sharing knowledge and creating learning material is a hobby for me. In addition to being a software developer, I'm also a teacher. As a Java trainer since 2009, I've taught Java to thousands of developers with various levels of experience, from university students to experienced developers in large corporations. In the past few years, I've come to consider Spring a must-learn for beginners. Apps today are no longer implemented with vanilla languages—almost everything relies on frameworks. Since Spring is the most popular application framework in the Java world today, Spring is something a developer needs to learn in their first software development steps.

In teaching Spring to beginners, I've realized that it is still treated as something you learn only when you already have some experience coding. When I started writing *Spring Start Here*, there were already plenty of tutorials, books, and articles on the topic, but my students continued to tell me they found those materials hard to understand. I realized the problem was not that the existing learning material wasn't excellent, but that there was no dedicated study guide for an absolute beginner, so I decided to write a book that doesn't consider Spring something you learn after you have some experience, but instead something you can learn with minimal foundational knowledge.

Technology changes quickly. But it's not only the technology changing. We also need to consider how we can improve the way we teach these technologies. Some years ago, one would start learning the language fundamentals and get employed as a developer without even knowing what a framework is. But today, these things are different. Learning all the details of a language up-front is no longer the way to quickly develop the skills you need to work in a software development team. Now, I recommend developers start with the fundamentals and, once they feel comfortable with the basics, start learning an application framework. Spring is, in my opinion, the best application framework to start learning. Understanding the Spring basics also opens doors to learning other technologies and changes the old, linear learning approach into something that looks more like a tree—and each branch of the tree is a new framework you learn in parallel with others.

I designed *Spring Start Here* to be the book you want to start learning the Spring framework with. This book leads you step-by-step, providing you with all the essential theoretical knowledge, accompanied by examples that practically apply the discussed topics. I hope this book will bring significant value to you, the reader, and help you quickly boost your Spring knowledge and open doors for further learning.

acknowledgments

This book wouldn't be possible without the large number of smart, professional, and friendly people who helped me throughout its development process.

First, a big thank you to my wife, Daniela, who was always there for me, and whose valuable opinions, continuous support, and encouragement were a huge help to me.

I'd also like to express my gratitude and send special thanks to all the colleagues and friends who helped me from the very first table of contents and proposal with their valuable advice.

A big thank you goes to the entire Manning team for their huge help in making this book a reality. I especially want to recognize Marina Michaels, Al Scherer, and Jean-François Morin for always being incredibly supportive and professional. Your advice has brought great value to this book.

I'd like to thank my friend Ioana Gŏz for the drawings she created for the book. She turned my thoughts into the cartoons in the book.

I also want to express my appreciation to all the reviewers who provided such useful feedback at every step. To Alain Lompo, Aleksandr Karpenko, Andrea Carlo Granata, Andrea Paciolla, Andres Damian Sacco, Andrew Oswald, Bobby Lin, Bonnie Malec, Christian Kreutzer-Beck, Daniel Carl, David Lisle Orpen, DeUndre' Rushon, Harinath Kuntamukkala, Håvard Wall, Jérôme Baton, Jim Welch, João Miguel Pires Dias, Lucian Enache, Matt D., Matthew Greene, Mikael Byström, Mladen Knežić, Nathan B.

Crocker, Pierre-Michel Ansel, Rajesh Mohanan, Ricardo Di Pasquale, Sunita Chowdhury, Tan Wee, and Zoheb Ainapore, your input has made this a much better book.

Finally, a special thank you to my friends, Maria Chițu, Andreea Tudose, Florin Ciuculescu, and Daniela Ileana for advising me along the way.

about this book

Since you've opened this book, I assume you're a software developer in the Java ecosystem who found out it's useful to learn Spring. This book teaches you the Spring foundations, assuming you know nothing in the first place about frameworks and, of course, about Spring.

You'll start with what a framework is and then gradually learn the basics of Spring with applied examples. You will not only learn to use the framework's components and capabilities, but you'll also learn the essentials of what happens behind the scenes in these capabilities. Knowing how the framework operates when you use a particular component helps you design better apps, and solve problems faster.

When you finish this book, you'll have learned the following skills, which are highly relevant in implementing apps:

- Configuring and using the Spring context and dependency injection with Spring
- Designing and using aspects
- Implementing web apps
- Implementing data exchange between apps
- Persisting data
- Testing implementations

You'll find this book is valuable for the following:

- Working on an app using Spring for your job
- Succeeding in a technical interview for a Java developer role
- Obtaining your Spring certification

Even if this book's first purpose is not to prepare you for a Spring certification, I consider it a must-read before digging into details a certification exam typically requires.

Who should read this book

This book is for developers who understand basic object-oriented programming and Java concepts and want to learn Spring or refresh their Spring fundamentals knowledge. You do not need to have previous experience with any framework, but you need to understand Java because this is the language we use throughout the book's examples.

Spring is one of the most encountered technologies in Java apps and will most likely be used even more in the future. For a Java developer, this makes Spring a must-know today. Learning what I teach you in this book will help you upskill, provide you with the Spring foundation knowledge and skills you need to successfully pass a Java interview, and work on an app using Spring technologies. The book also opens doors to further study Spring details that are more complex.

How this book is organized: A roadmap

This book is divided into two parts that cover 15 chapters. We'll start our discussion (in the first part of the book) with straightforward examples to show you how to make Spring aware of your application. We'll then build examples that enable you to understand the core of any real-world Spring app. Once we finish with Spring Core basics, we'll discuss Spring Data and Spring Boot basics.

From chapter 2 to the end of this book, you'll find that theoretical aspects are accompanied by projects in which we apply the notions we discuss. I explain the code in these examples snippet by snippet. My recommendation is you build these examples with me while reading. Then, you can compare your result with my solution.

As presented in the following figure, I designed the book's chapters to be read in the given order. In chapters 2 through 5, where we discuss the Spring context, you might find the examples predominantly theoretical. For anyone with little or no experience with Spring, it's essential to start this way. Don't worry! I present the foundations in the easiest possible way, and then our examples and discussions gradually become more sophisticated to reflect real-world, production-ready code.

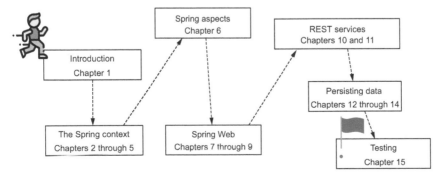

Figure 1   If you start with no (or very little) knowledge about Spring, the best way to read the book is to start with the first chapter and read everything in order.

If you already understand the Spring context and Spring AOP well, you can skip part 1 and go directly to part 2, "Implementation" (chapters 7–15), as presented in the next figure.

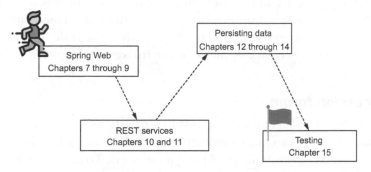

Figure 2 If you already understand the Spring framework's foundation and know how to use the Spring context and design aspects, you can start with part 2, where we use Spring capabilities to implement apps mirroring scenarios you face in real-world systems.

Once you finish reading this book, you'll have learned plenty of skills to develop apps like a professional. You'll learn to connect to databases using the most encountered techniques today, and you'll learn how to make apps communicate with each other. We'll end the book with teaching a critical topic: testing. I'll season the text here and there by adding stories of my experience and notes with valuable pieces of advice.

Remember that Spring is a vast universe, and one book won't teach you everything about it. With this book, you get started with the framework and learn the fundamental skills of using Spring's valuable components. Throughout the book, I refer, where appropriate, to other resources and books that detail the topics we discuss. I strongly recommend you read those additional resources and books to broaden your perspective on the discussed topics.

About the code

The book provides about 70 projects, which we'll work on in chapters 2 through 14. When working on a specific example, I mention the project's name, which implements that example. My recommendation is to try to write your example from scratch and then use the provided project only to compare your solution with mine. This approach will help you better understand the concepts you're learning.

Each of the projects is built with Maven, making it easy to import into any IDE. I used IntelliJ IDEA to write the projects, but you can choose to run them in Eclipse, Netbeans, or any other tool of your choice. Appendix F gives you an overview of the recommended tools.

This book contains many examples of source code, both in numbered listings and in line with normal text. In both cases, source code is formatted in a `fixed-width font like this` to separate it from ordinary text. Sometimes code is also **in bold** to highlight code that has changed from previous steps in the chapter, such as when a new feature adds to an existing line of code. In many cases, the original source code has been reformatted; we've added line breaks and reworked indentation to accommodate the available page space in the book. In rare cases, even this was not enough, and listings include line-continuation markers (➡). Additionally, comments in the source code have often been removed from the listings when the code is described in the text. Code annotations accompany many of the listings, highlighting important concepts.

liveBook discussion forum

Purchase of *Spring Start Here* includes free access to a private web forum run by Manning Publications where you can make comments about the book, ask technical questions, and receive help from the author and from other users. To access the forum, go to https://livebook.manning.com/#!/book/spring-start-here/discussion. You can also learn more about Manning's forums and the rules of conduct at https://livebook.manning.com/#!/discussion.

Manning's commitment to our readers is to provide a venue where a meaningful dialogue between individual readers and between readers and the author can take place. It is not a commitment to any specific amount of participation on the part of the author, whose contribution to the forum remains voluntary (and unpaid). We suggest you try asking the author some challenging questions lest his interest stray! The forum and the archives of previous discussions will be accessible from the publisher's website as long as the book is in print.

about the author

 **LAURENȚIU SPILCĂ** is a dedicated development lead and trainer at Endava, where he leads the development of projects in the financial market with users in Europe, the US, and Asia. He has over 10 years of experience. Laurenţiu believes it's important to not only deliver high-quality software, but also share knowledge and help others to upskill. These beliefs have driven him to design and teach courses related to Java technologies and deliver presentations and workshops. His Twitter handle is @laurspilca.

about the cover illustration

The figure on the cover of *Spring Start Here* is captioned "Femme d'ajaccio isle de Corse," or a woman from Ajaccio on the island of Corsica. The illustration is taken from a collection of dress costumes from various countries by Jacques Grasset de Saint-Sauveur (1757–1810), titled *Costumes de Différents Pays,* published in France in 1797. Each illustration is finely drawn and colored by hand. The rich variety of Grasset de Saint-Sauveur's collection reminds us vividly of how culturally apart the world's towns and regions were just 200 years ago. Isolated from each other, people spoke different dialects and languages. In the streets or in the countryside, it was easy to identify where they lived and what their trade or station in life was just by their dress.

The way we dress has changed since then and the diversity by region, so rich at the time, has faded away. It is now hard to tell apart the inhabitants of different continents, let alone different towns, regions, or countries. Perhaps we have traded cultural diversity for a more varied personal life—certainly for a more varied and fast-paced technological life.

At a time when it is hard to tell one computer book from another, Manning celebrates the inventiveness and initiative of the computer business with book covers based on the rich diversity of regional life of two centuries ago, brought back to life by Grasset de Saint-Sauveur's pictures.

Part 1

Fundamentals

Any building stands on a foundation. A framework is no different in this regard. In part 1, you'll learn to use the basic components that enable the Spring framework. These components are the Spring context and Spring aspects. Further in the book, you'll discover that all Spring capabilities rely on these essential components.

Spring in the real world

This chapter covers
- What a framework is
- When to use and when to avoid using frameworks
- What the Spring framework is
- Using Spring in real-world scenarios

The Spring framework (shortly, Spring) is an application framework that is part of the Java ecosystem. An *application framework* is a set of common software functionalities that provides a foundation structure for developing an application. An application framework eases the effort of writing an application by taking out the effort of writing all the program code from scratch.

We use Spring in the development of many kinds of applications nowadays, from large backend solutions to automation testing apps. According to many survey reports on Java technologies (like this one of JRebel from 2020: http://mng.bz/N4V7; or this one from JAXEnter: http://mng.bz/DK9a), Spring is the most used Java framework today.

Spring is popular, and developers have started to use it more often with other JVM languages than Java as well. In the last few years, we observed an impressive growth of developers using Spring with Kotlin (another appreciated language from the JVM family). In this book, we'll focus on the foundations of Spring, and I'll teach you essential skills for using Spring in real-world examples. To make the subject more comfortable for you and allow you to focus on Spring, we'll use only Java examples. Throughout the book, we'll discuss and apply, with examples, essential skills like connecting to a database, establishing communication between applications, and securing and testing an app.

Before diving into more technical details in the next chapters, let's talk about the Spring framework and where you'll actually use it. Why is Spring so appreciated, and when should you even use it?

In this chapter, we'll focus on what a framework is, referring in particular to the Spring framework. In section 1.1, we discuss the advantages of using a framework. In section 1.2, we discuss the Spring ecosystem with the components you need to learn to get started with Spring. Then I'll take you through possible usages of the Spring framework—in particular, real-world scenarios in section 1.3. In section 1.4, we'll discuss when using frameworks might not be the right approach. You need to understand all these things about the Spring framework before trying to use it. Otherwise, you might try to use a hammer to dig your garden.

Depending on your level, you might feel this chapter difficult. I might introduce some notions that you haven't heard about, and this aspect might disturb you. But don't worry; even if you don't understand some of the things now, they will be clarified later in the book. Sometimes, throughout the book, I'll refer to something said in earlier chapters. I use this approach because learning a framework like Spring doesn't always offer us a linear learning path, and sometimes you need to wait until you get more pieces of the puzzle before you see the complete picture. But in the end, you'll get a clear image, and you'll get the valuable skills you need to develop apps like a professional.

1.1 *Why should we use frameworks?*

In this section, we discuss frameworks. What are they? How did this concept appear, and why? To be motivated to use something, you need to know how that something brings you value. And that's also the case with Spring. I'll teach you these essential details by sharing the knowledge I gathered from my own experience and by studying and using various frameworks in real-world scenarios, including Spring.

An application framework is a set of functionalities on top of which we build applications. The application framework provides us a broad set of tools and functionalities that you can use to build apps. You don't need to use all the features the framework offers. Depending on the requirements of the app you make, you'll choose the right parts of the framework to use.

Here's an analogy I like for application frameworks. Did you ever buy a piece of furniture from a DIY store like Ikea? Say you buy a wardrobe—you won't get an assembled wardrobe, but the right components you need to build it and a manual on how to assemble your piece of furniture. Now imagine you ordered a wardrobe, but instead of getting only the right components you need, you get all the possible components you can use to assemble any piece of furniture: a table, a wardrobe, and so on. If you want a wardrobe, you have to find the right parts and assemble them. It's like an application framework. The application framework offers you various pieces of software you need to build your app. You need to know what features to choose and how to assemble them to achieve the right result (figure 1.1).

Figure 1.1 David ordered a wardrobe from the UAssemble store. But the store (framework) doesn't deliver to David (the programmer) just the components (software capabilities) he needs to build his new wardrobe (the app). The store ships him all the possible parts he might need to build the wardrobe. It's David's (the programmer's) choice on which components (software capabilities) are right and how to assemble them to get the right result (the application).

The idea of a framework isn't new. Throughout the history of software development, programmers observed they could reuse parts of code they'd written in multiple applications. Initially, when not so many applications were implemented, each application was unique and developed from scratch using a specific programming language. When the software development domain extended, and more and more applications started to be published on the market, it became easier to observe that many of these apps had similar requirements. Let's name a few of them:

- Logging error, warning, and info messages happen in every app.
- Most applications use transactions to process data changes. Transactions represent an important mechanism that takes care of data consistency. We'll discuss this subject in detail in chapter 13.

- Most applications use protection mechanisms against the same common vulnerabilities.
- Most applications use similar ways to communicate with each other.
- Most applications use similar mechanisms to improve their performance, like caching or data compression.

And the list continues. It turns out that the business logic code implemented in an app is significantly smaller than the wheels and belts that make the engine of the application (also often referred to as "the plumbing").

When I say "business logic code," I refer to the code that implements the business requirements of the application. This code is what implements the user's expectations in an application. For example, "clicking on a specific link will generate an invoice" is something users expect to happen. Some code of the application you develop implements this functionality, and this part of code is what developers call the business logic code. However, any app takes care of several more aspects: security, logging, data consistency, and so on (figure 1.2).

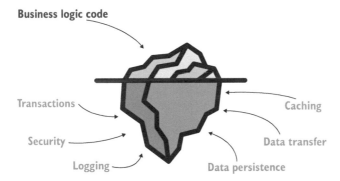

Figure 1.2   The user's perspective is similar to viewing an iceberg. Users mainly observe the results of the business logic code, but this is only a small part of what builds the app's complete functionality. Like an iceberg that is mostly underwater and hidden from view, we don't see most of the code in an enterprise app because it's provided by dependencies.

Moreover, the business logic code is what makes an application different from another from the functionality point of view. If you take two different apps, say a ridesharing system and a social networking app, they have different use cases.

> **NOTE**   A *use case* represents the reason a person uses the app. For example, in a ridesharing app, a use case is "requesting a car." For an app managing food delivery, a use case is "ordering a pizza."

You take different actions, but they both need data storing, data transfer, logging, security configurations, probably caching, and so on. Various applications can reuse these nonbusiness implementations. Is it then efficient to rewrite the same functionalities every time? Of course not:

- You spare a lot of time and money by reusing something rather than developing it yourself.
- An existing implementation that many apps already use has fewer chances to introduce bugs, as others have tested it.
- You benefit from the advice of a community because you now have a lot of developers understanding the same functionality. If you had implemented your own code, only a few people would know it.

A story of transition

One of the first applications I worked on was a huge system developed in Java. This system was composed of multiple applications designed around an old-fashioned architecture server, all of them written from scratch using Java SE. The development of this application started with the language about 25 years ago. This was the main reason for its shape. And almost no one could have imagined how big it would become. At that time, more advanced concepts of system architectures didn't exist, and things in general worked differently from the individual systems due to the slow internet connection.

But time passed, and years later, the app was more like a big ball of mud. For valid reasons I won't cover here, the team decided they had to go to a modern architecture. This change implied first cleaning up the code, and one of the main steps was using a framework. We decided to go with Spring. At that time, we had as an alternative Java EE (now named Jakarta EE), but most members of the team considered it's better to go with Spring, which offered a lighter alternative that was easier to implement and that we also considered easier to maintain.

The transition wasn't an easy one. Together with a few colleagues, experts in their domain and knowledgeable about the application itself, we invested a lot of effort into this transformation.

The result was amazing! We removed over 40% of the lines of code. This transition was the first moment I understood how significant the impact of using a framework could be.

NOTE Choosing and using a framework is linked to the design and architecture of an application. You'll find it useful to learn more about these subjects along with learning the Spring framework. In appendix A, you'll find a discussion about software architectures with excellent resources if you'd like to go into details.

1.2 The Spring ecosystem

In this section, we will discuss Spring and related projects like Spring Boot or Spring Data. You'll learn all about these in this book, and the links among them. In real-world scenarios, it's common to use different frameworks together, where each framework is designed to help you implement a specific part of the app faster.

We refer to Spring as a framework, but it is much more complex. Spring is an eco-system of frameworks. Usually, when developers refer to the Spring framework, they refer to a part of the software capabilities that include the following:

1 *Spring Core*—One of the fundamental parts of Spring that includes foundational capabilities. One of these features is the Spring context. As you'll learn in detail in chapter 2, the Spring context is a fundamental capability of the Spring frame-work that enables Spring to manage instances of your app. Also, as part of Spring Core, you find the Spring aspects functionality. Aspects help Spring inter-cept and manipulate methods you define in your app. We discuss more details of the aspects in chapter 6. The Spring Expression Language (SpEL) is another capability you'll find as part of Spring Core, which enables you to describe con-figurations for Spring using a specific language. All of these are new notions, and I don't expect you to know them yet. But soon you'll understand that Spring Core holds the mechanisms Spring uses to integrate into your app.

2 *Spring model-view-controller (MVC)*—The part of the Spring framework that enables you to develop web applications that serve HTTP requests. We'll use Spring MVC starting in chapter 7.

3 *Spring Data Access*—Also one of the fundamental parts of Spring. It provides basic tools you can use to connect to SQL databases to implement the per-sistence layer of your app. We'll use Spring Data Access starting in chapter 13.

4 *Spring testing*—The part holding the tools you need to write tests for your Spring application. We'll discuss this subject in chapter 15.

You can initially imagine the Spring framework as a solar system, where Spring Core represents the star in the middle, which holds all the framework together (figure 1.3).

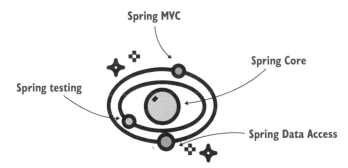

Figure 1.3 You can imagine the Spring framework as a solar system with the Spring Core in the center. The software capabilities are planets around Spring Core kept close to it by its gravitational field.

1.2.1 *Discovering Spring Core: The foundation of Spring*

Spring Core is the part of the Spring framework that provides the foundational mech-anisms to integrate into apps. Spring works based on the principle *inversion of control* (IoC). When using this principle, instead of allowing the app to control the execution, we give control to some other piece of software—in our case, the Spring framework. Through configurations, we instruct the framework on how to manage the code we write, which defines the logic of the app. Here's where the "inversion" in IoC comes from: you don't let the app control the execution by its own code and use dependencies. Instead, we allow the framework (the dependency) to control the app and its code (figure 1.4).

> **NOTE** In this context the term "controls" refers to actions like "creating an instance" or "calling a method." A framework can create objects of the classes you define in your app. Based on the configurations that you write, Spring intercepts the method to augment it with various features. For example, Spring can intercept a specific method to log any error that might appear during the method's execution.

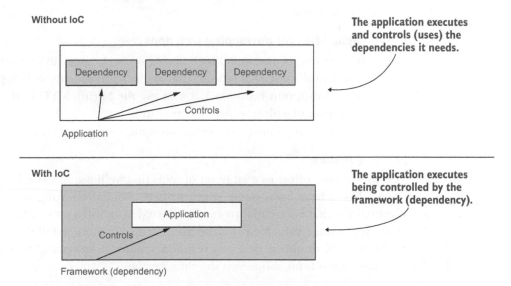

Figure 1.4 Inversion of control. Instead of executing its own code, which makes use of several other dependencies, in case of an IoC scenario, the app execution is controlled by the dependency. The Spring framework controls an app during its execution. Therefore, it implements an IoC scenario of execution.

You will start learning Spring with Spring Core by discussing the Spring IoC functionality in chapters 2 through 5. The IoC container glues Spring components and components of your application to the framework together. Using the IoC container, to which you often refer as the Spring context, you make certain objects known to Spring, which enables the framework to use them in the way you configured.

In chapter 6, we'll continue our discussion with Spring aspect-oriented programming (AOP). Spring can control instances added to its IoC container, and one of the things it can do is intercept methods that represent the behavior of these instances. This capability is called *aspecting* the method. Spring AOP is one of the most common ways the framework interacts with what your app does. This trait makes Spring AOP part of the essentials as well. Part of the Spring Core, we also find resource management, internationalization (i18n), type conversion, and SpEL. We'll encounter aspects of these features in examples throughout the book.

1.2.2   Using Spring Data Access feature to implement the app's persistence

For most applications, it's critical to persist part of the data they process. Working with databases is a fundamental subject, and in Spring, it's the Data Access module that you'll use to take care of data persistence in many cases. The Spring Data Access includes using JDBC, integrating with *object-relational mapping* (ORM) frameworks like Hibernate (don't worry if you don't yet know what an ORM framework is or haven't heard about Hibernate; we'll discuss these aspects later in the book), and managing transactions. In chapters 12 through 14, we'll cover everything needed to get you started with Spring Data Access.

1.2.3   The Spring MVC capabilities for developing web apps

The most common applications developed with Spring are web apps, and within the Spring ecosystem, you'll find a large set of tools that enables you to write web applications and web services in different fashions. You can use the Spring MVC to develop apps using a standard servlet fashion, which is common in a vast number of applications today. In chapter 7, we'll go into more detail on using the Spring MVC.

1.2.4   The Spring testing feature

The Spring testing module offers us a large set of tools that we'll use to write unit and integration tests. There have been many pages written about the testing topic, but we'll discuss everything that is essential to get you started with Spring testing in chapter 15. I'll also refer to some valuable resources you need to read to get all the details of this topic. My rule of thumb is that you're not a mature developer if you don't understand testing, so this topic is one you should care about.

1.2.5   Projects from the Spring ecosystem

The Spring ecosystem is so much more than just the capabilities discussed earlier in this section. It includes a big collection of other frameworks that integrate well and form a larger universe. Here we have projects like Spring Data, Spring Security, Spring Cloud, Spring Batch, Spring Boot, and so on. When you develop an app, you can use more of these projects together. For example, you can build an app using all of Spring Boot, Spring Security, and Spring Data. In the next few chapters, we'll work on smaller projects that make use of various projects of the Spring ecosystem. When I say project, I refer to a part of the Spring ecosystem that is independently developed. Each of these projects has a separate team that works on extending its capabilities. Also, each project is separately described and has its own reference on the Spring official website: https://spring.io/projects.

Out of this vast universe created by Spring, we'll also refer to Spring Data and Spring Boot. These projects are often encountered in apps, so it's important to get to know them from the beginning.

EXTENDING THE PERSISTENCE CAPABILITIES WITH SPRING DATA

The Spring Data project implements a part of the Spring ecosystem that enables you to easily connect to databases and use the persistence layer with a minimum number of lines of code written. The project refers to both SQL and NoSQL technologies and creates a high-level layer, which simplifies the way you work with data persistence.

> **NOTE** We have Spring Data Access, which is a module of Spring Core, and we also have an independent project in the Spring ecosystem named Spring Data. Spring Data Access contains fundamental data access implementations like the transaction mechanism and JDBC tools. Spring Data enhances access to databases and offers a broader set of tools, which makes development more accessible and enables your app to connect to different kinds of data sources. We'll discuss this subject in chapter 14.

SPRING BOOT

Spring Boot is a project part of the Spring ecosystem that introduces the concept of "convention over configuration." The main idea of this concept is that instead of setting up all the configurations of a framework yourself, Spring Boot offers you a default configuration that you can customize as needed. The result, in general, is that you write less code because you follow known conventions and your app differs from others in few or small ways. So instead of writing all the configurations for each and every app, it's more efficient to start with a default configuration and only change what's different from the convention. We'll discuss more about Spring Boot starting in chapter 7.

The Spring ecosystem is vast and contains many projects. Some of them you encounter more often than others, and some you may not use at all if you're building an application without a particular need. In this book, we refer only to the projects that are essential for you to get started: Spring Core, Spring Data, and Spring Boot. You can find a full list of projects that are part of the Spring ecosystem on the official Spring website: https://spring.io/projects/.

Alternatives for using Spring

We can't really discuss alternatives to Spring because someone could misunderstand them as alternatives to the entire ecosystem. But for many of the individual components and projects that create the Spring ecosystem, you can find other options like other open source or commercial frameworks or libraries.

For example, let's take the Spring IoC container. Years ago, the Java EE specification was a solution very much appreciated by the developers. With a slightly different philosophy, Java EE (which in 2017 was open sourced and remade in Jakarta EE, https://jakarta.ee/) offered specifications like Context and Dependency Injection (CDI) or Enterprise Java Beans (EJB). You could use CDI or EJB to manage a context of object instances and implement aspects (named "interceptors" in the EE terminology). Also, throughout history, Google Guice (https://github.com/google/guice) was an appreciated framework for the management of object instances in a container.

(continued)

For some of the projects taken individually, you could find one or more alternatives. For example, you could choose to use Apache Shiro (https://shiro.apache.org/) instead of Spring Security. Or you could decide to implement your web app using the Play framework (https://www.playframework.com/) instead of Spring MVC and Spring-related technologies.

A more recent project that looks promising is Red Hat Quarkus. Quarkus is designed for cloud native implementations and becomes more and more mature with rapid steps. I wouldn't be surprised to see it as one of the lead projects in developing enterprise apps in the Java ecosystem in the future (https://quarkus.io/).

My advice for you is to always take into consideration your alternatives. In software development, you need to be open-minded and never trust one solution as being "the one." You'll always find scenarios in which a specific technology works better than another.

1.3   Spring in real-world scenarios

Now that you have an overview of Spring, you're aware of when and why you should use a framework. In this section, I'll give you some application scenarios in which using the Spring framework might be an excellent fit. Too often, I've seen developers only refer to backend applications for using a framework like Spring. I've even seen a trend of restricting, even more, the scenario to backend web applications. While it's true that in plenty of cases we see Spring used in this way, it's important to remember that the framework isn't limited to this scenario. I've seen teams successfully using Spring in different kinds of applications, such as the development of an automation testing app or even in standalone desktop scenarios.

I'll further describe to you some common real-world scenarios in which I've seen Spring used successfully. These are not the only possible scenarios, and Spring might not work all the time in these cases. Remember what we discussed in section 1.2: a framework is not always a good choice. But these are common cases in which generally Spring is a good fit:

1   The development of a backend app
2   The development of an automation testing framework
3   The development of a desktop app
4   The development of a mobile app

1.3.1   Using Spring in the development of a backend app

A backend application is the part of a system that executes on the server side and has the responsibility of managing data and serving client applications' requests. The users access functionalities by using the client apps directly. Further, the client apps make requests to the backend app to work with the users' data. The backend app might use databases to store data or communicate with other backend apps in different fashions.

You can imagine, in a real-world scenario, that the app would be the backend application managing the transactions in your bank accounts. Users may access their accounts and manage them via a web application (online banking) or a mobile app. Both the mobile apps and the web apps represent clients for the backend application. To manage users' transactions, the backend application needs to communicate with other backend solutions, and part of the data it manages needs to be persisted in a database. In figure 1.5, you can visualize the architecture of such a system.

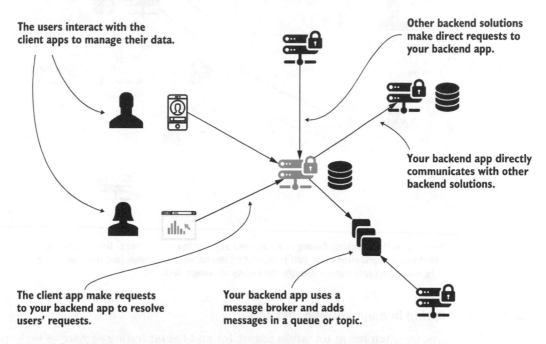

The users interact with the client apps to manage their data.

Other backend solutions make direct requests to your backend app.

Your backend app directly communicates with other backend solutions.

The client app make requests to your backend app to resolve users' requests.

Your backend app uses a message broker and adds messages in a queue or topic.

Figure 1.5 A backend app interacts in several ways with other apps and uses databases to manage data. Usually, a backend app is complex and may require the use of various technologies. Frameworks simplify the implementation by providing tools you can use to implement the backend solution faster.

> **NOTE** Don't worry if you don't understand all the details of figure 1.5. I don't expect you to know what a message broker is and not even how to establish the data exchange among the components. What I want you to see is that such a system can become complex in the real world and then understand that projects from the Spring ecosystem were built to help you eliminate this complexity as much as possible.

Spring offers an excellent set of tools for implementing backend applications. It makes your life easier with the different functionalities you generally implement in a backend solution, from integration with other apps to persistence in various database technologies. It's no wonder developers often use Spring for such applications. The framework basically offers you everything you need in such implementations and is an excellent fit for any kind of architectural style. Figure 1.6 indicates the possibilities of using Spring for a backend app.

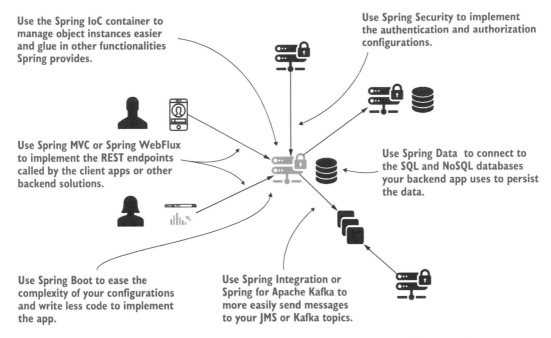

Use the Spring IoC container to manage object instances easier and glue in other functionalities Spring provides.

Use Spring Security to implement the authentication and authorization configurations.

Use Spring MVC or Spring WebFlux to implement the REST endpoints called by the client apps or other backend solutions.

Use Spring Data to connect to the SQL and NoSQL databases your backend app uses to persist the data.

Use Spring Boot to ease the complexity of your configurations and write less code to implement the app.

Use Spring Integration or Spring for Apache Kafka to more easily send messages to your JMS or Kafka topics.

Figure 1.6   The possibilities of using Spring in a backend application are endless, from exposing functionalities that other applications can call to managing the database access, and from securing the application to managing integration though third-party message brokers.

1.3.2   *Using Spring in a automation test app*

Nowadays, we often use automation testing for end-to-end testing of systems we implement. Automation testing refers to implementing software that development teams use to make sure an application behaves as expected. A development team can schedule the automation testing implementation to frequently test the app and notify the developers if something is wrong. Having such functionality gives developers confidence because they know they'll be notified if they break anything in the existing capabilities of the app while developing new features.

While with small systems you can do the testing manually, it's always a good idea to automate the test cases. For more complex systems, manually testing all the flows isn't even an option. Because the flows are so numerous, it'd require a massive number of hours and too much energy to cover it completely.

It turns out that the most efficient solution is to have a separate team implement an app that has the responsibility of validating all the flows of the tested system. While developers add new functionalities to the system, this testing app is also enhanced to cover what's new, and the teams use it to validate that everything still works as desired. The developers eventually use an integration tool and schedule the app to run regularly to get feedback as soon as possible for their changes (figure 1.7).

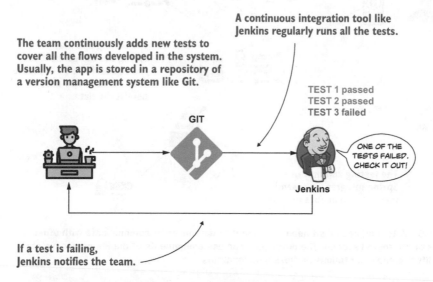

Figure 1.7 The team deploys the testing app in a test environment. A continuous integration tool like Jenkins executes the app regularly and sends feedback to the team. This way, the team is always aware of the system's status, and they know if they break something during development.

Such an application might become as complex as a backend app. In order to validate the flows, the app needs to communicate with the components of the system and even connect to databases. Sometimes the app mocks external dependencies to simulate different execution scenarios. For writing the test scenarios, developers use frameworks like Selenium, Cucumber, Gauge, and others. But, together with these frameworks, the app could still benefit in several ways from Spring's tools. For example, the app could manage the object instances to make the code more maintainable using the Spring IoC container. It could use Spring Data to connect to the databases where it needs to validate the data. It could send messages to queues or topics of a broker system to simulate specific scenarios or simply use Spring to call some REST endpoints (figure 1.8). (Remember, it's okay if this looks too advanced; meaning will be clarified as you progress through the book).

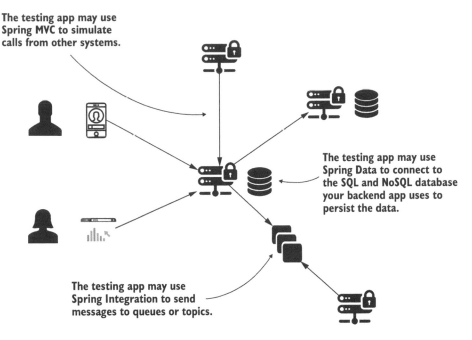

The testing app may use Spring MVC to simulate calls from other systems.

The testing app may use Spring Data to connect to the SQL and NoSQL database your backend app uses to persist the data.

The testing app may use Spring Integration to send messages to queues or topics.

Figure 1.8   A testing app might need to connect to databases or communicate with other systems or the tested system. The developers can use components of the Spring ecosystem to simplify the implementations of these functionalities.

1.3.3   *Using Spring for the development of a desktop app*

Today, desktop applications are not that frequently developed, as web or mobile apps have taken the role of interacting with the user. However, there's still a small number of desktop applications, and components of the Spring ecosystem could be a good choice in the development of their features. A desktop app could successfully use the Spring IoC container to manage the object instances. This way, the app's implementation is cleaner and improves its maintainability. Additionally, the app could potentially use Spring's tools to implement different features, for example to communicate with a backend or other components (calling web services or using other techniques for remote calls) or implement a caching solution.

1.3.4   *Using Spring in mobile apps*

With its Spring for Android project (https://spring.io/projects/spring-android), the Spring community tries to help the development of mobile applications. Even though you'll probably rarely encounter this situation, it's worth mentioning that you can use Spring's tools to develop Android apps. This Spring project provides a REST client for Android and authentication support for accessing secured APIs.

1.4   *When not to use frameworks*

In this section, we discuss why you should sometimes avoid using frameworks. It's essential you know when to use a framework and when to avoid using them. Sometimes, using a tool that's too much for the job might consume more energy and also obtain a worse result. Imagine using a chainsaw to cut bread. While you could try to and even achieve a final result, it'd be more difficult and energy-consuming than using a regular knife (and you may end up with nothing but breadcrumbs instead of sliced bread). We'll discuss a few scenarios in which using a framework isn't a great idea, and then I'll tell you a story about a team I was part of that failed in the implementation of an app because of using a framework.

It turns out that, like everything else in software development, you shouldn't apply a framework in all cases. You'll find situations in which a framework is not a good fit—or maybe a framework is a good fit, but not the Spring framework. In which of the following scenarios should you consider not using a framework?

1 You need to implement a particular functionality with a footprint as small as possible. By footprint, I mean the storage memory occupied by the app's files.
2 Specific security requirements force you to implement only custom code in your app without making use of any open source framework.
3 You'd have to make so many customizations over the framework that you'd write more code than if you'd simply not used it at all.
4 You already have a functional app, and by changing it to use a framework you don't gain any benefit.

Let's discuss these points in more detail.

1.4.1   *You need to have a small footprint*

For point one, I refer to situations in which you need to make your application small. In today's systems, we find more and more cases in which the services are delivered in containers. You've likely heard about containers, such as Docker, Kubernetes, or other terms related to this subject (if not, again, that's okay).

Containers in their entirety is a topic beyond the scope of this book, so for now the only thing I need you to know is that when you use such a deployment fashion, you want your application to be as small as possible. A container is like a box in which your application lives. One crucial principle regarding app deployment in containers is that the containers should be easily disposable: they can be destroyed and recreated as fast as possible. The size of the app (footprint) matters a lot here. You can save seconds from the app initialization by making it smaller. That doesn't mean you won't use frameworks for all the apps deployed in containers.

But for some apps, which are usually also quite small, it makes more sense to improve their initialization and make their footprint smaller rather than adding dependencies to different frameworks. Such a case is a kind of application called *server-less function*. These server-less functions are tiny applications deployed in containers.

Because you don't have too much access to the way they're deployed, it looks like they execute without a server (hence their name). These apps need to be small, and that's why, for this specific case of apps, you'll want to avoid adding a framework as much as possible. Because of its size, it's also possible that you won't need a framework anyway.

1.4.2   *Security needs dictate custom code*

I said in point two that in specific situations, apps could not use frameworks because of security requirements. This scenario usually happens with apps in the field of defense or governmental organizations. Again, it doesn't mean all the apps used in governmental organizations are prohibited from using frameworks, but for some, restrictions are applied. You may wonder why. Well, say an open source framework like Spring is used. If someone finds a specific vulnerability, it will become known, and a hacker could use this knowledge to exploit it. Sometimes, stakeholders of such apps want to make sure the chances of someone hacking into their system is as close to zero as possible. This could lead to even rebuilding a functionality instead of using it from a third-party source.

> **NOTE**   Wait! Earlier I said that it's more secure to use an open source framework because if a vulnerability exists, someone will likely discover it. Well, if you invest enough time and money, you probably can achieve this yourself as well. In general, it's cheaper to use a framework, of course. And if you don't want to be extra cautious, it makes more sense to use a framework. But in some projects, the stakeholders really want to make sure no information becomes public.

1.4.3   *Abundant existing customizations make a framework impractical*

Another case (point three) in which you might want to avoid using a framework is when you'd have to customize its components so much that you end up writing more code than if it hadn't been used. As I specified in section 1.1, a framework provides you parts that you assemble with your business code to obtain an app. These components, provided by the framework, don't fit perfectly, and you need to customize them in different ways. It's perfectly normal to customize the framework's components and the style in which they assemble than if you'd developed the functionality from scratch. If you find yourself in such a situation, you have probably chosen the wrong framework (search for alternatives) or you shouldn't use a framework at all.

1.4.4   *You won't benefit from switching to a framework*

In point four, I mentioned that a potential mistake could be trying to use a framework to replace something that already exists and is working in an app. Sometimes we are tempted to replace an existing architecture with something new. A new framework appears, and it's popular, and everyone uses it, so why shouldn't we change our app as well to use this framework? You can, but you need to attentively analyze what you want to achieve by changing something that works. In some cases, like my story from section

1.1, it could be helpful to change your app and make it rely on a specific framework. As long as this change brings a benefit, do it! A reason could be that you want to make the app more maintainable, more performant, or more secure. But if this change doesn't bring you a benefit, and sometimes it might even bring incertitude, then, in the end, you might discover you invested the time and money for a worse result. Let me tell you a story from my own experience.

An avoidable mistake

Using frameworks isn't always the best choice, and I had to learn that the hard way. Years earlier, we were working on the backend of a web application. Times influence many things, including software architectures. The app was using JDBC to directly connect to an Oracle database. The code was quite ugly. Everywhere the app needed to execute a query on the database it opened a statement and then sent a query that was sometimes written on multiple rows. You might be young enough not to have encountered JDBC direct usage in apps, but trust me, it's a long and ugly code.

At that time, some frameworks using another methodology to work with the database were becoming more and more popular. I remember when I first encountered Hibernate. This is an ORM framework, which allows you to treat the tables and their relationships in a database as objects and relationships among objects. When used correctly, it enables you to write less code and more intuitive functionality. When misused, it may slow down your app, make the code less intuitive, and even introduce bugs.

The application we were developing needed a change. We knew we could improve that ugly JDBC code. In my mind, we could at least minimize the number of lines. This change would have brought great benefits to maintainability. Together with other developers, we suggested using a tool provided by Spring called `JdbcTemplate` (you'll learn this tool in chapter 12). But others strongly pushed the decision to use Hibernate. It was quite popular, so why not to use it? (Actually it still is one of the most popular frameworks of its kind, and you'll learn about integrating it with Spring in chapter 13.) I could see changing that code to a completely new methodology would be a challenge. Moreover, I could see no benefits. The change also implied a greater risk of introducing bugs.

Fortunately, the change started with a proof of concept. After a couple of months, lots of effort, and stress, the team decided to quit.

After analyzing our options, we finished the implementation using `JdbcTemplate`. We managed to write cleaner code by eliminating a large number of lines of code, and we didn't need to introduce any new framework for this change.

1.5 What will you learn in this book

Since you opened this book, I assume you're probably a software developer in the Java ecosystem who found out it's useful to learn Spring. The purpose of this book is to teach you the foundations of Spring, assuming you know nothing at all about frameworks and, of course, about Spring. When I say Spring, I refer to the Spring ecosystem, not just the core part of the framework.

When you finish the book, you will have learned how to do the following:

- Use the Spring context and implement aspects around objects managed by the framework.
- Implement the mechanism of a Spring app to connect to a database and work with the persisted data.
- Establish data exchange between apps using REST APIs implemented with Spring.
- Build basic apps that use the convention-over-configuration approach.
- Use best practices in the standard class design of a Spring application.
- Properly test your Spring implementations.

Summary

- An application framework is a set of common software functionalities that provides a foundational structure for developing an application. A framework acts as the skeletal support to build an application.
- A framework helps you build an app more efficiently by providing functionality that you assemble to your implementation instead of developing it yourself. Using a framework saves you time and helps ensure there are fewer chances of implementing buggy features.
- Using a widely known framework like Spring opens a door to a large community, which makes it more likely that others will faces similar problems. You then have an excellent opportunity to learn about how others solved something similar to an issue you need to address, which will spare you the time of individual research.
- When implementing an application, always think of all possibilities, including not using a framework. If you decide to use one or more frameworks, take into consideration all their alternatives. You should think about the purpose of the framework, who else is using it (how big the community is), and for how long it's been on the market (maturity).
- Spring is not just a framework. We often refer to Spring as "Spring framework" to indicate the core functionalities, but Spring offers an entire ecosystem formed of many projects used in application development. Each project is dedicated to a specific domain, and when implementing an app, you might use more of these projects to implement the functionality you desire. The projects of the Spring ecosystem we'll use in this book are as follows:
  - Spring Core, which builds the foundation of Spring and provides features like the context, aspects, and basic data access.
  - Spring Data, which provides a high-level, comfortable-to-use set of tools to implement the persistence layer of your apps. You'll find how easy it is to use Spring Data to work with both SQL and NoSQL databases.
  - Spring Boot, which is a project of the Spring ecosystem that helps you apply a "convention over-configuration" approach.

- Quite often, learning materials (like books, articles, or video tutorials) offer examples with Spring only for backend applications. While it's true that it's widespread to use Spring with backend apps, you can use Spring with other kinds of apps as well, even in desktop applications and automation testing apps.

The Spring context: Defining beans

This chapter covers

- Understanding the need for Spring context
- Adding new object instances to the Spring context

In this chapter, you start learning how to work with a crucial Spring framework element: the context (also known as the application context in a Spring app). Imagine the context as a place in the memory of your app in which we add all the object instances that we want the framework to manage. By default, Spring doesn't know any of the objects you define in your application. To enable Spring to see your objects, you need to add them to the context. Later in this book we discuss using different capabilities provided by Spring in apps. You'll learn that plugging in such features is done through the context by adding object instances and establishing relationships among them. Spring uses the instances in the context to connect your app to various functionalities it provides. You'll learn the basics of the most important features (e.g., transactions, testing, etc.) throughout the book.

Learning what Spring context is and how it works is the first step in learning to use Spring, because without knowing how to manage the Spring context, almost nothing else you'll learn to do with it will be possible. The context is a complex mechanism that enables Spring to control instances you define. This way, it allows you to use the capabilities the framework offers.

We start in this chapter by learning how to add object instances to the Spring context. In chapter 3, you'll learn how to refer to the instances you added and establish relationships among them.

We'll name these object instances "beans." Of course, for the syntaxes you need to learn we'll write code snippets, and you can find all these snippets in the projects provided with the book (you can download the projects from the "Book resources" section of the live book). I'll enhance the code examples with visuals and detailed explanations of the approaches.

Because I want to make your introduction to Spring progressive and take everything step by step, in this chapter we focus on the syntaxes you need to know for working with the Spring context. You'll find out later that not all the objects of an app need to be managed by Spring, so you don't need to add all the object instances of your app to the Spring context. For the moment, I invite you to focus on learning the approaches for adding an instance for Spring to manage.

2.1 *Creating a Maven project*

In this section, we'll discuss creating a Maven project. Maven is not a subject directly related to Spring, but it's a tool you use to easily manage an app's build process regardless of the framework you use. You need to know Maven project basics to follow the coding examples. Maven is also one of the most used building tools for Spring projects in real-world scenarios (with Gradle, another build tool, taking second place, but we won't discuss it in this book). Because Maven's such a well-known tool, you may already know how to create a project and add dependencies to it using its configuration. In this case, you can skip this section and go directly to section 2.2.

A build tool is software we use to build apps more easily. You configure a build tool to do the tasks that are part of building the app instead of manually doing them. Some examples of tasks that are often part of building the app are as follows:

- Downloading the dependencies needed by your app
- Running tests
- Validating that the syntax follows rules that you define
- Checking for security vulnerabilities
- Compiling the app
- Packaging the app in an executable archive

So that our examples can easily manage dependencies, we need to use a build tool for the projects we develop. This section teaches only what you need to know for developing the examples in this book; we'll go step by step through the process of creating a

Maven project, and I'll teach you the essentials regarding its structure. If you'd like to learn more details about using Maven, I recommend *Introducing Maven: A Build Tool for Today's Java Developers* by Balaji Varanasi (APress, 2019).

Let's start at the very beginning. First, as with developing any other app, you need an integrated development environment (IDE). Any professional IDE nowadays offers support for Maven projects, so you can choose any you'd like: IntelliJ IDEA, Eclipse, Spring STS, Netbeans, and so on. For this book, I use IntelliJ IDEA, which is the IDE I use most often. Don't worry—the structure of the Maven project is the same regardless of which IDE you choose.

Let's start by creating a new project. You create a new project in IntelliJ from File > New > Project. This will get you to a window like the one in figure 2.1.

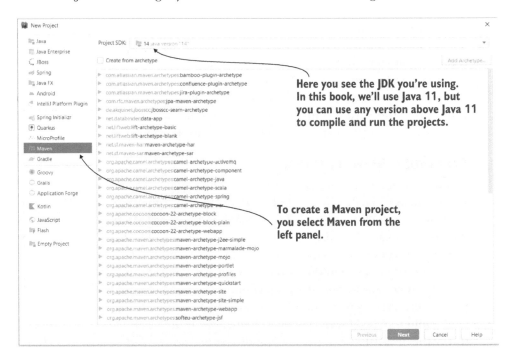

Figure 2.1   Creating a new Maven project. After going to File > New > Project, you get to this window, where you need to select the type of the project from the left panel. In our case, we choose Maven. In the upper part of the window, you select the JDK you wish to use to compile and run the project.

Once you've selected the type of your project, in the next window (figure 2.2) you need to give it a name. In addition to the project name and choosing the location in which to store it, for a Maven project you can also specify the following:

- A group ID, which we use to group multiple related projects
- An artifact ID, which is the name of the current application
- A version, which is an identifier of the current implementation state

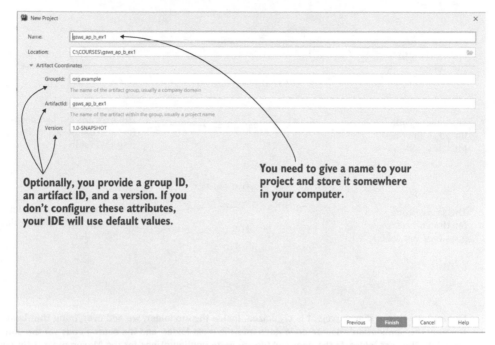

Figure 2.2 Before you finish creating your project, you need to give it a name and specify where you want your IDE to store the project. Optionally, you can give your project a group ID, an artifact ID, and a version. You then press the Finish button in the lower right corner to complete creating the project.

In a real-world app, these three attributes are essential details, and it's important to provide them. But in our case, because we only work on theoretical examples, you can omit them and leave your IDE to fill in some default values for these characteristics.

Once you've created the project, you'll find its structure looks like the one presented in figure 2.3. Again, the Maven project structure does not depend on the IDE you choose for developing your projects. When you look first at your project, you observe two main things:

- The "src" folder (also known as the source folder), where you'll put everything that belongs to the app.
- The pom.xml file, where you write the configurations of your Maven project, like adding new dependencies.

Maven organizes the "src" folder into the following folders:

- The "main" folder, where you store the application's source code. This folder contains the Java code and the configurations separately into two different subfolders named "java" and "resources."
- The "test" folder, where you store the unit tests' source code (we discuss more about unit tests and how to define them in chapter 15).

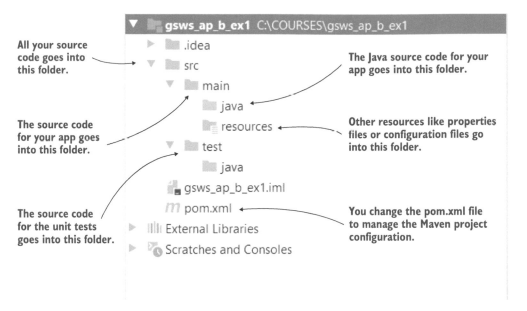

All your source code goes into this folder.

The source code for your app goes into this folder.

The source code for the unit tests goes into this folder.

The Java source code for your app goes into this folder.

Other resources like properties files or configuration files go into this folder.

You change the pom.xml file to manage the Maven project configuration.

Figure 2.3   **How a Maven project is organized. Inside the src folder, we add everything that belongs to the app: the application's source code goes into the main folder, and the source code for the unit tests goes into the test folder. In the pom.xml file we write configurations for the Maven project (in our examples we'll primarily use it to define the dependencies).**

Figure 2.4 shows you how to add new source code to the "main/java" folder of the Maven project. New classes of the app go into this folder.

Inside the "java" folder you create your usual Java packages and classes. Here, I've created a package named "main" and a new Main class inside it.

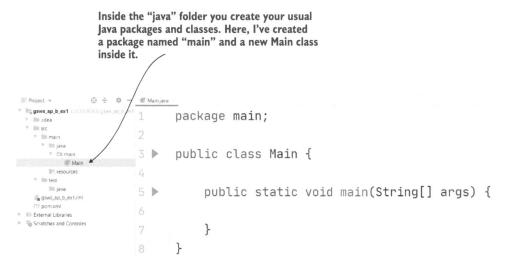

Figure 2.4   **Inside the "java" folder, you create the usual Java packages and classes of your application. These are the classes that define the whole logic of your app and make use of the dependencies you provide.**

In the projects we create in this book, we use plenty of external dependencies: libraries or frameworks we use to implement the functionality of the examples. To add these dependencies to your Maven projects, we need to change the content of the pom.xml file. In the following listing, you find the default content of the pom.xml file immediately after creating the Maven project.

Listing 2.1   The default content of the pom.xml file

```xml
<?xml version="1.0" encoding="UTF-8"?>
<project xmlns="http://maven.apache.org/POM/4.0.0"
         xmlns:xsi="http://www.w3.org/2001/XMLSchema-instance"
         xsi:schemaLocation="http://maven.apache.org/POM/4.0.0
         http://maven.apache.org/xsd/maven-4.0.0.xsd">

  <modelVersion>4.0.0</modelVersion>

  <groupId>org.example</groupId>
  <artifactId>sq-ch2-ex1</artifactId>
  <version>1.0-SNAPSHOT</version>

</project>
```

With this pom.xml file, the project doesn't use any external dependency. If you look in the project's external dependencies folder, you should only see the JDK (figure 2.5).

Initially, inside the External Libraries section of your project, you only have the JDK. Once you add more dependencies to your project, other files will appear here, represented as external dependencies.

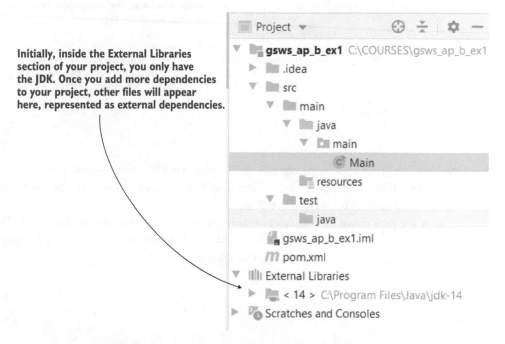

Figure 2.5   With a default pom.xml file, your project only uses the JDK as an external dependency. One of the reasons you change the pom.xml file (and the one we'll use in this book) is to add new dependencies your app needs.

The following listing shows you how to add external dependencies to your project. You write all the dependencies between the <dependencies> </dependencies> tags. Each dependency is represented by a <dependency> </dependency> group of tags where you write the dependency's attributes: the dependency's group ID, artifact name, and version. Maven will search for the dependency by the values you provided for these three attributes and will download the dependencies from a repository. I won't go into detail on how to configure a custom repository. You just need to be aware that Maven will download the dependencies (usually jar files) by default from a repository named the Maven central. You can find the downloaded jar files in your project's external dependencies folder, as presented in figure 2.6.

Listing 2.2   Adding a new dependency in the pom.xml file

```
<?xml version="1.0" encoding="UTF-8"?>
<project xmlns="http://maven.apache.org/POM/4.0.0"
        xmlns:xsi="http://www.w3.org/2001/XMLSchema-instance"
        xsi:schemaLocation="http://maven.apache.org/POM/4.0.0
        http://maven.apache.org/xsd/maven-4.0.0.xsd">

  <modelVersion>4.0.0</modelVersion>

  <groupId>org.example</groupId>
  <artifactId>sq_ch2_ex1</artifactId>              You need to write the dependencies for the
  <version>1.0-SNAPSHOT</version>                  project between the <dependencies> and
                                                   </dependecies> tags.
  <dependencies>        ◁
    <dependency>  .          ◁
      <groupId>org.springframework</groupId>       A dependency is represented
      <artifactId>spring-jdbc</artifactId>         by a group of <dependency>
      <version>5.2.6.RELEASE</version>             </dependency> tags.
    </dependency>
  </dependencies>

</project>
```

Once you've added the dependency in the pom.xml file, as presented in the previous listing, the IDE downloads them, and you'll now find these dependencies in the "External Libraries" folder (figure 2.6).

Now we can move to the next section, where we discuss the basics of the Spring context. You'll create Maven projects, and you'll learn to use a Spring dependency named spring-context, to manage the Spring context.

**Adding the Spring context dependency
adds multiple files as external dependencies.**

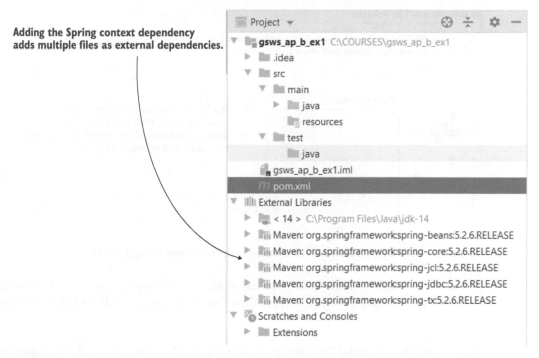

**Figure 2.6   When you add a new dependency to the pom.xml file, Maven downloads the jar files representing
that dependency. You find these jar files in the External Libraries folder of the project.**

2.2   *Adding new beans to the Spring context*

In this section, you'll learn how to add new object instances (i.e., beans) to the Spring context. You'll find out that you have multiple ways to add beans in the Spring context such that Spring can manage them and plug features it provides into your app. Depending on the action, you'll choose a specific way to add the bean; we'll discuss when to select one or another. You can add beans in the context in the following ways (which we'll describe later in this chapter):

- Using the @Bean annotation
- Using stereotype annotations
- Programmatically

Let's first create a project with a reference to no framework—not even Spring. We'll then add the dependencies needed to use the Spring context and create it (figure 2.7). This example will serve as a prerequisite to adding beans to the Spring context examples that we're going to work on in sections 2.2.1 through 2.2.3.

We create a Maven project and define a class. Because it's funny to imagine, I'll consider a class named Parrot with only a String attribute representing the name of the parrot (listing 2.3). Remember, in this chapter, we only focus on adding beans to the Spring context, so it's okay to use any object that helps you better remember the

What you want to achieve

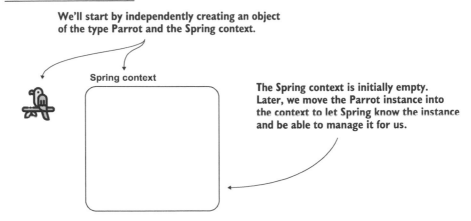

We'll start by independently creating an object
of the type Parrot and the Spring context.

Spring context

The Spring context is initially empty.
Later, we move the Parrot instance into
the context to let Spring know the instance
and be able to manage it for us.

Figure 2.7   **To start, we create an object instance and the empty Spring context.**

syntaxes. You find the code for this example in the project "sq-ch2-ex1" (you can download the projects from the "Resources" section of the live book). For your project, you can use the same name or choose the one you prefer.

Listing 2.3   **The** `Parrot` **class**

```
public class Parrot {

  private String name;

  // Omitted getters and setters
}
```

You can now define a class containing the main method and create an instance of the class `Parrot`, as presented in the following listing. I usually name this class `Main`.

Listing 2.4   **Creating an instance of the** `Parrot` **class**

```
public class Main {

  public static void main(String[] args) {
    Parrot p = new Parrot();
  }
}
```

It's now time to add the needed dependencies to our project. Because we're using Maven, I'll add the dependencies in the pom.xml file, as presented in the following listing.

Listing 2.5   **Adding the dependency for Spring context**

```
<project xmlns="http://maven.apache.org/POM/4.0.0"
  xmlns:xsi="http://www.w3.org/2001/XMLSchema-instance"
  xsi:schemaLocation="http://maven.apache.org/POM/4.0.0
```

```
                  http://maven.apache.org/xsd/maven-4.0.0.xsd">

    <modelVersion>4.0.0</modelVersion>

    <groupId>org.example</groupId>
    <artifactId>sq-ch2-ex1</artifactId>
    <version>1.0-SNAPSHOT</version>

    <dependencies>
       <dependency>
          <groupId>org.springframework</groupId>
          <artifactId>spring-context</artifactId>
          <version>5.2.6.RELEASE</version>
       </dependency>
    </dependencies>

</project>
```

A critical thing to observe is that Spring is designed to be modular. By modular, I mean that you don't need to add the whole Spring to your app when you use something out of the Spring ecosystem. You just need to add those parts that you use. For this reason, in listing 2.5, you see that I've only added the spring-context dependency, which instructs Maven to pull the needed dependencies for us to use the Spring context. Throughout the book, we'll add various dependencies to our projects according to what we implement, but we'll always only add what we need.

> **NOTE** You might wonder how I knew which Maven dependency I should add. The truth is that I've used them so many times I know them by heart. However, you don't need to memorize them. Whenever you work with a new Spring project, you can search for the dependencies you need to add directly in the Spring reference (https://docs.spring.io/spring-framework/docs/current/spring-framework-reference/core.html). Generally, Spring dependencies are part of the org.springframework group ID.

With the dependency added to our project, we can create an instance of the Spring context. In the next listing, you can see how I've changed the main method to create the Spring context instance.

Listing 2.6 Creating the instance of the Spring context

```
public class Main {

    public static void main(String[] args) {
        var context =
            new AnnotationConfigApplicationContext();     ◁── Creates an instance of
                                                              the Spring context
        Parrot p = new Parrot();
    }
}
```

NOTE   We use the `AnnotationConfigApplicationContext` class to create the Spring context instance. Spring offers multiple implementations. Because in most cases you'll use the `AnnotationConfigApplicationContext` class (the implementation that uses the most used today's approach: annotations), we'll focus on this one in this book. Also, I only tell you what you need to know for the current discussion. If you're just getting started with Spring, my recommendation is to avoid getting into details with context implementations and these classes' inheritance chains. Chances are that if you do you'll get lost with unimportant details instead of focusing on the essential things.

As presented in figure 2.8, you created an instance of `Parrot`, added the Spring context dependencies to your project, and created an instance of the Spring context. Your objective is to add the `Parrot` object to the context, which is the next step.

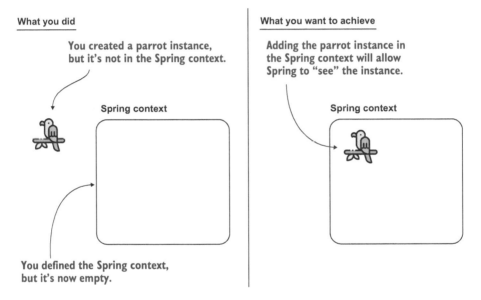

What you did

You created a parrot instance, but it's not in the Spring context.

Spring context

You defined the Spring context, but it's now empty.

What you want to achieve

Adding the parrot instance in the Spring context will allow Spring to "see" the instance.

Spring context

Figure 2.8   You created the Spring context instance and a `Parrot` instance. Now, you want to add the `Parrot` instance inside the Spring context to make Spring aware of this instance.

We just finished creating the prerequisite (skeleton) project, which we'll use in the next sections to understand how to add beans to the Spring context. In section 2.2.1, we continue learning how to add the instance to the Spring context using the `@Bean` annotation. Further, in sections 2.2.2 and 2.2.3, you'll also learn the alternatives of adding the instance using stereotype annotations and doing it programmatically. After discussing all three approaches, we'll compare them, and you'll learn the best circumstances for using each.

2.2.1 *Using the @Bean annotation to add beans into the Spring context*

In this section, we'll discuss adding an object instance to the Spring context using the `@Bean` annotation. This makes it possible for you to add the instances of the classes defined in your project (like `Parrot` in our case), as well as classes you didn't create yourself but you use in your app. I believe this approach is the easiest to understand when starting out. Remember that the reason you learn to add beans to the Spring context is that Spring can manage only the objects that are part of it. First, I'll give you a straightforward example of how to add a bean to the Spring context using the `@Bean` annotation. Then I'll show you how to add multiple beans of the same or different type.

The steps you need to follow to add a bean to the Spring context using the `@Bean` annotation are as follows (figure 2.9):

1. Define a configuration class (annotated with `@Configuration`) for your project, which, as we'll discuss later, we use to configure the context of Spring.
2. Add a method to the configuration class that returns the object instance you want to add to the context and annotate the method with the `@Bean` annotation.
3. Make Spring use the configuration class defined in step 1. As you'll learn later, we use configuration classes to write different configurations for the framework.

Let's follow these steps and apply them in the project named "sq-c2-ex2." To keep all the steps we discuss separated, I recommend you create new projects for each example.

> **NOTE** Remember, you can find the book's projects in the "Resources" section of the live book.

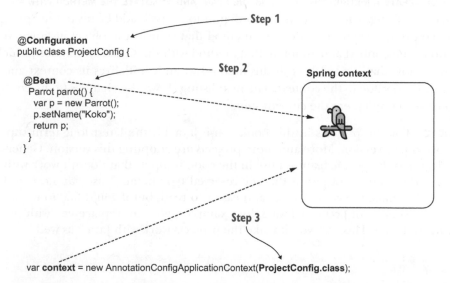

Figure 2.9 Steps for adding the bean to the context using the `@Bean` annotation. By adding the instance to the Spring context, you make the framework aware of the object, enabling it to manage the instance.

> **NOTE**   A configuration class is a special class in Spring applications that we use to instruct Spring to do specific actions. For example, we can tell Spring to create beans or to enable certain functionalities. You will learn different things you can define in configuration classes throughout the rest of the book.

STEP 1: DEFINING A CONFIGURATION CLASS IN YOUR PROJECT

The first step is to create a configuration class in the project. A Spring configuration class is characterized by the fact that it is annotated with the @Configuration annotation. We use the configuration classes to define various Spring-related configurations for the project. Throughout the book, you'll learn different things you can configure using the configuration classes. For the moment we focus only on adding new instances to the Spring context. The next listing shows you how to define the configuration class. I named this configuration class ProjectConfig.

Listing 2.7   Defining a configuration class for the project

```
@Configuration
public class ProjectConfig {
}
```

We use the @Configuration annotation to define this class as a Spring configuration class.

> **NOTE**   I separate the classes into different packages to make the code easier to understand. For example, I create the configuration classes in a package named config, and the Main class in a package named main. Organizing the classes into packages is a good practice; I recommend you follow it in your real-world implementations as well.

STEP 2: CREATE A METHOD THAT RETURNS THE BEAN, AND ANNOTATE THE METHOD WITH @BEAN

One of the things you can do with a configuration class is add beans to the Spring context. To do this, we need to define a method that returns the object instance we wish to add to the context and annotate that method with the @Bean annotation, which lets Spring know that it needs to call this method when it initializes its context and adds the returned value to the context. The next listing shows the changes to the configuration class to implement the current step.

> **NOTE**   For the projects in this book, I use Java 11: the latest long-term supported Java version. More and more projects are adopting this version. Generally, the only specific feature I use in the code snippets that doesn't work with an earlier version of Java is the var reserved type name. I use var here and there to make the code shorter and easier to read, but if you'd like to use an earlier version of Java (say Java 8, for example), you can replace var with the inferred type. This way, you'll make the projects work with Java 8 as well.

Listing 2.8   Defining the @Bean method

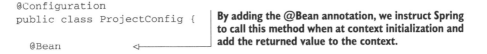

```
@Configuration
public class ProjectConfig {

    @Bean
```

By adding the @Bean annotation, we instruct Spring to call this method when at context initialization and add the returned value to the context.

```
Parrot parrot() {
  var p = new Parrot();
  p.setName("Koko");
  return p;
}
}
```

Set a name for the parrot we'll use later when we test the app.

Spring adds to its context the Parrot instance returned by the method.

Observe that the name I used for the method doesn't contain a verb. You probably learned that a Java best practice is to put verbs in method names because the methods generally represent actions. But for methods we use to add beans in the Spring context, we don't follow this convention. Such methods represent the object instances they return and that will now be part of the Spring context. The method's name also becomes the bean's name (as in listing 2.8, the bean's name is now "parrot"). By convention, you can use nouns, and most often they have the same name as the class.

STEP 3: MAKE SPRING INITIALIZE ITS CONTEXT USING THE NEWLY CREATED CONFIGURATION CLASS
We've implemented a configuration class in which we tell Spring the object instance that needs to become a bean. Now we need to make sure Spring uses this configuration class when initializing its context. The next listing shows you how to change the instantiation of the Spring context in the main class to use the configuration class we implemented in the first two steps.

Listing 2.9 Initializing the Spring context based on the defined configuration class

```
public class Main {

  public static void main(String[] args) {
    var context =
      new AnnotationConfigApplicationContext(
        ProjectConfig.class);
  }
}
```

When creating the Spring context instance, send the configuration class as a parameter to instruct Spring to use it.

To verify the Parrot instance is indeed part of the context now, you can refer to the instance and print its name in the console, as presented in the following listing.

Listing 2.10 Referring to the Parrot instance from the context

```
public class Main {

  public static void main(String[] args) {
    var context =
      new AnnotationConfigApplicationContext(
        ProjectConfig.class);

    Parrot p = context.getBean(Parrot.class);

    System.out.println(p.getName());
  }
}
```

Gets a reference of a bean of type Parrot from the Spring context

Now you'll see the name you gave to the parrot you added in the context in the console, in my case Koko.

> **NOTE**   In real-world scenarios, we use unit and integration tests to validate that our implementations work as desired. The projects in this book implement unit tests to validate the discussed behavior. Because this is a "getting started" book, you might not yet be aware of unit tests. To avoid creating confusion and allow you to focus on the discussed subject, we won't discuss unit tests until chapter 15. However, if you already know how to write unit tests and reading them helps you better understand the subject, you can find all the unit tests implemented in the test folder of each of our Maven projects. If you don't yet know how unit tests work, I recommend focusing only on the discussed subject.

As in the previous example, you can add any kind of object to the Spring context (figure 2.10). Let's also add a String and an Integer and see that it's working.

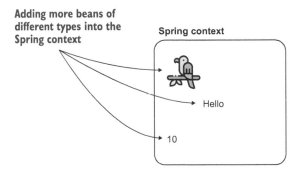

Adding more beans of different types into the Spring context

Spring context

Hello

10

Figure 2.10   You can add any object to the Spring context to make Spring aware of it.

The next listing shows you how I changed the configuration class to also add a bean of type String and a bean of type Integer.

Listing 2.11   Adding two more beans to the context

```
@Configuration
public class ProjectConfig {

  @Bean
  Parrot parrot() {
    var p = new Parrot();
    p.setName("Koko");
    return p;
  }

  @Bean                          Adds the string "Hello"
  String hello() {          ⟵    to the Spring context
    return "Hello";
  }
```

```
@Bean                    ◁──┐  Adds the integer 10
Integer ten() {             │  to the Spring context
    return 10;
}
}
```

NOTE Remember the Spring context's purpose: we add the instances we expect Spring needs to manage. (This way, we plug in functionalities offered by the framework.) In a real-world app, we won't add every object to the Spring context. Starting with chapter 4, when our examples will become closer to code in a production-ready app, we'll also focus more on which objects Spring needs to manage. For the moment, focus on the approaches you can use to add beans to the Spring context.

You can now refer to these two new beans in the same way we did with the parrot. The next listing shows you how to change the main method to print the new beans' values.

> **Listing 2.12   Printing the two new beans in the console**

```
public class Main {

  public static void main(String[] args) {
    var context = new AnnotationConfigApplicationContext(
                    ProjectConfig.class);

    Parrot p = context.getBean(Parrot.class);      ◁──┐  You don't need to do any explicit
    System.out.println(p.getName());                   │  casting. Spring looks for a bean
                                                       │  of the type you requested in its
    String s = context.getBean(String.class);          │  context. If such a bean doesn't exist,
    System.out.println(s);                             │  Spring will throw an exception.

    Integer n = context.getBean(Integer.class);
    System.out.println(n);
  }
}
```

Running the app now, the values of the three beans will be printed in the console, as shown in the next code snippet.

```
Koko
Hello
10
```

Thus far we added one or more beans of different types to the Spring context. But could we add more than one object of the same type (figure 2.11)? If yes, how can we individually refer to these objects? Let's create a new project, "sq-ch2-ex3," to demonstrate how you can add multiple beans of the same type to the Spring context and how you can refer to them afterward.

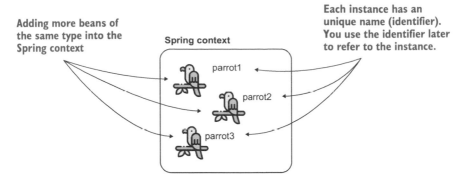

Adding more beans of the same type into the Spring context

Spring context

Each instance has an unique name (identifier). You use the identifier later to refer to the instance.

parrot1

parrot2

parrot3

Figure 2.11   You can add more beans of the same type to the Spring context by using multiple methods annotated with @Bean. Each instance will have a unique identifier. To refer to them afterward, you'll need to use the beans' identifiers.

NOTE   Don't confuse the name of the bean with the name of the parrot. In our example, the beans' names (or identifiers) in the Spring context are parrot1, parrot2, and parrot3 (like the name of the @Bean methods defining them). The names I gave to the parrots are Koko, Miki, and Riki. The parrot name is just an attribute of the Parrot object, and it doesn't mean anything to Spring.

You can declare as many instances of the same type as you wish by simply declaring more methods annotated with the @Bean annotation. The following listing shows you how I've declared three beans of type Parrot in the configuration class. You find this example with the project "sq-ch2-ex3."

Listing 2.13   Adding multiple beans of the same type to the Spring context

```
@Configuration
public class ProjectConfig {

  @Bean
  Parrot parrot1() {
    var p = new Parrot();
    p.setName("Koko");
    return p;
  }

  @Bean
  Parrot parrot2() {
    var p = new Parrot();
    p.setName("Miki");
    return p;
  }

  @Bean
  Parrot parrot3() {
    var p = new Parrot();
```

```
        p.setName("Riki");
        return p;
    }
}
```

Of course, you can't get the beans from the context anymore by only specifying the type. If you do, you'll get an exception because Spring cannot guess which instance you've declared you refer to. Look at the following listing. Running such a code throws an exception in which Spring tells you that you need to be precise, which is the instance you want to use.

Listing 2.14 Referring to a `Parrot` instance by type

```
public class Main {

  public static void main(String[] args) {
    var context = new
      AnnotationConfigApplicationContext(ProjectConfig.class);

    Parrot p = context.getBean(Parrot.class);      ◁──┐  You'll get an exception on this line
                                                        because Spring cannot guess which
    System.out.println(p.getName());                    of the three Parrot instances you
                                                        refer to.
  }
}
```

When running your application, you'll get an exception similar to the one presented by the next code snippet.

```
Exception in thread "main"
org.springframework.beans.factory.NoUniqueBeanDefinitionException: No
qualifying bean of type 'main.Parrot' available: expected single matching
bean but found 3:
    parrot1,parrot2,parrot3    ◁──┐  Names of the Parrot
    at …                            beans in the context
```

To solve this ambiguity problem, you need to refer precisely to one of the instances by using the bean's name. By default, Spring uses the names of the methods annotated with @Bean as the beans' names themselves. Remember that's why we don't name the @Bean methods using verbs. In our case, the beans have the names parrot1, parrot2, and parrot3 (remember, the method represents the bean). You can find these names in the previous code snippet in the message of the exception. Did you spot them? Let's change the main method to refer to one of these beans explicitly by using its name. Observe how I referred to the parrot2 bean in the following listing.

Listing 2.15 Referring to a bean by its identifier

```
public class Main {

  public static void main(String[] args) {
    var context = new
```

```
AnnotationConfigApplicationContext(ProjectConfig.class);

Parrot p = context.getBean("parrot2", Parrot.class);     ◁     First parameter is the
System.out.println(p.getName());                                name of the instance
                                                                to which we refer
  }
}
```

Running the app now, you'll no longer get an exception. Instead, you'll see in the console the name of the second parrot, `Miki`.

If you'd like to give another name to the bean, you can use either one of the name or the value attributes of the `@Bean` annotation. Any of the following syntaxes will change the name of the bean in `"miki"`:

- `@Bean(name = "miki")`
- `@Bean(value = "miki")`
- `@Bean("miki")`

In the next code snippet, you can observe the change as it appears in code, and if you'd like to run this example, you find it in the project named "sq-ch2-ex4":

```
@Bean(name = "miki")     ◁———  Sets the name of the bean
Parrot parrot2() {
  var p = new Parrot();
  p.setName("Miki");     ◁———  Sets the name of the parrot
  return p;
}
```

Defining a bean as primary

Earlier in this section we discussed that you could have multiple beans of the same kind in the Spring context, but you need to refer to them using their names. There's another option when referring to beans in the context when you have more of the same type.

When you have multiple beans of the same kind in the Spring context you can make one of them *primary*. You mark the bean you want to be primary using the `@Primary` annotation. A primary bean is the one Spring will choose if it has multiple options and you don't specify a name; the primary bean is simply Spring's default choice. The next code snippet shows you what the `@Bean` method annotated as primary looks like:

```
@Bean
@Primary
Parrot parrot2() {
  var p = new Parrot();
  p.setName("Miki");
  return p;
}
```

If you refer to a `Parrot` without specifying the name, Spring will now select `Miki` by default. Of course, you can only define one bean of a type as primary. You find this example implemented in the project "sq-ch2-ex5."

2.2.2 Using stereotype annotations to add beans to the Spring context

In this section, you'll learn a different approach for adding beans to the Spring context (later in this chapter, we also compare the approaches and discuss when to choose one or another). Remember, adding beans to the Spring context is essential because it's how you make Spring aware of the object instances of your application, which need to be managed by the framework. Spring offers you more ways to add beans to its context. In different scenarios, you'll find using one of these approaches is more comfortable than another. For example, with stereotype annotations, you'll observe you write less code to instruct Spring to add a bean to its context.

Later you'll learn that Spring offers multiple stereotype annotations. But in this section, I want you to focus on how to use a stereotype annotation in general. We'll take the most basic of these, `@Component`, and use it to demonstrate our examples.

With stereotype annotations, you add the annotation above the class for which you need to have an instance in the Spring context. When doing so, we say that you've marked the class as a component. When the app creates the Spring context, Spring creates an instance of the class you marked as a component and adds that instance to its context. We'll still have a configuration class when we use this approach to tell Spring where to look for the classes annotated with stereotype annotations. Moreover, you can use both the approaches (using `@Bean` and stereotype annotations together; we'll work on these types of complex examples in later chapters).

The steps we need to follow in the process are as follows (figure 2.12):

1   Using the `@Component` annotation, mark the classes for which you want Spring to add an instance to its context (in our case `Parrot`).
2   Using `@ComponentScan` annotation over the configuration class, instruct Spring on where to find the classes you marked.

Let's take our example with the `Parrot` class. We can add an instance of the class in the Spring context by annotating the `Parrot` class with one of the stereotype annotations, say `@Component`.

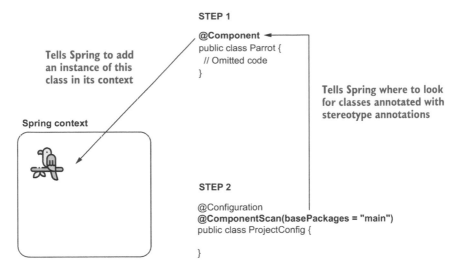

Figure 2.12   **When using stereotype annotations, consider two steps. First, use the stereotype annotation (@Component) to annotate the class for which you want Spring to add a bean to its context. Second, use the @ComponentScan annotation to tell Spring where to look for classes annotated with stereotype annotations.**

The next listing shows you how to use the @Component annotation for the Parrot class. You can find this example in the project "sq-ch2-ex6."

Listing 2.16   **Using a stereotype annotation for the Parrot class**

```
@Component
public class Parrot {

  private String name;

  public String getName() {
    return name;
  }

  public void setName(String name) {
    this.name = name;
  }
}
```

By using the @Component annotation over the class, we instruct Spring to create an instance of this class and add it to its context.

But wait! This code won't work just yet. By default, Spring doesn't search for classes annotated with stereotype annotations, so if we just leave the code as-is, Spring won't add a bean of type Parrot in its context. To tell Spring it needs to search for classes annotated with stereotype annotations, we use the @ComponentScan annotation over the configuration class. Also, with the @ComponentScan annotation, we tell Spring where to look for these classes. We enumerate the packages where we defined the classes with stereotype annotations. The next listing shows you how to use the @ComponentScan annotation over the configuration class of the project. In my case, the name of the package is "main."

Listing 2.17   Using the @ComponentScan annotation to tell Spring where to look

```
@Configuration
@ComponentScan(basePackages = "main")
public class ProjectConfig {

}
```

Using the basePackages attribute of the annotation, we tell Spring where to look for classes annotated with stereotype annotations.

Now you told Spring the following:

1   Which classes to add an instance to its context (`Parrot`)
2   Where to find these classes (using `@ComponentScan`)

NOTE   We don't need methods anymore to define the beans. And it now looks like this approach is better because you achieve the same thing by writing less code. But wait until the end of this chapter. You'll learn that both approaches are useful, depending on the scenario.

You can continue writing the main method as presented in the following listing to prove that Spring creates and adds the bean in its context.

Listing 2.18   Defining the main method to test the Spring configuration

Prints the default String representation of the instance taken from the Spring context

```
public class Main {

  public static void main(String[] args) {
    var context = new
      AnnotationConfigApplicationContext(ProjectConfig.class);

    Parrot p = context.getBean(Parrot.class);

    System.out.println(p);
    System.out.println(p.getName());
  }
}
```

Prints null because we did not assign any name to the parrot instance added by Spring in its context

Running this application, you'll observe Spring added a `Parrot` instance to its context because the first value printed is the default `String` representation of this instance. However, the second value printed is `null` because we did not assign any name to this parrot. Spring just creates the instance of the class, but it's still our duty if we want to change this instance in any way afterward (like assigning it a name).

Now that we've covered the two most frequently encountered ways you add beans to the Spring context, let's make a short comparison of them (table 2.1).

What you'll observe is that in real-world scenarios you'll use stereotype annotations as much as possible (because this approach implies writing less code), and you'll only use the `@Bean` when you can't add the bean otherwise (e.g., you create the bean for a class that is part of a library so you cannot modify that class to add the stereotype annotation).

Table 2.1 Advantages and disadvantages: A comparison of the two ways of adding beans to the Spring context, which tells you when you would use either of them

Using the @Bean annotation	Using stereotype annotations
1 You have full control over the instance creation you add to the Spring context. It is your responsibility to create and configure the instance in the body of the method annotated with @Bean. Spring only takes that instance and adds it to the context as-is. 2 You can use this method to add more instances of the same type to the Spring context. Remember, in section 2.1.1 we added three Parrot instances into the Spring context. 3 You can use the @Bean annotation to add to the Spring context any object instance. The class that defines the instance doesn't need to be defined in your app. Remember, earlier we added a String and an Integer to the Spring context. 4 You need to write a separate method for each bean you create, which adds boilerplate code to your app. For this reason, we prefer using @Bean as a second option to stereotype annotations in our projects.	1 You only have control over the instance after the framework creates it. 2 This way, you can only add one instance of the class to the context. 3 You can use stereotype annotations only to create beans of the classes your application owns. For example, you couldn't add a bean of type String or Integer like we did in section 2.1.1 with the @Bean annotation because you don't own these classes to change them by adding a stereotype annotation. 4 Using stereotype annotations to add beans to the Spring context doesn't add boilerplate code to your app. You'll prefer this approach in general for the classes that belong to your app.

Using @PostConstruct to manage the instance after its creation

As we've discussed in this section, using stereotype annotations you instruct Spring to create a bean and add it to its context. But, unlike using the @Bean annotation, you don't have full control over the instance creation. Using @Bean, we were able to define a name for each of the Parrot instances we added to the Spring context, but using @Component, we didn't get a chance to do something after Spring called the constructor of the Parrot class. What if we want to execute some instructions right after Spring creates the bean? We can use the @PostConstruct annotation.

Spring borrows the @PostConstruct annotation from Java EE. We can also use this annotation with Spring beans to specify a set of instructions Spring executes after the bean creation. You just need to define a method in the component class and annotate that method with @PostConstruct, which instructs Spring to call that method after the constructor finishes its execution.

Let's add to pom.xml the Maven dependency needed to use the @PostConstruct annotation:

```
<dependency>
    <groupId>javax.annotation</groupId>
    <artifactId>javax.annotation-api</artifactId>
    <version>1.3.2</version>
</dependency>
```

You don't need to add this dependency if you use a Java version smaller than Java 11. Before Java 11, the Java EE dependencies were part of the JDK. With Java 11, the JDK was cleaned of the APIs not related to SE, including the Java EE dependencies.

If you wish to use functionalities that were part of the removed APIs (like @PostConstruct), you now need to explicitly add the dependency in your app.

Now you can define a method in the Parrot class, as presented in the next code snippet:

```
@Component
public class Parrot {

  private String name;

  @PostConstruct
  public void init() {
    this.name = "Kiki";
  }

  // Omitted code
}
```

You find this example in the project "sq-ch2-ex7." If you now print the name of the parrot in the console, you'll observe the app prints the value Kiki in the console.

Very similarly, but less encountered in real-world apps, you can use an annotation named @PreDestroy. With this annotation, you define a method that Spring calls immediately before closing and clearing the context. The @PreDestroy annotation is also described in JSR-250 and borrowed by Spring. But generally I recommend developers avoid using it and find a different approach to executing something before Spring clears the context, mainly because you can expect Spring to fail to clear the context. Say you defined something sensitive (like closing a database connection) in the @PreDestroy method; if Spring doesn't call the method, you may get into big problems.

2.2.3 *Programmatically adding beans to the Spring context*

In this section, we discuss adding beans programmatically to the Spring context. We've had the option of programmatically adding beans to the Spring context with Spring 5, which offers great flexibility because it enables you to add new instances in the context directly by calling a method of the context instance. You'd use this approach when you want to implement a custom way of adding beans to the context and the @Bean or the stereotype annotations are not enough for your needs. Say you need to register specific beans in the Spring context depending on specific configurations of your application. With the @Bean and stereotype annotations, you can implement most of the scenarios, but you can't do something like the code presented in the next snippet:

```
if (condition) {
    registerBean(b1);          ◁─── If the condition is true, add a
                                     specific bean to the Spring context.
} else {

    registerBean(b2);          ◁─── Otherwise, add another
                                     bean to the Spring context.
}
```

To keep using our parrots example, the scenario is as follows: The app reads a collection of parrots. Some of them are green; others are orange. You want the app to add to the Spring context only the parrots that are green (figure 2.13).

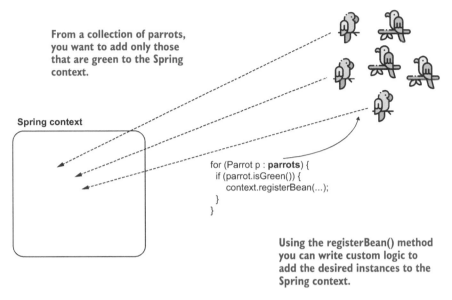

Figure 2.13   Using the `registerBean()` method to add specific object instances to the Spring context

Let's see how this method works. To add a bean to the Spring context using a programmatic approach, you just need to call the registerBean() method of the ApplicationContext instance. The registerBean() has four parameters, as presented in the next code snippet:

```
<T> void registerBean(
  String beanName,
  Class<T> beanClass,
  Supplier<T> supplier,
  BeanDefinitionCustomizer... customizers);
```

1 Use the first parameter beanName to define a name for the bean you add in the Spring context. If you don't need to give a name to the bean you're adding, you can use null as a value when you call the method.

2 The second parameter is the class that defines the bean you add to the context. Say you want to add an instance of the class Parrot; the value you give to this parameter is Parrot.class.

3 The third parameter is an instance of Supplier. The implementation of this Supplier needs to return the value of the instance you add to the context. Remember, Supplier is a functional interface you find in the java.util .function package. The purpose of a supplier implementation is to return a value you define without taking parameters.

4 The fourth and last parameter is a varargs of `BeanDefinitionCustomizer`. (If this doesn't sound familiar, that's okay; the `BeanDefinitionCustomizer` is just an interface you implement to configure different characteristics of the bean; e.g., making it primary.) Being defined as a varargs type, you can omit this parameter entirely, or you can give it more values of type `BeanDefinitionCustomizer`.

In the project "sq-ch2-ex8," you find an example of using the `registerBean()` method. You observe that this project's configuration class is empty, and the `Parrot` class we use for our bean definition example is just a plain old Java object (POJO); we use no annotation with it. In the next code snippet, you find the configuration class as I defined it for this example:

```
@Configuration
public class ProjectConfig {
}
```

I defined the class `Parrot` that we use to create the bean:

```
public class Parrot {

  private String name;

  // Omitted getters and setters
}
```

In the main method of the project, I've used the `registerBean()` method to add an instance of type `Parrot` to the Spring context. The next listing presents the code of the main method. Figure 2.14 focuses on the syntax for calling the `registerBean()` method.

Listing 2.19 Using the `registerBean()` method to add a bean to the Spring context

```
public class Main {

  public static void main(String[] args) {
    var context =
      new AnnotationConfigApplicationContext(
        ProjectConfig.class);
                                          We create the instance we want
    Parrot x = new Parrot();   ←——       to add to the Spring context.
    x.setName("Kiki");
                                                     We define a Supplier to
    Supplier<Parrot> parrotSupplier = () -> x;   ←—— return this instance.

    context.registerBean("parrot1",            We call the registerBean() method to add
      Parrot.class, parrotSupplier);   ←——     the instance to the Spring context.

    Parrot p = context.getBean(Parrot.class);
    System.out.println(p.getName());       ⎤ To verify the bean is now in the
  }                                        ⎟ context, we refer to the parrot bean
}                                          ⎦ and print its name in the console.
```

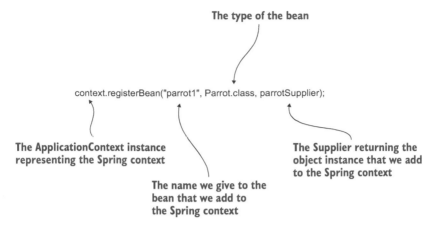

Figure 2.14 Calling the `registerBean()` method to add a bean to the Spring
context programmatically

Use one or more bean configurator instances as the last parameters to set different
characteristics of the beans you add. For example, you can make the bean primary by
changing the `registerBean()` method call, as shown in the next code snippet. A primary bean defines the instance Spring selects by default if you have multiple beans of
the same type in the context:

```
context.registerBean("parrot1",
                Parrot.class,
                parrotSupplier,
                bc -> bc.setPrimary(true));
```

You've just made a first big step into the Spring world. Learning how to add beans to
the Spring context might not seem like much, but it's more important than it looks.
With this skill, you can now proceed to referring to the beans in the Spring context,
which we discuss in chapter 3.

> **NOTE**   In this book, we use only modern configuration approaches. However,
> I find it essential for you also to be aware of how the developers configured
> the framework in the early days of Spring. At that time, we were using XML to
> write these configurations. In appendix B, a short example is provided to give
> you a feeling on how you would use XML to add a bean to the Spring context.

Summary

- The first thing you need to learn in Spring is adding object instances (which we
  call beans) to the Spring context. You can imagine the Spring context as a
  bucket in which you add the instances you expect Spring to be able to manage.
  Spring can see only the instances you add to its context.

- You can add beans to the Spring context in three ways: using the @Bean annotation, using stereotype annotations, and doing it programmatically.
  - Using the @Bean annotation to add instances to the Spring context enables you to add any kind of object instance as a bean and even multiple instances of the same kind to the Spring context. From this point of view, this approach is more flexible than using stereotype annotations. Still, it requires you to write more code because you need to write a separate method in the configuration class for each independent instance added to the context.
  - Using stereotype annotations, you can create beans for only the application classes with a specific annotation (e.g., @Component). This configuration approach requires writing less code, which makes your configuration more comfortable to read. You'll prefer this approach over the @Bean annotation for classes that you define and can annotate.
  - Using the registerBean() method enables you to implement custom logic for adding beans to the Spring context. Remember, you can use this approach only with Spring 5 and later.

The Spring context: Wiring beans

This chapter covers

- Establishing relationships among beans
- Using dependency injection
- Accessing the beans from the Spring context through dependency injection

In chapter 2, we discussed the Spring context: the place in the app's memory where we add the object instances we want Spring to manage. Because Spring uses the IoC principle, as we discussed in chapter 1, we need to tell Spring which objects of our app it needs to control. Spring needs control over some of the objects of our app to augment them with the capabilities it provides. In chapter 2, you learned multiple ways to add object instances to the Spring context. You also learned that we add these instances (beans) into the Spring context to make Spring aware of them.

In this chapter, we discuss how to access the beans, which we've added to the Spring context. In chapter 2, we used the `getBean()` method of the context instance directly to access the beans. But in apps, we need to refer from one bean to another in a straightforward fashion—by telling Spring to provide a reference to an instance from its context where we need it. This way, we establish relationships among the beans (one bean will have a reference to another to delegate calls when it needs). As you probably already know, often in any object-oriented programming language, an object needs to delegate specific responsibilities to others when implementing their behavior, so you need to know how to establish such relationships among objects when you use Spring as a framework as well.

You'll learn you have more ways you can access the objects you added to the Spring context, and we'll study each with examples, visuals, and, of course, code snippets. At the end of this chapter, you'll have the needed skills to use the Spring context and configure beans and relationships among them. This skill is the foundation of using Spring; you won't find any Spring app in which you wouldn't apply the approaches we discuss in this chapter. For this reason, everything in this book (and everything you'll learn from any other book, article, or video tutorials) relies on properly understanding the approaches we discuss in chapters 2 through 5.

In chapter 2, you learned to use the @Bean annotation to add beans in the Spring context. In section 3.1, we start by implementing a relationship between two beans you'll define in the configuration class by using the @Bean annotation. Here we discuss two ways you can establish the relationships among beans:

- Link the beans by directly calling the methods that create them (which we'll call *wiring*).
- Enable Spring to provide us a value using a method parameter (which we'll call *auto-wiring*).

Then, in section 3.2, we discuss a third approach, which is a technique supported by the IoC principle: *dependency injection* (DI). We'll discuss how to use DI in Spring, applying the @Autowired annotation to implement the relationship between two beans (which is also an example of auto-wiring). You'll use both these approaches together in real-world projects.

> **NOTE** You might think that the examples in chapters 2 and 3 are not close enough to the production code. In the end, real apps don't manage parrots and persons! But I want to start smoothly with the most straightforward examples and make sure you focus on these essential syntaxes, which you'll use in virtually every Spring app. This way, I make sure you properly understand how the discussed approaches work and focus only on them. Starting in chapter 4, our class design will become closer to what you'll find in real-world projects.

3.1 *Implementing relationships among beans defined in the configuration file*

In this section, you will learn to implement the relationship between two beans defined in the configuration class annotating methods with the @Bean annotation. You'll often encounter this approach for establishing the relationships among beans using the Spring configuration. In chapter 2, we discussed that we use the @Bean annotation to add beans to the Spring context in the cases in which we cannot change the class for which we want to add the bean, for example, if the class is part of the JDK or another dependency. And to establish relationships among these beans, you need to learn the approaches we discuss in this section. We'll discuss how these approaches work, I'll give you the steps you need to implement the relationships among beans, and then we'll apply these steps with small code projects.

Say we have two instances in the Spring context: a parrot and a person. We'll create and add these instances to the context. We want to make the person own the parrot. In other words, we need to link the two instances. This straightforward example helps us discuss the two approaches for linking the beans in the Spring context without adding unnecessary complexity and enables you to focus on the Spring configurations only.

So, for each of the two approaches (wiring and auto-wiring), we have two steps (figure 3.1):

1   Add the person and parrot beans to the Spring context (as you learned in chapter 2).

2   Establish a relationship between the person and the parrot.

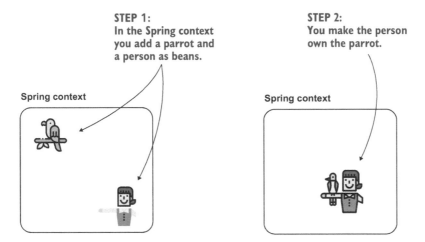

STEP 1:
In the Spring context
you add a parrot and
a person as beans.

STEP 2:
You make the person
own the parrot.

Spring context

Spring context

Figure 3.1   Having two beans in the Spring context, we want to establish a relationship between them. We do this so that one object can then delegate to the other in the implementation of their responsibilities. You can do this using a wiring approach, which implies directly calling the methods that declare the beans to establish the link between them, or through auto-wiring. You use the framework's dependency injection capabilities.

Figure 3.2 presents the "has-A" relationship between the person and the parrot object in a more technical way than figure 3.1.

Before diving into either of the approaches, let's start with the first example of this chapter ("sq-ch3-ex1") to remember how to add the beans into the Spring context using methods annotated with @Bean in the configuration class, as we discussed in section 2.2.1 (step 1). We'll add a parrot instance and a person instance. Once we have

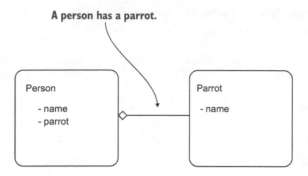

A person has a parrot.

Figure 3.2 Implementing the relationship between the beans. This is a simplified diagram representing the "has-A" relationship between the Person and the Parrot objects. We'll implement this relationship through wiring and auto-wiring.

this project ready, we change it to establish the relationship between the two instances (step 2). In section 3.1.1, we implement wiring, and in section 3.1.2, we implement auto-wiring for @Bean annotated methods. In the pom.xml file of the Maven project, we add the dependency for Spring context as you find it in the next code snippet:

```
<dependency>
    <groupId>org.springframework</groupId>
    <artifactId>spring-context</artifactId>
    <version>5.2.7.RELEASE</version>
</dependency>
```

We then define a class to describe the Parrot object and one to describe the Person. In the next code snippet, you find the definition of the Parrot class:

```
public class Parrot {

  private String name;

  // Omitted getters and setters

  @Override
  public String toString() {
    return "Parrot : " + name;
  }
}
```

In the next code snippet, you find the definition of the Person class:

```
public class Person {

  private String name;
  private Parrot parrot;

  // Omitted getters and setters
}
```

The following listing shows you how to define the two beans using the @Bean annotation in the configuration class.

Listing 3.1 Defining the Person and the Parrot beans

```
@Configuration
public class ProjectConfig {

  @Bean
  public Parrot parrot() {
    Parrot p = new Parrot();
    p.setName("Koko");
    return p;
  }

  @Bean
  public Person person() {
    Person p = new Person();
    p.setName("Ella");
    return p;
  }
}
```

You can now write a Main class, as presented in the following listing, and check that the two instances aren't yet linked to one another.

Listing 3.2 The definition of the Main class

Creates an instance of the Spring context based on the configuration class

```
public class Main {

  public static void main(String[] args) {
    var context = new AnnotationConfigApplicationContext
      (ProjectConfig.class);

    Person person =
      context.getBean(Person.class);      ← Gets a reference to the Person bean from the Spring context

    Parrot parrot =
      context.getBean(Parrot.class);      ← Gets a reference to the Parrot bean from the Spring context

    System.out.println(
      "Person's name: " + person.getName());   ← Prints the person's name to prove that the Person bean is in the context

    System.out.println(
      "Parrot's name: " + parrot.getName());   ← Prints the parrot's name to prove that the Parrot bean is in the context

    System.out.println(
      "Person's parrot: " + person.getParrot());  ← Prints the person's parrot to prove that there's not yet a relationship between the instances
}}
```

When running this app, you'll see a console output similar to the one presented in the next code snippet:

The Person bean is in the Spring context.

The Parrot bean is in the Spring context.

```
Person's name: Ella
Parrot's name: Koko
Person's parrot: null
```

The relationship between the person and the parrot isn't established.

The most important thing to observe here is that the person's parrot (third output line) is null. Both the person and the parrot instances are in the context, however. This output is null, which means there's not yet a relationship between the instances (figure 3.3).

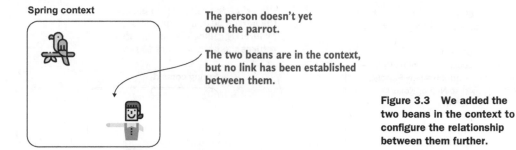

Spring context

The person doesn't yet own the parrot.

The two beans are in the context, but no link has been established between them.

Figure 3.3 We added the two beans in the context to configure the relationship between them further.

3.1.1 *Wiring the beans using a direct method call between the @Bean methods*

In this section, we establish the relationship between the two instances of Person and Parrot. The first way (wiring) to achieve this is to call one method from another in the configuration class. You'll find this often used because it's a straightforward approach. In the next listing, you find the small change I had to make in my configuration class to establish a link between the person and the parrot (see figure 3.4). To keep all the steps separate and help you easier understand the code, I have also separated this change in a second project: "sq-ch3-ex2."

Listing 3.3 Making a link between the beans with a direct method call

```java
@Configuration
public class ProjectConfig {

  @Bean
  public Parrot parrot() {
    Parrot p = new Parrot();
    p.setName("Koko");
    return p;
  }

  @Bean
  public Person person() {
    Person p = new Person();
```

```
    p.setName("Ella");
    p.setParrot(parrot());      Setting the reference of the parrot
    return p;                   bean to the person's parrot attribute
  }
}
```

Running the same app, you'll observe the output changed in the console. Now you find (see next snippet) that the second line shows that Ella (the person in the Spring context) owns Koko (the parrot in the Spring context):

```
Person's name: Ella             We now observe the relationship between the
Person's parrot: Parrot : Koko  person and the parrot has been established.
```

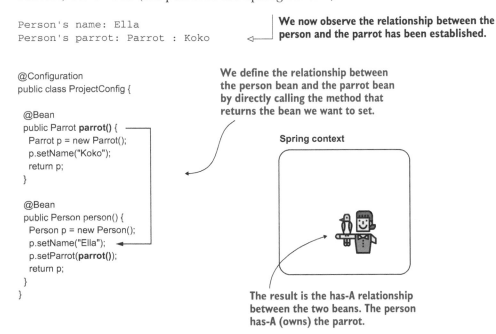

Figure 3.4   **We establish the relationship between the beans using direct wiring. This approach implies calling the method that returns the bean you want to set directly. You need to call this method from the one that defines the bean for which you set the dependency.**

Whenever I teach this approach in a class, I know some have the question: doesn't this mean that we create two instances of Parrot (figure 3.5)—one instance Spring creates and adds into its context and another one when the person() method makes the direct call to the parrot() method? No, we actually have only one parrot instance in this application overall.

It might look strange at first, but Spring is smart enough to understand that by calling the parrot() method, you want to refer to the parrot bean in its context. When we use the @Bean annotation to define beans into the Spring context, Spring controls how the methods are called and can apply logic above the method call (you'll learn more about how Spring intercepts methods in chapter 6). For the moment, remember that when the person() method calls the parrot() method, Spring will apply logic, as described next.

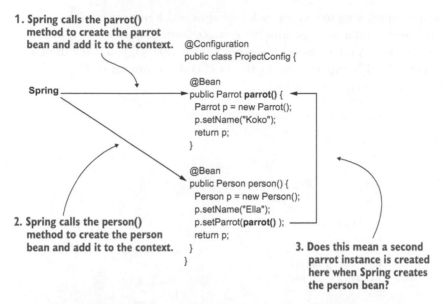

1. Spring calls the parrot() method to create the parrot bean and add it to the context.

```
@Configuration
public class ProjectConfig {

    @Bean
    public Parrot parrot() {
        Parrot p = new Parrot();
        p.setName("Koko");
        return p;
    }

    @Bean
    public Person person() {
        Person p = new Person();
        p.setName("Ella");
        p.setParrot(parrot() );
        return p;
    }
}
```

Spring

2. Spring calls the person() method to create the person bean and add it to the context.

3. Does this mean a second parrot instance is created here when Spring creates the person bean?

Figure 3.5   Spring creates a parrot instance when it calls the first @Bean annotated method `parrot()`. Then, Spring creates a person instance when it calls the second @Bean annotated method `person()`. The second method, `person()`, directly calls the first method, `parrot()`. Does this mean two instances of type `parrot` are created?

If the parrot bean already exists in the context, then instead of calling the `parrot()` method, Spring will directly take the instance from its context. If the parrot bean does not yet exist in the context, Spring calls the `parrot()` method and returns the bean (figure 3.6).

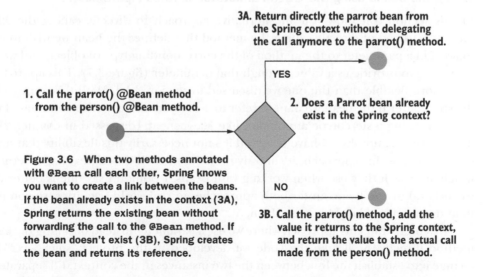

1. Call the parrot() @Bean method from the person() @Bean method.

2. Does a Parrot bean already exist in the Spring context?

YES

3A. Return directly the parrot bean from the Spring context without delegating the call anymore to the parrot() method.

NO

3B. Call the parrot() method, add the value it returns to the Spring context, and return the value to the actual call made from the person() method.

Figure 3.6   When two methods annotated with @Bean call each other, Spring knows you want to create a link between the beans. If the bean already exists in the context (3A), Spring returns the existing bean without forwarding the call to the @Bean method. If the bean doesn't exist (3B), Spring creates the bean and returns its reference.

It's actually quite easy to test this behavior. Just add a no-args constructor to the Parrot class and print a message into the console from it. How many times will the message be printed in the console? If the behavior is correct, you'll see the message only once. Let's do this experiment. In the next code snippet, I've changed the Parrot class to add a no-args constructor:

```java
public class Parrot {

  private String name;

  public Parrot() {
    System.out.println("Parrot created");
  }

  // Omitted getters and setters

  @Override
  public String toString() {
    return "Parrot : " + name;
  }
}
```

Rerun the app. The output changed (see next code snippet), and now the "Parrot created" message appears as well. You'll observe it appears only once, which proves that Spring manages the bean creation and calls the parrot() method only once:

```
Parrot created
Person's name: Ella
Person's parrot: Parrot : Koko
```

3.1.2   *Wiring the beans using the @Bean annotated method's parameters*

In this section, I'll show you an alternative approach to directly calling the @Bean method. Instead of directly calling the method that defines the bean we wish to refer to, we add a parameter to the method of the corresponding type of object, and we rely on Spring to provide us a value through that parameter (figure 3.7). This approach is a bit more flexible than the one we discussed in section 3.1.1. With this approach, it doesn't matter if the bean we want to refer to is defined with a method annotated with @Bean or using a stereotype annotation like @Component (discussed in chapter 2). In my experience, however, I have observed it's not necessarily this flexibility that makes developers use this approach; it's mostly the taste of each developer that determines which approach they use when working with beans. I wouldn't say one is better than the other, but you'll encounter both approaches in real-world scenarios, so you need to understand and be able to use them.

To demonstrate this approach where we use a parameter instead of calling the @Bean method directly, we'll take the code we developed in the project "sq-ch3-ex2" and change it to establish the link between the two instances in the context. I'll separate the new example in a project named "sq-ch3-ex3."

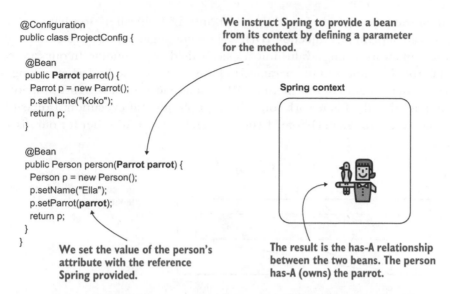

```
@Configuration
public class ProjectConfig {

  @Bean
  public Parrot parrot() {
    Parrot p = new Parrot();
    p.setName("Koko");
    return p;
  }

  @Bean
  public Person person(Parrot parrot) {
    Person p = new Person();
    p.setName("Ella");
    p.setParrot(parrot);
    return p;
  }
}
```

We instruct Spring to provide a bean from its context by defining a parameter for the method.

Spring context

We set the value of the person's attribute with the reference Spring provided.

The result is the has-A relationship between the two beans. The person has-A (owns) the parrot.

Figure 3.7 By defining a parameter to the method, we instruct Spring to provide us a bean of the type of that parameter from its context. We can then use the provided bean (`parrot`) when creating the second one (`person`). This way we establish the has-A relationship between the two beans.

In the next listing, you find the definition of the configuration class. Take a look at the `person()` method. It now receives a parameter of type `Parrot`, and I set the reference of that parameter to the returned person's attribute. When calling the method, Spring knows it has to find a parrot bean in its context and inject its value into the parameter of the `person()` method.

Listing 3.4 Injecting bean dependencies by using parameters of the methods

```
@Configuration
public class ProjectConfig {

  @Bean
  public Parrot parrot() {
    Parrot p = new Parrot();
    p.setName("Koko");
    return p;
  }

  @Bean
  public Person person(Parrot parrot) {                    Spring injects the parrot
    Person p = new Person();                                bean into this parameter.
    p.setName("Ella");
    p.setParrot(parrot);
    return p;
  }
}
```

In the previous paragraph, I used the word "inject." I refer here to what we will from now on call dependency injection (DI). As its name suggests, DI is a technique involving the framework setting a value into a specific field or parameter. In our case, Spring sets a particular value into the parameter of the person() method when calling it and resolves a dependency of this method. DI is an application of the IoC principle, and IoC implies that the framework controls the application at execution. I repeat figure 3.8, which you also saw in chapter 1 (figure 1.4), here as a refresher for our discussion on IoC.

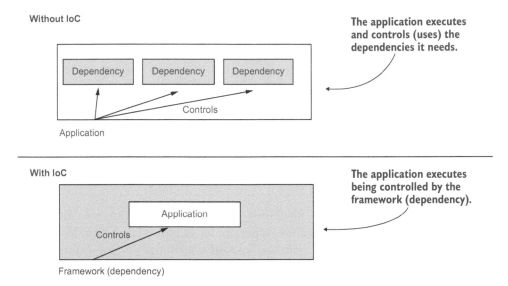

Figure 3.8   An application that's not using the IoC principle controls the execution and makes use of various dependencies. An application using the IoC principle allows a dependency to control its execution. The DI is such an example of control. The framework (a dependency) sets a value into a field of an object of the app.

You'll often use DI (and not only in Spring) because it's a very comfortable way to manage object instances that are created and help us minimize the code we write when developing our apps.

When running the app, the output in your console will be similar to the next code snippet. You observe that the parrot Koko is indeed linked to the person Ella:

```
Parrot created
Person's name: Ella
Person's parrot: Parrot : Koko
```

3.2   *Using the @Autowired annotation to inject beans*

In this section, we discuss another approach used to create a link between beans in the Spring context. You'll often encounter this technique, which refers to an annotation named @Autowired, when you can change the class for which you define the bean (when this class is not part of a dependency). Using the @Autowired annotation, we mark an object's property where we want Spring to inject a value from the context, and we mark this intention directly in the class that defines the object that needs the dependency. This approach makes it easier to see the relationship between the two objects than the alternatives we discussed in section 3.1. As you'll see, there are three ways we can use the @Autowired annotation:

- Injecting the value in the field of the class, which you usually find in examples and proofs of concept
- Injecting the value through the constructor parameters of the class approach that you'll use most often in real-world scenarios
- Injecting the value through the setter, which you'll rarely use in production-ready code

Let's discuss these in more detail and write an example for each.

3.2.1   *Using @Autowired to inject the values through the class fields*

In this section, we start by discussing the simplest of the three possibilities for using @Autowired, which is also the one developers often use in examples: using the annotation over the field (figure 3.9). As you'll learn, even if this approach is very straightforward, it has its sins, which is why we avoid using it when writing production code. However, you'll see it often used in examples, proofs of concept, and in writing tests, as we'll discuss in chapter 15, so you need to know how to use this approach.

Let's develop a project ("sq-ch3-ex4") in which we annotate the parrot field of the Person class with the @Autowired annotation to tell Spring we want to inject a value there from its context. Let's start with the classes defining our two objects: Person and Parrot. You find the definition of the Parrot class in the next code snippet:

```
@Component
public class Parrot {

  private String name = "Koko";

  // Omitted getters and setters

  @Override
  public String toString() {
    return "Parrot : " + name;
  }
}
```

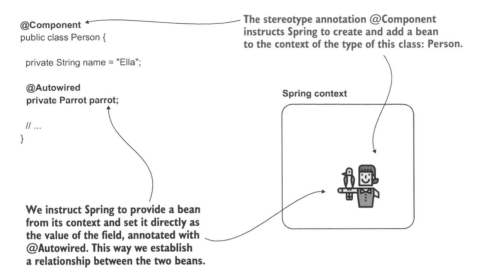

Figure 3.9   **Using the @Autowired annotation over the field, we instruct Spring to provide a value for that field from its context. Spring creates the two beans, person and parrot, and injects the parrot object to the field of the bean of type Person.**

We use the stereotype annotation @Component here, which you learned in chapter 2 (section 2.2.2). We use the stereotype annotation as an alternative to creating the bean using the configuration class. When annotating a class with @Component, Spring knows it has to create an instance of that class and add it to its context. The next code snippet shows the definition of the Person class:

```
@Component
public class Person {

    private String name = "Ella";

    @Autowired
    private Parrot parrot;

    // Omitted getters and setters
}
```

> Annotating the field with @Autowired, we instruct Spring to inject an appropriate value from its context.

NOTE   I've used stereotype annotations to add the beans in the Spring context for this example. I could have defined the beans using @Bean, but most often, in real-world scenarios, you'll encounter @Autowired used together with stereotype annotations, so let's focus on the approach that's most useful for you.

To continue our example, we define a configuration class. I'll name the configuration class ProjectConfig. Over this class, I'll use the @ComponentScan annotation to tell Spring where to find the classes I've annotated with @Component, as you learned in chapter 2 (section 2.2.2). The next code snippet shows the definition of the configuration class:

```
@Configuration
@ComponentScan(basePackages = "beans")
public class ProjectConfig {

}
```

I'll then use the main class, the same way I've used in the previous examples of this chapter, to prove that Spring injected the parrot bean's reference correctly:

```
public class Main {

  public static void main(String[] args) {
    var context = new AnnotationConfigApplicationContext
                        (ProjectConfig.class);

    Person p = context.getBean(Person.class);

    System.out.println("Person's name: " + p.getName());
    System.out.println("Person's parrot: " + p.getParrot());
  }
}
```

This will print in the app's console something similar to the output presented next. The second line of the output proves that the parrot (in my case, named Koko) belongs to the person bean (named Ella):

```
Person's name: Ella
Person's parrot: Parrot : Koko
```

Why is this approach not desired in production code? It's not totally wrong to use it, but you want to make sure you make your app maintainable and testable in production code. By injecting the value directly in the field:

- you don't have the option to make the field final (see next code snippet), and this way, make sure no one can change its value after initialization:

```
@Component
public class Person {

  private String name = "Ella";

  @Autowired
  private final Parrot parrot;         ◁─┐ This doesn't compile. You cannot define
                                          a final field without an initial value.
}
```

- it's more difficult to manage the value yourself at initialization.

As you'll learn in chapter 15, you sometimes need to create instances of the objects and easily manage the unit tests' dependencies.

3.2.2   *Using @Autowired to inject the values through the constructor*

The second option you have for injecting values into the object's attributes when Spring creates a bean is using the class's constructor defining the instance (figure 3.10). This approach is the one used most often in production code and the one I recommend. It enables you to define the fields as final, ensuring no one can change their value after Spring initializes them. The possibility to set the values when calling the constructor also helps you when writing specific unit tests where you don't want to rely on Spring making the field injection for you (but more on this subject later).

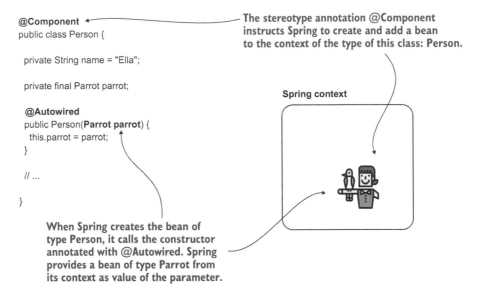

Figure 3.10   When you define a parameter of the constructor, Spring provides a bean from its context as a value to that parameter when calling the constructor.

We can quickly change the project's implementation from section 3.2.1 to use constructor injection instead of field injection. You only need to change the Person class, as presented in the following listing. You need to define a constructor for the class and annotate it with @Autowired. Now we can also make the parrot field final. You don't need to make any changes to your configuration class.

Listing 3.5   Injecting the values through constructor

```
@Component
public class Person {

  private String name = "Ella";
```

```
private final Parrot parrot;

@Autowired
public Person(Parrot parrot) {
  this.parrot = parrot;
}

// Omitted getters and setters

}
```

We can now make the field final to ensure its value cannot be changed after initialization.

We use the @Autowired annotation over the constructor.

To keep all the steps and changes, I've separated this example in the project "sq-ch3-ex5." You can already start the app and observe that it displays the same result as in the example in section 3.2.1. As you can see in the next code snippet, the person owns the parrot, so Spring established the link between the two instances correctly:

```
Person's name: Ella
Person's parrot: Parrot : Koko
```

> **NOTE** Starting with Spring version 4.3, when you only have one constructor in the class, you can omit writing the @Autowired annotation.

3.2.3 *Using dependency injection through the setter*

You won't often find developers applying the approach of using the setter for dependency injection. This approach has more disadvantages than advantages: it's more challenging to read, it doesn't allow you to make the field final, and it doesn't help you in making the testing easier. Even so, I wanted to mention this possibility. You might encounter it at some point, and I don't want you to wonder about its existence then. Even if it's not something I recommend, I have seen this used in a couple of old apps.

In the project "sq-ch3-ex6," you'll find an example of using the setter injection. You'll find that I only needed to change the Person class to implement this. In the next code snippet, I used the @Autowired annotation on the setter:

```
@Component
public class Person {

  private String name = "Ella";

  private Parrot parrot;

  // Omitted getters and setters

  @Autowired
  public void setParrot(Parrot parrot) {
    this.parrot = parrot;
  }
}
```

When running the app, you'll get the same output as the previously discussed examples of this section.

3.3   *Dealing with circular dependencies*

It's comfortable to let Spring build and set the dependencies to the objects of your application. Letting Spring do this job for you saves you from writing a bunch of lines of code and makes the app easier to read and understand. But Spring can also get confused in some cases. A scenario often encountered in practice is generating a circular dependency by mistake.

A circular dependency (figure 3.11) is a situation in which, to create a bean (let's name it Bean A), Spring needs to inject another bean that doesn't exist yet (Bean B). But Bean B also requests a dependency to Bean A. So, to create Bean B, Spring needs first to have Bean A. Spring is now in a deadlock. It cannot create Bean A because it needs Bean B, and it cannot create Bean B because it needs Bean A.

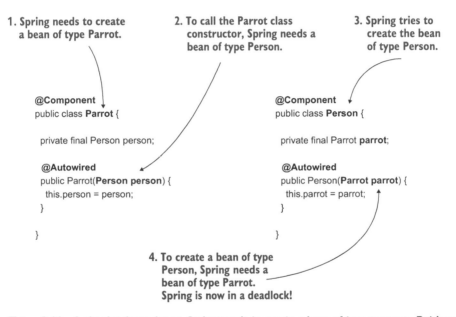

Figure 3.11   A circular dependency. Spring needs to create a bean of type `Parrot`. But because `Parrot` has as a dependency a `Person`, Spring needs first to create a `Person`. However, to create a `Person`, Spring already needs to have built a `Parrot`. Spring is now in a deadlock. It cannot create a `Parrot` because it needs a `Person`, and it cannot create a `Person` because it needs a `Parrot`.

A circular dependency is easy to avoid. You just need to make sure you don't define objects whose creation depends on the other. Having dependencies from one object to another like this is a bad design of classes. In such a case, you need to rewrite your code.

I don't think I know any Spring developer who didn't at least once create a circular dependency in an app. You need to be aware of this scenario so that when you encounter it, you know its cause and you'll solve it fast.

In the project "sq-ch3-ex7," you'll find an example of circular dependency. As presented in the next code snippets, I made the Parrot bean's instantiation dependent on the `Person` bean and vice-versa.

The `Person` class:

```
@Component
public class Person {

  private final Parrot parrot;

  @Autowired
  public Person(Parrot parrot) {      ◁──┐ To create the Person instance,
    this.parrot = parrot;                  Spring needs to have a Parrot bean.
  }

  // Omitted code

}
```

The `Parrot` class:

```
public class Parrot {

  private String name = "Koko";

  private final Person person;

  @Autowired
  public Parrot(Person person) {      ◁──┐ To create the Parrot instance, Spring
    this.person = person;                  needs to have a Person bean.
  }

  // Omitted code
}
```

Running the app with such a configuration will lead to an exception like the one presented in the next snippet:

```
Caused by:
org.springframework.beans.factory.BeanCurrentlyInCreationException: Error
creating bean with name 'parrot': Requested bean is currently in creation:
Is there an unresolvable circular reference?
    at
org.springframework.beans.factory.support.DefaultSingletonBeanRegistry.before
SingletonCreation(DefaultSingletonBeanRegistry.java:347)
```

With this exception, Spring tries to tell you the problem it encountered. The exception message is quite clear: Spring deals with a circular dependency and the classes that caused the situation. Whenever you find such an exception, you need to go to the classes specified by the exception and eliminate the circular dependency.

3.4   *Choosing from multiple beans in the Spring context*

In this section, we discuss the scenario in which Spring needs to inject a value into a parameter or class field but has multiple beans of the same type to choose from. Say you have three Parrot beans in the Spring context. You configure Spring to inject a value of type Parrot into a parameter. How will Spring behave? Which of the beans of the same type would the framework choose to inject in such a scenario?

Depending on your implementation, you have the following cases:

1 The identifier of the parameter matches the name of one of the beans from the context (which, remember, is the same as the name of the method annotated with @Bean that returns its value). In this case, Spring will choose the bean for which the name is the same as the parameter.

2 The identifier of the parameter doesn't match any of the bean names from the context. Then you have the following options:

   a You marked one of the beans as primary (as we discussed in chapter 2, using the @Primary annotation). In this case, Spring will select the primary bean for injection.

   b You can explicitly select a specific bean using the @Qualifier annotation, which we discuss in this chapter.

   c If none of the beans is primary and you don't use @Qualifier, the app will fail with an exception, complaining that the context contains more beans of the same type and Spring doesn't know which one to choose.

Let's try further in the project "sq-ch3-ex8," a scenario in which we have more than one instance of a type in the Spring context. The next listing shows you a configuration class that defines two Parrot instances and uses injection through the method parameters.

Listing 3.6   Using parameter injection for more than one bean

```
@Configuration
public class ProjectConfig {

  @Bean
  public Parrot parrot1() {
    Parrot p = new Parrot();
    p.setName("Koko");
    return p;
  }

  @Bean
  public Parrot parrot2() {
    Parrot p = new Parrot();
    p.setName("Miki");
    return p;
  }

  @Bean
  public Person person(Parrot parrot2) {
```

The name of the parameter matches the name of the bean representing parrot Miki.

```
    Person p = new Person();
    p.setName("Ella");
    p.setParrot(parrot2);
    return p;
  }
}
```

Running the app with this configuration, you'd observe a console output similar to the next code snippet. Observe that Spring linked the person bean to the parrot named Miki because the bean representing this parrot has the name parrot2 (figure 3.12):

```
Parrot created
Person's name: Ella
Person's parrot: Parrot : Miki
```

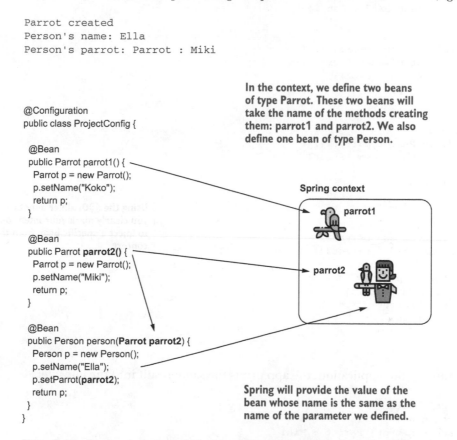

Figure 3.12   One way to instruct Spring to provide you a specific instance from its context, when the context contains more than one instance of the same type, is to rely on the name of this instance. Just name the parameter the same as the instance you'd like Spring to provide you.

In a real-world scenario, I prefer to avoid relying on the name of the parameter, which could be easily refactored and changed by mistake by another developer. To feel more comfortable, I usually choose a more visible approach to express my intention to inject a specific bean: using the @Qualifier annotation. Again, in my experience, I found developers arguing for and against using the @Qualifier annotation. I feel it is better to use in this case because it clearly defines your intention. Other developers believe adding this annotation creates unneeded (boilerplate) code.

The following listing provides an example using the @Qualifier annotation. Observe that instead of having a specific identifier of the parameter, I now specify the bean I want to inject using the value attribute of the @Qualifier annotation.

Listing 3.7   Using the @Qualifier annotation

```
@Configuration
public class ProjectConfig {

  @Bean
  public Parrot parrot1() {
    Parrot p = new Parrot();
    p.setName("Koko");
    return p;
  }

  @Bean
  public Parrot parrot2() {
    Parrot p = new Parrot();
    p.setName("Miki");
    return p;
  }

  @Bean
  public Person person(
    @Qualifier("parrot2") Parrot parrot) {     ◁─┐  Using the @Qualifier annotation,
                                                 │  you clearly mark your intention
    Person p = new Person();                     │  to inject a specific bean from the
    p.setName("Ella");                           ┘  context.
    p.setParrot(parrot);
    return p;
  }
}
```

Rerunning the application, the app prints the same result into the console:

```
Parrot created
Person's name: Ella
Person's parrot: Parrot : Miki
```

A similar situation can also happen when using the @Autowired annotation. To show you this case, I created another project, "sq-ch3-ex9." In this project, we define two beans of type Parrot (using the @Bean annotation) and an instance of Person (using stereotype annotations). I'll configure Spring to inject one of the two parrot beans in the bean of type Person.

As presented in the next code snippet, I didn't add the @Component annotation to the Parrot class because I intend to define the two beans of type Parrot using the @Bean annotation in the configuration class:

```
public class Parrot {

  private String name;

  // Omitted getters, setters, and toString()
}
```

We define a bean of type `Person` using the `@Component` stereotype annotation. Observe the identifier I gave to the parameter of the constructor in the next code snippet. The reason I gave the identifier "parrot2" is this is the name I'll also configure for the bean in the context I want Spring to inject into that parameter:

```
@Component
public class Person {

  private String name = "Ella";

  private final Parrot parrot;

  public Person(Parrot parrot2) {
    this.parrot = parrot2;
  }

  // Omitted getters and setters

}
```

I define two beans of type `Parrot` using the `@Bean` annotation in the configuration class. Don't forget we still have to add `@ComponentScan` to tell Spring where to find the classes annotated with stereotype annotations. In our case, we annotated class `Person` with the `@Component` stereotype annotation. The next listing shows the definition of the configuration class.

> **Listing 3.8 Defining the beans of type `Parrot` in the configuration class**

```
@Configuration
@ComponentScan(basePackages = "beans")
public class ProjectConfig {

  @Bean
  public Parrot parrot1() {
    Parrot p = new Parrot();
    p.setName("Koko");
    return p;
  }

  @Bean
  public Parrot parrot2() {        ◁─────  With the current setup, the bean named
    Parrot p = new Parrot();               parrot2 is the one that Spring injects into
    p.setName("Miki");                     the Person bean.
    return p;
  }
}
```

What happens if you run a main method as the one presented in the next code snippet? Our person owns which parrot? Because the name of the constructor's parameter matches one of the bean's names in the Spring context (parrot2), Spring injects that bean (figure 3.13), so the name of the parrot the app prints in the console is Miki:

```
public class Main {

  public static void main(String[] args) {
    var context = new
        AnnotationConfigApplicationContext(ProjectConfig.class);

    Person p = context.getBean(Person.class);

    System.out.println("Person's name: " + p.getName());
    System.out.println("Person's parrot: " + p.getParrot());
  }
}
```

Running this app, the console shows the following output:

```
Person's name: Ella
Person's parrot: Parrot : Miki
```

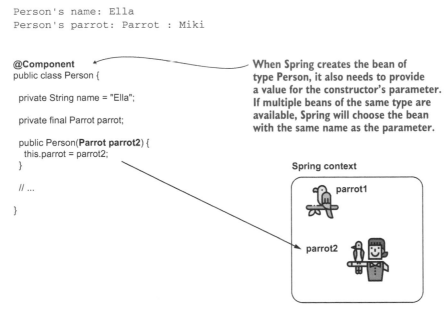

Figure 3.13   When the Spring context contains multiple beans of the same type, Spring will select the bean whose name matches the name of the parameter.

As we discussed for the @Bean annotated method parameter, I recommend against relying on the name of the variable. Instead, I prefer using the @Qualifier annotation to express my intention clearly: I inject a specific bean from the context. This way, we minimize the chance that someone would refactor the name of the variable and thus affect how the app works. Look at the change I made to the Person class in the next code snippet. Using the @Qualifier annotation, I specify the name of the bean I want Spring to inject from the context, and I don't rely on the identifier of the constructor's parameter (see the change in the project named "sq-ch3-ex10"):

```
@Component
public class Person {

  private String name = "Ella";

  private final Parrot parrot;

  public Person(@Qualifier("parrot2") Parrot parrot) {
    this.parrot = parrot;
  }

 // Omitted getters and setters

}
```

The behavior of the app doesn't change, and the output remains the same. This approach makes your code less subject to mistakes.

Summary

- The Spring context is a place in the app's memory that the framework uses to keep the objects it manages. You need to add any object that needs to be augmented to the Spring context with a feature the framework offers.
- When implementing an app, you need to refer from one object to another. This way, an object can delegate actions to other objects when executing their responsibilities. To implement this behavior, you need to establish relationships among the beans in the Spring context.
- You can establish a relationship between two beans using one of three approaches:
  - Directly referring to the @Bean annotated method that creates one of them from the method that creates the other. Spring knows you refer to the bean in the context, and if the bean already exists, it doesn't call the same method again to create another instance. Instead, it returns the reference to the existing bean in the context.
  - Defining a parameter to the method annotated with @Bean. When Spring observes the @Bean method has a parameter, it searches a bean of that parameter's type in its context and provides that bean as a value to the parameter.
  - Using the @Autowired annotation in three ways:
    - Annotate the field in the class where you want to instruct Spring to inject the bean from the context. You'll find this approach often used in examples and proofs of concept.

- ◆ Annotate the constructor you'd like Spring to call to create the bean. Spring will inject other beans from the context in the constructor's parameters. You'll find this approach the most used in real-world code.
- ◆ Annotate the setter of the attribute where you'd like Spring to inject the bean from the context. You won't find this approach often used in production-ready code.

- Whenever you allow Spring to provide a value or reference through an attribute of the class or a method or constructor parameter, we say Spring uses DI, a technique supported by the IoC principle.

- The creation of two beans that depend on one another generates a circular dependency. Spring cannot create the beans with a circular dependency, and the execution fails with an exception. When configuring your beans, make sure you avoid circular dependencies.

- When Spring has more than one bean of the same type in its context, it can't decide which of those beans need to be injected. You can tell Spring which is the instance it needs to inject by
  - using the @Primary annotation, which marks one of the beans as the default for dependency injection, or
  - naming the beans and injecting them by name using the @Qualifier annotation.

The Spring context: Using abstractions

This chapter covers

- Using interfaces to define contracts
- Using abstractions for beans in the Spring context
- Using dependency injection with abstractions

In this chapter, we discuss using abstraction with Spring beans. This topic is essential because in real-world projects, we often use abstractions to decouple implementations. As you'll learn in this chapter, we ensure our application is comfortable to maintain and test by decoupling implementations.

We'll start with a refresher on how to use interfaces to define contracts in section 4.1. To approach this subject, we begin by discussing objects' responsibilities and find out how they fit in a standard class design of an app. We'll use our coding skills to implement a small scenario in which we don't use Spring, but we focus on implementing a requirement and using abstractions to decouple the app's dependent objects.

We then discuss Spring's behavior when using DI with abstractions in section 4.2. We'll start from the implementation we worked on in section 4.1 and add Spring to the app's dependencies. We then use the Spring context to implement dependency injection. With this example, we get closer to what you expect to find in production-ready implementations: objects with typical responsibilities for real-world scenarios and abstraction used with DI and the Spring context.

4.1 Using interfaces to define contracts

In this section, we discuss using interfaces to define contracts. In Java, the interface is an abstract structure you use to declare a specific responsibility. An object implementing the interface has to define this responsibility. More objects implementing the same interface can define the responsibility declared by that interface in different ways. We can say that the interface specifies the "what needs to happen," while every object implementing the interface specifies the "how it should happen."

When I was a kid, my dad gave me an old radio I could disassemble and play with (I was quite enthusiastic about disassembling things). Looking at it, I realized I needed something to unscrew the bolts of the case. After thinking a while, I decided I could use a knife for this job, so I asked my father for a knife. He asked me, "What do you need a knife for?" I said I needed it to open the case. "Oh!" he said. "You better use a screwdriver; here it is!" At that time, I learned that it's always smarter to ask for what you need instead of for a solution when you have no idea what you're doing. Interfaces are the way objects ask for what they need.

4.1.1 Using interfaces for decoupling implementations

This section discusses what contracts are and how you can define them in a Java app using interfaces. I'll start with an analogy, and then I'll use some visuals to explain the concept and when using interfaces is useful. We'll then continue with the requirements of a problem in section 4.1.2 and solve this scenario without a framework in section 4.1.3. Further, in section 4.2, we add Spring to our recipe, and you'll learn how dependency injection in Spring works when using contracts to decouple functionalities.

An analogy: Suppose you use a ride-sharing app because you need to get somewhere. When you order a trip, you usually don't care how the car looks or who the driver is. You just need to get somewhere. In my case, I don't care whether a car or a spaceship comes to pick me up if I reach the destination in time. The ride-sharing app is an interface. The customer doesn't request a car or a driver, but a trip. Any driver with a car who can offer the service can answer the customer's request. The customer and the driver are decoupled through the app (interface); the customer doesn't know who the driver is nor which car will pick them up before a car responds to their request, and the driver doesn't need to know who they do the service for. Using this analogy, you can deduce the role of interfaces in relationship with objects in Java.

An implementation example: Say you implement an object that needs to print packages' details to be delivered for a shipping app. The printed details must be

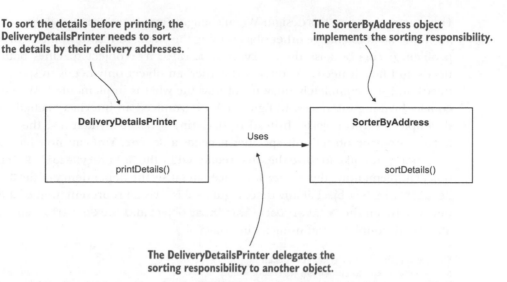

Figure 4.1 The `DeliveryDetailsPrinter` object delegates the responsibility of sorting the delivery details by the delivery addresses to another object named `SorterByAddress`.

sorted by their destination address. The object dealing with printing the details needs to delegate to some other object the responsibility of sorting the packages by their delivery addresses (figure 4.1).

As shown in figure 4.1, the DeliveryDetailsPrinter directly delegates the sorting responsibility to the SorterByAddress object. If we keep this class design, we may face difficulties later if we need to change this functionality. Let's imagine you need to change the printed details order later, and the new order is by the sender's name. You'd need to replace the SorterByAddress object with another one implementing the new responsibility, but you'd also need to change the DeliveryDetailsPrinter object that uses the sorting responsibility (figure 4.2).

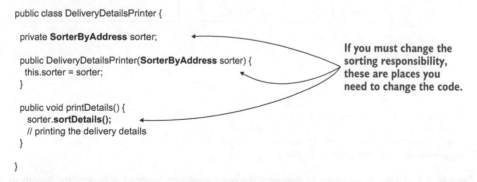

Figure 4.2 Because the two objects are strongly coupled, if you want to change the sorting responsibility, you also need to change the object using this responsibility. A better design would allow you to change the sorting responsibility without changing the object that uses the responsibility.

How can we improve this design? When changing an object's responsibility, we want to avoid the need to change other objects using the changed responsibility. This design's problem occurs because the DeliveryDetailsPrinter object specifies both what it needs and how it needs. As discussed earlier, an object only needs to specify what it needs and stay completely unaware of how the what is implemented. We do this, of course, by using interfaces. In figure 4.3, I introduced an interface named Sorter to decouple the two objects. Instead of declaring a SorterByAddress, the Delivery-DetailsPrinter object only specifies it needs a Sorter. You can now have as many objects as you'd like to solve the what requested by the DeliveryDetailsPrinter. Any object implementing the Sorter interface can satisfy the dependency of the Delivery-DetailsPrinter object at any time. Figure 4.3 is a visual representation of the dependency between the DeliveryDetailsPrinter object and the SorterByAddress object after we decoupled them using an interface.

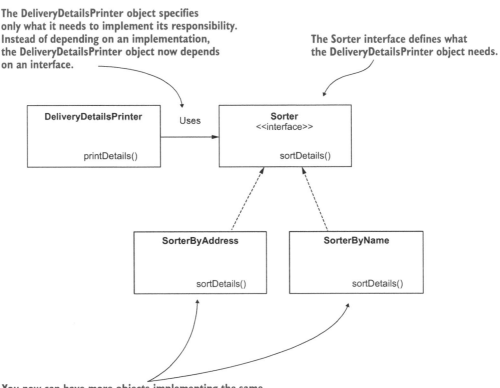

The DeliveryDetailsPrinter object specifies only what it needs to implement its responsibility. Instead of depending on an implementation, the DeliveryDetailsPrinter object now depends on an interface.

The Sorter interface defines what the DeliveryDetailsPrinter object needs.

You now can have more objects implementing the same interface. This allows you to change the implementation (the how) without affecting the object that consumes the implementation (DeliveryDetailsPrinter).

Figure 4.3   Using an interface to decouple the responsibilities. Instead of depending directly on an implementation, the DeliveryDetailsPrinter object depends on an interface (a contract). DeliveryDetailsPrinter can use any object implementing this interface instead of being stuck to a specific implementation.

In the next code snippet, you find the `Sorter` interface definition:

```
public interface Sorter {
  void sortDetails();
}
```

Look at figure 4.4 and compare it with figure 4.2. Because the `DeliveryDetails-Printer` object depends on the interface instead of the implementation directly, you don't need to change it further if you change the way the delivery details are sorted.

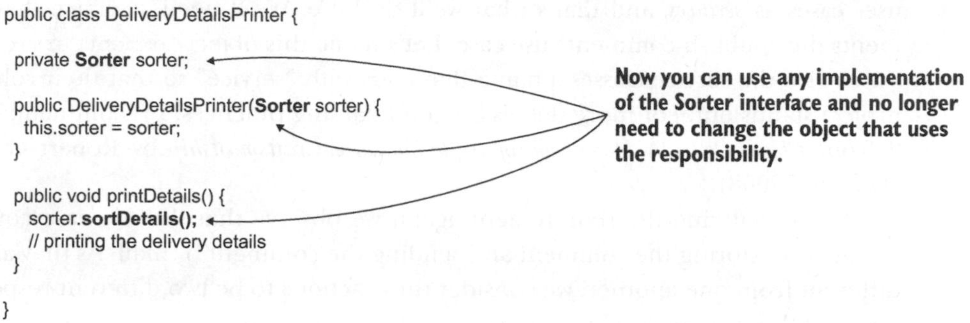

```
public class DeliveryDetailsPrinter {

  private Sorter sorter;

  public DeliveryDetailsPrinter(Sorter sorter) {
    this.sorter = sorter;
  }

  public void printDetails() {
    sorter.sortDetails();
    // printing the delivery details
  }

}
```

Now you can use any implementation of the Sorter interface and no longer need to change the object that uses the responsibility.

Figure 4.4 The `DeliveryDetailsPrinter` object depends on the `Sorter` interface. You can change the implementation of the `Sorter` interface and avoid making more changes to the object using this responsibility (`DeliveryDetailsPrinter`).

With this theoretical introduction, you are now aware of why we use interfaces to decouple the objects that depend on each other in the class design. Next, we implement a requirement for a scenario. We'll implement this requirement using plain Java, without any framework, and we'll focus on objects' responsibilities and using interfaces to decouple them. At the end of this section, we'll have a project defining some objects that collaborate to implement a use case.

In section 4.2, we'll change the project and add Spring to it to manage the objects as well as the relationships among them with dependency injection. By taking this step-by-step approach, you'll more easily observe the changes needed to add Spring to an app, as well as the benefits that would come with this change.

4.1.2   *The requirement of the scenario*

Thus far, we've used simple examples and we've chosen simple objects (like `Parrot`). Even if they aren't close to what a production-ready application uses, they help you focus on the syntaxes you need to learn. Now it's time you take a step forward and use what you've learned in the previous chapters with an example closer to what happens in the real world.

Say you are implementing an app a team uses to manage their tasks. One of the app's features is allowing the users to leave comments for the tasks. When a user publishes a comment, it is stored somewhere (e.g., in a database), and the app sends an email to a specific address configured in the app.

We need to design the objects and find the right responsibilities and abstractions for implementing this feature.

4.1.3   *Implementing the requirement without using a framework*

In this section, we focus on implementing the requirement described in section 4.1.1. You will do this by using what you've learned about interfaces thus far. First, we need to identify the objects (responsibilities) to implement.

In standard real-world applications, we usually refer to the objects implementing uses cases as *services*, and that's what we'll do here. We'll need a service that implements the "publish comment" use case. Let's name this object CommentService. I prefer to give the service classes a name that ends with "service" so that their role in the project stands out. For more details on good naming practices, I recommend chapter 2 from *Clean Code: A Handbook of Agile Software Craftsmanship* by Robert C. Martin (Pearson, 2008).

When analyzing the requirement again, we observe that the use case consists of two actions: storing the comment and sending the comment by mail. As they are quite different from one another, we consider these actions to be two different responsibilities, and thus we need to implement two different objects.

When we have an object working directly with a database, we generally name such an object *repository*. Sometimes you also find such objects referred to as *data access objects* (DAO). Let's name the object that implements the storing comment responsibility CommentRepository.

Finally, in a real-world app, when implementing objects whose responsibility is to establish communication with something outside the app, we name these objects *proxies*, so let's name the object whose responsibility is sending the email Comment-NotificationProxy. Figure 4.5 shows the relationship among the three responsibilities.

But wait! Didn't we say we shouldn't use direct coupling between implementations? We need to make sure we decouple the implementations by using interfaces. In the end, the CommentRepository might now use a database to store the comments. But in the future, maybe this needs to be changed to use some other technology or an external service. We can say the same for the CommentNotificationProxy object. Now it sends the notification by email, but maybe in a future version the comment notification needs to be sent through some other channel. We certainly want to make sure we decouple the CommentService from the implementations of its dependencies so that when we need to change the dependencies, we don't need to change the object using them as well.

Figure 4.6 shows how to decouple this class design by using abstractions. Instead of designing CommentRepository and CommentNotificationProxy as classes, we design them as interfaces that we can implement to define the functionality.

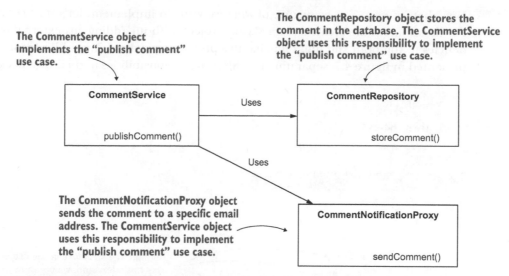

The CommentService object implements the "publish comment" use case.

The CommentRepository object stores the comment in the database. The CommentService object uses this responsibility to implement the "publish comment" use case.

The CommentNotificationProxy object sends the comment to a specific email address. The CommentService object uses this responsibility to implement the "publish comment" use case.

Figure 4.5 The CommentService object implements the "publish comment" use case. To do this, it needs to delegate to the responsibilities implemented by the CommentRepository and the CommentNotificationProxy objects.

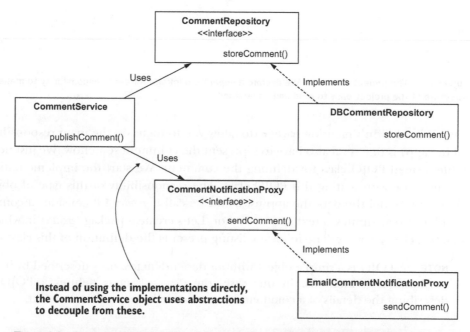

Instead of using the implementations directly, the CommentService object uses abstractions to decouple from these.

Figure 4.6 The CommentService object depends on the abstractions provided by CommentRepository and CommentNotificationProxy interfaces. The classes DBCommentRepository and EmailCommentNotificationProxy further implement these interfaces. This design decouples the implementation of the "publish comment" use case from its dependencies and makes the application easier to change for future developments.

Now that we have a clear picture of what we want to implement, let's start coding it. For the moment, we create a plain Maven project, without adding any external dependencies to the pom.xml file. I'll name this project "sq-ch4-ex1," and I'll organize it as presented in figure 4.7, separating the different responsibilities in their own packages.

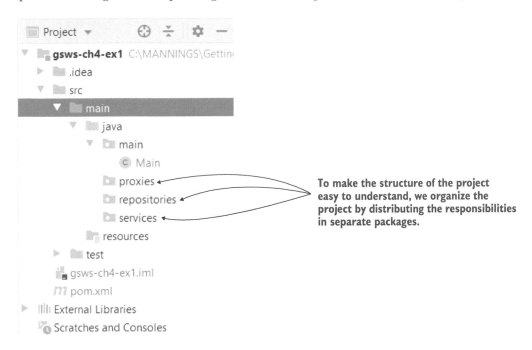

Figure 4.7   The project structure. We declare a separate package for each responsibility to make the structure of the project easy to read and understand.

One thing I didn't mention earlier (to allow you to focus on the main responsibilities of the app) is that we'll also have to represent the comment somehow. We just need to write a small POJO class for defining the comment. We start the implementation of the use case with writing this POJO class. The responsibility of this type of object is simply to model the data the app uses, and we call it *model*. I'll consider a comment that has two attributes: a text and an author. Let's create a package model in which we define a class Comment. The following listing presents the definition of this class.

> **NOTE**   A POJO is a simple object without dependencies, only described by its attributes and methods. In our case, the Comment class defines a POJO describing the details of a comment by its two attributes: author and text.

Listing 4.1   Defining the comment

```
public class Comment {

  private String author;
```

```
  private String text;

  // Omitted getters and setters
}
```

We can now define the responsibilities of repository and proxy. In the next listing, you can see the definition of the `CommentRepository` interface. The contract defined by this interface declares the `storeComment(Comment comment)` method, which the `CommentService` object needs to implement the use case. We store this interface and the class implementing it in the `repositories` package of the project.

Listing 4.2   Defining the `CommentRepository` interface

```
public interface CommentRepository {

  void storeComment(Comment comment);
}
```

The interface only gives the what the `CommentService` object needs for implementing the use case: store a comment. When you define an object that implements this contract, it needs to override the `storeComment(Comment comment)` method to define the how. In the next listing, you find the definition of the `DBCommentRepository` class. We don't know yet how to connect to a database, so we'll only write a text in the console to simulate this action. Later, starting with chapter 12, you'll also learn how to connect your application to a database.

Listing 4.3   Implementing the `CommentRepository` interface

```
public class DBCommentRepository implements CommentRepository {

  @Override
  public void storeComment(Comment comment) {
    System.out.println("Storing comment: " + comment.getText());
  }
}
```

Similarly, we define an interface for the second responsibility the `CommentService` object needs: `CommentNotificationProxy`. We define this interface and the class implementing it in the `proxies` package of the project. The following listing presents this interface.

Listing 4.4   Define a `CommentNotificationProxy` interface

```
public interface CommentNotificationProxy {

  void sendComment(Comment comment);
}
```

In the next listing, you find the implementation for this interface, which we'll use in our demonstration.

Listing 4.5 Implementation of the `CommentNotificationProxy` interface

```java
public class EmailCommentNotificationProxy
  implements CommentNotificationProxy {

  @Override
  public void sendComment(Comment comment) {
    System.out.println("Sending notification for comment: "
                       + comment.getText());
  }
}
```

We can now implement the object itself with the two dependencies of the Comment-Service object (the `CommentRepository` and the `CommentNotificationProxy`). In the service package, we write the `CommentService` class as presented in the following listing.

Listing 4.6 Implementing the `CommentService` object

```java
public class CommentService {                               We define the two dependencies
                                                            as attributes of the class.
  private final CommentRepository commentRepository;
  private final CommentNotificationProxy commentNotificationProxy;

  public CommentService(                                    We provide the
          CommentRepository commentRepository,              dependencies
          CommentNotificationProxy commentNotificationProxy) {   when the object is
                                                            built through the
    this.commentRepository = commentRepository;            parameters of the
    this.commentNotificationProxy = commentNotificationProxy;  constructor.
  }

  public void publishComment(Comment comment) {             We implement the use case that
    commentRepository.storeComment(comment);                delegates the "store comment" and
    commentNotificationProxy.sendComment(comment);          "send notification" responsibilities
  }                                                         to the dependencies.
}
```

Let's now write a `Main` class, as presented in the next listing, and test the whole class design.

Listing 4.7 Calling the use case in the `Main` class

```java
public class Main {

  public static void main(String[] args) {
    var commentRepository =
      new DBCommentRepository();                  Creates the instance for
    var commentNotificationProxy =                the dependencies
      new EmailCommentNotificationProxy();
```

```
    var commentService =
      new CommentService(
        commentRepository, commentNotificationProxy);

    var comment = new Comment();
    comment.setAuthor("Laurentiu");
    comment.setText("Demo comment");

    commentService.publishComment(comment);
  }
}
```

Creates the instance of the service class and providing the dependencies

Creates an instance of comment to send as a parameter to the publish comment use case

◁—— **Calls the publish comment use case**

When running this application, you'll observe the two lines in the console printed by the CommentRepository and the CommentNotificationProxy objects. The next code snippet presents this output:

```
Storing comment: Demo comment
Sending notification for comment: Demo comment
```

4.2 Using dependency injection with abstractions

In this section, we apply the Spring framework over the class design we implemented in section 4.1. Using this example, we can discuss how Spring manages dependency injection when using abstractions. This subject is essential because in most projects, you'll implement dependencies between objects using abstractions. In chapter 3, we discussed dependency injection, and we used concrete classes to declare the variables where we wanted Spring to set the values of beans from its context. But as you'll learn in this chapter, Spring also understands abstractions.

We'll start by adding the Spring dependency to our project, and then we'll decide which of the objects of this application need to be managed by Spring. You'll learn to decide which objects you need to make Spring aware of.

We'll then adapt the project we implemented in section 4.1 to use Spring and its dependency injection capabilities. We'll focus on discussing various situations that can appear when using dependency injection with abstractions. At the end of the section, we'll discuss more on the stereotype annotations. You'll find out @Component is not the only stereotype annotation you can use and when you should use other annotations.

4.2.1 Deciding which objects should be part of the Spring context

When we discussed Spring in chapters 2 and 3, we focused on syntax, and we didn't have a use case to mirror something you can find in a real-world scenario. This is also why we didn't discuss whether you need to add an object to the Spring context. Based on our discussion, you might think you need to add all the app objects in the Spring context, but this is not the case.

Remember, you learned that the main reason to add an object to the Spring context is to allow Spring to control it and further augment it with functionalities the framework provides. So the decision should be easy and based on the question, "Does this object need to be managed by the framework?"

It's not difficult to answer this question for our scenario, as the only Spring feature we use is the DI. In our case, we need to add the object to the Spring context if it either has a dependency we need to inject from the context or if it's a dependency itself. Looking at our implementation, you'll observe that the only object that doesn't have a dependency and is also not a dependency itself is Comment. The other objects in our class design are as follows:

- CommentService—Has two dependencies, the CommentRepository and the CommentNotificationProxy
- DBCommentRepository—Implements the CommentRepository interface and is a dependency of the CommentService
- EmailCommentNotificationProxy—Implements the CommentNotification-Proxy interface and is a dependency of the CommentService

But why not add the Comment instances as well? I'm often asked this question when I teach Spring courses. Adding objects to the Spring context without needing the framework to manage them adds unnecessary complexity to your app, making the app both more challenging to maintain and less performant. When you add an object to the Spring context, you allow the framework to manage it with some specific functionality the framework provides. If you add the object to be managed by Spring without getting any benefit from the framework, you just over-engineer your implementation.

In chapter 2, we discussed that using stereotype annotations (@Component) is the most comfortable way to add beans to the Spring context when the classes belong to your project, and you can change them. We'll use this approach here as well.

Observe that the two interfaces in figure 4.8 remain white (we don't mark them with @Component). I often see students confused about where they should use the stereotype annotations when they also use interfaces in their implementations. We use stereotype annotations for the classes that Spring needs to create instances and add these instances to its context. It doesn't make sense to add stereotype annotations on interfaces or abstract classes because these cannot be instantiated. Syntactically, you can do this, but it is not useful.

Let's change the code and add the @Component annotation to these classes. In the following listing, you find the change for the DBCommentRepository class.

Listing 4.8   Adding @Component to the DBCommentRepository class

```
@Component                                              ◁─────────   Marking
public class DBCommentRepository implements CommentRepository {        the class with
                                                                       @Component
  @Override                                                            instructs Spring
  public void storeComment(Comment comment) {                          to instantiate the
    System.out.println("Storing comment: " + comment.getText());       class and add an
  }                                                                     instance as a bean
}                                                                      in its context.
```

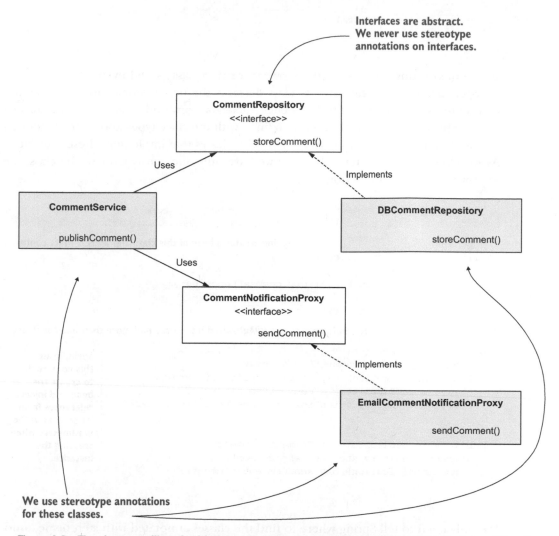

Figure 4.8 The classes we'll mark with the @Component stereotype annotation are shaded gray. When the context is loaded, Spring creates instances of these classes and adds them to its context.

In the next listing, you find the changes for the EmailCommentNotificationProxy class.

Listing 4.9   Adding @Component to the EmailCommentNotificationProxy class

```
@Component
public class EmailCommentNotificationProxy
  implements CommentNotificationProxy {

  @Override
  public void sendComment(Comment comment) {
    System.out.println(
      "Sending notification for comment: " +
```

```
                    comment.getText());
  }
}
```

In the next listing, we change the `CommentService` class as well by annotating it with `@Component`. The `CommentService` class declares the dependencies to the other two components through the interfaces `CommentRepository` and `CommentNotification-Proxy`. Spring sees the attributes are defined with interface types and is smart enough to search in its context for beans created with classes that implement these interfaces. As we discussed in chapter 2, because we have only one constructor in the class, the `@Autowired` annotation is optional.

Listing 4.10   Making the `CommentService` class a component

```
@Component                        ◄——— Spring creates a bean of this class and adds it to its context.
public class CommentService {

  private final CommentRepository commentRepository;

  private final CommentNotificationProxy commentNotificationProxy;
```
            ◄————————⌐ **We would have to use @Autowired if the class had more than one constructor.**
```
  public CommentService(                             ◄————————————————┐   Spring uses
    CommentRepository commentRepository,                               │   this constructor
    CommentNotificationProxy commentNotificationProxy) {               │   to create the
    this.commentRepository = commentRepository;                        │   bean and injects
    this.commentNotificationProxy = commentNotificationProxy;          │   references from
  }                                                                    │   its context in the
                                                                       │   parameters when
  public void publishComment(Comment comment) {                        │   creating the
    commentRepository.storeComment(comment);                           │   instance.
    commentNotificationProxy.sendComment(comment);
  }
}
```

We only need to tell Spring where to find the classes annotated with stereotype annotations and test the app. The next listing presents the project's configuration class where we use the `@ComponentScan` annotation to tell Spring where to find the classes annotated with `@Component`. We discussed `@ComponentScan` in chapter 2.

Listing 4.11   Using `@ComponentScan` in the configuration class

The @Configuration annotation marks the configuration class.

We use the @ComponentScan annotation to tell Spring in which packages to search for the classes annotated with stereotype annotations. Observe that the model package is not specified because it doesn't contain classes annotated with stereotype annotations.

```
└─▷ @Configuration
    @ComponentScan(          ◄——┘
      basePackages = {"proxies", "services", "repositories"}
    )
    public class ProjectConfiguration {
    }
```

NOTE In this example, I use the `basePackages` attribute of the `@Component-Scan` annotation. Spring also offers the feature of directly specifying the classes (by using the `basePackageClasses` attribute of the same annotation). The advantage of defining the packages is that you only have to mention the package name. In case it contains 20 component classes, you write only one line (the name of the package) instead of 20. The disadvantage is that if a developer renames the package, they might not realize they also have to change the value of the `@ComponentScan` annotation. Mentioning the classes directly, you might write more, but when someone changes the code, they immediately see they also need to change the `@ComponentScan` annotation; otherwise, the app doesn't compile. In a production application, you might find both approaches, and, in my experience, one is not better than the other.

To test our setup, let's create a new main method, as presented in the following listing. We'll spin the Spring context, grab the bean of type `CommentService` out of it, and call the `publishComment(Comment comment)` method.

Listing 4.12 The `Main` class

```
public class Main {

  public static void main(String[] args) {
    var context =
      new AnnotationConfigApplicationContext(
        ProjectConfiguration.class);

    var comment = new Comment();
    comment.setAuthor("Laurentiu");
    comment.setText("Demo comment");

    var commentService = context.getBean(CommentService.class);
    commentService.publishComment(comment);
  }
}
```

Running the application, you'll observe the output presented in the following code snippet, which demonstrates that the two dependencies were accessed and correctly called by the `CommentService` object:

```
Storing comment: Demo comment
Sending notification for comment: Demo comment
```

It's a small example, and it might not look like Spring improves a lot the experience, but look again. By using the DI feature, we don't create the instance of the `Comment-Service` object and its dependencies ourselves, and we don't need to explicitly make the relationship between them. In a real-world scenario, where you have more than three classes, letting Spring manage the objects and dependencies among them really makes a difference. It eliminates code that can be implied (which developers also name *boilerplate code*), which allows you to focus on what the application does. And remember that adding these instances to the context enables Spring to control and augment them with features that we'll discuss in the next chapters.

Different ways of using dependency injection with abstraction

In chapter 3, you've learned multiple ways you can use auto-wiring. We discussed the `@Autowired` annotation, through which you can make field, constructor, or setter injection. We also discussed using auto-wiring within the configuration class using the parameters of the methods annotated with `@Bean` (which Spring uses to create beans in the context).

Of course, in the current section, I started with the most used approach in real-world examples, constructor injection. But I consider it essential for you to be aware of different approaches that you might encounter as well. In this sidebar, I'd like to highlight that DI with abstractions (as you saw in this section) works the same with all the DI fashions you learned in chapter 3. To prove this, let's try to change project "sq-ch4-ex2" and make it first use field dependency injection with `@Autowired`. We can then change the project again and test how DI with abstraction works if we use `@Bean` methods in the configuration class.

To keep all the steps we work on, I'll create a new project named "sq-ch4-ex3" for the first demonstration. Fortunately, the only thing we need to change is the `CommentService` class. We remove the constructor and mark the fields of the class with the `@Autowired` annotation, as presented by the next code snippet:

```
@Component
public class CommentService {

  @Autowired
  private CommentRepository commentRepository;

  @Autowired
  private CommentNotificationProxy commentNotificationProxy;

  public void publishComment(Comment comment) {
    commentRepository.storeComment(comment);
    commentNotificationProxy.sendComment(comment);
  }
}
```

Fields are no longer final, and they are marked with @Autowired. Spring uses the default constructor to create the instance of the class and then injects the two dependencies from its context.

As you probably expect now, you can use auto-wiring through the parameters of the `@Bean` annotated methods with abstractions as well. I have separated these examples in the project "sq-ch4-ex4." In this project, I completely removed the stereotype annotation (`@Component`) of the `CommentService` class and its two dependencies.

Further, I changed the configuration class to create these beans and establish the relationships among them. The next code snippet shows the new look of the configuration class:

```
@Configuration                              ◄───  Because we don't use stereotype
public class ProjectConfiguration {               annotations, we no longer need to use
                                                  the @ComponentScan annotation.

  @Bean
  public CommentRepository commentRepository() {   ◄─
    return new DBCommentRepository();                    We create a bean
  }                                                      for each of the two
                                                         dependencies.
  @Bean
  public CommentNotificationProxy commentNotificationProxy() {   ◄─
    return new EmailCommentNotificationProxy();
  }

  @Bean
  public CommentService commentService(
    CommentRepository commentRepository,
    CommentNotificationProxy commentNotificationProxy) {   ◄─
    return new CommentService(commentRepository,
            commentNotificationProxy);
  }
}
```

We use parameters of the @Bean method (which are now defined with the interface type) to instruct Spring to provide references for beans from its context, compatible with the type of the parameters.

4.2.2 *Choosing what to auto-wire from multiple implementations of an abstraction*

Thus far, we have focused on Spring's behavior when using DI with abstractions. But we used an example in which we made sure to add only one instance for each kind of abstraction we requested for injection.

Let's go one step further and discuss what happens if the Spring context contains more instances that match a requested abstraction. This scenario can happen in real-world projects, and you need to know how to handle these cases to make your app work as expected.

Suppose we have two beans created with two different classes that implement the CommentNotificationProxy interface (figure 4.9). Fortunately for us, Spring uses a mechanism for deciding which bean to choose that we discussed in chapter 3. In chapter 3, you learned that if more than one bean of the same type exists in the Spring context, you need to tell Spring which of these beans to inject. You also learned the following approaches:

- Using the @Primary annotation to mark one of the beans for implementation as the default
- Using the @Qualifier annotation to name a bean and then refer to it by its name for DI

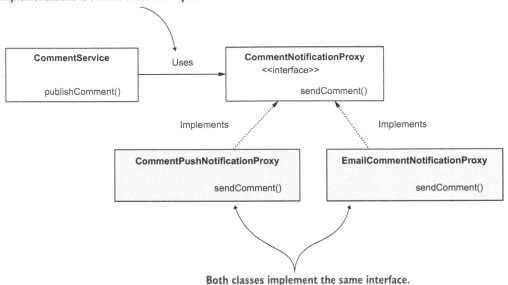

When CommentService requests a dependency of the type CommentNotificationProxy, Spring needs to decide which of the multiple existing implementations it should choose to inject.

Both classes implement the same interface.

Figure 4.9   Sometimes, in real-world scenarios, we have multiple implementations of the same interface. When using dependency injection on the interface, you need to instruct Spring which is the implementation it should inject.

Now we want now to prove that these two approaches work with abstractions as well. Let's add a new class, CommentPushNotificationProxy (which implements the CommentNotificationProxy interface), to our application and test the approaches one by one, as shown in the following listing. To keep the examples separated, I created a new project named "sq-ch4-ex5." I started this example with the code in the project "sq-ch4-ex2."

Listing 4.13   A new implementation of the `CommentNotificationProxy` interface

```
@Component
public class CommentPushNotificationProxy
  implements CommentNotificationProxy {        ⟵─┐ The class implements the
                                                  │ CommentNotificationProxy interface
  @Override
  public void sendComment(Comment comment) {
    System.out.println(
      "Sending push notification for comment: "
        + comment.getText());
  }
}
```

If you run this application as-is, you'll get an exception because Spring doesn't know which of the two beans in its context to choose for injection. I have extracted the most interesting part of the exception message in the next code snippet. The exception clearly states the problem Spring encounters. As you can see, it's a NoUniqueBean-DefinitionException with the message "expected single matching but found 2." This is how the framework tells us it needs guidance regarding the existing beans it should inject from the context:

```
Caused by: org.springframework.beans.factory.NoUniqueBeanDefinitionException:

No qualifying bean of type 'proxies.CommentNotificationProxy' available:
    expected single matching bean but found 2:

commentPushNotificationProxy,emailCommentNotificationProxy
```

MARKING AN IMPLEMENTATION AS DEFAULT FOR INJECTION WITH @PRIMARY
The first solution is using @Primary. The only thing you need to do is add @Primary near the @Component annotation to mark the implementation provided by this class as the default for implementation, as shown in the following listing.

Listing 4.14   Using @Primary to mark the implementation as default

```
@Component
@Primary                                          ⮜──────   Using @Primary, we mark this
public class CommentPushNotificationProxy                  implementation as a default
  implements CommentNotificationProxy {                    for dependency injection.

  @Override
  public void sendComment(Comment comment) {
    System.out.println(
      "Sending push notification for comment: "
          + comment.getText());
  }
}
```

With just this small change, your app has a more friendly output, as presented in the next code snippet. Observe that Spring indeed injected the implementation provided by the newly created class:

```
Storing comment: Demo comment
Sending push notification for comment: Demo comment   ⮜──┐
```
Spring injected the new implementation because we marked it as primary.

The question I usually hear at this moment is, "Now we have two implementations, but Spring will always inject only one of them? Why have both classes in this case?"

Let's discuss how you can get into such a situation in a real-world scenario. As you are already aware, apps are complex and use plenty of dependencies. It's possible that, at some point, you use a dependency that provides an implementation for a specific

You need to create a custom implementation
for the interface defined by the dependency.
But you also need to mark it as primary so
that when you use DI, Spring injects your
custom implementation and not the one
provided by the dependency.

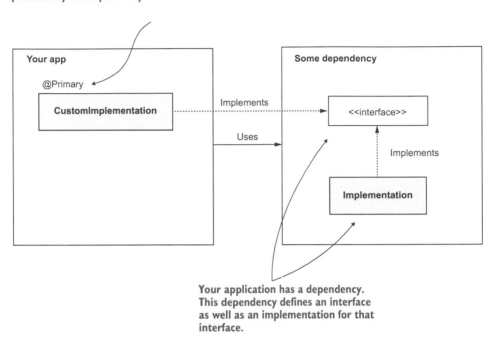

Your application has a dependency.
This dependency defines an interface
as well as an implementation for that
interface.

Figure 4.10 Sometimes you use dependencies that already provide implementations for specific
interfaces. When you need to have custom implementations of those interfaces, you can use
@Primary to mark your implementation as a default for DI. This way, Spring knows to inject the
implementation you define and not the one provided by the dependency.

interface (figure 4.10), but the provided implementation is not suitable for your app,
and you choose to define your custom implementation. Then @Primary is your simplest solution.

NAMING IMPLEMENTATION FOR DEPENDENCY INJECTION WITH @QUALIFIER

Sometimes, in production apps, you need to define more implementations of the
same interface, and different objects use these implementations. Imagine we need to
have two implementations for comment notification: by email or by push notification
(figure 4.11). These are still implementations of the same interface, but they depend
on different objects in the app.

Let's change the code to test this approach. You can find this implementation in
the project "sq-ch4-ex6." The following code snippets show you how to use the @Qual-
ifier annotation to name specific implementations.

More objects declare the dependency on the CommentNotificationProxy interface.

This service needs to use the implementation that sends the notification by email.

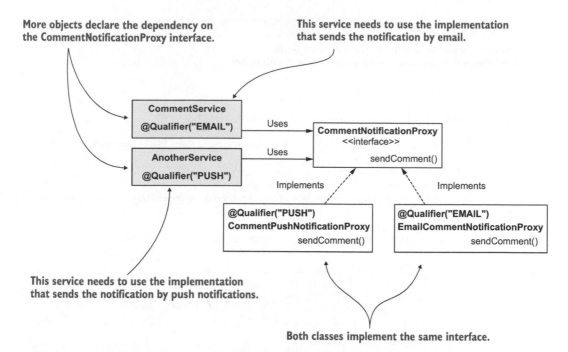

This service needs to use the implementation that sends the notification by push notifications.

Both classes implement the same interface.

Figure 4.11 If different objects need to use different implementations of the same contract, we can use @Qualifier to name them and tell Spring where and what it needs to inject.

The CommentPushNotification class:

```
@Component
@Qualifier("PUSH")
public class CommentPushNotificationProxy
  implements CommentNotificationProxy {
  // Omitted code
}
```

Using @Qualifier, we name this implementation "PUSH."

The EmailCommentNotificationProxy class:

```
@Component
@Qualifier("EMAIL")
public class EmailCommentNotificationProxy
  implements CommentNotificationProxy {
  // Omitted code
}
```

Using @Qualifier, we name this implementation "EMAIL."

When you want Spring to inject one of these, you just need to specify the implementation's name using the @Qualifier annotation again. In the next listing, you find out how to inject a specific implementation as a dependency of the CommentService object.

Listing 4.15   Specifying the implementation Spring needs to inject with @Qualifier

For each parameter where we want to use a specific implementation, we annotate the parameter with @Qualifier.

```
@Component
public class CommentService {

  private final CommentRepository commentRepository;

  private final CommentNotificationProxy commentNotificationProxy;

  public CommentService(
      CommentRepository commentRepository,
      @Qualifier("PUSH") CommentNotificationProxy commentNotificationProxy) {

      this.commentRepository = commentRepository;
      this.commentNotificationProxy = commentNotificationProxy;
  }

  // Omitted code
}
```

Spring injects the dependency you specified using @Qualifier when you run the app. Observe the output in the console:

```
Storing comment: Demo comment
Sending push notification for comment: Demo comment
```

Observe that Spring injected the implementation for push notifications.

4.3   *Focusing on object responsibilities with stereotype annotations*

Thus far, when discussing stereotype annotations, we have only used @Component in our examples. But with real-world implementations, you'll find out that developers sometimes use other annotations for the same purpose. In this section, I'll show you how to use two more stereotype annotations: @Service and @Repository.

In real-world projects, it's a common practice to define the component's purpose using the stereotype annotation explicitly. Using @Component is generic and gives you no detail about the responsibility of the object you're implementing. But developers generally use objects with some known responsibilities. Two of the responsibilities we discussed in section 4.1 are the service and the repository.

The services are the objects with the responsibility of implementing the use cases, while repositories are the objects managing the data persistence. Because these responsibilities are so common in projects, and they are important in the class design, having a distinctive way of marking them helps the developer better understand the app design.

Spring offers us the @Service annotation to mark a component that takes the responsibility of a service and the @Repository annotation to mark a component that implements a repository responsibility (figure 4.12). All three (@Component, @Service, and @Repository) are stereotype annotations and instruct Spring to create and add an instance of the annotated class to its context.

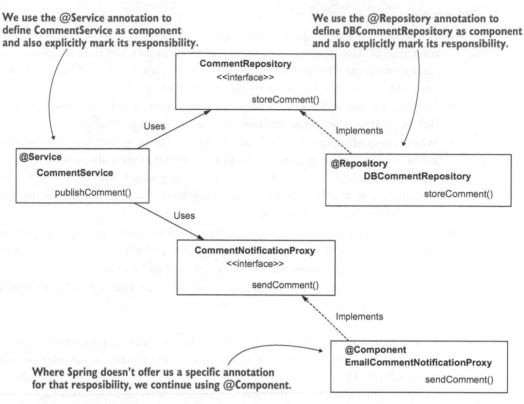

We use the @Service annotation to define CommentService as component and also explicitly mark its responsibility.

We use the @Repository annotation to define DBCommentRepository as component and also explicitly mark its responsibility.

Where Spring doesn't offer us a specific annotation for that resposibility, we continue using @Component.

Figure 4.12 We use the `@Service` and `@Repository` annotations to explicitly mark the responsibilities of the components in our class design. Where Spring doesn't offer a specific annotation for that responsibility, we continue to use `@Component`.

In the examples in this chapter, you would mark the CommentService class with @Service instead of @Component. This way, you explicitly mark the object's responsibility and make this aspect more visible for any developer reading the class. The next code snippet shows this class annotated with the @Service stereotype annotation:

```
@Service
public class CommentService {
  // Omitted code
}
```
We use @Service to define this object as a component having the responsibility of service.

Similarly, you explicitly mark the repository class's responsibility using the @Repository annotation:

```
@Repository
public class DBCommentRepository implements CommentRepository {
  // Omitted code
}
```
We use @Repository to define this object as a component with the responsibility of the repository.

You can find this example ("sq-ch4-ex7") in the projects provided with the book.

Summary

- Decoupling implementations through abstractions is a good practice in implementing a class design. Decoupling objects makes implementations easy to change without affecting too many parts of the application. This aspect makes your application more easily extended and maintained.

- In Java, we use interfaces to decouple implementations. We also say that we define contracts between implementations through interfaces.

- When using abstraction with dependency injection, Spring knows to search for a bean created with an implementation of the requested abstraction.

- You use stereotype annotations on classes for which Spring needs to create instances and add these instances as beans to its context. You never use stereotype annotations on interfaces.

- When the Spring context has more beans created with multiple implementations of the same abstraction, to instruct Spring which bean to inject, you can
  - use the @Primary annotation to mark one of them as default, or
  - use the @Qualifier annotation to name the bean and then instruct Spring to inject that bean by name.

- When we have service responsibility components, we use the @Service stereotype annotation instead of @Component. Likewise, when a component has repository responsibility, we use the @Repository stereotype annotation instead of @Component. This way, we mark the component's responsibility explicitly, and we make the class design more comfortable to read and understand.

The Spring context: Bean scopes and life cycle

This chapter covers

- Using the singleton bean scope
- Using eager and lazy instantiation for singleton beans
- Using the prototype bean scope

Thus far we have discussed several essential things about object instances managed by Spring (beans). We covered the important syntaxes you need to know to create beans, and we discussed establishing relationships among beans (including the necessity of using abstractions). But we didn't focus on how and when Spring creates the beans. From this perspective, we've only relied on the framework's default approaches.

I chose not to discuss this aspect earlier in the book because I wanted you to focus on the syntaxes you'll need up-front in your projects. However, production apps' scenarios are complex, and sometimes relying on the framework's default behavior is not enough. For this reason, in this chapter we need to go a bit deeper with our discussion on how Spring manages the beans in its context.

Spring has multiple different approaches for creating beans and managing their life cycle, and in the Spring world we name these approaches *scopes*. In this chapter, we discuss two scopes you'll often find in Spring apps: *singleton* and *prototype*.

> **NOTE**   Later, in chapter 9, we discuss three more bean scopes that apply to web applications: request, session, and application.

Singleton is the default scope of a bean in Spring, and it's what we've been using up to now. In section 5.1, we discuss the singleton bean scope. We'll deal first with how Spring manages singleton beans and then discuss essential things you need to know about using the singleton scope in real-world apps.

In section 5.2, we continue by discussing the prototype bean scope. Our focus will be on how the prototype scope is different from singleton and real-world situations in which you'd need to apply one or another.

5.1   *Using the singleton bean scope*

The singleton bean scope defines Spring's default approach for managing the beans in its context. It is also the bean scope you'll most encounter in production apps.

In section 5.1.1, we start our discussion by learning how Spring creates and manages singleton beans, which is essential for understanding where you should use them. For this purpose, we'll take two examples that employ the different approaches you can use to define beans (which you learned in chapter 2) and analyze Spring's behavior for these beans. We'll then discuss (in section 5.1.2) the critical aspects of using singleton beans in real-world scenarios. We end this section by discussing two singleton bean instantiation approaches (eager and lazy) and where you should use them in production apps.

5.1.1   *How singleton beans work*

Let's start with Spring's behavior for managing singleton-scoped beans. You need to know what to expect when using this scope, especially because singleton is the default (and the most used) bean scope in Spring. In this section, I'll describe the link between the code you write and the Spring context to make Spring's behavior easy to understand. We'll then test the behavior with a couple of examples.

Spring creates a singleton bean when it loads the context and assigns the bean a name (sometimes also referred to as bean ID). We name this scope singleton because you always get the same instance when you refer to a specific bean. But be careful! You can have more instances of the same type in the Spring context if they have different names. I highlight this aspect because you might be aware of and have possibly used the "singleton" design pattern in the past. If you don't know the singleton design pattern, you are not susceptible to confusion and you can skip the following paragraph.

But if you know what singleton pattern is, the way it works in Spring might look strange to you because you have only one instance of a type in the app. For Spring, the singleton concept allows multiple instances of the same type, and singleton means unique per name but not unique per app (figure 5.1).

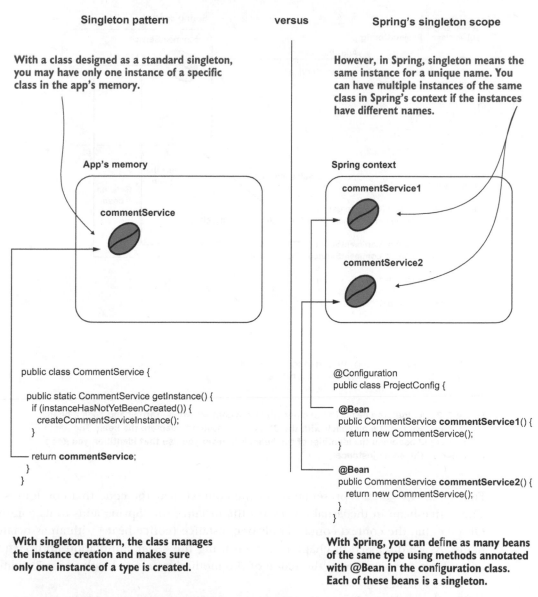

Figure 5.1 When one refers to a singleton class in an app, they mean a class that offers only one instance to the app and manages the creation of that instance. In Spring, however, singleton doesn't mean the context has only one instance of that type. It just means that a name is assigned to the instance, and the same instance will always be referred through that name.

DECLARING SINGLETON-SCOPED BEANS WITH @BEAN

Let's demonstrate a singleton bean's behavior with an example using the @Bean annotation to add an instance to the Spring context and then simply refer to it multiple times in a main class. We do this to prove we get the same instance every time we refer to the bean.

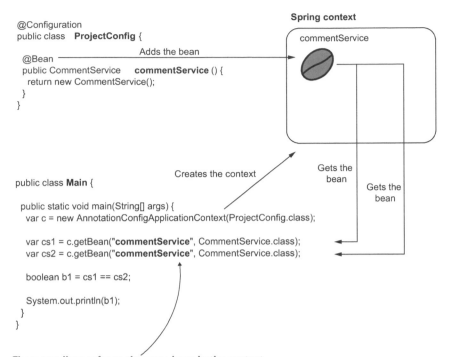

Figure 5.2   A singleton bean. The app initializes the context when starting and adds a bean. In this case, we use the approach with the @Bean annotation to declare the bean. The name of the method becomes the identifier of the bean. Wherever you use that identifier, you get a reference to the same instance.

Figure 5.2 is a visual representation of the context near the code that configures it. The coffee bean in the visual represents the instance that Spring adds to its context. Observe that the context contains only one instance (coffee bean) with an associated name. As we discussed in chapter 2, when using the @Bean annotation approach to add a bean to the context, the name of the method annotated with @Bean becomes the bean's name.

In this example, I used the @Bean annotation approach to add the bean to the Spring context. But I don't want you to think a singleton bean can only be created using the @Bean annotation. The result would have been the same if we used stereotype annotations (like @Component) to add the bean to the context. We'll demonstrate this fact with the next example.

Also, note that I've explicitly used the bean name when getting the bean from the Spring context in this demonstration. You learned in chapter 2 that when you have only one bean of a kind in the Spring context, you no longer need to use its name. You can get that bean by its type. In this example, I used the name simply to enforce that we refer to the same bean. As we discussed in chapter 2, I could have just referred to the type, and in both cases where we get the bean from the context we would get the reference to the same (and only) instance of CommentService in the context.

Let's write the code and run it to conclude this example. You can find this example in the project named "sq-ch5-ex1." We need to define an empty CommentService class, as presented in the next code snippet. You then write the configuration class and the main class, as presented in figure 5.2:

```
public class CommentService {
}
```

In the next listing, you find the configuration class definition, which uses a method annotated with @Bean to add an instance of type CommentService to the Spring context.

Listing 5.1 Adding a bean to the Spring context

```
@Configuration
public class ProjectConfig {

  @Bean                                          Adds the CommentService bean
  public CommentService commentService() {       to the Spring context
    return new CommentService();
  }
}
```

In the next listing, you find the Main class we use to test Spring's behavior for our singleton bean. We get the reference to the CommentService bean twice, and we expect to get the same reference each time.

Listing 5.2 The Main class used to test Spring's behavior for the singleton bean

```
public class Main {

  public static void main(String[] args) {
    var c = new AnnotationConfigApplicationContext(ProjectConfig.class);

    var cs1 = c.getBean("commentService", CommentService.class);
    var cs2 = c.getBean("commentService", CommentService.class);

    boolean b1 = cs1 == cs2;              Because the two variables hold
                                          the same reference, the result
    System.out.println(b1);              of this operation is true.
  }
}
```

Running the app will print "true" in the console because, being a singleton bean, Spring returns the same reference every time.

DECLARING SINGLETON BEANS USING STEREOTYPE ANNOTATIONS

As mentioned earlier, Spring's behavior for singleton beans isn't any different when using stereotype annotations than when you declared them with the @Bean annotation. But in this section, I'd like to enforce this statement with an example.

Consider a class design scenario where two service classes depend on a repository. Say we have both CommentService and UserService depending on a repository named CommentRepository, as presented in figure 5.3.

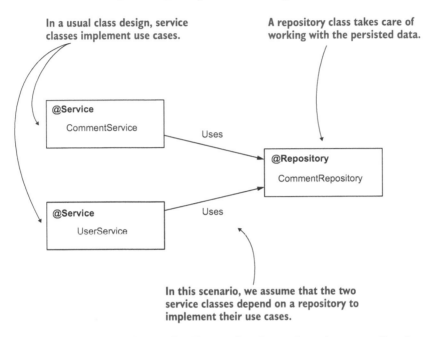

Figure 5.3 **A scenario class design. Two service classes depend on a repository to implement their use cases. When designed as singleton beans, Spring's context will have one instance of each of these classes.**

The reason these classes are dependent on one another isn't important, and our services won't do anything (it's just a scenario). We assume this class design is part of a more complicated app, and we focus on the relationship between beans and how Spring establishes the links in its context. Figure 5.4 is a visual representation of the context near the code that configures it.

Let's prove this behavior by creating the three classes and comparing the references Spring injects in the service beans. Spring injects the same reference in both service beans. In the following code snippet, you find the definition of the Comment-Repository class (project "sq-ch5-ex2"):

```
@Repository
public class CommentRepository {
}
```

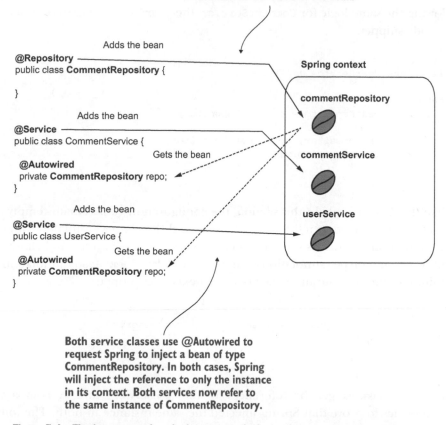

Because of the @Repository stereotype annotation, Spring adds a bean of type CommentRepository to its context. By default the bean is singleton, so Spring creates one instance and assignes a name to it. When using stereotype annotations, the name of the class becomes the name of the bean.

Both service classes use @Autowired to request Spring to inject a bean of type CommentRepository. In both cases, Spring will inject the reference to only the instance in its context. Both services now refer to the same instance of CommentRepository.

Figure 5.4 The beans are also singleton-scoped when using stereotype annotations to create them. When using @Autowired to request Spring to inject a bean reference, the framework injects the reference to the singleton bean in all the requested places.

The next code snippet presents the definition of the CommentService class. Observe that I used @Autowired to instruct Spring to inject an instance of type Comment-Repository in an attribute declared in the class. I also defined a getter method that I intend to use later to prove Spring injects the same object reference in both service beans:

```
@Service
public class CommentService {

   @Autowired
   private CommentRepository commentRepository;
```

```
    public CommentRepository getCommentRepository() {
      return commentRepository;
    }
}
```

Following the same logic for `CommentService`, the `UserService` class is defined in the next code snippet:

```
@Service
public class UserService {

  @Autowired
  private CommentRepository commentRepository;

  public CommentRepository getCommentRepository() {
    return commentRepository;
  }
}
```

Unlike the first example in this section, the configuration class remains empty in this project. We only need to tell Spring where to find the classes annotated with stereotype annotations. As discussed in chapter 2, to tell Spring where to find classes annotated with stereotype annotations we use the `@ComponentScan` annotation. The definition of the configuration class is in the next code snippet:

```
@Configuration
@ComponentScan(basePackages = {"services", "repositories"})
public class ProjectConfig {

}
```

In the `Main` class, we get the references for the two services, and we compare their dependencies to prove that Spring injected the same instance in both. The following listing presents the main class.

Listing 5.3   Testing Spring's behavior for injecting the singleton bean in the `Main` class

Creates the Spring context based on the configuration class

```
public class Main {

  public static void main(String[] args) {
    var c = new AnnotationConfigApplicationContext(
      ProjectConfig.class);

    var s1 = c.getBean(CommentService.class);
    var s2 = c.getBean(UserService.class);

    boolean b =
      s1.getCommentRepository() == s2.getCommentRepository();
```

Gets the references of the two service beans in the Spring context

Compares the references for the repository dependency injected by Spring

```
        System.out.println(b);
    }
}
```

> Because the dependency (CommentRepository) is singleton, both services contain the same reference, so this line always prints "true."

5.1.2 Singleton beans in real-world scenarios

Thus far we've discussed how Spring manages singleton beans. It's time to also discuss things you need to be aware of when working with singleton beans. Let's start by considering some scenarios where you should or shouldn't use singleton beans.

Because the singleton bean scope assumes that multiple components of the app can share an object instance, the most important thing to consider is that these beans must be immutable. Most often, a real-world app executes actions on multiple threads (e.g., any web app). In such a scenario, multiple threads share the same object instance. If these threads change the instance, you encounter a *race-condition* scenario (figure 5.5).

A race condition is a situation that can happen in multithreaded architectures when multiple threads try to change a shared resource. In case of a race condition, the developer needs to properly synchronize the threads to avoid unexpected execution results or errors.

If you want mutable singleton beans (whose attributes change), you need to make these beans concurrent by yourself (mainly by employing thread synchronization). But singleton beans aren't designed to be synchronized. They're commonly used to define an app's backbone class design and delegate responsibilities one to another. Technically, synchronization is possible, but it's not a good practice. Synchronizing the thread

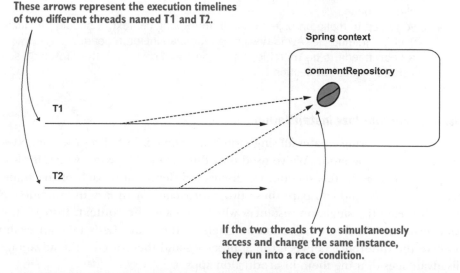

These arrows represent the execution timelines of two different threads named T1 and T2.

Spring context

commentRepository

T1

T2

If the two threads try to simultaneously access and change the same instance, they run into a race condition.

Figure 5.5 When multiple threads access a singleton bean, they access the same instance. If these threads try to change the instance simultaneously, they run into a race condition. The race condition causes unexpected results or execution exceptions if the bean is not designed for concurrency.

on a concurrent instance can dramatically affect the app's performance. In most cases, you will find other means to solve the same problem and avoid thread concurrency.

Do you remember our discussion in chapter 3, where I told you that constructor DI is a good practice and preferred over field injection? One of the advantages of constructor injection is that it allows you to make the instance immutable (define the bean's fields as final). In our previous example, we can enhance the CommentService class's definition by replacing the field injection with constructor injection. A better design of the class would look like the following code snippet:

```
@Service
public class CommentService {

  private final CommentRepository commentRepository;

  public CommentService(CommentRepository commentRepository) {
    this.commentRepository = commentRepository;
  }

  public CommentRepository getCommentRepository() {
    return commentRepository;
  }
}
```

> Making the field final highlights that this field was intended not to be changed.

> **Using beans boils down to three points**
> - Make an object bean in the Spring context only if you need Spring to manage it so that the framework can augment that bean with a specific capability. If the object doesn't need any capability offered by the framework, you don't need to make it a bean.
> - If you need to make an object bean in the Spring context, it should be singleton only if it's immutable. Avoid designing mutable singleton beans.
> - If a bean needs to be mutable, an option could be to use the prototype scope, which we discuss in section 5.2.

5.1.3   *Using eager and lazy instantiation*

In most cases, Spring creates all singleton beans when it initializes the context—this is Spring's default behavior. We've used only this default behavior, which is also called *eager instantiation*. In this section, we discuss a different approach of the framework, *lazy instantiation*, and compare these two approaches. With lazy instantiation, Spring doesn't create the singleton instances when it creates the context. Instead, it creates each instance the first time someone refers to the bean. Let's take an example to observe the difference between the approaches and then discuss the advantages and disadvantages of using them in production apps.

In our initial scenario, we only need a bean to test the default (eager) initialization (project "sq-ch5-ex3"). I'll keep the namings we've been using, and I'll name this class

CommentService. You make this class a bean, either using the @Bean annotation approach or a stereotype annotation, as I've done in the next code snippet. But either way, make sure to add an output to the console in the class's constructor. This way, we'll easily observe if the framework calls it:

```
@Service
public class CommentService {

  public CommentService() {
    System.out.println("CommentService instance created!");
  }
}
```

If you use a stereotype annotation, don't forget to add the @ComponentScan annotation in the configuration class. My configuration class in the next code snippet:

```
@Configuration
@ComponentScan(basePackages = {"services"})
public class ProjectConfig {

}
```

In the Main class, we only instantiate the Spring context. A critical aspect to observe is that no one uses the CommentService bean. However, Spring will create and store the instance in the context. We know that Spring creates the instance because we'll see the output from the CommentService bean class's constructor when running the app. The next code snippet presents the Main class:

```
public class Main {

  public static void main(String[] args) {    ◁——
    var c = new AnnotationConfigApplicationContext(ProjectConfig.class);
  }
}
```

> **This app creates the Spring context, but it doesn't use the CommentService bean anywhere.**

Even if the app doesn't use the bean anywhere, when running the app you'll find the following output in the console:

```
CommentService instance created!
```

Now change the example (project "sq-ch5-ex4") by adding the @Lazy annotation above the class (for stereotype annotations approach) or above the @Bean method (for the @Bean method approach). You'll observe the output no longer appears in the console when running the app because we instructed Spring to create the bean only when someone uses it. And, in our example, nobody uses the CommentService bean.

```
@Service
@Lazy                                    ◁——
public class CommentService {
```

> **The @Lazy annotation tells Spring that it needs to create the bean only when someone refers to the bean for the first time.**

```
  public CommentService() {
    System.out.println("CommentService instance created!");
  }
}
```

Change the Main class and add a reference to the CommentService bean, as presented in the next code snippet:

```
public class Main {

  public static void main(String[] args) {
    var c = new AnnotationConfigApplicationContext(ProjectConfig.class);

    System.out.println("Before retrieving the CommentService");
    var service = c.getBean(CommentService.class);
    System.out.println("After retrieving the CommentService");
  }
}
```

At this line, where Spring needs to provide a reference to the CommentService bean, Spring also creates the instance.

Rerun the app, and you'll find the output again in the console. The framework creates the bean only if it's used:

```
Before retrieving the CommentService
CommentService instance created!
After retrieving the CommentService
```

When should you use eager instantiation and when should you use lazy? In most cases, it's more comfortable to let the framework create all the instances at the beginning when the context is instantiated (eager); this way, when one instance delegates to another, the second bean already exists in any situation.

In a lazy instantiation, the framework has to first check if the instance exists and eventually create it if it doesn't, so from the performance point of view, it's better to have the instances in the context already (eager) because it spares some checks the framework needs to do when one bean delegates to another. Another advantage of eager instantiation is when something is wrong and the framework cannot create a bean; we can observe this issue when starting the app. With lazy instantiation, someone would observe the issue only when the app is already executing and it reaches the point that the bean needs to be created.

But lazy instantiation is not all evil. Some time ago, I worked on a vast monolithic application. This app was installed in different locations where it was used in various scopes by its clients. In most cases, a specific client didn't use a big part of the functionality, so instantiating the beans together with the Spring context unnecessarily occupied a lot of memory. For that app, the developers designed most of the beans to be lazily instantiated so that the app would create only the necessary instances.

My advice is to go with the default, which is an eager instantiation. This approach generally brings more benefits. If you find yourself in a situation like the one I presented with the monolithic app, first see if you can do something about the app's design. Often, the need for using lazy instantiation is a sign something might be wrong with the app's design. For example, in my story, it would have been better if the app had been designed in a modular way or as microservices. Such an architecture would have helped the developers deploy only what specific clients needed, and then making the instantiation of the beans lazy wouldn't have been necessary. But in the real world, not everything is possible due to other factors like cost or time. If you cannot treat the real cause of the problem, you can sometimes treat at least some of the symptoms.

5.2 Using the prototype bean scope

In this section, we discuss the second bean scope Spring offers: prototype. In some cases, which we'll analyze in this section, you'd go with prototype-scoped beans instead of singleton. We'll discuss the framework's behavior for beans declared as prototype in section 5.2.1. You'll then learn how to change the bean's scope to prototype, and we'll try it with a couple of examples. Finally, in section 5.2.2, we'll discuss real-world situations you need to know when using the prototype scope.

5.2.1 How prototype beans work

Let's figure out the Spring behavior for managing prototype beans before discussing where you'd use them in apps. As you'll see, the idea is straightforward. Every time you request a reference to a prototype-scoped bean, Spring creates a new object instance. For prototype beans, Spring doesn't create and manage an object instance directly. The framework manages the object's type and creates a new instance every time someone requests a reference to the bean. In figure 5.6, I represented the bean as a coffee plant (every time you request a bean, you get a new instance). We still use the bean terminology, but I use the coffee plant because I want to help you quickly understand and remember Spring's behavior for prototype beans.

As you can see in figure 5.6, we need to use a new annotation named @Scope to change the bean's scope. When you create the bean using the @Bean annotation approach, @Scope goes together with @Bean over the method that declares the bean. When declaring the bean with stereotype annotations, you use the @Scope annotation and the stereotype annotation over the class that declares the bean.

With prototype beans, we no longer have concurrency problems because each thread that requests the bean gets a different instance, so defining mutable prototype beans is not a problem (figure 5.7).

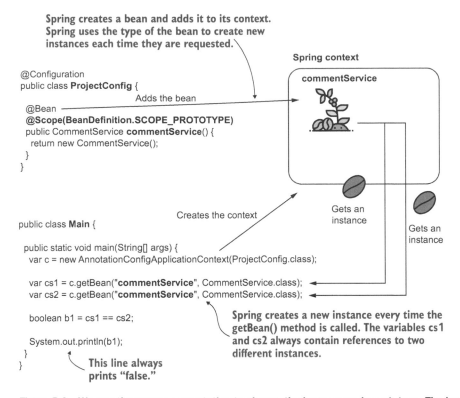

Spring creates a bean and adds it to its context. Spring uses the type of the bean to create new instances each time they are requested.

Spring context

commentService

```
@Configuration
public class ProjectConfig {
                            Adds the bean
    @Bean
    @Scope(BeanDefinition.SCOPE_PROTOTYPE)
    public CommentService commentService() {
      return new CommentService();
    }
}
```

Creates the context

Gets an instance

Gets an instance

```
public class Main {

    public static void main(String[] args) {
      var c = new AnnotationConfigApplicationContext(ProjectConfig.class);

      var cs1 = c.getBean("commentService", CommentService.class);
      var cs2 = c.getBean("commentService", CommentService.class);

      boolean b1 = cs1 == cs2;

      System.out.println(b1);
    }
}
```

This line always prints "false."

Spring creates a new instance every time the getBean() method is called. The variables cs1 and cs2 always contain references to two different instances.

Figure 5.6   We use the @Scope annotation to change the bean scope in prototype. The bean is now represented as a coffee plant because you get a new object instance each time you refer to it. For this reason, variables cs1 and cs2 will always contain different references, so the output of the code is always "false."

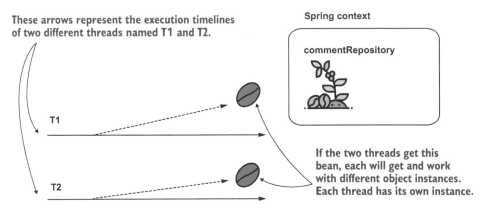

These arrows represent the execution timelines of two different threads named T1 and T2.

Spring context

commentRepository

T1

T2

If the two threads get this bean, each will get and work with different object instances. Each thread has its own instance.

Figure 5.7   When multiple threads request a certain prototype bean, each thread gets a different instance. This way, the threads cannot run into a race condition.

DECLARING PROTOTYPE-SCOPED BEANS WITH @BEAN

To enforce our discussion, let's write a project ("sq-ch5-ex5") and prove Spring's behavior for managing prototype beans. We create a bean named CommentService and declare it as prototype to prove we get a new instance every time we request that bean. The next code snippet presents the CommentService class:

```
public class CommentService {
}
```

We define a bean with the CommentService class in the configuration class, as presented in the following listing.

Listing 5.4 Declaring the prototype bean in the configuration class

```
@Configuration
public class ProjectConfig {

  @Bean
  @Scope(BeanDefinition.SCOPE_PROTOTYPE)      <--- Makes this bean prototype-scoped
  public CommentService commentService() {
    return new CommentService();
  }
}
```

To prove that every time we request the bean we get a new instance, we create a Main class and request the beans twice from the context. We observe that the references we get are different. You find the definition of the Main class in the following listing.

Listing 5.5 Testing Spring's behavior for the prototype bean in the Main class

The two variables cs1 and cs2 contain references to different instances.
```
public class Main {

  public static void main(String[] args) {
    var c = new AnnotationConfigApplicationContext(ProjectConfig.class);

    var cs1 = c.getBean("commentService", CommentService.class);
    var cs2 = c.getBean("commentService", CommentService.class);

    boolean b1 = cs1 == cs2;
                                           This line always prints
    System.out.println(b1);         <--┘  "false" in the console.
  }
}
```

When you run the app, you'll see it always displays "false" in the console. This output proves that the two instances received when calling the getBean() method are different.

DECLARING PROTOTYPE-SCOPED BEANS USING STEREOTYPE ANNOTATIONS

Let's also create a project ("sq-ch5-ex6") to observe the behavior for auto-wiring prototype-scoped beans. We'll define a `CommentRepository` prototype bean, and we inject the bean using `@Autowired` in two other service beans. We will observe that each service bean has a reference to a different instance of `CommentRepository`. This scenario is similar to the example we used in section 5.1 for singleton-scoped beans, but now the `CommentRepository` bean is prototype. Figure 5.8 describes the relationships between the beans.

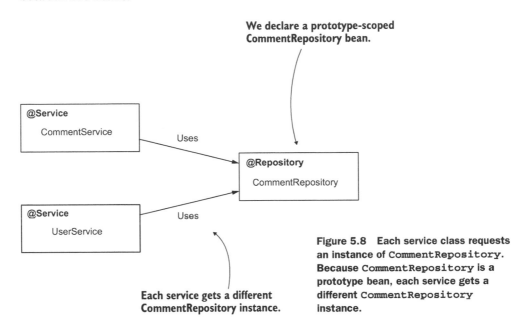

Figure 5.8 Each service class requests an instance of `CommentRepository`. Because `CommentRepository` is a prototype bean, each service gets a different `CommentRepository` instance.

The next code snippet gives definition of the `CommentRepository` class. Observe the `@Scope` annotation used over the class to change the scope of the bean to prototype:

```
@Repository
@Scope(BeanDefinition.SCOPE_PROTOTYPE)
public class CommentRepository {
}
```

The two service classes request an instance of type `CommentRepository` using the `@Autowired` annotation. The next code snippet presents the `CommentService` class:

```
@Service
public class CommentService {

  @Autowired
  private CommentRepository commentRepository;

  public CommentRepository getCommentRepository() {
```

```
    return commentRepository;
  }
}
```

In the previous code snippet, the UserService class also requests an instance of the CommentRepository bean. In the configuration class, we need to use the @Component-Scan annotation to tell Spring where to find the classes annotated with stereotype annotations:

```
@Configuration
@ComponentScan(basePackages = {"services", "repositories"})
public class ProjectConfig {

}
```

We add the Main class to our project and test how Spring injects the CommentRepository bean. The Main class is shown in the following listing.

> **Listing 5.6 Testing Spring's behavior for injecting the prototype bean in the Main class**

```
public class Main {

  public static void main(String[] args) {
    var c = new AnnotationConfigApplicationContext(ProjectConfig.class);

    var s1 = c.getBean(CommentService.class);      Gets references from the
    var s2 = c.getBean(UserService.class);         context for the service beans

    boolean b =                                    ◄─────────────
      s1.getCommentRepository() == s2.getCommentRepository();

    System.out.println(b);              Compares the references for the injected
  }                                     CommentRepository instances. Because
}                                       CommentRepository is a prototype bean,
                                        the result of the comparison is always false.
```

5.2.2 *Prototype beans in real-world scenarios*

So far we've discussed how Spring manages prototype beans by focusing on the behavior. In this section, we focus more on the use cases and where you should use prototype-scoped beans in production apps. Just as we did with singleton apps in section 5.1.2, we'll consider the discussed characteristics and analyze which scenarios prototype beans are good for and where should you avoid them (by using singleton beans).

   You won't find prototype beans as often as you'll find singleton beans. But there is a good pattern you can use to decide if a bean should be prototype. Remember that singleton beans are not quite good friends with mutating objects. Say you design an object named CommentProcessor that processes the comments and validates them. A service uses the CommentProcessor object to implement a use case. But the Comment-Processor object stores the comment to be processed as an attribute, and its methods change this attribute (figure 5.9).

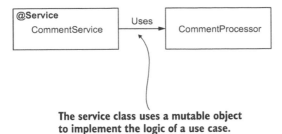

The service class uses a mutable object
to implement the logic of a use case.

Figure 5.9   **A service class uses a mutable
object to implement the logic of a use case.**

The next listing shows the implementation of the CommentProcessor bean.

Listing 5.7   A mutable object; a potential candidate to the prototype scope

```java
public class CommentProcessor {
  private Comment comment;

  public void setComment(Comment comment) {
    this.comment = comment;
  }

  public void getComment() {
    return this.comment;
  }

  public void processComment() {
    // changing the comment attribute
  }

  public void validateComment() {
    // validating and changing the comment attribute
  }
}
```

**These two methods alter the
value of the Comment attribute.**

The next listing presents this service that uses the CommentProcessor class to implement a use case. The service method creates an instance of CommentProcessor using
the class's constructor and then uses the instance in the method's logic.

Listing 5.8   A service using a mutable object to implement a use case

```java
@Service
public class CommentService {

  public void sendComment(Comment c) {
    CommentProcessor p = new CommentProcessor();

    p.setComment(c);
    p.processComment(c);
    p.validateComment(c);
```

**Creates a CommentProcessor
instance**

**Uses the CommentProcessor instance
to alter the Comment instance**

```
    c = p.getComment();        Gets the modified Comment
    // do something further     instance and uses it further
  }
}
```

The CommentProcessor object is not even a bean in the Spring context. Does it need to be a bean? It's critical you ask yourself this question before deciding to make any object a bean. Remember that an object needs to be a bean in the context only if Spring needs to manage it to augment the object with some capability the framework offers. If we leave our scenario like this, the CommentProcessor object doesn't need to be a bean at all.

But let's suppose further that the CommentProcessor bean needs to use an object CommentRepository to persist some data, and CommentRepository is a bean in the Spring context (figure 5.10).

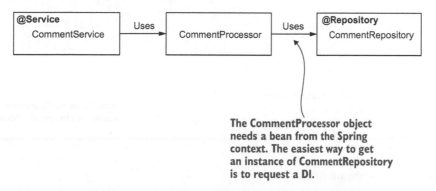

Figure 5.10 **If the** CommentProcessor **object needs to use an instance of** CommentRepository, **the easiest way to get an instance is to request a DI. But to do this, Spring needs to know about** CommentProcessor, **so the** CommentProcessor **object needs to be a bean in the context.**

In this scenario, the CommentProcessor bean needs to become a bean to benefit from the DI capability Spring offers. In general, in any case where we want Spring to augment the object with a specific capability, it needs to be a bean.

We make CommentProcessor a bean in the Spring context. But can it be singleton-scoped? No. If we define this bean as singleton and multiple threads use it concurrently, we get into a race condition (as discussed in section 5.1.2). We would not be sure which comment provided by which thread is processed and if the comment was processed correctly. In this scenario, we want each method call to get a different instance of the CommentProcessor object. We can change the CommentProcessor class to be a prototype bean, as presented in the next code snippet:

```
@Component
@Scope(BeanDefinition.SCOPE_PROTOTYPE)
public class CommentProcessor {
```

```
    @Autowired
    private CommentRepository commentRepository;

    // Omitted code
}
```

You can now get an instance of `CommentProcessor` from the Spring context. But be careful! You need this instance for every call of the `sendComment()` method, so the request to the bean should be inside the method itself. To achieve such a result, you can directly inject the Spring context (`ApplicationContext`) into the `Comment-Service` bean using `@Autowired`. In the `sendComment()` method, you retrieve the `CommentProcessor` instance using `getBean()` from the application context, as presented in the next listing.

Listing 5.9   Using `CommentProcessor` as prototype bean

```
@Service
public class CommentService {

    @Autowired
    private ApplicationContext context;

    public void sendComment(Comment c) {
        CommentProcessor p =
            context.getBean(CommentProcessor.class);    ⟵⎤ A new CommentProcessor
                                                          ⎦ instance is always provided here.
        p.setComment(c);
        p.processComment(c);
        p.validateComment(c);

        c = p.getComment();
        // do something further
    }
}
```

Don't make the mistake of injecting the `CommentProcessor` directly in the `Comment-Service` bean. The `CommentService` bean is a singleton, which means that Spring creates only an instance of this class. As a consequence, Spring will also inject the dependencies of this class just once when it creates the `CommentService` bean itself. In this case, you'll end up with only an instance of the `CommentProcessor`. Each call of the `sendComment()` method will use this unique instance, so with multiple threads you'll run into the same race condition issues as with a singleton bean. The next listing presents this approach. Use this as an exercise to try out and prove this behavior.

Listing 5.10 Injecting a prototype into a singleton

```
@Service
public class CommentService {

  @Autowired
  private CommentProcessor p;

  public void sendComment(Comment c) {

    p.setComment(c);
    p.processComment(c);
    p.validateComment(c);

    c = p.getComment();
    // do something further
  }
}
```

Spring injects this bean when creating the CommentService bean. But because CommentService is singleton, Spring will also create and inject the CommentProcessor just once.

I conclude this section by giving you my opinion about using prototype beans. I generally prefer to avoid using them, and mutable instances in general, in the apps I develop. But sometimes you need to refactor or work with old applications. In my case, I faced such a scenario when I worked in an app refactoring for adding Spring to an old application. That app used mutating objects in many places, and refactoring all these places in a short time was impossible. We needed to use prototype bean, which allowed the team to refactor each of these cases progressively.

As a recap, let's have a quick comparison between singleton and prototype scopes. Table 5.1 shows their characteristics side-by-side.

Table 5.1 A quick comparison between singleton and prototype bean scopes

Singleton	Prototype
1 The framework associates a name with an actual object instance.	**1** A name is associated with a type.
2 Every time you refer to a bean name you'll get the same object instance.	**2** Every time you refer to a bean name, you get a new instance.
3 You can configure Spring to create the instances when the context is loaded or when first referred.	**3** The framework always creates the object instances for the prototype scope when you refer to the bean.
4 Singleton is the default bean scope in Spring.	**4** You need to explicitly mark a bean as a prototype.
5 It's not recommended that a singleton bean to have mutable attributes.	**5** A prototype bean can have mutable attributes.

Summary

- In Spring, the scope of beans defines how the framework manages the object instances.
- Spring offers two bean scopes: singleton and prototype.
  - With singleton, Spring manages the object instances directly in its context. Each instance has a unique name, and using that name you always refer to that specific instance. Singleton is Spring's default.
  - With prototype, Spring considers only the object type. Each type has a unique name associated with it. Spring creates a new instance of that type every time you refer to the bean name.
- You can configure Spring to create a singleton bean either when the context is initialized (eager) or when the bean is referred for the first time (lazy). By default, a bean is eagerly instantiated.
- In apps, we most often use singleton beans. Because anyone referring to the same name gets the same object instance, multiple different threads could access and use this instance. For this reason, it's advisable to have the instance immutable. If, however, you prefer to have mutating operations on the bean's attribute, it's your responsibility to take care of the thread synchronization.
- If you need to have a mutable object like a bean, using the prototype scope could be a good option.
- Be careful with injecting a prototype-scoped bean into a singleton-scoped bean. When you do something like this, you need to be aware that the singleton instance always uses the same prototype instance, which Spring injects when it creates the singleton instance. This is usually a vicious design because the point of making a bean prototype-scoped is to get a different instance for every use.

Using aspects with Spring AOP

This chapter covers

- Aspect-oriented programming (AOP)
- Using aspects
- Using the aspect execution chain

Thus far, we have discussed the Spring context, and the only Spring capability we have used is DI, which is supported by the IoC principle. With DI, the framework manages objects you define, and you can request to use these objects where you need them. As we discussed in chapters 2 through 5, to request a bean's reference, in most cases, you use the @Autowired annotation. When you request such an object from the Spring context, we say that Spring "injects" the object where you requested it. In this chapter, you'll learn how to use another powerful technique supported by the IoC principle: *aspects*.

Aspects are a way the framework intercepts method calls and possibly alters the execution of methods. You can affect the execution of specific method calls you select. This technique helps you extract part of the logic belonging to the executing method. In certain scenarios, decoupling a part of the code helps make that method easier to understand (figure 6.1). It allows the developer to focus only on the relevant details discussed when reading the method logic. In this chapter, we'll discuss how to implement aspects and when you should use them. Aspects are a powerful tool, and, as Peter Parker's uncle says, "With great power comes great responsibility!" If you don't use aspects carefully, you might end up with a less maintainable app, which is quite the opposite of what you want to achieve. This approach is called *aspect-oriented programming* (AOP).

Figure 6.1   Sometimes it's not relevant to have parts of the code in the same place with the business logic because it makes the app more difficult to understand. A solution is to move part of the code aside from the business logic implementation using aspects. In this scene, Jane, the programmer, is discouraged by the logging lines written together with the business code. Count Dracula shows her the magic of aspects by decoupling the logs into an aspect.

Another important reason for learning aspects is that Spring uses them in implementing a lot of the crucial capabilities it offers. Understanding how the framework works can save you many hours of debugging later when you face a specific problem. A pertinent example of Spring capability that uses aspects is *transactionality*, which we'll discuss in chapter 13. Transactionality is one of the main capabilities most apps use today to keep the persisted data's consistency. Another important capability relying on aspects is security configurations, which help your app protect its data and make sure data cannot be seen or changed by unwanted individuals. To properly understand what happens in apps using these functionalities, you first need to learn aspects.

We'll start with a theoretical introduction to aspects in section 6.1. You'll learn how aspects work. Once you understand these basics, in section 6.2, you'll learn how to implement an aspect. We'll start with a scenario, and we'll develop an example that we'll use to discuss the most practical syntaxes for using aspects. In section 6.3, you'll learn what happens when you define multiple aspects to intercept the same method and deal with such scenarios.

6.1 *How aspects work in Spring*

In this section, you'll learn how aspects work and the essential terminology you'll encounter when using aspects. By learning to implement aspects, you'll be able to use new techniques to make your app more maintainable. Moreover, you'll also understand how certain Spring features are plugged into apps. We discuss these things first and then go straight into an implementation example in section 6.2. But it helps if you have an idea of what we're implementing before diving into writing code.

An aspect is simply a piece of logic the framework executes when you call specific methods of your choice. When designing an aspect, you define the following:

- *What* code you want Spring to execute when you call specific methods. This is named an *aspect*.
- *When* the app should execute this logic of the aspect (e.g., before or after the method call, instead of the method call). This is named the *advice*.
- *Which* methods the framework needs to intercept and execute the aspect for them. This is named a *pointcut*.

With aspects terminology, you'll also find the concept of a *join point*, which defines the event that triggers the execution of an aspect. But with Spring, this event is always a method call.

As in the case of the dependency injection, to use aspects you need the framework to manage the objects for which you want to apply aspects. You'll use the approaches you learned in chapter 2 to add beans to the Spring context to enable the framework to control them and apply aspects you define. The bean that declares the method intercepted by an aspect is named the *target object*. Figure 6.2 summarizes these terms.

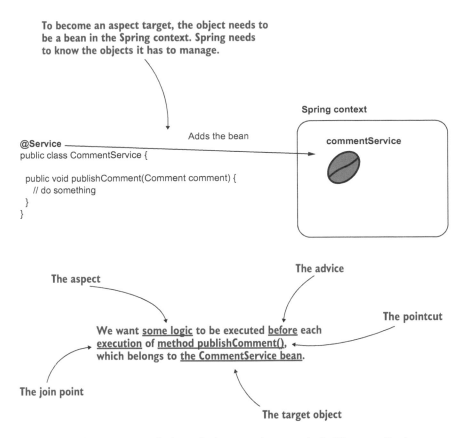

To become an aspect target, the object needs to be a bean in the Spring context. Spring needs to know the objects it has to manage.

Spring context

Adds the bean

commentService

@Service
public class CommentService {

 public void publishComment(Comment comment) {
  // do something
 }
}

The aspect

The advice

The pointcut

We want some logic to be executed before each
execution of method publishComment(),
which belongs to the CommentService bean.

The join point

The target object

Figure 6.2   The aspect terminology. Spring executes some logic (the aspect) when someone calls a specific method (the pointcut). We need to specify when the logic is executed according to the pointcut (e.g., before). The when is the advice. For Spring to intercept the method, the object that defines the intercepted method needs to be a bean in the Spring context. So, the bean becomes the target object of the aspect.

But how does Spring intercept each method call and apply the aspect logic? As discussed earlier in this section, the object needs to be a bean in the Spring context. But because you made the object an aspect target, Spring won't directly give you an instance reference for the bean when you request it from the context. Instead, Spring gives you an object that calls the aspect logic instead of the actual method. We say that Spring gives you a *proxy* object instead of the real bean. You will now receive the proxy instead of the bean anytime you get the bean from the context, either if you directly use the getBean() method of the context or if you use DI (figure 6.3). This approach is named *weaving*.

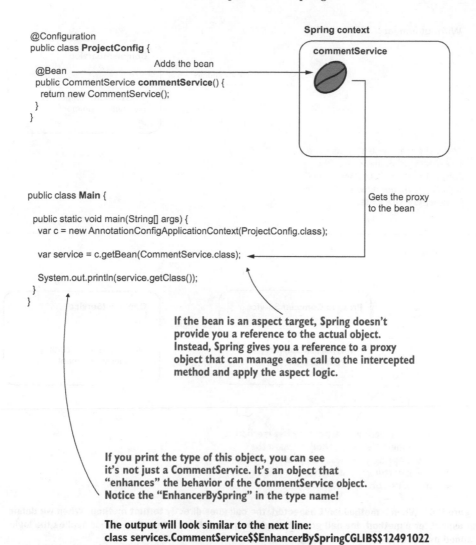

```
@Configuration
public class ProjectConfig {

  @Bean ————————— Adds the bean
  public CommentService commentService() {
    return new CommentService();
  }
}
```

Spring context

commentService

Gets the proxy
to the bean

```
public class Main {

  public static void main(String[] args) {
    var c = new AnnotationConfigApplicationContext(ProjectConfig.class);

    var service = c.getBean(CommentService.class);

    System.out.println(service.getClass());
  }
}
```

**If the bean is an aspect target, Spring doesn't
provide you a reference to the actual object.
Instead, Spring gives you a reference to a proxy
object that can manage each call to the intercepted
method and apply the aspect logic.**

**If you print the type of this object, you can see
it's not just a CommentService. It's an object that
"enhances" the behavior of the CommentService object.
Notice the "EnhancerBySpring" in the type name!**

**The output will look similar to the next line:
class services.CommentService$$EnhancerBySpringCGLIB$$12491022**

**Figure 6.3 Weaving an aspect. Instead of giving you a reference to the real bean, Spring gives
you a reference to a proxy object, intercepts the method calls, and manages the aspect logic.**

In figure 6.4, you find a comparison between calling the method when it isn't intercepted by an aspect versus an aspect intercepting the method call. You observe that calling an aspected method assumes you call the method through the proxy object provided by Spring. The proxy applies the aspect logic and delegates the call to the actual method.

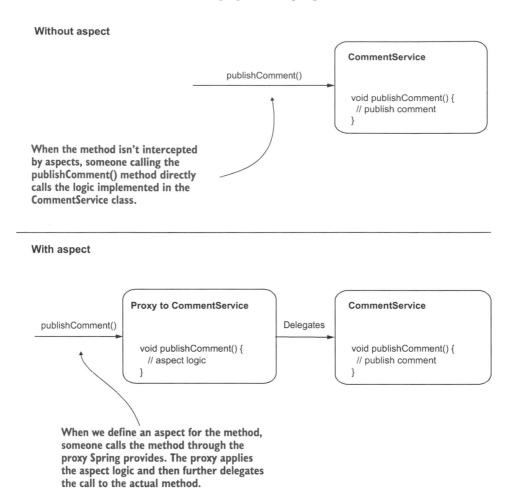

Without aspect

When the method isn't intercepted by aspects, someone calling the publishComment() method directly calls the logic implemented in the CommentService class.

With aspect

When we define an aspect for the method, someone calls the method through the proxy Spring provides. The proxy applies the aspect logic and then further delegates the call to the actual method.

Figure 6.4   When a method isn't aspected, the call goes directly to that method. When we define an aspect for a method, the call goes through the proxy object. The proxy object applies the logic defined by the aspect and then delegates the call to the real method.

Now that you have the big picture of aspects and how Spring manages them, we go further and discuss the syntaxes you need to implement aspects with Spring. In section 6.2, I describe a scenario, and then we implement the requirements of the scenario using aspects.

6.2   *Implementing aspects with Spring AOP*

In this section, you'll learn the most relevant aspect syntaxes used in real-world examples. We'll consider a scenario and implement its requirements with aspects. At the end of this section, you'll be able to apply aspect syntaxes to solve the most frequent problems in real-world scenarios.

Suppose you have an application that implements multiple use cases in its service classes. Some new regulations require your app to store the time it started and ended for each use case execution. In your team, you decided to take responsibility for implementing a functionality to log all the events where a use case begins and ends.

In section 6.2.1, we'll use an aspect to solve this scenario in the simplest way possible. By doing so, you'll learn what you need to implement an aspect. Further, in this chapter, I'll progressively add more details in regard to using aspects. In section 6.2.2, we'll discuss how an aspect uses or even alters the intercepted method's parameters or the value returned by the method. In section 6.2.3, you'll learn how to use annotations to mark methods you want to intercept for a specific purpose. Developers often use annotations to mark the method an aspect needs to intercept. Many features in Spring use annotations, as you'll learn in the next chapters. Section 6.2.4 will give you more alternatives for advice annotations you can use with Spring aspects.

6.2.1 *Implementing a simple aspect*

In this section, we discuss implementing a simple aspect to solve our scenario. We'll create a new project and define a service class containing a method that we'll use to test our implementation and prove the aspect we define works as desired in the end.

You find this example in the project named "sq-ch6-ex1." In addition to the `spring-context` dependency, for this example we also need the `spring-aspects` dependency. Make sure to update your pom.xml file and add the needed dependencies, as presented in the next code snippet:

```
<dependency>
    <groupId>org.springframework</groupId>
    <artifactId>spring-context</artifactId>
    <version>5.2.8.RELEASE</version>
</dependency>
<dependency>
    <groupId>org.springframework</groupId>
    <artifactId>spring-aspects</artifactId>
    <version>5.2.8.RELEASE</version>
</dependency>
```

We need this dependency to implement the aspects.

To make our example shorter and allow you to focus on the syntax related to aspects, we'll only consider one service object named `CommentService` and a use case it defines named `publishComment(Comment comment)`. This method, defined in the `Comment-Service` class, receives a parameter of type `Comment`. `Comment` is a model class and is presented in the next code snippet:

```
public class Comment {

  private String text;
  private String author;

  // Omitted getters and setters
}
```

NOTE   Remember from chapter 4 that a model class is a class that models the data processed by the app. In our case, the `Comment` class describes a comment with its attributes: text and author. A service class implements use cases of an app. In chapter 4, we discussed more of these responsibilities, and we used them in examples.

In listing 6.1, you find the definition of the `CommentService` class. We annotate the `CommentService` class with the `@Service` stereotype annotation to make it a bean in the Spring context. The `CommentService` class defines the `publishComment(Comment comment)` method, representing our scenario's use case.

You also observe in this example that instead of using `System.out`, I used an object of type `Logger` to write messages in the console. In real-world apps, you don't use `System.out` to write messages in the console. You'll generally use a logging framework that offers you more flexibility in customizing the logging features and standardizing the logging messages. Some good options for a logging framework are as follows:

- Log4j (https://logging.apache.org/log4j/2.x/)
- Logback (http://logback.qos.ch/)
- Java Logging API, which comes with the JDK (http://mng.bz/v4Xq)

The logging frameworks are compatible with any Java app, whether it's using Spring or not. As they are not related to Spring, I haven't use them in our examples to avoid distracting you. But we are far enough now with Spring that we can start to use these additional frameworks in our examples to familiarize you with syntaxes closer to production-ready apps.

Listing 6.1   The `Service` class used in the examples

We use the stereotype annotation to make this a bean in the Spring context.

To log a message in the app's console every time someone calls the use case, we use a logger object.

This method defines the use case for our demonstration.

```
@Service
public class CommentService {

  private Logger logger =
    Logger.getLogger(CommentService.class.getName());

  public void publishComment(Comment comment) {
    logger.info("Publishing comment:" + comment.getText());
  }
}
```

In this example, I use the JDK logging capabilities to avoid adding other dependencies to our project. When declaring a logger object, you need to give it a name as a parameter. This name then appears in the logs and makes it easy for you to observe the log message source. Often, we use the class name, which I did in our example: `CommentService.class.getName()`.

We also need to add a configuration class to tell Spring where to look for the classes annotated with stereotype annotations. In my case, I added the service class in the package named `"services"`, and this is what I need to specify with the @ComponentScan annotation, as you observe from the next code snippet:

```
@Configuration
@ComponentScan(basePackages = "services")    ◄┐   We use @ComponentScan to tell Spring
public class ProjectConfig {                       where to search for classes annotated
                                                   with stereotype annotations.
}
```

Let's write the Main class that calls the publishComment() method in the service class and observe the current behavior, as shown in the following listing.

> **Listing 6.2   The Main class we use to test the app's behavior**

```
public class Main {

  public static void main(String[] args) {
    var c = new AnnotationConfigApplicationContext(ProjectConfig.class);

    var service = c.getBean(CommentService.class);    ◄─┤   Gets the CommentService
                                                           bean from the context
    Comment comment = new Comment();          ◄┐
    comment.setText("Demo comment");            │  Creates a Comment instance
    comment.setAuthor("Natasha");               │  to give as a parameter to the
                                                │  publishComment() method
    service.publishComment(comment);    ◄─┐
  }                                          │  Calls the publishComment() method
}
```

If you run the app, you'll observe an output in the console similar to what you see in the next snippet:

```
Sep 26, 2020 12:39:53 PM services.CommentService publishComment
INFO: Publishing comment:Demo comment
```

You will see the output generated by the publishComment() method. This is how the app looks before we solve the example we discussed. Remember, we need to print messages in the console before and after the service method call. Let's now enhance the project with an aspect class that intercepts the method call and adds an output before and after the call.

To create an aspect, you follow these steps (figure 6.5):

1 Enable the aspect mechanism in your Spring app by annotating the configuration class with the @EnableAspectJAutoProxy annotation.

2 Create a new class, and annotate it with the @Aspect annotation. Using either @Bean or stereotype annotations, add a bean for this class in the Spring context.

3 Define a method that will implement the aspect logic and tell Spring when and which methods to intercept using an advice annotation.

4 Implement the aspect logic.

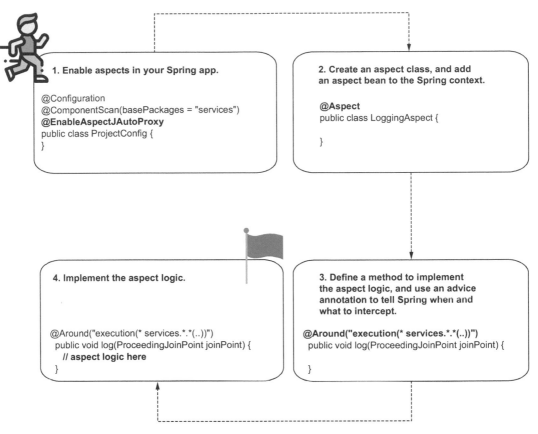

Figure 6.5   To implement an aspect, you follow four easy steps. First, you need to enable the aspect capability in your app. Then you create an aspect class, define a method, and instruct Spring when and what to intercept. Finally, you implement the aspect logic.

STEP 1: ENABLING THE ASPECTS MECHANISM FOR YOUR APPLICATION

For the first step, you need to tell Spring you'll use aspects in your app. Whenever you use a specific mechanism provided by Spring, you have to explicitly enable it by annotating your configuration class with a particular annotation. In most cases, the names of these annotations start with "Enable." You will learn more such annotations that enable different Spring capabilities as you progress through the book. In this example, we need to use the @EnableAspectJAutoProxy annotation to enable the aspect capabilities. The configuration class needs to look like the one presented in the following listing.

Listing 6.3   Enabling the aspects mechanism in a Spring app

```
@Configuration
@ComponentScan(basePackages = "services")
@EnableAspectJAutoProxy
public class ProjectConfig {
}
```

◁—— **Enables the aspects mechanism in our Spring app**

STEP 2: CREATE A CLASS THAT DEFINES THE ASPECT, AND ADD AN INSTANCE FOR THIS CLASS IN THE SPRING CONTEXT

We need to create a new bean in the Spring context that defines the aspect. This object holds the methods, which will intercept specific method calls and augment them with specific logic. In the next listing, you find the definition of this new class.

Listing 6.4   Defining an aspect class

```
@Aspect
public class LoggingAspect {
  public void log() {
    // To implement later
  }
}
```

You can use any of the approaches you learned in chapter 2 to add an instance of this class to the Spring context. If you decide to use the @Bean annotation, you have to change the configuration class, as presented in the next code snippet. Of course, you can also use stereotype annotations if you'd like:

```
@Configuration
@ComponentScan(basePackages = "services")
@EnableAspectJAutoProxy
public class ProjectConfig {

  @Bean
  public LoggingAspect aspect() {
    return new LoggingAspect();
  }
}
```

◁—— **Adds an instance of the LoggingAspect class to the Spring context**

Remember, you need to make this object a bean in the Spring context because Spring needs to know about any object it needs to manage. This is why I strongly emphasized the approaches to manage the Spring context in chapters 2 through 5. You'll use these skills almost everywhere when developing a Spring app.

Also, the @Aspect annotation isn't a stereotype annotation. Using @Aspect, you tell Spring that the class implements the definition of an aspect, but Spring won't also create a bean for this class. You need to explicitly use one of the syntaxes you learned in chapter 2 to create a bean for your class and allow Spring to manage it this way. It's a common mistake to forget that annotating the class with @Aspect doesn't also add a bean to the context, and I've seen much frustration caused by forgetting this.

STEP 3: USE AN ADVICE ANNOTATION TO TELL SPRING WHEN AND WHICH METHOD CALLS TO INTERCEPT

Now that we have defined the aspect class, we choose the advice and annotate the method accordingly. In the next listing, you see how I annotated the method with the @Around annotation.

Listing 6.5 Using an advice annotation to weave the aspect to specific methods

```
@Aspect
public class LoggingAspect {

  @Around("execution(* services.*.*(..))")        ← Defines which are the
  public void log(ProceedingJoinPoint joinPoint) {    intercepted methods
    joinPoint.proceed();        ←
  }                                  Delegates to the actual intercepted method
}
```

Other than using the @Around annotation, you also observe I've written an unusual string expression as the value of the annotation, and I have added a parameter to the aspect method. What are these?

Let's take them one by one. The peculiar expression used as a parameter to the @Around annotation tells Spring which method calls to intercept. Don't be intimidated by this expression! This expression language is called AspectJ pointcut language, and you won't need to learn it by heart to use it. In practice, you don't use complex expressions. When I need to write such an expression, I always refer to the documentation (http://mng.bz/4K9g).

Theoretically, you can write very complex AspectJ pointcut expressions to identify a particular set of method calls to be intercepted. This language is really powerful. But as we'll discuss later in this chapter, it's always better to avoid writing complex expressions. In most cases, you can find simpler alternatives.

Look at the expression I used (figure 6.6). It means Spring intercepts any method defined in a class that is in the services package, regardless of the method's return type, the class it belongs to, the name of the method, or the parameters the method receives.

On second look, the expression doesn't seem so complicated, does it? I know these AspectJ pointcut expressions tend to scare beginners, but trust me, you don't have to become an AspectJ expert to use these expressions in Spring apps.

Now let's look at the second element I've added to the method: the Proceeding-JoinPoint parameter, which represents the intercepted method. The main thing you do with this parameter is tell the aspect when it should delegate further to the actual method.

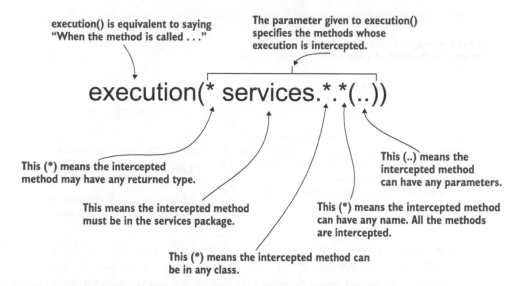

execution() is equivalent to saying
"When the method is called . . ."

The parameter given to execution()
specifies the methods whose
execution is intercepted.

execution(* services.*.*(..))

This (*) means the intercepted
method may have any returned type.

This means the intercepted method
must be in the services package.

This (*) means the intercepted method can
be in any class.

This (*) means the intercepted method
can have any name. All the methods
are intercepted.

This (..) means the
intercepted method
can have any parameters.

Figure 6.6   The AspectJ pointcut expression used in the example. It tells Spring to intercept the calls for all the methods in the services package, regardless of their return type, the class they belong to, name, or the parameters they receive.

STEP 4: IMPLEMENT THE ASPECT LOGIC

In listing 6.6, I've added the logic for our aspect. Now the aspect

1. Intercepts the method
2. Displays something in the console before calling the intercepted method
3. Calls the intercepted method
4. Displays something in the console after calling the intercepted method

Figure 6.7 visually presents the aspect's behavior.

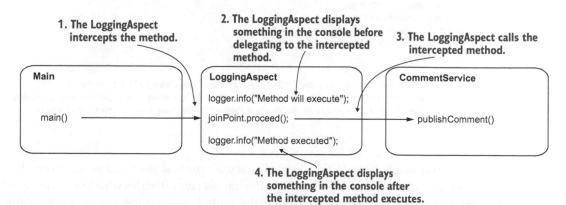

1. The LoggingAspect
intercepts the method.

2. The LoggingAspect displays
something in the console before
delegating to the intercepted
method.

3. The LoggingAspect calls the
intercepted method.

Main	LoggingAspect	CommentService

main()	logger.info("Method will execute");
	joinPoint.proceed();
	logger.info("Method executed");
		publishComment()

4. The LoggingAspect displays
something in the console after
the intercepted method executes.

Figure 6.7   The aspect behavior. `LoggingAspect` wraps the method execution by displaying something before and after the method call. This way, you observe a simple implementation of an aspect.

Listing 6.6   Implementing the aspect logic

Prints a message in the console before the intercepted method's execution

```
@Aspect
public class LoggingAspect {

  private Logger logger = Logger.getLogger(LoggingAspect.class.getName());

  @Around("execution(* services.*.*(..))")
  public void log(ProceedingJoinPoint joinPoint) throws Throwable {
    logger.info("Method will execute");
    joinPoint.proceed();                          ← Calls the intercepted method
    logger.info("Method executed");      ←
  }                                              Prints a message in the console after
}                                                the intercepted method's execution
```

The method `proceed()` of the `ProceedingJoinPoint` parameter calls the intercepted method, `publishComment()`, of the `CommentService` bean. If you don't call `proceed()`, the aspect never delegates further to the intercepted method (figure 6.8).

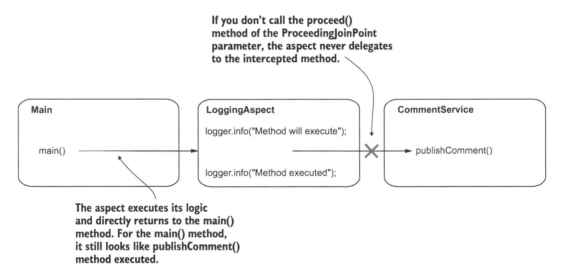

If you don't call the proceed() method of the ProceedingJoinPoint parameter, the aspect never delegates to the intercepted method.

The aspect executes its logic and directly returns to the main() method. For the main() method, it still looks like publishComment() method executed.

Figure 6.8   If you don't call the `proceed()` method of the `ProceedingJoinPoint` parameter of the aspect, the aspect never delegates further to the intercepted method. In this case, the aspect simply executes instead of the intercepted method. The caller of the method doesn't know that the real method is never executed.

You can even implement logic where the actual method isn't called anymore. For example, an aspect that applies some authorization rules decides whether to delegate further to a method the app protects. If the authorization rules aren't fulfilled, the aspect doesn't delegate to the intercepted method it protects (figure 6.9).

Figure 6.9   An aspect can decide not to delegate at all to the method it intercepts. This behavior looks like the aspect applies a mind trick to the caller of the method. The caller ends up executing another logic than the one it actually called.

Also, observe that the `proceed()` method throws a `Throwable`. The method `proceed()` is designed to throw any exception coming from the intercepted method. In this example, I chose the easy way to propagate it further, but you can use a `try-catch-finally` block to treat this throwable if you need it.

Rerun the application ("sq-ch6-ex1"). In the console output, you'll find the logs from both the aspect and the intercepted method. The output you see should look similar to the one presented in the following snippet:

```
Sep 27, 2020 1:11:11 PM aspects.LoggingAspect log          This line is printed from the aspect.
INFO: Method will execute
Sep 27, 2020 1:11:11 PM services.CommentService publishComment
INFO: Publishing comment:Demo comment
Sep 27, 2020 1:11:11 PM aspects.LoggingAspect log          This line is printed from
INFO: Method executed                                       the actual method.
                          This line is printed from the aspect.
```

6.2.2   *Altering the intercepted method's parameters and the returned value*

I told you aspects are really powerful. Not only can they intercept a method and alter its execution, but they can also intercept the parameters used to call the method and possibly alter them or the value the intercepted method returns. In this section, we'll change the example we've been working on to prove how an aspect can affect the parameters and the value returned by the intercepted method. Knowing how to do this gives you even more opportunities in what you can implement using aspects.

Suppose you want to log the parameters used to call the service method and what the method returned. To demonstrate how to implement such a scenario, I separated this example into a project named "sq-ch6-ex2." Because we also refer to what the method returns, I changed the service method and made it return a value, as presented in the next code snippet:

```
@Service
public class CommentService {

  private Logger logger = Logger.getLogger(CommentService.class.getName());

  public String publishComment(Comment comment) {
    logger.info("Publishing comment:" + comment.getText());
    return "SUCCESS";        ◁        For our demonstration, the
  }                                   method now returns a value.
}
```

The aspect can easily find the name of the intercepted method and the method parameters. Remember that the ProceedingJoinPoint parameter of the aspect method represents the intercepted method. You can use this parameter to get any information related to the intercepted method (parameters, method name, target object, and so on). The next code snippet shows you how to get the method name and the parameters used to call the method before intercepting the call:

```
String methodName = joinPoint.getSignature().getName();
Object [] arguments = joinPoint.getArgs();
```

Now we can change the aspect also to log these details. In the next listing, you find the change you need to make to the aspect method.

Listing 6.7 Obtaining the method name and parameters in the aspect logic

```
@Aspect
public class LoggingAspect {

  private Logger logger = Logger.getLogger(LoggingAspect.class.getName());

  @Around("execution(* services.*.*(..))")
  public Object log(ProceedingJoinPoint joinPoint) throws Throwable {
    String methodName =
      joinPoint.getSignature().getName();          Obtains the name and parameters
    Object [] arguments = joinPoint.getArgs();     of the intercepted method

    logger.info("Method " + methodName +       ◁         Logs the name and
      " with parameters " + Arrays.asList(arguments) +    parameters of the
      " will execute");                                   intercepted method
Calls the
intercepted
method
    └──▷   Object returnedByMethod = joinPoint.proceed();

    logger.info("Method executed and returned " + returnedByMethod);

    return returnedByMethod;     ◁       Returns the value returned by
  }                                      the intercepted method
}
```

The main() method calls publishComment() of the CommentService bean, but an aspect intercepts the call.

The aspect logs the call as well as the parameters of the method and the value it returns.

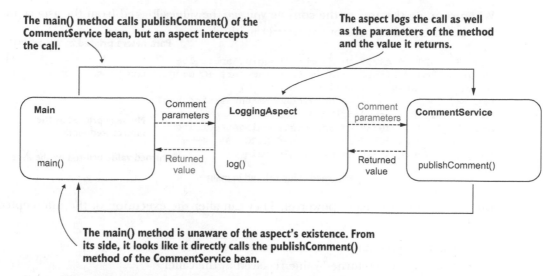

The main() method is unaware of the aspect's existence. From its side, it looks like it directly calls the publishComment() method of the CommentService bean.

Figure 6.10   The aspect intercepts the method call, so it can access the parameters and the value returned by the intercepted method after execution. For the `main()` method, it looks like it directly calls the `publishComment()` method of the `CommentService` bean. The caller isn't aware that an aspect intercepted the call.

Figure 6.10 makes it easier to visualize the flow. Observe how the aspect intercepts the call and can access the parameters and the returned value.

I've changed the main() method to print the value returned by publishComment(), as presented in the following listing.

Listing 6.8   Printing the returned value to observe the aspect's behavior

```
public class Main {

  private static Logger logger = Logger.getLogger(Main.class.getName());

  public static void main(String[] args) {
    var c = new AnnotationConfigApplicationContext(ProjectConfig.class);

    var service = c.getBean(CommentService.class);

    Comment comment = new Comment();
    comment.setText("Demo comment");
    comment.setAuthor("Natasha");

    String value = service.publishComment(comment);

    logger.info(value);        ⟵   Prints the value returned by the
  }                                 publishComment() method
}
```

When running the app, in the console you see the values logged from the aspect and the returned value logged by the `main()` method:

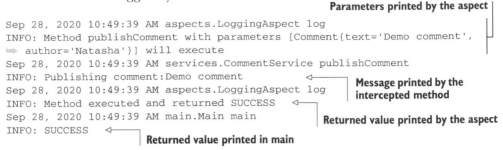

Parameters printed by the aspect

```
Sep 28, 2020 10:49:39 AM aspects.LoggingAspect log
INFO: Method publishComment with parameters [Comment{text='Demo comment',
➥ author='Natasha'}] will execute
Sep 28, 2020 10:49:39 AM services.CommentService publishComment
INFO: Publishing comment:Demo comment          ◄──── Message printed by the
Sep 28, 2020 10:49:39 AM aspects.LoggingAspect log    intercepted method
INFO: Method executed and returned SUCCESS     ◄────
Sep 28, 2020 10:49:39 AM main.Main main         Returned value printed by the aspect
INFO: SUCCESS   ◄────
            Returned value printed in main
```

But aspects are even more powerful. They can alter the execution of the intercepted method by

- Changing the value of the parameters sent to the method
- Changing the returned value received by the caller
- Throwing an exception to the caller or catching and treating an exception thrown by the intercepted method

You can be extremely flexible in altering the call of an intercepted method. You can even change its behavior completely (figure 6.11). But be careful! When you alter the logic through an aspect, you make a part of the logic transparent. Make sure you don't

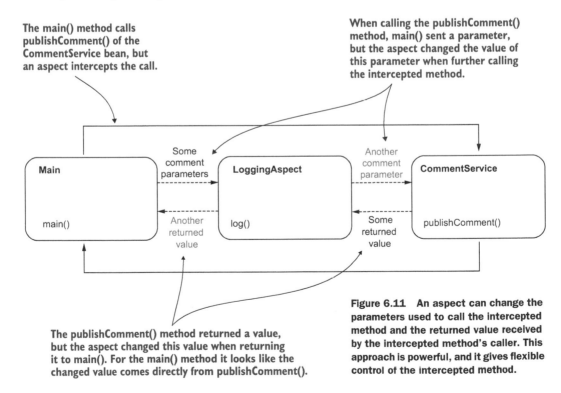

The main() method calls publishComment() of the CommentService bean, but an aspect intercepts the call.

When calling the publishComment() method, main() sent a parameter, but the aspect changed the value of this parameter when further calling the intercepted method.

The publishComment() method returned a value, but the aspect changed this value when returning it to main(). For the main() method it looks like the changed value comes directly from publishComment().

Figure 6.11   An aspect can change the parameters used to call the intercepted method and the returned value received by the intercepted method's caller. This approach is powerful, and it gives flexible control of the intercepted method.

hide things that aren't obvious. The whole idea of decoupling a part of the logic is to avoid duplicating code and hide what's irrelevant, so a developer can easily focus on the business logic code. When considering writing an aspect, put yourself in the developer's shoes. Someone who needs to understand the code should easily realize what's happening.

In the project "sq-ch6-ex3," we demonstrate how aspects can alter the call by changing the parameters or the value returned by the intercepted method. The following listing shows that when you call the proceed() method without sending any parameters, the aspect sends the original parameters to the intercepted method. But you can choose to provide a parameter when calling the proceed() method. This parameter is an array of objects that the aspect sends to the intercepted method instead of the original parameter values. The aspect logs the value returned by the intercepted method, but it returns to the caller a different value.

Listing 6.9   Altering the parameters and the returned value

```
@Aspect
public class LoggingAspect {

  private Logger logger =
  Logger.getLogger(LoggingAspect.class.getName());

  @Around("execution(* services.*.*(..))")
  public Object log(ProceedingJoinPoint joinPoint) throws Throwable {
    String methodName = joinPoint.getSignature().getName();
    Object [] arguments = joinPoint.getArgs();


    logger.info("Method " + methodName +
        " with parameters " + Arrays.asList(arguments) +
        " will execute");

    Comment comment = new Comment();                      We send a different comment
    comment.setText("Some other text!");                  instance as a value to the
    Object [] newArguments = {comment};                   method's parameter.

    Object returnedByMethod = joinPoint.proceed(newArguments);   ◄──────────

    logger.info("Method executed and returned " + returnedByMethod);

    return "FAILED";   ◄──────┐  We log the value returned by the intercepted method,
  }                           │  but we return a different value to the caller.
}
```

Running the app generates an output like the one in the next snippet. The values of the parameters received by the publishComment() method are different than the ones sent when calling the method. The publishComment() method returns a value, but main() gets a different one:

The publishComment() method is called with a
comment having the text "Demo comment."

```
Sep 29, 2020 10:43:51 AM aspects.LoggingAspect log
INFO: Method publishComment with parameters [Comment{text='Demo comment',
   author='Natasha'}] will execute
Sep 29, 2020 10:43:51 AM services.CommentService publishComment
INFO: Publishing comment:Some other text!
Sep 29, 2020 10:43:51 AM aspects.LoggingAspect log
INFO: Method executed and returned SUCCESS
Sep 29, 2020 10:43:51 AM main.Main main
INFO: FAILED
```

The publishComment() method
receives a comment with the text
"Some other text!"

The method publishComment()
returns "SUCCESS."

The returned value main()
receives is "FAILED."

> **NOTE** I know I repeat myself, but this point is quite important. Be careful
> with using aspects! You should only use them to hide irrelevant lines of code
> that can easily be implied. Aspects are so powerful they can bring you to the
> "dark side" of hiding relevant code and make your app more difficult to main-
> tain. Use aspects with caution!

Okay, but would we ever want to have an aspect that changes the parameters of the
intercepted method? Or its returned value? Yes. Sometimes it happens that such an
approach is useful. I explained all these approaches because in the next chapters we'll
use certain Spring capabilities that rely on aspects. For example, in chapter 13 we'll
discuss transactions. Transactions in Spring rely on aspects. When we get to that subject, you'll find understanding aspects very useful.

By first understanding how aspects work you gain a significant advantage in understanding Spring. I often see developers starting to use a framework without understanding what's behind the functionalities they use. Not surprisingly, in many cases,
these developers introduce bugs or vulnerabilities to their apps, or they make them
less performant and maintainable. My advice is to always learn how things work before
using them.

6.2.3 *Intercepting annotated methods*

In this section, we discuss an important approach, often used in Spring apps, for
marking the methods that need to be intercepted by aspects: using annotations. Have
you observed how many annotations we've already used in our examples? Annotations
are comfortable to use, and since they appeared with Java 5, they became the de facto
approach in configuring apps that use specific frameworks. There's probably no Java
framework today that doesn't use annotations. You can also use them to mark the
methods you want an aspect to intercept with a comfortable syntax that allows you also
to avoid writing complex AspectJ pointcut expressions.

We'll create a separate example to learn this approach, similar to those we've
discussed so far in this chapter. In the CommentService class, we'll add three methods:
publishComment(), deleteComment(), and editComment(). You find this example in
the project "sq-ch6-ex4." We want to define a custom annotation and log only the

execution of the methods we mark using the custom annotation. To achieve this objective, you need to do the following:

1. Define a custom annotation, and make it accessible at runtime. We'll call this annotation `@ToLog`.
2. Use a different AspectJ pointcut expression for the aspect method to tell the aspect to intercept the methods annotated with the custom annotation.

Figure 6.12 visually represents these steps.

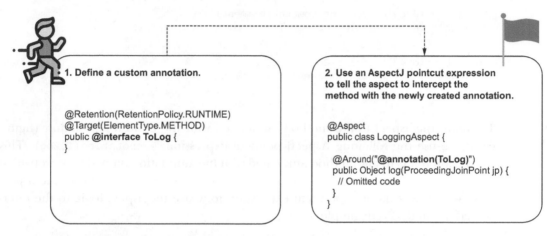

Figure 6.12   **The steps for intercepted annotated methods. You need to create a custom annotation you want to use to annotate the methods your aspect needs to intercept. Then you use a different AspectJ pointcut expression to configure the aspect to intercept the methods annotated with the custom annotation you created.**

We don't need to change the logic of the aspect. For this example, our aspect does the same thing as the previous examples: logs the intercepted method's execution.

In the next code snippet, you find the declaration of the custom annotation. The definition of the retention policy with `@Retention(RetentionPolicy.RUNTIME)` is critical. By default, in Java annotations cannot be intercepted at runtime. You need to explicitly specify that someone can intercept annotations by setting the retention policy to `RUNTIME`. The `@Target` annotation specifies which language elements we can use this annotation for. By default, you can annotate any language elements, but it's always a good idea to restrict the annotation to only what you make it for—in our case, methods:

```
@Retention(RetentionPolicy.RUNTIME)      Enables the annotation to
@Target(ElementType.METHOD)              be intercepted at runtime
public @interface ToLog {
}                              Restricts this annotation to only be used with methods
```

In the following listing, you find the definition of the `CommentService` class, which now defines three methods. We annotated only the `deleteComment()` method, so we expect the aspect will intercept only this one.

Listing 6.10   The `CommentService` class defining three methods

```
@Service
public class CommentService {

  private Logger logger = Logger.getLogger(CommentService.class.getName());

  public void publishComment(Comment comment) {
    logger.info("Publishing comment:" + comment.getText());
  }
  @ToLog
  public void deleteComment(Comment comment) {
    logger.info("Deleting comment:" + comment.getText());
  }

  public void editComment(Comment comment) {
    logger.info("Editing comment:" + comment.getText());
  }
}
```

> We use the custom annotation for the methods we want the aspect to intercept.

To weave the aspect to the methods annotated with the custom annotation (figure 6.13), we use the following AspectJ pointcut expression: `@annotation(ToLog)`. This expression refers to any method annotated with the annotation named `@ToLog` (which is, in this case, our custom annotation). In the next listing, you now find the aspect class, which uses the new pointcut expression to weave the aspect logic to the intercepted methods. Pretty simple, isn't it?

Listing 6.11   Changing the pointcut expression to weave aspect to annotated methods

```
@Aspect
public class LoggingAspect {

  private Logger logger = Logger.getLogger(LoggingAspect.class.getName());

  @Around("@annotation(ToLog)")
  public Object log(ProceedingJoinPoint joinPoint) throws Throwable {
    // Omitted code
  }
}
```

> Weaving the aspect to the methods annotated with @ToLog

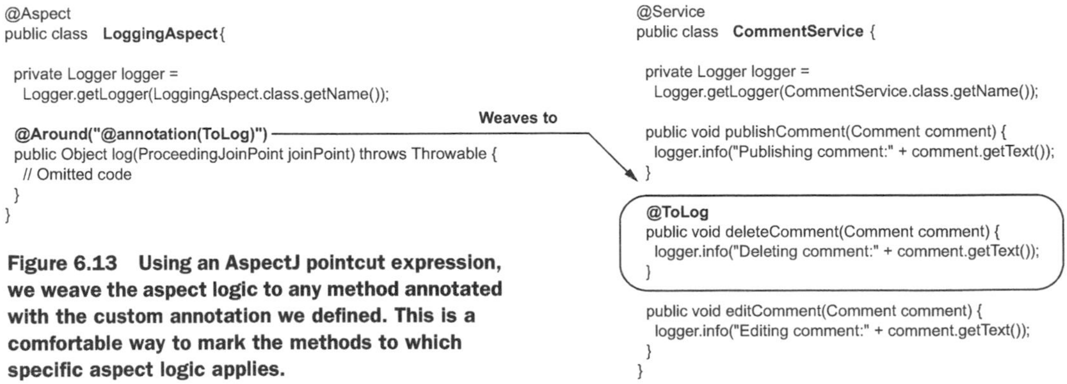

Figure 6.13   Using an AspectJ pointcut expression, we weave the aspect logic to any method annotated with the custom annotation we defined. This is a comfortable way to mark the methods to which specific aspect logic applies.

When you run the app, only the annotated method (deleteComment(), in our case) is intercepted, and the aspect logs the execution of this method in the console. You should see an output in the console similar to the one presented in the next snippet:

```
Sep 29, 2020 2:22:42 PM services.CommentService publishComment
INFO: Publishing comment:Demo comment
Sep 29, 2020 2:22:42 PM aspects.LoggingAspect log
INFO: Method deleteComment with parameters [Comment{text='Demo comment',
   author='Natasha'}] will execute
Sep 29, 2020 2:22:42 PM services.CommentService deleteComment
INFO: Deleting comment:Demo comment
Sep 29, 2020 2:22:42 PM aspects.LoggingAspect log
INFO: Method executed and returned null
Sep 29, 2020 2:22:42 PM services.CommentService editComment
INFO: Editing comment:Demo comment
```

**The aspect intercepts only the deleteComment()
method, which we annotated with the custom
@ToLog annotation.**

6.2.4 Other advice annotations you can use

In this section, we discuss alternative advice annotation for aspects in Spring. So far in this chapter, we've used the advice annotation @Around. This is indeed the most used of the advice annotations in Spring apps because you can cover any implementation case: you can do things before, after, or even instead of the intercepted method. You can alter the logic any way you want from the aspect.

But you don't necessarily always need all this flexibility. A good idea is to look for the most straightforward way to implement what you need to implement. Any app implementation should be defined by simplicity. By avoiding complexity, you make the app easier to maintain. For simple scenarios, Spring offers four alternative advice annotations that are less powerful than @Around. It's recommended you use these when their capabilities are enough to keep the implementation simple.

Other than @Around, Spring offers the following advice annotations:

- @Before—Calls the method defining the aspect logic before the execution of the intercepted method.
- @AfterReturning—Calls the method defining the aspect logic after the method successfully returns, and provides the returned value as a parameter to the aspect method. The aspect method isn't called if the intercepted method throws an exception.
- @AfterThrowing—Calls the method defining the aspect logic if the intercepted method throws an exception, and provides the exception instance as a parameter to the aspect method.
- @After—Calls the method defining the aspect logic only after the intercepted method execution, whether the method successfully returned or threw an exception.

You use these advice annotations the same way as for @Around. You provide them with an AspectJ pointcut expression to weave the aspect logic to specific method executions.

The aspect methods don't receive the `ProceedingJoinPoint` parameter, and they cannot decide when to delegate to the intercepted method. This event already happens based on the annotation's purpose (for example, for `@Before`, the intercepted method call will always happen after the aspect logic execution).

You find an example that uses `@AfterReturning` in the project named "sq-ch6-ex5." In the next code snippet, you find the `@AfterReturning` annotation used. Observe that we use it the same way we did with `@Around`.

The AspectJ pointcut expression specifies which methods this aspect logic weaves to.

Optionally, when you use @AfterReturning, you can get the value returned by the intercepted method. In this case, we add the "returning" attribute with a value that corresponds to the name of the method's parameter where this value will be provided.

```
@Aspect
public class LoggingAspect {

  private Logger logger = Logger.getLogger(LoggingAspect.class.getName());

  @AfterReturning(value = "@annotation(ToLog)",
              returning = "returnedValue")
  public void log(Object returnedValue) {
    logger.info("Method executed and returned " + returnedValue);
  }
}
```

The parameter name should be the same as the value of the "returning" attribute of the annotation or missing if we don't need to use the returned value.

6.3 *The aspect execution chain*

In all our examples thus far, we discussed what happens when one aspect intercepts a method. In a real-world app, a method is often intercepted by more than one aspect. For example, we have a method for which we want to log the execution and apply some security constraints. We often have aspects taking care of such responsibilities, so we have two aspects acting on the same method's execution in this scenario. There's nothing wrong with having as many aspects as we need, but when this happens, we need to ask ourselves the following questions:

- In which order does Spring execute these aspects?
- Does the execution order matter?

In this section, we'll analyze an example to answer these two questions.

Suppose, for a method, we need to apply some security restrictions as well as log its executions. We have two aspects that take care of these responsibilities:

- `SecurityAspect`—Applies the security restrictions. This aspect intercepts the method, validates the call, and in some conditions doesn't forward the call to the intercepted method (the details about how the `SecurityAspect` works aren't relevant for our current discussion; just remember that sometimes this aspect doesn't call the intercepted method).
- `LoggingAspect`—Logs the beginning and end of the intercepted method execution.

When you have multiple aspects weaved to the same method, they need to execute one after another. One way is to have the `SecurityAspect` execute first and then delegate to the `LoggingAspect`, which further delegates to the intercepted method. The second option is to have the `LoggingAspect` execute first and then delegate to the `Security-Aspect`, which eventually delegates further to the intercepted method. This way, the aspects create an execution chain.

The order in which the aspects execute is important because executing the aspects in different orders can have different results. Take our example: we know that the `SecurityAspect` doesn't delegate the execution in all the cases, so if we choose this aspect to execute first, sometimes the `LoggingAspect` won't execute. If we expect the `LoggingAspect` to log the executions that failed due to security restrictions, this isn't the way we need to go (figure 6.14).

In some cases, the SecurityAspect doesn't further delegate. So if the SecurityAspect is executed first, the LoggingAspect won't always have the chance to execute. In such a case, the method calls won't be logged.

Aspect execution chains

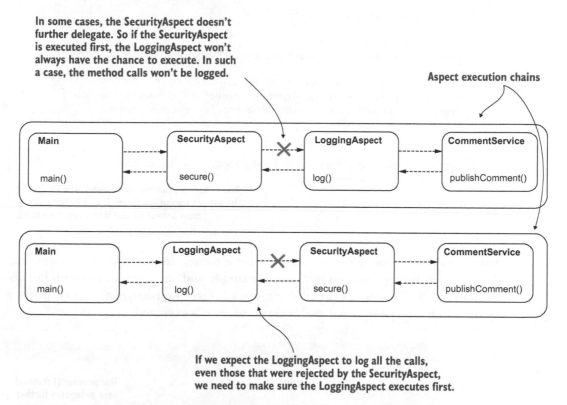

If we expect the LoggingAspect to log all the calls, even those that were rejected by the SecurityAspect, we need to make sure the LoggingAspect executes first.

Figure 6.14 The aspect execution order matters. Depending on your app's requirements, you need to choose a specific order for the aspects to execute. In this scenario, the `LoggingAspect` cannot log all the method executions if the `SecurityAspect` executes first.

Okay, the execution order of the aspects is sometimes relevant. But can we define this order then? By default, Spring doesn't guarantee the order in which two aspects in the same execution chain are called. If the execution order is not relevant, then you just need to define the aspects and leave the framework to execute them in whatever order. If you need to define the aspects' execution order, you can use the `@Order` annotation. This annotation receives an ordinal (a number) representing the order in the execution chain for a specific aspect. The smaller the number, the earlier that aspect executes. If two values are the same, the order of execution is again not defined. Let's try the @Order annotation in an example.

In the project named "sq-ch6-ex6," I define two aspects that intercept the publish-Comment() method of a CommentService bean. In the next listing, you find the aspect named LoggingAspect. We don't initially define any order for our aspects.

Listing 6.12 The implementation of the LoggingAspect class

```
@Aspect
public class LoggingAspect {

  private Logger logger =
    Logger.getLogger(LoggingAspect.class.getName());

  @Around(value = "@annotation(ToLog)")
  public Object log(ProceedingJoinPoint joinPoint) throws Throwable {
    logger.info("Logging Aspect: Calling the intercepted method");

    Object returnedValue = joinPoint.proceed();          ⟵

    logger.info("Logging Aspect: Method executed and returned " +
                returnedValue);

    return returnedValue;
  }
}
```

The proceed() method here delegates further in the aspect execution chain. It can either call the next aspect or the intercepted method.

The second aspect we define for our example is named SecurityAspect, as shown in the following listing. To keep our example simple and allow you to focus on the discussion, this aspect doesn't do anything special. Like the LoggingAspect, it prints a message in the console, so we easily observe when it is executed.

Listing 6.13 The implementation of the SecurityAspect class

The proceed() method here delegates further in the aspect execution chain. It can call either the next aspect or the intercepted method.

```
@Aspect
public class SecurityAspect {

  private Logger logger =
    Logger.getLogger(SecurityAspect.class.getName());

  @Around(value = "@annotation(ToLog)")
  public Object secure(ProceedingJoinPoint joinPoint) throws Throwable {
    logger.info("Security Aspect: Calling the intercepted method");

    Object returnedValue = joinPoint.proceed();          ⟵

    logger.info("Security Aspect: Method executed and returned " +
                returnedValue);
```

```
    return returnedValue;
  }
}
```

The CommentService class is similar to the one we defined in the previous examples. But to make your reading more comfortable, you can also find it in the following listing.

Listing 6.14 The implementation of the CommentService class

```
@Service
public class CommentService {

  private Logger logger =
    Logger.getLogger(CommentService.class.getName());

  @ToLog
  public String publishComment(Comment comment) {
    logger.info("Publishing comment:" + comment.getText());
    return "SUCCESS";
  }

}
```

Also, remember that both aspects need to be beans in the Spring context. For this example, I chose to use the @Bean approach to add the beans in the context. My configuration class is presented next.

Listing 6.15 Declaring the aspect beans in the Configuration class

```
@Configuration
@ComponentScan(basePackages = "services")
@EnableAspectJAutoProxy
public class ProjectConfig {

  @Bean
  public LoggingAspect loggingAspect() {        ◁─┐
    return new LoggingAspect();                    │  Both aspects need to be added as
  }                                                │  beans in the Spring context.
                                                   │
  @Bean                                            │
  public SecurityAspect securityAspect() {      ◁─┘
    return new SecurityAspect();
  }
}
```

The main() method calls the publishComment() method of the CommentService bean. In my case, the output after the execution looks like the one in the next code snippet:

The LoggingAspect is called first and delegates to the SecurityAspect.

```
Sep 29, 2020 6:04:22 PM aspects.LoggingAspect log
INFO: Logging Aspect: Calling the intercepted method
Sep 29, 2020 6:04:22 PM aspects.SecurityAspect secure
INFO: Security Aspect: Calling the intercepted method
Sep 29, 2020 6:04:22 PM services.CommentService publishComment
INFO: Publishing comment:Demo comment
Sep 29, 2020 6:04:22 PM aspects.SecurityAspect secure
INFO: Security Aspect: Method executed and returned SUCCESS
Sep 29, 2020 6:04:22 PM aspects.LoggingAspect log
INFO: Logging Aspect: Method executed and returned SUCCESS
```

The SecurityAspect is called second and delegates to the intercepted method.

The intercepted method executes.

The intercepted method returns to the SecurityAspect.

The SecurityAspect returns to the LoggingAspect.

Figure 6.15 helps you visualize the execution chain and understand the logs in the console.

1. The LoggingAspect is the first to intercept the call.

2. The LoggingAspect delegates to SecurityAspect.

3. The SecurityAspect executes and delegates to the intercepted method.

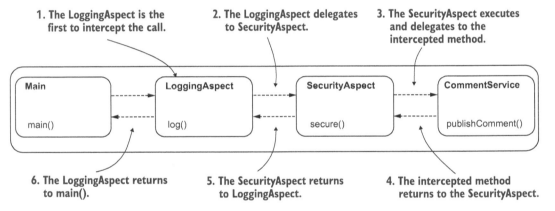

6. The LoggingAspect returns to main().

5. The SecurityAspect returns to LoggingAspect.

4. The intercepted method returns to the SecurityAspect.

Figure 6.15 The execution flow. The `LoggingAspect` was first to intercept the method call. The `LoggingAspect` delegates further in the execution chain to the `SecurityAspect`, which further delegates the call to the intercepted method. The intercepted method returns to the `SecurityAspect`, which returns further to the `LoggingAspect`.

To reverse the order in which `LoggingAspect` and `SecurityAspect` execute, we use the `@Order` annotation. Observe in the next code snippet how I used the `@Order` annotation to specify an execution position for `SecurityAspect` (see this example in the project "sq-ch6-ex7"):

```
@Aspect
@Order(1)                  ◁——— Gives an execution order
public class SecurityAspect {          position to the aspect

  // Omitted code
}
```

For the `LoggingAspect`, I use `@Order` to place the aspect in a higher order position, as presented in the next snippet:

```
@Aspect
@Order(2)          ◁─────┐   Places the LoggingAspect
public class LoggingAspect {   as second to be executed
  // Omitted code
}
```

Rerun the application and observe that the order in which the aspects execute has changed. The logging should now look like the one in the next snippet:

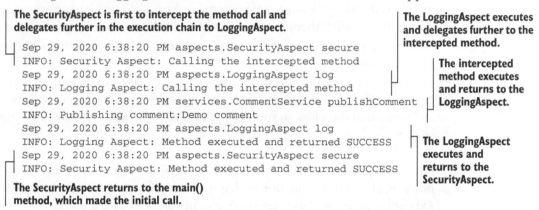

The SecurityAspect is first to intercept the method call and delegates further in the execution chain to LoggingAspect.

The LoggingAspect executes and delegates further to the intercepted method.

```
Sep 29, 2020 6:38:20 PM aspects.SecurityAspect secure
INFO: Security Aspect: Calling the intercepted method
Sep 29, 2020 6:38:20 PM aspects.LoggingAspect log
INFO: Logging Aspect: Calling the intercepted method
Sep 29, 2020 6:38:20 PM services.CommentService publishComment
INFO: Publishing comment:Demo comment
Sep 29, 2020 6:38:20 PM aspects.LoggingAspect log
INFO: Logging Aspect: Method executed and returned SUCCESS
Sep 29, 2020 6:38:20 PM aspects.SecurityAspect secure
INFO: Security Aspect: Method executed and returned SUCCESS
```

The intercepted method executes and returns to the LoggingAspect.

The LoggingAspect executes and returns to the SecurityAspect.

The SecurityAspect returns to the main() method, which made the initial call.

Figure 6.16 helps you visualize the execution chain and understand the logs in the console.

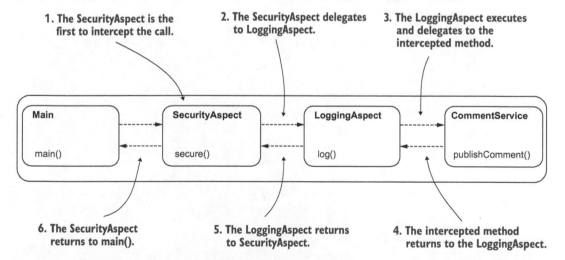

1. The SecurityAspect is the first to intercept the call.

2. The SecurityAspect delegates to LoggingAspect.

3. The LoggingAspect executes and delegates to the intercepted method.

6. The SecurityAspect returns to main().

5. The LoggingAspect returns to SecurityAspect.

4. The intercepted method returns to the LoggingAspect.

Figure 6.16 The execution flow after changing the order of the aspects. The `SecurityAspect` was first to intercept the method call and delegates further in the execution chain to the `LoggingAspect`, which further delegates the call to the intercepted method. The intercepted method returns to the `LoggingAspect`, which returns further to the `SecurityAspect`.

Summary

- An aspect is an object that intercepts a method call and can execute logic before, after, and even instead of executing the intercepted method. This helps you decouple part of the code from the business implementation and makes your app easier to maintain.

- Using an aspect, you can write logic that executes with a method execution while being completely decoupled from that method. This way, someone who reads the code only sees what's relevant regarding the business implementation.

- However, aspects can be a dangerous tool. Overengineering your code with aspects will make your app less maintainable. You don't need to use aspects everywhere. When using them, make sure they really help your implementation.

- Aspects support many essential Spring capabilities like transactions and securing methods.

- To define an aspect in Spring, you annotate the class implementing the aspect logic with the @Aspect annotation. But remember that Spring needs to manage an instance of this class, so you need to also add a bean of its type in the Spring context.

- To tell Spring which methods an aspect needs to intercept, you use AspectJ pointcut expressions. You write these expressions as values to advice annotations. Spring offers you five advice annotations: @Around, @Before, @After, @AfterThrowing, and @AfterReturning. In most cases we use @Around, which is also the most powerful.

- Multiple aspects can intercept the same method call. In this case, it's recommended that you define an order for the aspects to execute using the @Order annotation.

Part 2

Implementation

In part 2, you'll learn to implement apps using Spring capabilities you'll often need in the real world. We'll start by discussing web apps. Further, you'll learn how to exchange data between apps and work with persisted data. You'll find that Spring makes this straightforward and easy. We'll end the book with writing unit and integration tests for the functionalities you implement in your Spring apps.

The skills you'll learn in part 2 rely on understanding the foundation that supports Spring: the Spring context and aspects. You can start directly with part 2 if you already know how Spring context and aspects work and you're eager to implement apps that use Spring capabilities. However, if you are not yet confident with the Spring context and aspects, it is a better idea to start with part 1 and learn these things first.

Understanding Spring Boot and Spring MVC

7

This chapter covers

- Implementing your first web app
- Using Spring Boot in developing Spring apps
- Understanding the Spring MVC architecture

Now that you know all the needed Spring basics, let's focus on web apps and how you use Spring to implement them. You can use all the Spring capabilities we've discussed to implement any kind of app. But often with Spring, the applications you implement are web apps. In chapters 1 through 6, we discussed the Spring context and aspects that are mandatory for understanding what comes next in the book (including what you'll find in this chapter). If you jumped directly to this chapter, and you don't know yet how to work with the Spring context and aspects, you might find our discussion difficult to understand. I strongly recommend you make sure you know the basics of using the framework before going further.

Spring makes web app development straightforward. We'll start this chapter by discussing what web apps are and how they work.

To implement web apps, we'll use a project in the Spring ecosystem named Spring Boot. In section 7.2, we'll discuss Spring Boot and why it's essential in app implementations. In section 7.3, we'll discuss the standard architecture of a simple Spring web app, and we'll implement a web app using Spring Boot. At the end of this chapter, you'll understand how a web app works, and you'll be able to implement a basic web app with Spring.

This chapter's main purpose is to help you understand the foundation that supports web apps' implementation. In chapters 8 and 9, we will implement the major capabilities you find in most web apps in production. But everything we discuss in these next chapters relies on the foundation in this chapter.

7.1   *What is a web app?*

In this section, we look at what a web app is. I'm sure you use web apps daily. You probably just left a few tabs open in a web browser before starting to read this chapter. Maybe you don't even read this book on paper and use the Manning liveBook web app for this.

Any app you access through your web browser is a web app. Years ago, we used desktop apps installed on our computers for almost anything we were doing (figure 7.1). With time, most of these apps became accessible via a web browser. Accessing an app in a browser makes it more comfortable to use. You don't have to install anything, and you can use it from any device that has access to the internet, such as a tablet or smartphone.

Figure 7.1   Times change. In the 1990s, we used a desktop app for everything. Today, almost any application we use is a web app. As developers, it's essential you learn how to implement web apps.

In this section, I want to make sure you have a clear overview of what we're going to implement. What is a web app, and what do we need to build and execute such an app? Once you have a clear picture of a web app, we continue implementing one with Spring.

7.1.1 A general overview of a web app

In this section, we take a high-level look at what a web app is from the technical standpoint. This overview allows us to discuss in further detail our options for creating web apps.

First, a web app is composed of two parts:

- *The client side* is what the user directly interacts with. A web browser represents the client side of a web app. The browser sends requests to a web server, receives responses from it, and provides a way for the user to interact with the app. We also refer to the client side of a web app as the *frontend*.
- *The server side* receives requests from the client and sends back data in response. The server side implements logic that processes and sometimes stores the client requested data before sending a response. We also refer to the server side of a web app as the *backend*.

Figure 7.2 presents the big picture of a web app.

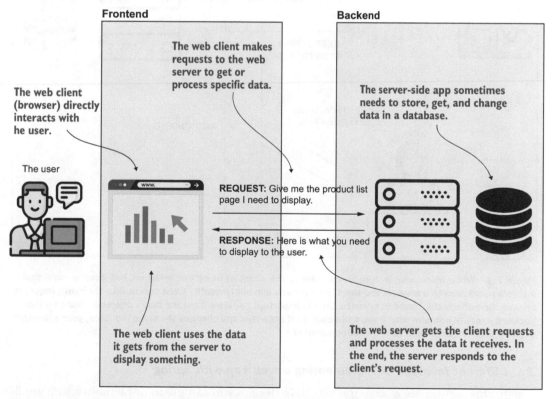

Figure 7.2 The big picture of a web app. The user interacts with the app through its frontend. The frontend communicates with the backend to execute logic at the user's request and get the data to display. The backend executes business logic and sometimes persists data in a database or communicates with other external services.

When discussing web apps, we usually refer to a client and a server, but it's important to keep in mind that the backend serves multiple clients concurrently. Numerous people may use the same app at the same time on different platforms. Users can access the app through a browser on a computer, phone, tablet, and so on (figure 7.3).

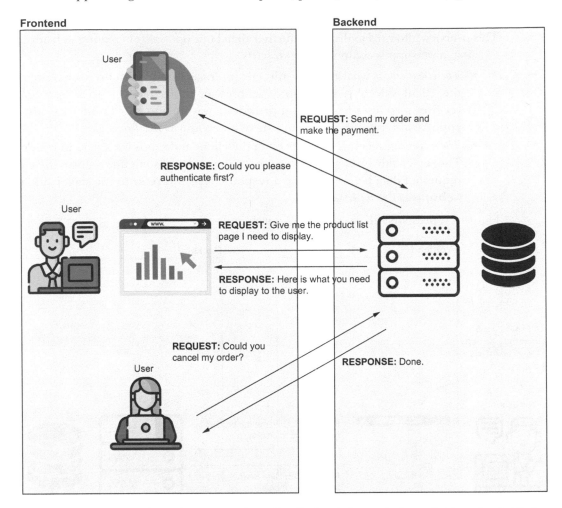

Figure 7.3   When discussing web apps, we refer to the client as being one instance, but keep in mind that multiple users access a browser and use the same web app concurrently. Each user makes their own requests on specific actions they need to execute. This is important because it means that some operations on the backend execute concurrently. If you write code that accesses and changes the same resource, your app might wrongly behave because of race condition scenarios.

7.1.2   *Different fashions of implementing a web app with Spring*

In this section, we discuss the two main designs you can use to implement a web application. We'll implement apps in both these ways in chapters 8 through 10, and we'll discuss the implementation details when we go deeper into implementing each. But for now I want you to be aware of your choices and have a general understanding of these options. It's important to know how you can create your web app to avoid getting confused later when implementing examples.

We classify the approaches of creating a web app as the following:

1 *Apps where the backend provides the fully prepared view in response to a client's request.* The browser directly interprets the data received from the backend and displays this information to the user in these apps. We discuss this approach and implement a simple app to prove it in this chapter. We then continue our discussion with more complex details relevant to production apps in chapters 8 and 9.

2 *Apps using frontend-backend separation.* For these apps, the backend only serves raw data. The browser doesn't display the data in the backend's response directly. The browser runs a separate frontend app that gets the backend responses, processes the data, and instructs the browser what to display. We discuss this approach and implement examples of it in chapter 9.

Figure 7.4 presents the first approach in which the app doesn't use a frontend-backend separation. For these apps, almost everything happens on the backend side. The backend gets requests representing user actions and executes some logic. In the end, the server responds with what the browser needs to display. The backend responds with the data in formats that the browser can interpret and display, such as HTML, CSS, images, and so on. It can also send scripts written in languages that the browser can understand and execute (such as JavaScript).

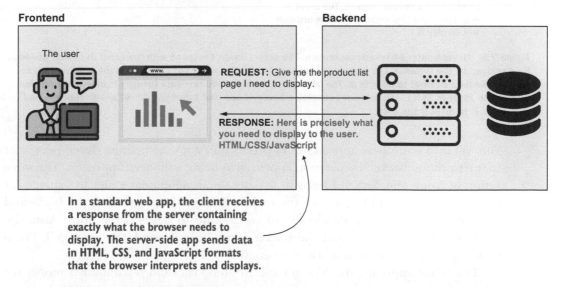

In a standard web app, the client receives a response from the server containing exactly what the browser needs to display. The server-side app sends data in HTML, CSS, and JavaScript formats that the browser interprets and displays.

Figure 7.4 When a web app doesn't provide frontend-backend separation, the browser precisely displays what it gets from the server. The server gets requests from the browser, executes some logic, and then responds. In response, the backend provides content formatted as HTML, CSS, and other fashions that the browser interprets to display.

Figure 7.5 shows an app using frontend-backend separation. Compare the server's response in figure 7.5 with the response the server sends back in figure 7.4. Instead of telling the browser precisely what to display, the server now only sends raw data. The browser runs an independent frontend app it loads at an initial request from the server. This frontend app takes the server's raw response, interprets it, and decides how the information is displayed. We'll discuss more details about this approach in chapter 9.

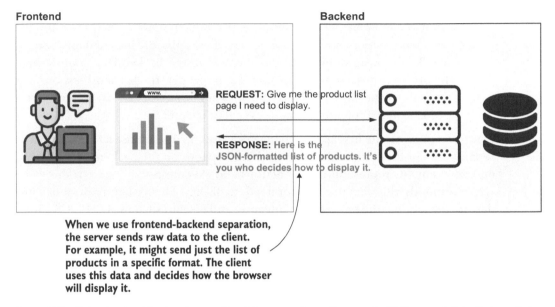

Figure 7.5   Using frontend-backend separation. The server doesn't respond with the exact data that needs to be displayed by the browser. The backend sends the data to the client but doesn't tell the browser how to display this data or what to do with it. The backend now only sends raw data (usually in an easily parsable format like JSON or XML). The browser executes a frontend app that takes the server's raw response and processes it to display the data.

You will find both these approaches in production apps. Sometimes developers refer to the frontend-backend separation approach as being a modern approach. The separation of front- and backend helps in making the development easier to manage for larger apps. Different teams take the responsibility of implementing the back- and frontend, allowing more developers to collaborate to develop the apps. Also, the deployment of the front- and the backend can be independently managed. For a larger app, this flexibility is also a nice benefit.

The other approach that doesn't use frontend-backend separation is mostly for small apps. After discussing both approaches in detail, I'll teach you the advantages of both methods, and you'll know when to choose an approach based on your app's needs.

7.1.3 *Using a servlet container in web app development*

In this section, we more deeply analyze what and why you need to build a web app with Spring. Thus far we've seen that a web app has a frontend and a backend. But we didn't explicitly discuss implementing a web app with Spring. Of course, our purpose is to learn Spring and to implement apps with it, so we have to take a step forward and find out what we need to implement web apps with the framework.

One of the most important things to consider is the communication between the client and the server. A web browser uses a protocol named Hypertext Transfer Protocol (HTTP) to communicate with the server over the network. This protocol accurately describes how the client and the server exchange data over the network. But unless you are passionate about networking, you don't need to understand how HTTP works in detail to write web apps. As a software developer, you're expected to know that the web app components use this protocol to exchange data in a request-response fashion. The client sends a request to the server, and the server responds. The client waits for the response after every request it sends. In appendix C, you'll find all the details you need to know about HTTP to understand the discussion in chapters 7 through 9.

But does that mean your app needs to know how to process the HTTP messages? Well, you can implement this capability if you wish, but unless you want to have some fun writing low-level functionalities, you'll use a component already designed to understand HTTP.

In fact, what you need is not only something that understands HTTP, but something that can translate the HTTP request and response to a Java app. This something is a *servlet container* (sometimes referred to as a web server): a translator of the HTTP messages for your Java app. This way, your Java app doesn't need to take care of implementing the communication layer. One of the most appreciated servlet container implementations is Tomcat, which is also the dependency we'll use for the examples in this book.

> **NOTE** We use Tomcat for the examples in this book, but you can use its alternatives for your Spring app. The list of solutions used in real-world apps is long. Among these, you find Jetty (https://www.eclipse.org/jetty/), JBoss (https://www.jboss.org/), and Payara (https://www.payara.fish/).

Figure 7.6 is a visual representation of a servlet container (Tomcat) in our app's architecture.

But if this is everything a servlet container does, why name it "servlet" container? What is a servlet? A servlet is nothing more than a Java object that directly interacts with the servlet container. When the servlet container gets an HTTP request, it calls a servlet object's method and provides the request as a parameter. The same method also gets a parameter representing the HTTP response used by the servlet to set the response sent back to the client that made the request.

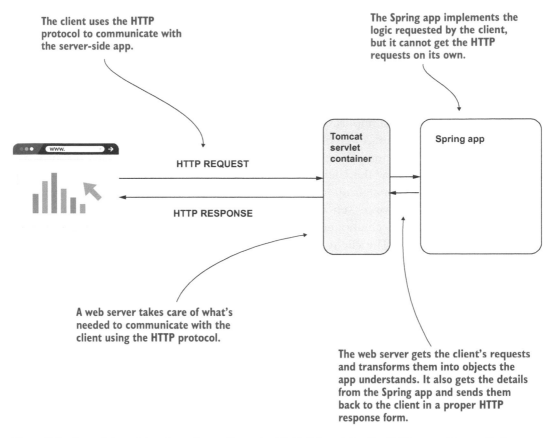

The client uses the HTTP protocol to communicate with the server-side app.

The Spring app implements the logic requested by the client, but it cannot get the HTTP requests on its own.

Tomcat servlet container

Spring app

HTTP REQUEST

HTTP RESPONSE

A web server takes care of what's needed to communicate with the client using the HTTP protocol.

The web server gets the client's requests and transforms them into objects the app understands. It also gets the details from the Spring app and sends them back to the client in a proper HTTP response form.

Figure 7.6   A servlet container (e.g., Tomcat) speaks HTTP. It translates the HTTP request to our Spring app and the app's response into an HTTP response. This way, we don't need to care about the protocol used for communication on the network, as we simply write everything as Java objects and methods.

Some time ago, the servlet was the most critical component of a backend web app from the developer's point of view. Suppose a developer had to implement a new page accessible at a specific path in the URL (e.g., /home/profile/edit, etc.) for a web app. The developer needed to create a new servlet instance, configure it in the servlet container, and assign it to a specific path (figure 7.7). The servlet contained the logic associated with the user's request and the ability to prepare a response, including info for the browser on how to display the response. For any path the web client could call, the developer needed to add the instance in the servlet container and configure it. Because such a component manages servlet instances you add into its context, we name it a servlet container. It basically has a context of servlet instances it controls, just as Spring does with its beans. For this reason, we call a component such as Tomcat a servlet container.

As you'll learn in this chapter, we don't typically create servlet instances. We'll use a servlet with the Spring apps we develop with Spring, but you won't need to write this

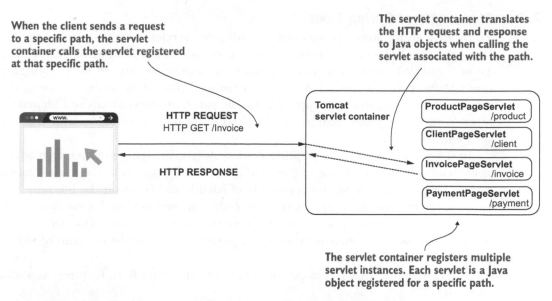

When the client sends a request to a specific path, the servlet container calls the servlet registered at that specific path.

The servlet container translates the HTTP request and response to Java objects when calling the servlet associated with the path.

HTTP REQUEST
HTTP GET /Invoice

HTTP RESPONSE

Tomcat servlet container

ProductPageServlet
/product

ClientPageServlet
/client

InvoicePageServlet
/invoice

PaymentPageServlet
/payment

The servlet container registers multiple servlet instances. Each servlet is a Java object registered for a specific path.

Figure 7.7   The servlet container (Tomcat) registers multiple servlet instances. Each servlet is associated with a path. When the client sends a request, Tomcat calls a method of the servlet associated with the path the client requested. The servlet gets the values on the request and builds the response that Tomcat sends back to the client.

yourself, so you don't have to focus on learning to implement servlets. But you do need to remember the servlet is the entry point to your app's logic. It's the component the servlet container (Tomcat, in our case) directly interacts with. It's how the request data enters your app and how the response goes through Tomcat back to the client (figure 7.8).

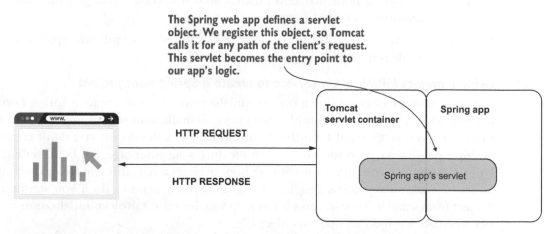

The Spring web app defines a servlet object. We register this object, so Tomcat calls it for any path of the client's request. This servlet becomes the entry point to our app's logic.

Tomcat servlet container

Spring app

HTTP REQUEST

HTTP RESPONSE

Spring app's servlet

Figure 7.8   The Spring app defines a servlet object and registers it into the servlet container. Now both Spring and the servlet container know this object and can manage it. The servlet container calls this object for any client request, allowing the servlet to manage the request and the response.

7.2   *The magic of Spring Boot*

To create a Spring web app, we need to configure a servlet container, create a servlet instance, and then make sure we correctly configure this servlet instance such that Tomcat calls it for any client request. What a headache to write so many configurations! Many years ago, when I was teaching Spring 3 (the latest Spring version at that time) and we configured web apps, this was the part both the students and I hated the most. Fortunately, times changed, and today I don't have to bother you by teaching such configurations.

In this section, we'll discuss Spring Boot, a tool for implementing modern Spring apps. Spring Boot is now one of the most appreciated projects in the Spring ecosystem. It helps you create Spring apps more efficiently and focus on the business code you write by eliminating a huge part of the code you used to write for configurations. Especially in a world of service-oriented architectures (SOA) and microservices, where you create apps more often (discussed in appendix A), avoiding the pain of writing configurations is helpful.

Listed here are what I consider the most critical Spring Boot features, and what they offer:

- *Simplified project creation*—You can use a project initialization service to get an empty but configured skeleton app.
- *Dependency starters*—Spring Boot groups certain dependencies used for a specific purpose with dependency starters. You don't need to figure out all the must-have dependencies you need to add to your project for one particular purpose nor which versions you should use for compatibility.
- *Autoconfiguration based on dependencies*—Based on the dependencies you added to your project, Spring Boot defines some default configurations. Instead of writing all the configurations yourself, you only need to change the ones provided by Spring Boot that don't match what you need. Changing the configs likely requires less code (if any).

Let's discuss these essential features of Spring Boot more in-depth and apply them. The first example is the first Spring web app we write.

7.2.1   *Using a project initialization service to create a Spring Boot project*

In this section, we discuss using a project initialization service to create a Spring Boot project. Some people don't consider the project initialization service as much, but I can't tell you how thankful I am this feature exists. As a developer, you don't create multiple projects a day, so you don't see this feature's big advantage. For both students and teachers who write numerous Spring Boot projects a day, this feature spares you hours of work on repetitive, insignificant actions you'd need to do if you started a project from scratch. To learn how it can help you, let's use a project initialization service to create a project named "sq-ch7-ex1."

Some IDEs integrate directly with a project initialization service, and some don't. For example, in IntelliJ Ultimate or STS, you'll find this feature available when creating a new project (figure 7.9)—but if you use IntelliJ Community, you don't.

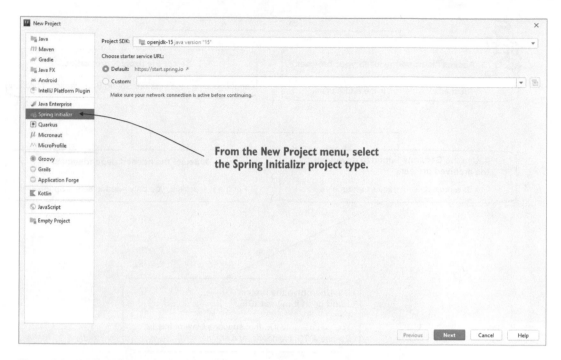

Figure 7.9 Some IDEs integrate with a project initializer service directly. For example, in IntelliJ Ultimate, you can select Spring Initializr from the New Project menu to create a Spring Boot app with a project initializer service.

If your IDE supports this feature, you'll probably find it named Spring Initializr in your project creation menu. But if your IDE doesn't support direct integration with a Spring Boot project initialization service, you can use this feature by accessing http://start.spring.io directly in your browser. This service will help you create a project you can import into any IDE. Let's use this approach to create our first project.

The following list summarizes the steps we'll take to create the Spring Boot project using start.spring.io (figure 7.10):

1 Access start.spring.io in a web browser.
2 Select the project properties (language, the version, the build tool, and so on).
3 Select the needed dependencies you want to add to your project.
4 Use the Generate button to download the archived project.
5 Unarchive the project and open it in your IDE.

Once you access start.spring.io in a web browser, you'll find an interface similar to the one in figure 7.11. You have to specify some project properties, like the build tool you prefer between Maven and Gradle and the Java version you want to use. Spring Boot even offers you the possibility to change the syntax of your app to Kotlin or Groovy.

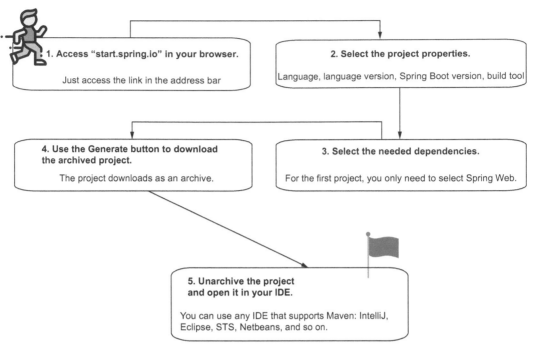

Figure 7.10   Steps to generate a Spring Boot project using start.spring.io. Access start.spring.io in your browser, select the properties and the needed dependencies, and download the archived project. Then open the project in your browser.

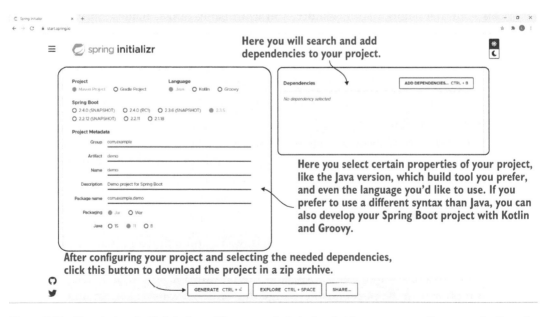

Figure 7.11   The start.spring.io interface. After accessing start.spring.io, you can specify your project's main configurations, select the dependencies, and download the archived project.

Spring Boot offers us many options, but we'll continue using Maven and Java 11 throughout the book to keep the examples consistent. Figure 7.12 shows you an example of filling the fields for generating a new Spring Boot project for our example. In this example, we only need to add a dependency named Spring Web. This dependency adds everything our project needs to become a Spring web app.

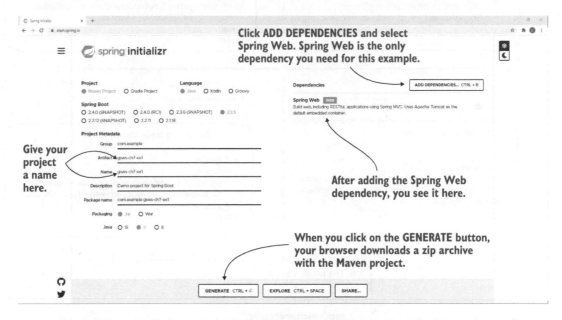

Figure 7.12 For our example, we need to add the Spring Web dependency. You can add it using the Add Dependencies button on the right upper-hand side of the window. You also need to give a name to your project.

When you click the Generate button, the browser downloads a zip archive containing a Spring Boot project. Now we discuss the main things Spring Initializr configured into your Maven project (figure 7.13):

- The Spring app main class
- The Spring Boot POM parent
- The dependencies
- The Spring Boot Maven plugin
- The properties file

You need to be aware of how your project looks. For this reason, we'll discuss each configuration.

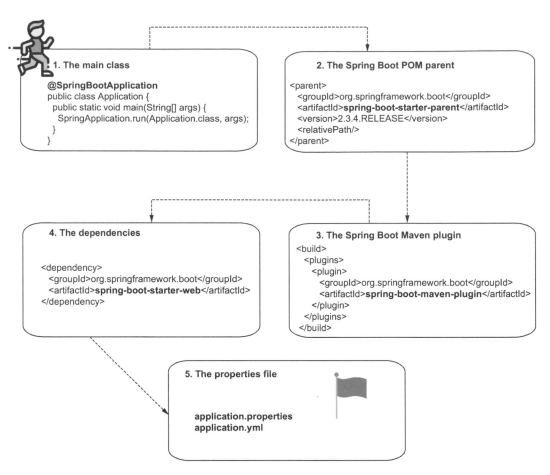

Figure 7.13   When generating a Spring Boot project with Spring Initializr, it makes some configurations to the project that you don't find in a plain Maven project.

THE APP'S MAIN CLASS CREATED BY START.SPRING.IO

The first thing to look at is the application's main class. Unarchive the downloaded file and open it in your IDE. You can observe that Spring Initializr added the Main class to your app and also some configurations in the pom.xml file. The Main class of a Spring Boot app is annotated with the @SpringBootApplication annotation, and it looks similar to the next code snippet:

```
@SpringBootApplication
public class Main {              This annotation defines the Main
                                 class of a Spring Boot app.
  public static void main(String[] args) {
    SpringApplication.run(Main.class, args);
  }

}
```

Spring Initializr generated all this code. In this book, we'll only focus on what's relevant to our examples. For example, I won't detail what the `SpringApplication.run()` method does and how precisely Spring Boot uses the `@SpringBootApplication` annotation. These details aren't relevant to what you're learning now. Spring Boot is a subject for a whole book. But at some point you'll undoubtedly want to understand how Spring Boot apps work in detail, and for this I recommend you read Craig Walls's *Spring Boot in Action* (Manning, 2015) and Mark Heckler's *Spring Boot: Up and Running* O'Reilly Media, 2021).

THE SPRING BOOT MAVEN PARENT CONFIGURED BY START.SPRING.IO

Second, we look at the pom.xml file. If you open your project's pom.xml file, you'll find that the project initialization service also added some details here. One of the most important details you'll find is the Spring Boot parent node, which looks similar to the next code snippet:

```
<parent>
   <groupId>org.springframework.boot</groupId>
   <artifactId>spring-boot-starter-parent</artifactId>
   <version>2.3.4.RELEASE</version>
   <relativePath/>
</parent>
```

One of the essential things this parent does is provide you with compatible versions for the dependencies you'll add to your project. You'll observe that we don't specify a version for a dependency we use in most cases. We let (and it's recommended) Spring Boot choose the version of a dependency to make sure we don't run into incompatibilities.

THE SPRING BOOT MAVEN PLUGIN CONFIGURED BY START.SPRING.IO

Next we look at the Spring Boot Maven plugin configured by start.spring.io when creating the project. You find this plugin also configured in the pom.xml file. The next code snippet shows the plugin declaration, which you usually find at the end of the pom.xml file inside the `<build> <plugins> ... </plugins></build>` tags. This plugin is responsible for adding part of the default configurations you'll observe in your project:

```
<build>
   <plugins>
      <plugin>
         <groupId>org.springframework.boot</groupId>
         <artifactId>spring-boot-maven-plugin</artifactId>
      </plugin>
   </plugins>
 </build>
```

THE MAVEN DEPENDENCIES ADDED BY START.SPRING.IO WHEN CREATING THE PROJECT

Also in the pom.xml file, you find the dependency you added when creating the project in start.spring.io, Spring Web. You'll find this dependency provided, as shown in the next code snippet. It is a dependency starter named spring-boot-starter-web. We discuss what a dependency starter is in detail in section 7.2.2. For now, know that it doesn't specify a version.

For all the examples we have written, we also specified a version for each dependency. The reason you don't specify one now is to let Spring Boot choose the right one for you. As we discussed earlier in this section, this is why we need the Spring Boot parent to the pom.xml file:

```
<dependency>
    <groupId>org.springframework.boot</groupId>
    <artifactId>spring-boot-starter-web</artifactId>
</dependency>
```

THE APPLICATION PROPERTIES FILE

The last essential thing Spring Initializr added to your project is a file named "application.properties." You find this file in the resources folder of your Maven project. Initially, this file is empty, and for this first example we'll keep it this way. Later, we'll discuss using this file to configure property values your app needs during its execution.

7.2.2 *Using dependency starters to simplify the dependency management*

Now that you learned how to use a Spring Boot project initialization service and have a better overview of the Spring Boot project you created, let's focus on the second essential advantage Spring Boot offers: *dependency starters*. Dependency starters save you plenty of time, and they're an invaluable feature Spring Boot offers.

A dependency starter is a group of dependencies you add to configure your app for a specific purpose. In your project's pom.xml file, the starter looks like a normal dependency, as presented in the next code snippet. Observe the name of the dependency: A starter name usually starts with "spring-boot-starter-" followed by a relevant name that describes the capabilities it added to the app:

```
<dependency>
    <groupId>org.springframework.boot</groupId>
    <artifactId>spring-boot-starter-web</artifactId>
</dependency>
```

Say you want to add web capabilities to your app. In the past, to configure a Spring web app you had to add all the needed dependencies to your pom.xml file yourself and make sure their versions were compatible one with the other. Configuring all the dependencies you need is not an easy job. Taking care of the version compatibility is even more complicated.

With dependency starters, we don't request dependencies directly. We request capabilities (figure 7.14). You add a dependency starter for a particular capability you need, say web functionalities, a database, or security. Spring Boot makes sure to add the right dependencies to your app with the proper compatible version for your requested capability. We can say that dependency starters are capability-oriented groups of compatible dependencies.

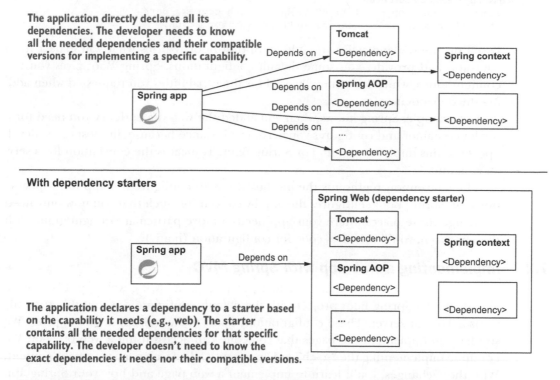

Without dependency starters

The application directly declares all its dependencies. The developer needs to know all the needed dependencies and their compatible versions for implementing a specific capability.

With dependency starters

The application declares a dependency to a starter based on the capability it needs (e.g., web). The starter contains all the needed dependencies for that specific capability. The developer doesn't need to know the exact dependencies it needs nor their compatible versions.

Figure 7.14 Using dependency starters. Instead of individually referring to specific dependencies, the app now depends on only a starter. The starter contains all the needed dependencies for implementing a specific capability. The starter also makes sure these dependencies are compatible with one another.

Look at your pom.xml file. You only added the spring-boot-starter-web dependency, no Spring context, no AOP, no Tomcat! But, if you look in the "External Libraries" folder of your app, you'll find JAR archives for all these. Spring Boot knew you would need them and downloaded them with specific versions it knows are compatible.

7.2.3   *Using autoconfiguration by convention based on dependencies*

Spring Boot also provides autoconfiguration for your application. We say that it applies the *convention-over-configuration* principle. In this section, we discuss what convention-over-configuration is and how Spring Boot helps us by applying this principle. Out of all the previous Spring Boot features discussed in this chapter, the autoconfiguration is probably the most appreciated and the most known.

Just start your app, and you'll understand why. Yes, I know, you didn't even write anything yet—only downloaded the project and opened it in your IDE. But you can start the app, and you'll find your app boots a Tomcat instance by default accessible on port 8080. In your console, you find something similar to the next snippet:

**Spring Boot configured Tomcat and
starts it by default on port 8080.**
```
Tomcat started on port(s): 8080 (http) with context path ''
Started Main in 1.684 seconds (JVM running for 2.306)
```

Based on the dependencies you added, Spring Boot realizes what you expect from your app and provides you some default configurations. Spring Boot gives you the configurations, which are generally used for the capabilities you requested when adding the dependencies.

For example, Spring knows when you added the web dependency you need for a servlet container and configures you a Tomcat instance because, in most cases, developers use this implementation. For Spring Boot, Tomcat is the convention for a servlet container.

The convention represents the most-used way to configure the app for a specific purpose. Spring Boot configures the app by convention such that you now only need to change those places where your app needs a more particular configuration. With this approach, you'll write less code for configuration (if any).

7.3   *Implementing a web app with Spring MVC*

In this section, we'll implement our first web page in a Spring web app. It's true we already have a Spring Boot project with the default configurations, but this app only starts a Tomcat server. These configurations don't make our app a web app yet! We still have to implement the pages that someone can access using a web browser. We continue implementing the "sq-ch7-ex1" project to add a web page with static content. With these changes, you'll learn to implement a web page and how your Spring app works behind the scenes.

To add a web page to your app, you follow two steps (figure 7.15):

1   Write an HTML document with the content you want to be displayed by the browser.

2   Write a controller with an action for the web page created at point 1.

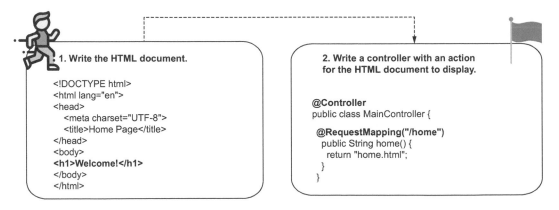

Figure 7.15   The steps for adding a static web page to your application. Add the HTML document containing the information the browser will display and then write a controller with an action assigned to it.

In the "sq-ch7-ex1" project, we first start adding a static web page with the content we want to display in the browser. This web page is just an HTML document, and for our example the page only displays a short text in a heading. The following listing shows you what the content of this file should look like. You need to add the file in the "resources/static" folder of your Maven project. This folder is the default place where the Spring Boot app expects to find the pages to render.

Listing 7.1 The content of the HTML file

```html
<!DOCTYPE html>
<html lang="en">
<head>
    <meta charset="UTF-8">
    <title>Home Page</title>
</head>
<body>
    <h1>Welcome!</h1>
</body>
</html>
```

> In a standard HTML document, we display a heading text.

The second step you take is writing a controller with a method that links the HTTP request to the page you want your app to provide in response. The controller is a component of the web app that contains methods (often named actions) executed for a specific HTTP request. In the end, the controller's action returns a reference to the web page the app returns in response. We'll keep our first example simple, and we won't make the controller execute any specific logic for the request for now. We'll just configure an action to return in response to the content of the home.html document we created and stored in the "resources/static" folder in the first step.

To mark a class as a controller, you only need to use the @Controller annotation, a stereotype annotation (like @Component and @Service, discussed in chapter 4). This means that Spring will also add a bean of this class to its context to manage it. Inside this class, you can define controller actions, which are methods associated with specific HTTP requests.

Say you want the browser to display this page's content when the user accesses the /home path. To achieve this result, you annotate the action method with the @RequestMapping annotation specifying the path as a value of the annotation: @RequestMapping("/home"). The method needs to return, as a string, the name of the document you want the app to send as a response. The following listing shows the controller class and the action it implements.

Listing 7.2 The definition of the controller class

```java
@Controller
public class MainController {

    @RequestMapping("/home")
    public String home() {
```

> `@Controller` ← **We annotate the class with the @Controller stereotype annotation.**

> `@RequestMapping("/home")` ← **We use the @RequestMapping annotation to associate the action with an HTTP request path.**

```
    return "home.html";
  }
}
```
We return the HTML document name that contains the details we want the browser to display.

I know you have plenty of questions now! All my students do at this point when I teach Spring in class—questions such as these:

1   Can this method do something other than return the HTML file name?
2   Can it get parameters?
3   I saw examples on the web using annotations other than `@RequestMapping`; are they better?
4   Can the HTML page contain dynamic content?

We will answer all these questions with examples in chapter 8. But for the moment, I ask that you focus on this simple app to understand what we just wrote. First, you need to know how Spring manages the request and calls this controller action we implemented. Correctly understanding the framework's way of managing the web request is a valuable skill that will help you later learn the details faster and implement any feature you need in a web app.

We now start the application, analyze its behavior, and discuss, with visuals, the mechanism behind the app that makes this result possible. When starting the app, you will see the log. It tells you Tomcat started and the port it uses in the app console. If you use the dcfault (you didn't configure something not explained in this chapter), Tomcat uses port 8080.

```
Tomcat started on port(s): 8080 (http) with context path ''
```

Open a browser window on the same computer where you run the app and write the following address in the address bar: http://localhost:8080/home (figure 7.16). Do not forget to write the path /home you mapped with the controller's action; otherwise, you'll get an error and an HTTP response with the status "404 Not Found."

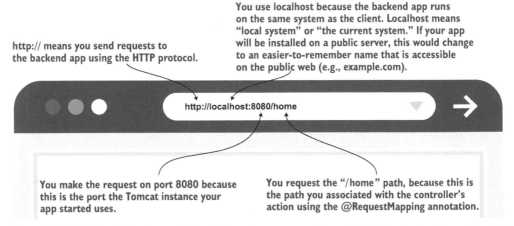

You use localhost because the backend app runs on the same system as the client. Localhost means "local system" or "the current system." If your app will be installed on a public server, this would change to an easier-to-remember name that is accessible on the public web (e.g., example.com).

http:// means you send requests to the backend app using the HTTP protocol.

http://localhost:8080/home

You make the request on port 8080 because this is the port the Tomcat instance your app started uses.

You request the "/home" path, because this is the path you associated with the controller's action using the @RequestMapping annotation.

Figure 7.16   Testing the implementation. Using a browser, send a request to the backend app. You need to use the port Tomcat opened and the path you specified with the @RequestMapping annotation.

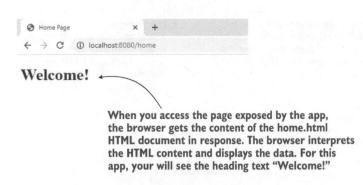

When you access the page exposed by the app, the browser gets the content of the home.html HTML document in response. The browser interprets the HTML content and displays the data. For this app, your will see the heading text "Welcome!"

Figure 7.17 Accessing the page in a browser, you'll see the heading text "Welcome!" The browser interprets and displays the HTML received in response from the backend.

Figure 7.17 shows you the result of accessing the web page in a browser.

Now that you've seen the app's behavior, let's discuss the mechanism behind it. Spring has a set of components that interact with each other to get the result you observed. Figure 7.18 presents these components and the flow in which they manage an HTTP request.

1 The client makes an HTTP request.

2 Tomcat gets the client's HTTP request. Tomcat has to call a servlet component for the HTTP request. In the case of Spring MVC, Tomcat calls a servlet Spring Boot configured. We name this servlet *dispatcher servlet.*

3 The dispatcher servlet is the entry point of the Spring web app. (It's that servlet we discussed in figure 7.8 earlier in this chapter; it's also in figure 7.18.) Tomcat calls the dispatcher servlet for any HTTP request it gets. Its responsibility is to manage the request further inside the Spring app. It has to find what controller action to call for the request and what to send back in response to the client. This servlet is also referred to as a "front controller."

4 The first thing the dispatcher servlet needs to do is find a controller action to call for the request. To find out which controller action to call, the dispatcher servlet delegates to a component named *handler mapping.* The handler mapping finds the controller action you associated with the request with the @Request-Mapping annotation.

5 After finding out which controller action to call, the dispatcher servlet calls that specific controller action. If the handler mapping couldn't find any action associated with the request, the app responds to the client with an HTTP "404 Not Found" status. The controller returns the page name it needs to render for the response to the dispatcher servlet. We refer to this HTML page also as "the view."

6 At this moment, the dispatcher servlet needs to find the view with the name received from the controller to get its content and send it as response. The dispatcher servlet delegates the responsibility of getting the view content to a component named "View Resolver."

7 The dispatcher servlet returns the rendered view in the HTTP response.

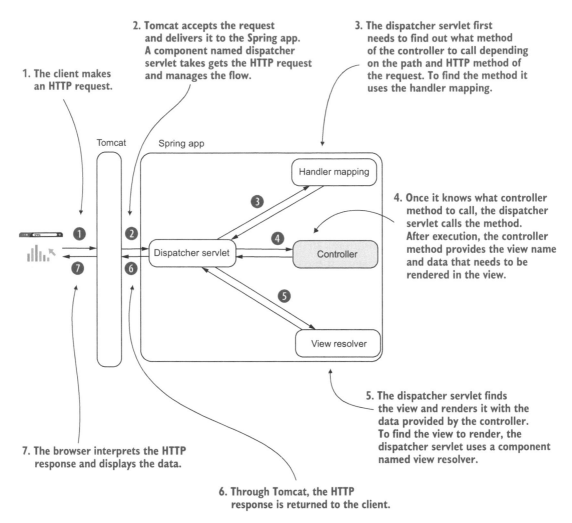

2. Tomcat accepts the request and delivers it to the Spring app. A component named dispatcher servlet takes gets the HTTP request and manages the flow.

3. The dispatcher servlet first needs to find out what method of the controller to call depending on the path and HTTP method of the request. To find the method it uses the handler mapping.

1. The client makes an HTTP request.

4. Once it knows what controller method to call, the dispatcher servlet calls the method. After execution, the controller method provides the view name and data that needs to be rendered in the view.

5. The dispatcher servlet finds the view and renders it with the data provided by the controller. To find the view to render, the dispatcher servlet uses a component named view resolver.

7. The browser interprets the HTTP response and displays the data.

6. Through Tomcat, the HTTP response is returned to the client.

Figure 7.18   The Spring MVC architecture. In the diagram, you find the main components of Spring MVC. These components and the way they collaborate are responsible for a web app's behavior. The controller (shaded differently) is the only component you implement. Spring Boot configures the other components.

NOTE   In this chapter, I described the handler mapping as the component that finds the controller action by the HTTP request path. The handler mapping also searches by something named the HTTP method, which I left it out of my explanations for the moment so that you can more easily focus on the flow. We'll discuss HTTP methods in more detail in chapter 8.

Spring (with Spring Boot) considerably simplifies the development of a web app by arranging this setup. You only need to write controller actions and map them to requests using annotations. A large part of the logic is hidden in the framework, and this helps you write the apps faster and cleaner.

In chapter 8, we continue with more details on what you can do with a controller class. Real-world apps are often more complex than just returning the content of a static HTML page. In most cases, the page displays dynamic details processed by the app before rendering the HTTP response. But take a moment now and review what you learned in this chapter. Understanding how Spring web apps work is essential for the next chapters' discussions and is definitely necessary for becoming a professional Spring developer. "Don't rush into learning details before properly understanding the basics" is a rule of thumb I use when learning any technology.

Summary

- People use web apps more often today than they use desktop apps. For this reason, you must understand how web apps work and learn to implement them.

- A web app is an application the user interacts with using a web browser. A web app has a client side and a server side where the data is processed and stored. The client side (frontend) sends requests to the server side (backend). The backend executes the action requested by the frontend and responds back.

- Spring offers you the capability of implementing web apps. To avoid writing many configurations, you can use Spring Boot: a Spring ecosystem project that applies the convention-over-configuration principle providing you default configurations for the capabilities your app needs.

- Spring Boot also helps you more easily configure your dependencies through the dependency starters it offers. A dependency starter is a group of dependencies with comparable versions to offer your app a specific capability.

- To get the HTTP requests and deliver the responses, a Java backend web app needs a servlet container (e.g., Tomcat): software with the capability to translate HTTP requests and responses to the Java app. With servlet containers, you don't need to implement the communication over the network using the HTTP protocol.

- You can easily create your web app project as a Spring Boot project, which auto-configures a servlet container and comes with the capabilities you need to write the use cases of your web app. Spring Boot also configures a set of components that intercept and manage HTTP requests. These components are part of a class design we name Spring MVC.

- Because Spring Boot autoconfigures the Spring MVC components and the servlet container, you only need to write the HTML document containing the data the app sends as a response and a controller class for a minimal HTTP request-response flow action.

- You use annotations to configure your controller and the controller's actions. To mark a class as a Spring MVC controller, use the `@Controller` stereotype annotation. To assign a controller action to a specific HTTP request, use the `@RequestMapping` annotation.

Implementing web apps with Spring Boot and Spring MVC

8

This chapter covers

- Using a template engine to implement dynamic views
- Sending data from client to server through HTTP requests
- Using GET and POST HTTP methods for your HTTP requests

In chapter 7, we made progress in understanding how to use Spring to write web apps. We've discussed a web app's components, the dependencies a web app needs, and the Spring MVC architecture. We even wrote a first web app to prove all these components work together.

In this chapter, we'll take a step further and implement some capabilities you'll find in any modern web app. We start with implementing pages whose content changes according to how your app processes the data for specific requests. Today we rarely see static pages on websites. You probably think, "There has to be a way to decide what content to add on the pages before delivering the HTTP response back to the browser." There are ways you can do this!

In section 8.1, we'll implement dynamic views using template engines. A template engine is a dependency that allows you to easily get and display variable data the controller sends. We'll demonstrate how the template engine works in an example after reviewing the Spring MVC flow.

In section 8.2, you'll learn how to send data from the client to the server through the HTTP request. We'll use that data in the controller's method and create the dynamic content on the view.

In section 8.3, we discuss HTTP methods, and you'll learn that the request path isn't enough to identify a client's request. Together with the request path, the client uses an HTTP method represented with a verb (GET, POST, PUT, DELETE, PATCH, etc.), which expresses the client's intention. In our example, we'll implement an HTML form that someone can use to send values the backend has to process. Later, in chapters 12 and 13, you'll learn to persist such data in a database, and your apps will get closer and closer to what a production-ready deliverable looks like.

8.1 Implementing web apps with a dynamic view

Suppose you implement the cart page of an online shop. This page shouldn't display the same data for everyone. It also doesn't even show the same information every time for the same user. This page shows precisely the products a particular user has added to their cart. In figure 8.1, you find an example of a dynamic view presented with the Manning website's cart functionality. Observe how requests to the same page *manning.com/cart* receive different data in response. The information displayed is different, even if the page is the same. The page has dynamic content!

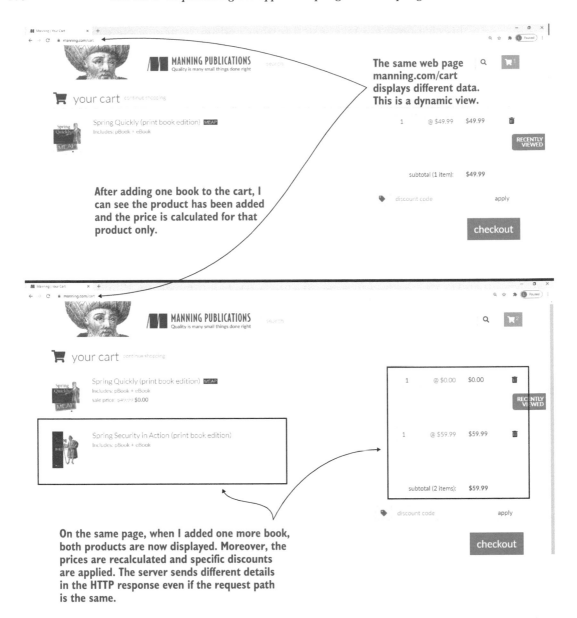

The same web page manning.com/cart displays different data. This is a dynamic view.

After adding one book to the cart, I can see the product has been added and the price is calculated for that product only.

On the same page, when I added one more book, both products are now displayed. Moreover, the prices are recalculated and specific discounts are applied. The server sends different details in the HTTP response even if the request path is the same.

Figure 8.1   A dynamic view presented with the Manning shopping cart functionality. Even if the requested page is the same, the content of the page is different. The backend sent different data in the response before and after adding one more product to the cart.

In this section, we implement a web app with a dynamic view. Most apps today need to display dynamic data to the user. Now, for a user's request expressed through an HTTP request sent by the browser, the web app receives some data, processes it, and then sends back an HTTP response that the browser needs to display (figure 8.2).

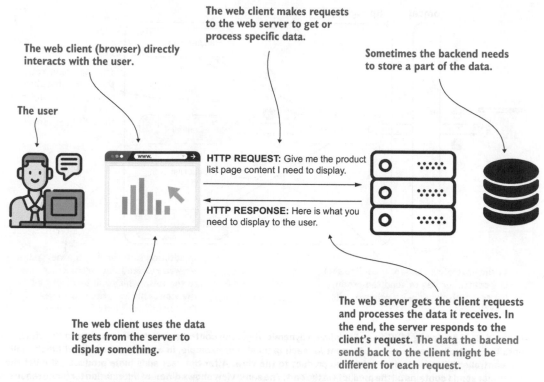

The web client makes requests to the web server to get or process specific data.

The web client (browser) directly interacts with the user.

Sometimes the backend needs to store a part of the data.

The user

HTTP REQUEST: Give me the product list page content I need to display.

HTTP RESPONSE: Here is what you need to display to the user.

The web client uses the data it gets from the server to display something.

The web server gets the client requests and processes the data it receives. In the end, the server responds to the client's request. The data the backend sends back to the client might be different for each request.

Figure 8.2 A client sends data through the HTTP request. The backend processes this data and builds a response to send back to the client. Depending on how the backend processed the data, different requests may result in other data displayed to the user.

We'll review the Spring MVC flow and then work on an example to demonstrate how the view can get dynamic values from the controller.

In the example we implemented at the end of chapter 7, the browser's content was the same for every HTTP request for our page. Remember the Spring MVC flow (figure 8.3):

1 The client sends an HTTP request to the web server.
2 The dispatcher servlet uses the handler mapping to find out what controller action to call.
3 The dispatcher servlet calls the controller's action.
4 After executing the action associated with the HTTP request, the controller returns the view name the dispatcher servlet needs to render into the HTTP response.
5 The response is sent back to the client.

Number 4 is where we need to make a change. We want the controller not only to return the view name but somehow also send data to the view. The view will incorporate

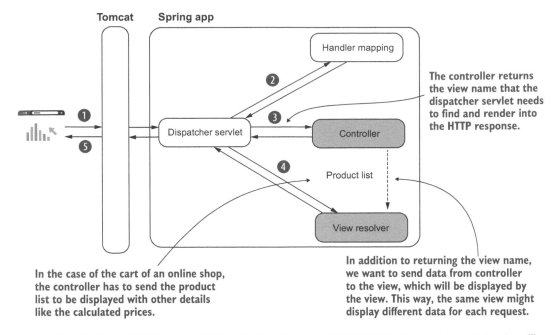

In the case of the cart of an online shop, the controller has to send the product list to be displayed with other details like the calculated prices.

The controller returns the view name that the dispatcher servlet needs to find and render into the HTTP response.

In addition to returning the view name, we want to send data from controller to the view, which will be displayed by the view. This way, the same view might display different data for each request.

Figure 8.3   The Spring MVC flow. To define a dynamic view, the controller needs to send data to the view. The data the controller sends can be different for each request. For example, in an online shop's cart functionality, the controller initially sends a list of one product to the view. After the user adds more products, the list the controller sends contains all the products in the cart. The same view shows different information for these requests.

this data to define the HTTP response. This way, if the server sends a list of one product, and the page displays the list, the page will display one product. If the controller sends two products for the same view, now the displayed data will be different because the page will show two products (the behavior you observed in figure 8.1).

Let me show you how to send data from the controller to the view in a project now. You can find this example in the project "sq-ch8-ex1." This example is simple to allow you to focus on the syntax. But you can use this approach to send any data from the controller to the view.

Let's assume for now we want to send a name and print it with a specific color. In a real-world scenario, you'd maybe need to print the name of the user somewhere on the page. How you do that? How do you get data that could be different from one request to another and print it on the page?

We'll create a Spring Boot project ("sq-ch8-ex1") and add a template engine to the dependencies in the pom.xml file. We'll use a template engine named Thymeleaf. The template engine is a dependency that allows us to easily send data from the controller to the view and display this data in a specific way. I chose Thymeleaf because it's less complex than others, and I find it easier to understand and learn. As you'll observe in our example, the templates used with Thymleaf are simple HTML static files. The next code snippet shows the dependency you need to add to the pom.xml file:

```
<dependency>
    <groupId>org.springframework.boot</groupId>
    <artifactId>spring-boot-starter-thymeleaf</artifactId>   <—
</dependency>
<dependency>
    <groupId>org.springframework.boot</groupId>
    <artifactId>spring-boot-starter-web</artifactId>   <—
</dependency>
```

> **The dependency starter that needs to be added to use Thymeleaf as a template engine**

> **Though you're building a web app, you still need to add the dependency starter for web apps.**

In listing 8.1, you find the definition of the controller. We annotate the method to map the action to a specific request path using @RequestMapping, as you learned in chapter 7. We now also define a parameter to the method. This parameter of type Model stores the data we want the controller to send to the view. In this Model instance, we add the values we want to send to the view and identify each of them with a unique name (also referred to as key). To add a new value that the controller sends to the view, we call the addAttribute() method. The first parameter of the addAttribute() method is the key; the second parameter is the value you send to the view.

Listing 8.1 The controller class defines the page action

The @Controller stereotype annotation marks this class as Spring MVC controller and adds a bean of this type to the Spring context.

We assign the controller's action to an HTTP request path.

The action method defines a parameter of type Model that stores the data the controller sends to the view.

```
@Controller
public class MainController {

    @RequestMapping("/home")   <—
    public String home(Model page) {   <—
        page.addAttribute("username", "Katy");
        page.addAttribute("color", "red");
        return "home.html";   <—
    }
}
```

We add the data we want the controller to send to the view.

The controller's action returns the view to be rendered into the HTTP response.

NOTE Students sometimes ask me why they get an error if they directly add to the browser's address bar "localhost:8080" without a path like "/home." It's correct that an error appears. The error is a default page you see displayed by a Spring Boot app when you get an HTTP 404 (Not Found) response status. When you call directly "localhost:8080" you refer to the path "/." Because you didn't assign any controller action to this path, it's normal to get an HTTP 404. If you wish to see something else instead, assign a controller action to this path as well using the @RequestMapping annotation.

To define the view, you need to add a new "home.html" file to your Spring Boot project's "resources/templates" folder. Be attentive to the small difference: in chapter 7, we added the HTML file in the "resources/static" folder because we created a static view. Now that we're using a template engine to create a dynamic view, you need to add the HTML file to the "resources/templates" folder instead.

Listing 8.2 shows the content of the "home.html" file I added to the project. The first important thing to notice in the file's content is the <html> tag where I added the attribute xmlns:th="http://www.thymeleaf.org". This definition is equivalent to an import in Java. It allows us further to use the prefix "th" to refer to specific features provided by Thymeleaf in the view.

A little bit further in the view, you find two places where I used this "th" prefix to refer to the controller's data to the view. With the ${attribute_key} syntax, you refer to any of the attributes you send from the controller using the Model instance. For example, I used the ${username} to get the value of the "username" attribute and ${color} to get the value of the "color" attribute.

> **Listing 8.2   The home.html file representing the dynamic view of the app**

```html
<!DOCTYPE html>
<html lang="en" xmlns:th="http://www.thymeleaf.org">      ⟵─┐ Defines the Thymeleaf
                                                              │  "th" prefix
  <head>
    <meta charset="UTF-8">
    <title>Home Page</title>
  </head>

  <body>
    <h1>Welcome
    <span th:style="'color:' + ${color}"        │ Uses the "th" prefix to use the
          th:text="${username}"></span>!</h1>    │ values sent by the controller
  </body>

</html>
```

To test if everything works, start the application and access the web page in a browser. Your page will look like the one in figure 8.4.

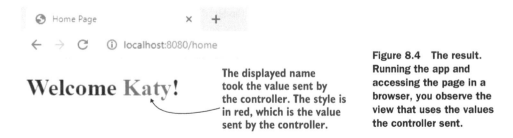

Figure 8.4   The result. Running the app and accessing the page in a browser, you observe the view that uses the values the controller sent.

The displayed name took the value sent by the controller. The style is in red, which is the value sent by the controller.

Now, whatever your controller sends, the view uses.

8.1.1   Getting data on the HTTP request

In this section, we discuss how the client sends data to the server through HTTP requests. In apps, we often need to give the client the ability to send information to the server. This data gets processed and then displayed on the view, as you learned in section 8.1. Here are some examples of use cases where the client has to send data to the server:

- You implement the order functionality of an online shop. The client needs to send to the server the products that the user orders. Further, the server takes care of the order.

- You implement a web forum where you allow users to add and edit new posts. The client sends the post details to the server, which stores or changes the details in a database.

- You implement the login functionality of an app. Users write their credentials, which need to be validated. The client sends the credentials to the server, and the server validates these credentials.

- You implement the contact page of a web app. The page displays a form where the user can write a message subject and body. These details need to be sent in an email to a specific address. The client sends these values to the server, and the server takes care of processing them and sending an email to the desired email address.

In most cases, to send data through the HTTP request you use one of the following ways:

- An *HTTP request parameter* represents a simple way to send values from client to server in a key-value(s) pair format. To send HTTP request parameters, you append them to the URI in a request query expression. They are also called *query parameters.* You should use this approach only for sending a small quantity of data.

- An *HTTP request header* is similar to the request parameters in that the request headers are sent through the HTTP header. The big difference is that they don't appear in the URI, but you still cannot send large quantities of data using HTTP headers.

- A *path variable* sends data through the request path itself. It is the same as for the request parameter approach: you use a path variable to send a small quantity of data. But we should use path variables when the value you send is mandatory.

- The *HTTP request body* is mainly used to send a larger quantity of data (formatted as a string, but sometimes even binary data such as a file). We'll discuss this approach in chapter 10, where you'll learn to implement REST endpoints.

8.1.2 Using request parameters to send data from client to server

In this section, we implement an example to demonstrate the use of HTTP request parameters—simple ways to send data from the client to the backend. You often encounter this approach in production apps. You use request parameters in the following scenarios:

- *The quantity of data you send is not large.* You set the request parameters using query variables (as shown in this section's example). This approach limits you to about 2,000 characters.

- *You need to send optional data.* A request parameter is a clean way to deal with a value the client might not send. The server can expect to not get a value for specific request parameters.

An often-encountered use case for request parameters used is defining some search and filtering criteria (figure 8.5). Say your app displays product details in a table. Each product is identified by a name, a price, and a brand. You want to allow the user to search for products by any of these. The user might decide to search by price or by name and brand. Any combination is possible. For such a scenario, request parameters are the right choice for implementation. The app sends each of these values (name, price, and brand) in optional request parameters. The client only needs to send the values by which the user decides to search.

Let's use a request parameter by changing the example we discussed in section 8.1 to get the color in which the username is displayed from the client. Listing 8.3 shows you how to change the controller class to get the client's color value in a request parameter. I separated this example into a project named "sq-ch8-ex2" so you can analyze the changes more easily. To get the value from a request parameter, you need to add one more parameter to the controller's action method and annotate that parameter with the @RequestParam annotation. The @RequestParam annotation tells Spring it

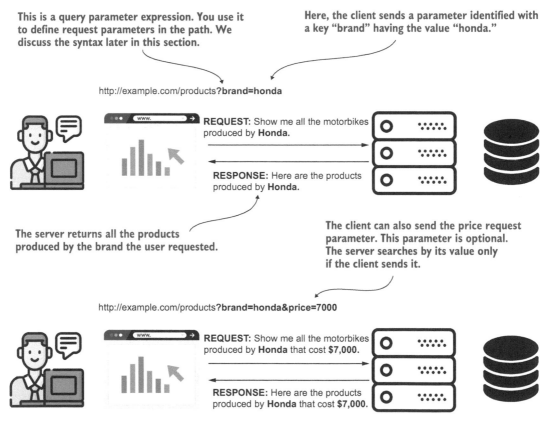

Figure 8.5 A request parameter can be optional. A common scenario for using request parameters is implementing a search functionality where the search criteria are optional. The client sends only some of the request parameters, and the server knows to use only the values it receives. You implement the server to consider it might not get values for some of the parameters.

needs to get the value from the HTTP request parameter with the same name as the method's parameter name.

Listing 8.3   Getting a value through a request parameter

```
@Controller
public class MainController {

  @RequestMapping("/home")
  public String home(
      @RequestParam String color,
      Model page) {
    page.addAttribute("username", "Katy");
    page.addAttribute("color", color);
    return "home.html";
  }
}
```

We define a new parameter for the controller's action method and annotate it with @RequestParam.

We also add the Model parameter that we use to send data from the controller to the view.

The controller passes the color sent by the client to the view.

Figure 8.6 shows how the color parameter value travels from the client to the controller's action on the backend to be used by the view.

The client sends the color through an HTTP request parameter.

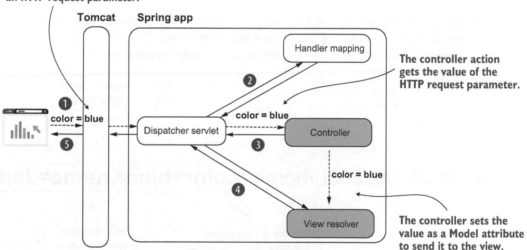

The controller action gets the value of the HTTP request parameter.

The controller sets the value as a Model attribute to send it to the view.

Figure 8.6   The value sent by the client from the Spring MVC perspective. The controller action gets the request parameters the client sends and can use them. In our example, the value is set on the Model **and delivered to the view.**

Run the application and access the /home path. To set the request parameter's value, you need to use the next snippet's syntax:

```
http://localhost:8080/home?color=blue
```

When setting HTTP request parameters, you extend the path with a ? symbol followed by pairs of key=value parameters separated by the & symbol. For example, if I want to also send the name as a request parameter, I write:

```
http://localhost:8080/home?color=blue&name=Jane
```

You can add a new parameter to the controller's action to get this parameter as well. The next code snippet shows this change. You can also find this example in the project "sq-ch8-ex3":

```
@Controller
public class MainController {

  @RequestMapping("/home")
  public String home(
      @RequestParam(required = false) String name,      ◁── Gets the new request parameter "name"
      @RequestParam(required = false) String color,
      Model page) {
    page.addAttribute("username", name);      ◁── Sends the "name" parameter's value to the view
    page.addAttribute("color", color);
    return "home.html";
  }
}
```

In the group key=value (for example, color=blue), "key" is the name of the request parameter, and its value is written right after the = symbol.

Figure 8.7 visually summarizes the syntax for request parameters.

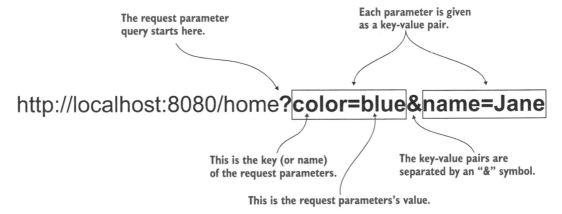

Figure 8.7   Sending data through request parameters. Each request parameter is a key-value pair. You provide the request parameters with the path in a query starting with the question mark symbol. If you set more than one request parameter, you separate each key-value pair with the "and" (&) symbol.

NOTE   A request parameter is mandatory by default. If the client doesn't provide a value for it, the server sends back a response with the status HTTP "400 Bad Request." If you wish the value to be optional, you need to explicitly specify this on the annotation using the optional attribute: @RequestParam(optional=true).

8.1.3 *Using path variables to send data from client to server*

Let's discuss the use of path variables and compare it to the approach you learned in section 8.2.1 for sending data from client to server. Using path variables is also a way of sending data from client to server. But instead of using the HTTP request parameters, you directly set variable values in the path, as presented in the next snippets.

Using request parameters:

```
http://localhost:8080/home?color=blue
```

Using path variables:

```
http://localhost:8080/home/blue
```

You don't identify the value with a key anymore. You just take that value from a precise position in the path. On the server side, you extract that value from the path from the specific position. You may have more than one value provided as a path variable, but it's generally better to avoid using more than a couple. You'll observe that the path becomes more challenging to read if you go with more than two path variables. I prefer using request parameters for more than two values instead of path variables, as you learned in section 8.2.1. Also, you shouldn't use path variables for optional values. I recommend you use path variables only for mandatory parameters. If you have optional values to send in the HTTP request, you should use request parameters, as we discussed in section 8.2.1. Table 8.1 compares the request parameters, and path variables approaches.

Table 8.1 A quick comparison of the request parameters and path variables approaches

Request parameters	Path variables
1 Can be used with optional values.	1 Should not be used with optional values.
2 It is recommended that you avoid a large number of parameters. If you need to use more than three, I recommend you use the request body, as you'll learn in chapter 10. Avoid sending more than three query parameters for readability.	2 Always avoid sending more than three path variables. It's even better if you keep a maximum of two.
3 Some developers consider the query expression more difficult to read than the path expression.	3 Easier to read than a query expression. For a publicly exposed website, it's also easier for search engines (e.g., Google) to index the pages. This advantage might make the website easier to find through a search engine.

When the page you write depends on only one or two values that are the core of the end result, it's better to write them directly in the path to make the request easier to read. The URL is also easier to find when you bookmark it in your browser and easier to index with a search engine (if it matters for your app).

Let's write an example to demonstrate the syntax you need to write in your controller for getting values as path variables. I changed the examples we implemented in section 8.2.1 but separated the code into another project, "sq-ch8-ex4," to make it easier for you to test it.

To reference a path variable in the controller's action, you simply give it a name and add it to the path between curly braces, as presented in the following listing. You then use the @PathVariable annotation to mark the controller's action parameter to get the path variable's value. Listing 8.4 shows you how to change the controller action to get the color value with a path variable (the rest of the example is the same as "sq-ch8-ex2," which we discussed in section 8.1.1).

Listing 8.4   Using path variables to get values from the client

```
@Controller
public class MainController {

  @RequestMapping("/home/{color}")       To define a path variable, you assign it
  public String home(                     a name and put it in the path between
      @PathVariable String color,         curly braces.
      Model page) {                       You mark the parameter where you
    page.addAttribute("username", "Katy");  want to get the path variable value
    page.addAttribute("color", color);      with the @PathVariable annotation.
    return "home.html";                     The name of the parameter must be
  }                                         the same as the name of the variable
}                                           in the path.
```

Run the app and access the page in your browser with different values for the color.

```
http://localhost:8080/home/blue
http://localhost:8080/home/red
http://localhost:8080/home/green
```

Each request colors the name displayed by the page in the given color. Figure 8.8 visually represents the link between the code and the request path.

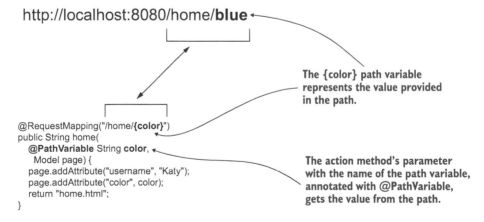

Figure 8.8   Using path variables. To get a value from a path variable, you give the variable a name between curly braces when defining the path on the controller action. You use a parameter annotated with @PathVariable to get the value of the path variable.

8.2   *Using the GET and POST HTTP methods*

In this section, we discuss HTTP methods and how the client uses them to express what action (create, change, retrieve, delete) it will apply to the requested resource. A path and a verb identify an HTTP request. Thus far we have only referred to the path, and, without noticing, we used the *HTTP GET* method. Its purpose is to define what action the client requests. For example, by using GET, we represent an action that only retrieves data. It's a way for the client to say it wants to obtain something from the server, but the call won't change data. But you'll need more than this. An app also needs to change, add, or delete data.

> **NOTE**   Be careful! You can use an HTTP method against its designed purpose, but this is incorrect. For example, you could use HTTP GET and implement a functionality that changes data. Technically, this is possible, but it's a bad, bad choice. Never use an HTTP method against its designed purpose.

We've relied on the request path to reach a specific action of the controller, but in a more complex scenario you can assign the same path to multiple actions of the controller as long as you use different HTTP methods. We'll work on an example to apply such a case.

The HTTP method is defined by a verb and represents the client's intention. If the client's request only retrieves data, we implement the endpoint with HTTP GET. But if the client's request somehow changes data on the server side, we use other verbs to represent the client's intention clearly.

Table 8.2 presents the essential HTTP methods you'll use in apps and which you should learn.

Table 8.2   Basic HTTP methods you'll often encounter in web apps

HTTP method	Description
GET	The client's request only retrieves data.
POST	The client's request sends new data to be added by the server.
PUT	The client's request changes a data record on the server side.
PATCH	The client's request partially changes a data record on the server side.
DELETE	The client's request deletes data on the server side.

Figure 8.9 visually presents the essential HTTP methods to help you remember them.

> **NOTE**   Even if it's a good practice to make a distinction between entirely replacing a record (PUT) and changing only a part of it (PATCH) in production apps, this distinction is not always made.

Now let's implement an example that uses more than just HTTP GET. The scenario is the following: We have to create an app that stores a list of products. Each product has

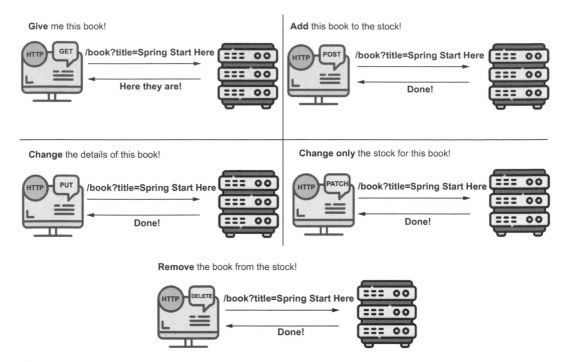

Figure 8.9   The basic HTTP methods. You use GET for retrieving data, POST for adding data, PUT for changing a record, PATCH for changing a part of the record, and DELETE to remove data. The client must use the appropriate HTTP method to express the action executed by a specific request.

a name and a price. The web app displays a list of all products and allows the user to add one more product through an HTML form.

Observe the two use cases described by the scenario. The user needs to do the following:

- View all products in the list; here, we'll continue using HTTP GET.
- Add products to the list; here, we'll use HTTP POST.

We create a new project, "sq-ch8-ex5," with the dependencies (in the pom.xml file) for web and Thymeleaf, as described by the next code snippet:

```
<dependency>
    <groupId>org.springframework.boot</groupId>
    <artifactId>spring-boot-starter-thymeleaf</artifactId>
</dependency>
<dependency>
    <groupId>org.springframework.boot</groupId>
    <artifactId>spring-boot-starter-web</artifactId>
</dependency>
```

In the project, we create a Product class to describe a product with its name and price attributes. The Product class is a model class, as we discussed in chapter 5, so we'll create it in a package named "model." The following listing presents the Product class.

Listing 8.5   The `Product` class describes a product with name and price as attributes

```
public class Product {

  private String name;
  private double price;

  // Omitted getters and setters
}
```

Now that we have a way to represent a product, let's create the list where the app stores the products. The web app will display the product in this list on a web page, and in this list the user can add more products. We will implement the two use cases (getting the list of products to display and adding a new product) as methods in a service class. Let's create a new service class named `ProductService` in a package named "service."

The next listing presents the service class, which instantiates a list and defines two methods for adding a new product and getting it.

Listing 8.6   The `ProductService` class implements the app's use cases

```
@Service
public class ProductService {

  private List<Product> products = new ArrayList<>();

  public void addProduct(Product p) {
    products.add(p);
  }

  public List<Product> findAll() {
    return products;
  }

}
```

NOTE   This design is a simplification to allow you to focus on the discussion of the HTTP methods. Remember that a Spring bean's scope by default is singleton, as we discussed in chapter 5, and a web application implies multiple threads (one for each request). Changing a list defined as an attribute of the bean would cause race condition situations in a real-world app where more clients add products simultaneously. For now, we'll keep our simplification, because in the next chapters we'll replace the list with a database, so this problem will no longer occur. But keep in mind this is a vicious approach, and, as we discussed in chapter 5, you shouldn't use something similar in a production-ready app. Singleton beans aren't thread-safe!

Chapter 12 discusses data sources; we'll use a database to store the data closer to how a production app looks. But for the moment, it's better to focus on the discussed subject, HTTP methods, and build our examples progressively.

A controller will call the use cases implemented by the service. The controller gets data about a new product from the client and adds it to the list by calling the service, and the controller gets the list of products and sends it to the view. You learned how to implement these capabilities earlier in this chapter. First, let's create a Product-Controller class in a package named "controllers" and allow this controller to inject the service bean. The following listing shows you the definition of the controller.

Listing 8.7   The `ProductController` class uses the service to call the use cases

```
@Controller
public class ProductsController {

  private final ProductService productService;        We use DI through the
                                                      controller's constructor
  public ProductsController(                          parameters to get the service
    ProductService productService) {    ←───────      bean from the Spring context.
    this.productService = productService;
  }

}
```

Now we expose the first use case: displaying the product list on a page. This functionality should be straightforward. We use a `Model` parameter to send the data from the controller to the view, as you learned in section 8.1. The following listing presents the implementation for the controller action.

Listing 8.8   Sending the list of products to the view

We map the controller action to the /products path. The @RequestMapping annotation, by default, uses the HTTP GET method.

```
@Controller
public class ProductsController {

  private final ProductService productService;

  public ProductsController(ProductService productService) {
    this.productService = productService;
  }
                                                      We define a Model parameter that we
                                                      use to send the data to the view.
  @RequestMapping("/products")
  public String viewProducts(Model model) {    ←──    We get the product list
    var products = productService.findAll();   ←──    from the service.
    model.addAttribute("products", products);  ←──
                                                      We send the product list to the view.
    return "products.html";    ←───
  }                                     We return the view name, which will be taken
}                                       and rendered by the dispatcher servlet.
```

To display the products in the view, we define the products.html page in the "resources/templates" folder of the project, as you learned in section 8.1. The following listing shows you the content of the "products.html" file, which takes the list of products the controller sends and displays it in an HTML table.

Listing 8.9   Displaying the products on the page

```
<!DOCTYPE html>
<html lang="en" xmlns:th="http://www.thymeleaf.org">    ◁──── We define the
    <head>                                                     "th" prefix to use the
        <meta charset="UTF-8">                                 Thymeleaf capabilities.
        <title>Home Page</title>
    </head>
    <body>
        <h1>Products</h1>

        <h2>View products</h2>

        <table>
            <tr>
                <th>PRODUCT NAME</th>         We define a static
                <th>PRODUCT PRICE</th>        header for our table.
            </tr>
            <tr th:each="p: ${products}" >   ◁────
                <td th:text="${p.name}"></td>       We use the th:each feature
                <td th:text="${p.price}"></td>      from Thymeleaf to iterate on
            </tr>                                    the collection and display a table
        </table>                                     row for each product in the list.
    </body>
</html>
```

We display the name and the price of each product on one row.

Figure 8.10 presents the flow for calling the /products path with HTTP GET on the Spring MVC diagram:

1 The client sends an HTTP request for the /products path.
2 The dispatcher servlet uses the handler mapping to find the controller's action to call for the /products path.
3 The dispatcher servlet calls the controller's action.
4 The controller requests the product list from the service and sends it to be rendered with the view.
5 The view is rendered into an HTTP response.
6 The HTTP response is sent back to the client.

But we still need to implement the second use case before we test the app's functionality. We'll see nothing more than an empty table if we don't have an option to add a product to the list. Let's change the controller and add an action to allow adding a product to the product list. Listing 8.10 presents the definition of this action.

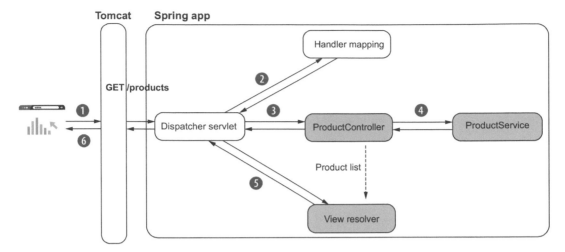

Figure 8.10   When calling /products with HTTP GET, the controller gets the product list from the service and sends it to the view. The HTTP response contains the HTML table with the products from the list.

Listing 8.10   Implementing the action method for adding a product

```
@Controller
public class ProductsController {

  // Omitted code

  @RequestMapping(path = "/products",
               method = RequestMethod.POST)
  public String addProduct(
     @RequestParam String name,
     @RequestParam double price,
     Model model
  ) {
    Product p = new Product();
    p.setName(name);
    p.setPrice(price);
    productService.addProduct(p);

    var products = productService.findAll();
    model.addAttribute("products", products);

    return "products.html";
  }
}
```

We map the controller action to the /products path. We use the method attribute of the @RequestMapping annotation to change the HTTP method to POST.

We get the name and the price for the product to add using request parameters.

We build a new Product instance and add it to the list by calling the service use case method.

We get the list of products and send it to the view.

We return the name of the view to be rendered.

We used the attribute method of the @RequestMapping annotation to specify the HTTP method. If you don't set a method, by default @RequestMapping uses HTTP GET. But because both the path and the method are essential for any HTTP call, we want to always confirm both. For this reason, developers usually use dedicated annotations for each HTTP method instead of @RequestMapping. For apps, you'll often find developers using @GetMapping to map a GET request to an action, @PostMapping for a request using HTTP POST, and so on. We'll also change our example to use these dedicated annotations for HTTP methods. The following listing presents the controller class's full content, including the changes on the mapping annotations for the actions.

Listing 8.11 The `ProductController` class

```java
@Controller
public class ProductsController {

  private final ProductService productService;

  public ProductsController(ProductService productService) {
    this.productService = productService;
  }

  @GetMapping("/products")
  public String viewProducts(Model model) {
    var products = productService.findAll();
    model.addAttribute("products", products);

    return "products.html";
  }

  @PostMapping("/products")
  public String addProduct(
      @RequestParam String name,
      @RequestParam double price,
      Model model
  ) {
    Product p = new Product();
    p.setName(name);
    p.setPrice(price);
    productService.addProduct(p);

    var products = productService.findAll();
    model.addAttribute("products", products);

    return "products.html";
  }
}
```

@GetMapping maps the HTTP GET request with a specific path to the controller's action.

@PostMapping maps the HTTP POST request with a specific path to the controller's action.

We can also change the view to allow the user to call the controller's HTTP POST action and add a product to the list. We'll use an HTML form to make this HTTP request. The following listing presents the changes we need to make on the products.html page (our view) to add the HTML form. The result of the page designed with listing 8.12 is shown in figure 8.11.

Listing 8.12   **Adding an HTML form to the view for adding a product to the list**

```
<!DOCTYPE html>
<html lang="en" xmlns:th="http://www.thymeleaf.org">
    <head>
        <meta charset="UTF-8">
        <title>Home Page</title>
    </head>
    <body>

        <!-- Omitted code -->

        <h2>Add a product</h2>
        <form action="/products" method="post">
          Name: <input
                    type="text"
                    name="name"><br />
          Price: <input
                    type="number"
                    step="any"
                    name="price"><br />
          <button type="submit">Add product</button>
        </form>
    </body>
</html>
```

When submitted, the HTML form makes a POST request for path /products.

An input component allows the user to set the name of the product. The value in the component is sent as a request parameter with the key "name."

The user uses a submit button to submit the form.

An input component allows the user to set the price of the product. The value in the component is sent as a request parameter with the key "price."

Run and test the app. You access the page in your browser on http://localhost:8080/products, and you should be able to add new products and see those already added. Figure 8.11 shows the result.

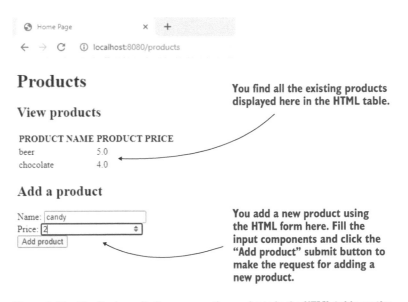

Figure 8.11   The final result. A user sees the products in the HTML table on the page and can add a new product through the HTML form.

In our example, I used the @RequestParameter annotation, which you learned in section 8.2.1. I used this annotation here to make it clear how the client sends the data. But sometimes Spring allows you to omit code. For example, you could use a Product as a parameter of the controller's action directly, as presented in listing 8.13. Because the request parameters' names are the same as the Product class attributes' names, Spring knows to match them and automatically creates the object. For someone who already knows Spring, this is excellent because it spares you from writing code lines. But beginners might get confused by all these details. Say you find an example in an article that uses this syntax. It might be unclear where the Product instance comes from. If you've just begun learning Spring and find yourself in such a situation, my advice is to be aware that Spring tends to have plenty of syntaxes to hide as much code as possible. Whenever you find a syntax you don't clearly understand in an example or article, try finding the framework specification details.

This small change is separated in a project named "sq-ch8-ex6" if you want to test and compare it with the project "sq-ch8-ex5."

> **Listing 8.13 Directly using the model as a parameter of the controller's action**

```
@Controller
public class ProductsController {

   // Omitted code

   @PostMapping("/products")
   public String addProduct(
       Product p,          ◁——
       Model model
   ) {
     productService.addProduct(p);

     var products = productService.findAll();
     model.addAttribute("products", products);

     return "products.html";
   }
}
```

You can use the model class as a parameter of the controller's action directly. Spring knows to create the instance based on the request attributes. The model class needs to have a default constructor to allow Spring to create the instance before calling the action method.

Summary

- Today's web apps have dynamic pages (also referred to as dynamic views). A dynamic page might display different content for different requests.
- To know what to display, a dynamic view gets the variable data from the controller.
- An easy way to implement dynamic pages in Spring apps is using a template engine such as Thymeleaf. Alternatives to Thymeleaf are Mustache, FreeMarker, and Java Server Pages (JSP).
- A template engine is a dependency that provides your app with the capability to easily get the data the controller sends and display it on the view.

- The client can send data to the server through request parameters or path variables. A controller's action gets the details the client sends in parameters annotated with `@RequestParam` or `@PathVariable`.
- A request parameter can be optional.
- You should only use path variables for mandatory data the client sends.
- A path and an HTTP method identify an HTTP request. The HTTP method is represented by a verb that identifies the client's intention. The essential HTTP methods you'll often find in production apps are GET, POST, PUT, PATCH, and DELETE.
    - GET expresses the client's intention to retrieve data without changing data on the backend.
    - POST expresses the client's intention to add new data on the server side.
    - PUT expresses the client's intention to change a data record on the backend entirely.
    - PATCH expresses the client's intention to change a part of a data record on the backend.
    - DELETE expresses the client's intention to remove data on the backend.
- Through a browser's HTML form process directly, you can use only HTTP GET and HTTP POST. To use other HTTP methods such as DELETE or PUT, you need to implement the call using a client language such as JavaScript.

Using the
Spring web scopes

9

This chapter covers

- Using the Spring web scopes
- Implementing a simple login functionality for a web app
- Redirecting from one page to another in a web app

In chapter 5, we discussed Spring bean scopes. You learned that Spring manages a bean's life cycle differently depending on how you declare the bean in the Spring context. In this chapter, we'll add some new ways Spring manages the beans in the context. You'll learn Spring has custom ways to manage instances for web apps by using the HTTP request as a point of reference. Spring is pretty cool, isn't it?

In any Spring app, you can choose to declare a bean as one of the following:

- *Singleton*—The default bean scope in Spring, for which the framework uniquely identifies each instance with a name in the context
- *Prototype*—The bean scope in Spring, for which the framework only manages the type and creates a new instance of that class every time someone requests it (directly from the context or through wiring or auto-wiring).

In this chapter, you'll learn that in web apps you can use other bean scopes that are relevant only to web applications. We call them *web scopes*:

- *Request scope*—Spring creates an instance of the bean class for every HTTP request. The instance exists only for that specific HTTP request.
- *Session scope*—Spring creates an instance and keeps the instance in the server's memory for the full HTTP session. Spring links the instance in the context with the client's session.
- *Application scope*—The instance is unique in the app's context, and it's available while the app is running.

To teach you how these web scopes work in a Spring application, we'll work on an example in which we implement a login functionality. Most of the web apps today offer their users the possibility to log in and access an account, so the example is also relevant from a real-world perspective.

In section 9.1, we'll use a request-scoped bean to take the user's credentials for login and make sure the app uses them only for the login request. Then, in section 9.2, we'll use a session-scoped bean to store all the relevant details we need to keep for the logged-in user as long as the user remains logged in. In section 9.3, we'll use the application-scoped bean to add a capability to count logins. Figure 9.1 shows you the steps we take to implement this app.

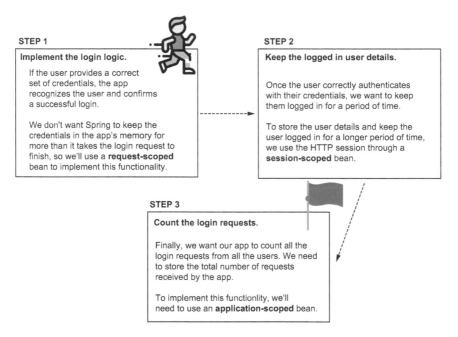

Figure 9.1   We'll implement the login functionality in three steps. For each step we implement, we'll need to use a different bean scope. In section 9.1, we'll use a request-scoped bean to implement the login logic without risking storing the credentials for longer than the login request. We'll then decide what details we need to store for the authenticated user in a session-scoped bean. Finally, we'll implement a feature to count all the login requests, and we'll use an application-scoped bean to keep the number.

9.1 Using the request scope in a Spring web app

In this section, you'll learn how to use request-scoped beans in Spring web apps. As you learned in chapters 7 and 8, web apps are focused on HTTP requests and responses. For this reason, and often in web apps, certain functionalities are easier to manage if Spring offers you a way to manage the bean life cycle in relationship with the HTTP request.

A request-scoped bean is an object managed by Spring, for which the framework creates a new instance for every HTTP request. The app can use the instance only for the request that created it. Any new HTTP request (from the same or other clients) creates and uses a different instance of the same class (figure 9.2).

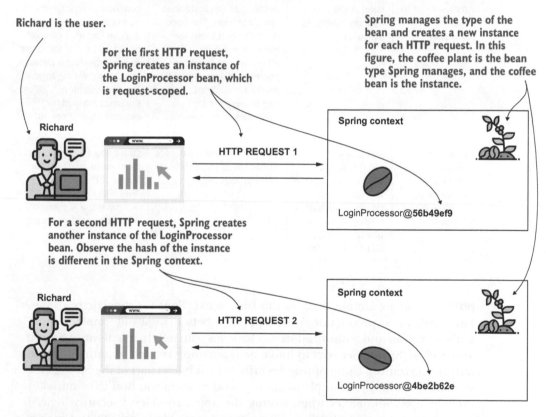

Figure 9.2 For every HTTP request, Spring provides a new instance for the request-scoped bean. When using a request-scoped bean, you can be sure the data you add on the bean is available only on the HTTP request that created the bean. Spring manages the bean type (the plant) and uses it to get instances (coffee beans) for each new request.

Let's demonstrate the use of a request-scoped bean in an example. We'll implement a web application's login functionality, and we'll use a request-scoped bean to manage the user's credentials for the login logic.

Key aspects of request-scoped beans

Before diving into implementing a Spring app that uses request-scoped beans, I'd like to shortly enumerate here the key aspects of using this bean scope. These aspects will help you analyze whether a request-scoped bean is the right approach in a real-world scenario. Keep in mind the very relevant aspects of request-scoped beans, explained in the following table.

Fact	Consequence	To consider	To avoid
Spring creates a new instance for every HTTP request from any client.	Spring creates a lot of instances of this bean in the app's memory during its execution.	The number of instances is usually not a big problem because these instances are short-lived. The app doesn't need them for more than the time the HTTP request needs to complete. Once the HTTP request completes, the app releases the instances, and they are garbage-collected.	However, make sure you don't implement a time-consuming logic Spring needs to execute to create the instance (like getting data from a database or implementing a network call). Avoid writing logic in the constructor or a @PostConstruct method for request-scoped beans.
Only one request can use an instance of a request-scoped bean.	Instances of request-scoped beans are not prone to multithread-related issues as only one thread (the one of the request) can access them.	You can use the instance's attributes to store data used by request.	Don't use synchronization techniques for the attributes of these beans. These techniques would be redundant, and they only affect the performance of your app.

NOTE   A login example, such as this one, is excellent for didactic purposes. However, in a production-ready app, it's better to avoid implementing authentication and authorization mechanisms yourself. In a real-world Spring app, we use Spring Security to implement anything related to authentication and authorization. Using Spring Security (which is also part of the Spring eco-system) simplifies your implementations and ensures you don't (by mistake) introduce vulnerabilities when writing the application-level security logic. I recommend you also read *Spring Security in Action* (Manning, 2020), which is another book I authored and that describes, in detail, how to use Spring Security to protect your Spring app.

To make things straightforward, we will consider a set of credentials that we bake into our application. In a real-world app, the app stores the users in a database. It also encrypts the passwords to protect them. For now, we focus only on the purpose of this chapter: discussing the Spring web bean scopes. Later, in chapters 11 and 12, you'll learn more about storing data in a database.

Let's create a Spring Boot project and add the needed dependencies. You will find this example in the project "sq-ch9-ex1." You can add the dependencies directly when creating the project (for example, using start.spring.io) or afterward in your pom.xml. For this example, we will use the web dependency and Thymeleaf as a templating engine (like we did in chapter 8). The next code snippet shows the dependencies you need to have in your pom.xml file:

```
<dependency>
    <groupId>org.springframework.boot</groupId>
    <artifactId>spring-boot-starter-thymeleaf</artifactId>
</dependency>
<dependency>
    <groupId>org.springframework.boot</groupId>
    <artifactId>spring-boot-starter-web</artifactId>
</dependency>
```

We'll create a page that contains a login form asking for a user's name and password. The app compares the username and the password with a set of credentials it knows (in my case, user "natalie" with password "password"). If we provide correct credentials (they match with the credentials the app knows), then the page displays a message "You are now logged in" under the login form. If the credentials we provide are not correct, then the app displays a message: "Login failed."

As you learned in chapters 7 and 8, we need to implement a page (representing our view) and a controller class. The controller sends the message it needs to display to the view according to the login's result (figure 9.3).

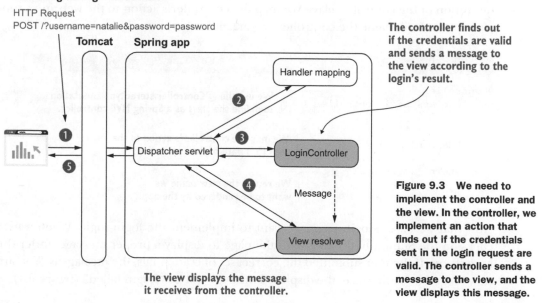

The client sends an HTTP request containing the login credentials.

HTTP Request
POST /?username=natalie&password=password

The controller finds out if the credentials are valid and sends a message to the view according to the login's result.

The view displays the message it receives from the controller.

Figure 9.3   We need to implement the controller and the view. In the controller, we implement an action that finds out if the credentials sent in the login request are valid. The controller sends a message to the view, and the view displays this message.

Listing 9.1 shows the HTML login page that defines the view in our app. As you
learned in chapter 8, you have to store the page in the resources/templates folder of
your Spring Boot project. Let's name the page "login.html." To display the message
with the logic's result, we need to send a parameter from the controller to the view. I
named this parameter "message," as you can see in the following listing, where I used
the syntax ${message} to display this in a paragraph under the login form.

Listing 9.1   The definition of the login page login.html

```
<!DOCTYPE html>
<html lang="en" xmlns:th="http://www.thymeleaf.org">
<head>
  <meta charset="UTF-8">
  <title>Login</title>
</head>
<body>
  <form action="/" method="post">
    Username: <input type="text" name="username" /><br />
    Password: <input type="password" name="password" /><br />
    <button type="submit">Log in</button>
  </form>

  <p th:text="${message}"></p>
</body>
</html>
```

We define the "th" Thymeleaf prefix to use the templating engine's capabilities.

We define an HTML form to send the credentials to the server.

The input fields are used to write the credentials, username, and password.

When the user clicks the Submit button, the client makes an HTTP POST request with the credentials.

We display a message with the result of the login request under the HTML form.

A controller action needs to get the HTTP request (from the dispatcher servlet, as you
learned in chapters 7 and 8), so let's define the controller and the action that receives
the HTTP request for the page we created in listing 9.1. In listing 9.2, you find the
definition of the controller class. We map the controller's action to the web app's root
path ("/"). I will name the controller LoginController.

Listing 9.2   The controller's action mapped to the root path

```
@Controller
public class LoginController {

  @GetMapping("/")
  public String loginGet() {
    return "login.html";
  }
}
```

We use the @Controller stereotype annotation to define the class as a Spring MVC controller.

We map the controller's action to the root ("/") path of the application.

We return the view name we want to be rendered by the app.

Now that we have a login page, we want to implement the login logic. When a user
clicks on the Submit button, we want the page to display a proper message under the
login form. If the user submitted the correct set of credentials, the message is "You are
now logged in"; otherwise, the displayed message will be "Login failed" (figure 9.4).

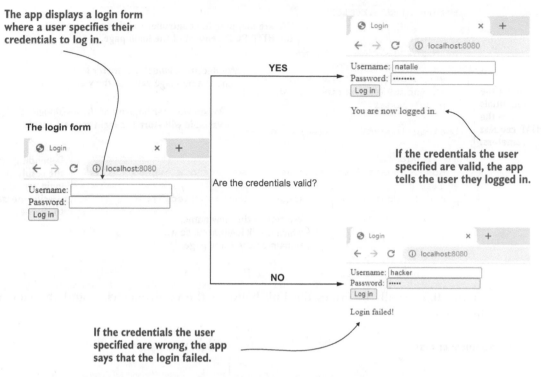

The app displays a login form where a user specifies their credentials to log in.

The login form

YES

Are the credentials valid?

If the credentials the user specified are valid, the app tells the user they logged in.

NO

If the credentials the user specified are wrong, the app says that the login failed.

Figure 9.4 The functionality we implement in this section. The page displays a login form for the user. Then the user provides valid credentials, and the app displays a message that they successfully logged in. If the user provides incorrect credentials, the app tells the user that the login failed.

To process the HTTP POST request that the HTML form creates when the user clicks on the Submit button, we need to add one more action to our LoginController. This action takes the client's request parameters (the username and the password) and sends a message to the view according to the login result. Listing 9.3 shows you the definition of the controller's action, which we'll map to the HTTP POST login request.

Notice that we haven't implemented the login logic. In the next listing, we take the request and send a message in response according to a variable representing the request's result. But this variable (in listing 9.3 named loggedIn) is always "false." In the next listings in this section, we complete this action by adding a call to the login logic. This login logic will return the login result based on the credentials the client sent in the request.

Listing 9.3 The controller's login action

```
@Controller
public class LoginController {

    @GetMapping("/")
    public String loginGet() {
```

```
        return "login.html";
    }                                    We are mapping the controller's action to
                                         the HTTP POST request of the login page.
    @PostMapping("/")      ◄
    public String loginPost(             We declare a Model parameter to
        @RequestParam String username,   send the message value to the view.
        @RequestParam String password,
        Model model          ◄
    ) {                                  When we later implement the login logic, this
        boolean loggedIn = false;   ◄    variable will store the login request result.

        if (loggedIn) {
            model.addAttribute("message", "You are now logged in.");
        } else {
            model.addAttribute("message", "Login failed!");
        }
                                   We return the view name,
                                   which is still login.html, so we
        return "login.html";  ◄    remain on the same page.
    }
}
```

We get the credentials from the HTTP request parameters.

Depending on the result of the login, we send a specific message to the view.

Figure 9.5 visually describes the link between the controller class and the view we implemented.

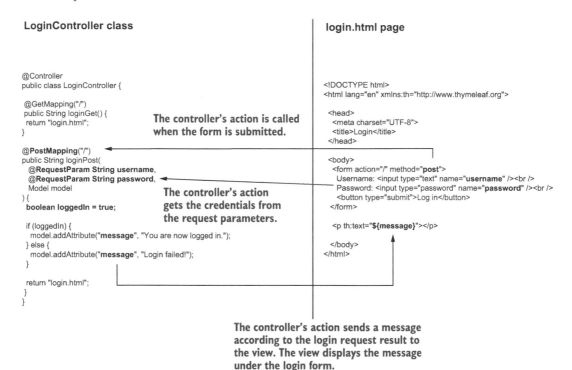

Figure 9.5   The dispatcher servlet calls the controller's action when someone submits the HTML login form. The controller's action gets the credentials from the HTTP request parameters. According to the login result, the controller sends a message to the view, and the view displays this message under the HTML form.

Now we have a controller and a view, but where is the request scope in all of this? The only class we wrote is the LoginController, and we left it a singleton, which is the default Spring scope. We don't need to change the scope for LoginController as long as it doesn't store any detail in its attributes. But remember, we need to implement the login logic. The login logic depends on the user's credentials, and we have to take into consideration two things about these credentials:

1 The credentials are sensitive details, and you don't want to store them in the app's memory for longer than the login request.
2 More users with different credentials might attempt to log in simultaneously.

Considering these two points, we need to make sure that if we use a bean for implementing the login logic, each instance is unique for each HTTP request. We need to use a request-scoped bean. We'll extend the app as presented in figure 9.5. We add a request-scoped bean LoginProcessor, which takes the credentials on the request and validates them (figure 9.6).

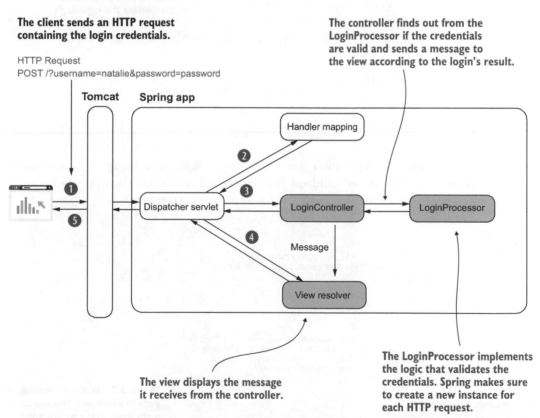

The client sends an HTTP request containing the login credentials.

HTTP Request
POST /?username=natalie&password=password

The controller finds out from the LoginProcessor if the credentials are valid and sends a message to the view according to the login's result.

The view displays the message it receives from the controller.

The LoginProcessor implements the logic that validates the credentials. Spring makes sure to create a new instance for each HTTP request.

Figure 9.6 The LoginProcessor bean is request-scoped. Spring makes sure to create a new instance for each HTTP request. The bean implements the login logic. The controller calls a method it implements. The method returns true if the credentials are valid and false otherwise. Based on the value the LoginProcessor returns, the LoginController sends the right message to the view.

Listing 9.4 shows the implementation of the LoginProcessor class. To change the scope of the bean, we use the @RequestScoped annotation. Of course, we still need to make a bean of this class type in the Spring context by using the @Bean annotation in either a configuration class or a stereotype annotation. I chose to annotate the class with the @Component stereotype annotation.

> **Listing 9.4   Request-scoped LoginProcessor bean implementing the login logic**

```
                    We annotate the class with a stereotype
                    annotation to tell Spring this is a bean.        We use the @RequestScope annotation to change the
                                                                     bean's scope to request scope. This way, Spring creates
     └─▷ @Component                                                  a new instance of the class for every HTTP request.
         @RequestScope              ◁──────────────────────
         public class LoginProcessor {

             private String username;         The bean stores the
             private String password;         credentials as attributes.

             public boolean login() {            ◁───────────
                 String username = this.getUsername();          The bean defines a method for
                 String password = this.getPassword();          implementing the login logic.

                 if ("natalie".equals(username) && "password".equals(password)) {
                     return true;
                 } else {
                     return false;
                 }
             }

             // omitted getters and setters
         }
```

You can run the application and access the login page using the localhost:8080 address in your browser's address bar. Figure 9.7 shows you the app's behavior after accessing the page and for using valid and incorrect credentials.

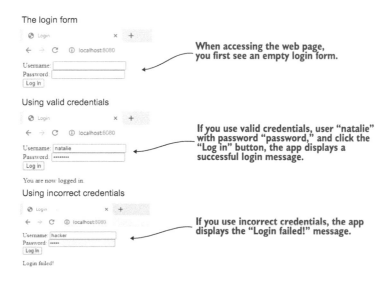

Figure 9.7   When accessing the page in a browser, the app shows a login form. You can use valid credentials, and the app displays a successful login message. If you use incorrect credentials, the app displays a "Login failed!" message.

9.2 *Using the session scope in a Spring web app*

In this section, we discuss session-scoped beans. When you enter a web app and log in, you expect to then surf through that app's pages, and the app still remembers you've logged in. A session-scoped bean is an object managed by Spring, for which Spring creates an instance and links it to the HTTP session. Once a client sends a request to the server, the server reserves a place in the memory for this request, for the whole duration of their session. Spring creates an instance of a session-scoped bean when the HTTP session is created for a specific client. That instance can be reused for the same client while it still has the HTTP session active. The data you store in the session-scoped bean attribute is available for all the client's requests throughout an HTTP session. This approach of storing the data allows you to store information about what users do while they're surfing through the pages of your app.

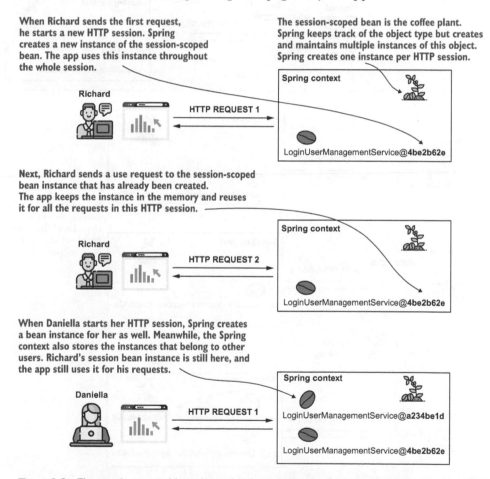

Figure 9.8   The session-scoped bean is used to keep a bean in the context throughout the client's full HTTP session. Spring creates an instance of a session-scoped bean for each HTTP session a client opens. The client accesses the same instance for all the requests sent through the same HTTP session. Each user has their own session and accesses different instances of the session-scoped bean.

Take time to compare figure 9.8, which presents the session-scoped bean, with figure 9.2, which presents the request-scoped bean. Figure 9.9 summarizes the comparison between the two approaches as well. While for a request-scoped bean Spring creates a

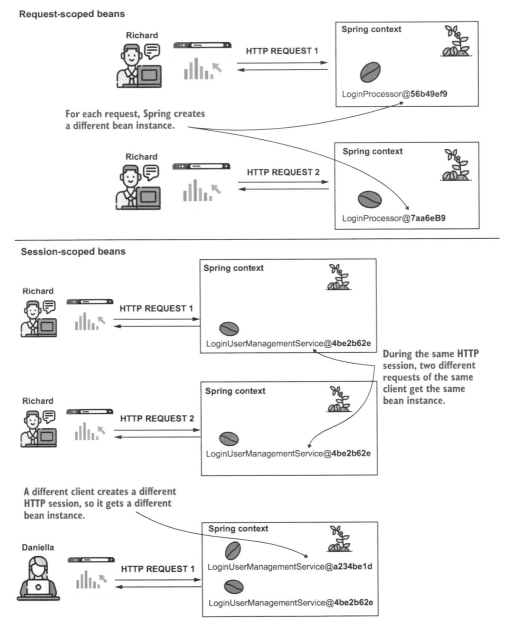

Figure 9.9   A comparison between the request-scoped and session-scoped beans to help you visualize the differences between these two web bean scopes. You use request-scoped beans when you want Spring to create a new instance for each request. You use a session-scoped bean when you want to keep the bean (together with any details it holds) throughout the client's HTTP session.

new instance for every HTTP request, for a session-scoped bean, Spring creates only one instance per HTTP session. A session-scoped bean allows us to store data shared by multiple requests of the same client.

A couple of features you can implement using session-scoped beans include the following examples:

- *A login*—Keeps details of the authenticated user while they visit different parts of your app and send multiple requests
- *An online shopping cart*—Users visit multiple places in your app, searching for products they add to the cart. The cart remembers all the products the client added.

Key aspects of session-scoped beans

Like we did for the request-scoped beans, let's analyze the key characteristics of the session-scoped beans you need to consider when planning to use them in a production app.

Fact	Consequence	To consider	To avoid
The session-scoped bean instances are kept for the entire HTTP session.	They have a longer life, and they are less frequently garbage-collected than the request-scoped beans.	The app keeps the data you store in the session-scoped beans for a more extended period.	Avoid keeping too much data on the session. It can potentially become a performance problem. Moreover, never store sensitive details (like passwords, private keys, or any other secret detail) in session-bean attributes.
Multiple requests can share the session-scoped bean instance.	If the same client issues multiple concurrent requests that change the data on the instance, you may encounter multithreading-related issues like race conditions.	When you know such a scenario is possible, you might need to use synchronization techniques to avoid concurrency. However, I generally recommend you see if this can be avoided and keep synchronization only as a last resort when it can't be avoided.	
The session-scoped beans are a way to share data among requests by keeping the data on the server side.	The logic you implement might imply requests become dependent one on the other.	When keeping details stateful in one app's memory, you make clients dependent on that specific app instance. Before deciding to implement some feature with a session-scoped bean, consider alternatives, such as storing the data you want to share in a database instead of the session. This way, you can leave the HTTP requests independent one from another.	

We continue to use a session-scoped bean to make our app aware that a user logged in and recognize them as a logged-in user while they access different pages of the app. This way, the example teaches you all the relevant details you need to know when working with production applications.

Let's change the application we implemented in section 9.1 to display a page that only logged-in users can access. Once a user logs in, the app redirects them to this page, which displays a welcome message containing the logged-in username and offers the user the option to log out by clicking a link.

These are the steps we need to take to implement this change (figure 9.10):

1 Create a session-scoped bean to keep the logged-in user's details.
2 Create the page a user can only access after login.
3 Make sure a user cannot access the page created at point 1 without logging in first.
4 Redirect the user from login to the main page after successful authentication.

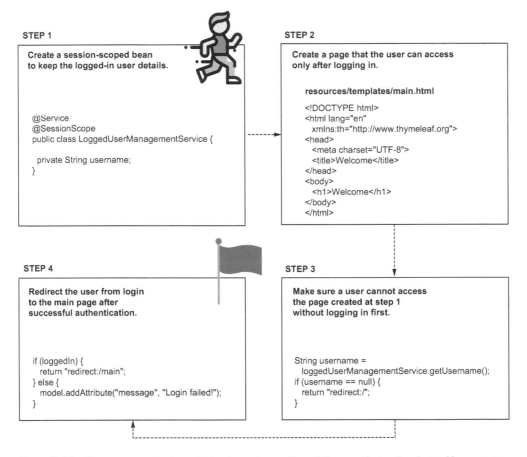

Figure 9.10 We use a session-bean to implement a section of the app that only a logged-in user can access. Once the user authenticates, the app redirects them to a page they can only access once authenticated. If the user tries to access this page before authentication, the app redirects them to the login form.

I separated the changes for this example in the project "sq-ch9-ex2."

Fortunately, creating a session-scoped bean in Spring is as simple as using the `@SessionScope` annotation with the bean class. Let's create a new class, `LoggedUser-ManagementService`, and make it session-scoped, as presented in the following listing.

Listing 9.5 Defining a session-scoped bean to keep the logged user details

We add the @Service stereotype annotation to instruct Spring to manage this class as a bean in its context.

We use the @SessionScope annotation to change the scope of the bean to session.

```
@Service
@SessionScope
public class LoggedUserManagementService {

  private String username;

  // Omitted getters and setters
}
```

Every time a user successfully logs in, we store its name in this bean's username attribute. We auto-wire the `LoggedUserManagementService` bean in the `LoginProcessor` class, which we implemented in section 9.1 to take care of the authentication logic, as shown in the following listing.

Listing 9.6 Using the `LoggedUserManagementService` bean in the login logic

```
@Component
@RequestScope
public class LoginProcessor {

  private final LoggedUserManagementService loggedUserManagementService;

  private String username;
  private String password;

  public LoginProcessor(
    LoggedUserManagementService loggedUserManagementService) {
    this.loggedUserManagementService = loggedUserManagementService;
  }

  public boolean login() {
    String username = this.getUsername();
    String password = this.getPassword();

    boolean loginResult = false;
    if ("natalie".equals(username) && "password".equals(password)) {
      loginResult = true;
      loggedUserManagementService.setUsername(username);
    }

    return loginResult;
  }

  // Omitted getters and setters
}
```

We auto-wire the LoggedUserManagementService bean.

We store the username on the LoggedUserManagementService bean.

Observe that the LoginProcessor bean stays request-scoped. We still use Spring to create this instance for each login request. We only need the username and password attributes' values during the request to execute the authentication logic.

Because the LoggedUserManagementService bean is session-scoped, the username value will now be accessible throughout the entire HTTP session. You can use this value to know if someone is logged in, and who. You don't have to worry about the case where multiple users are logged in; the application framework makes sure to link each HTTP request to the correct session. Figure 9.11 visually describes the login flow.

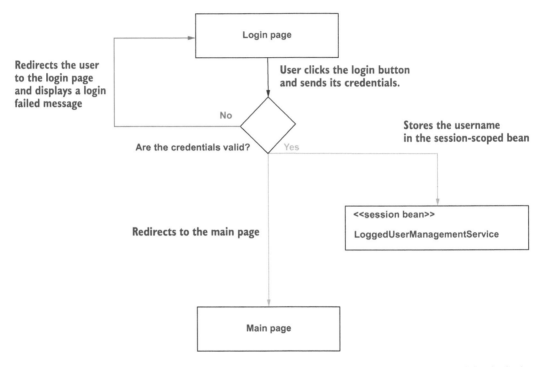

Figure 9.11   The login flow implemented in the example. When the user submits their credentials, the login process begins. If the user's credentials are correct, the username is stored in the session-scoped bean, and the app redirects the user to the main page. If the credentials are not valid, the app redirects the user back to the login page and displays a failed login message.

Now we create a new page and make sure a user can access it only if they have already logged in. We define a new controller (that we'll call MainController) for the new page. We'll define an action and map it to the /main path. To make sure a user can access this path only if they logged in, we check if the LoggedUserManagementService bean stores any username. If it doesn't, we redirect the user to the login page. To redirect the user to another page, the controller action needs to return the string "redirect:" followed by the path to which the action wants to redirect the user. Figure 9.12 visually presents the logic behind the main page.

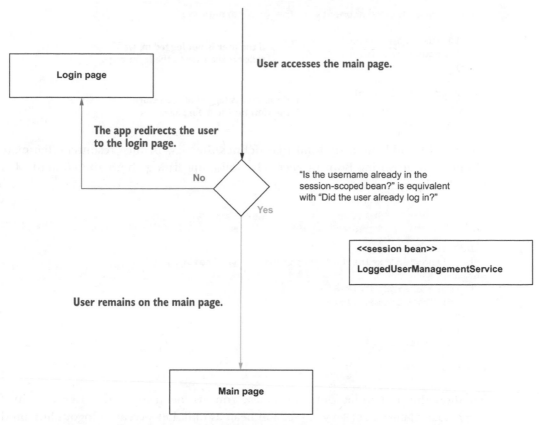

User accesses the main page.

Login page

**The app redirects the user
to the login page.**

No

"Is the username already in the
session-scoped bean?" is equivalent
with "Did the user already log in?"

Yes

<<session bean>>

LoggedUserManagementService

User remains on the main page.

Main page

**Figure 9.12 Someone can access the main page only after they are authenticated. When the app
authenticates the user, it stores the username in the session-scoped bean. This way, the app knows the user
had already logged in. When someone accesses the main page, and the username is not in the session-scoped
bean (they did not authenticate), the app redirects them to the login page.**

The following listing shows the `MainController` class.

Listing 9.7 The MainController class

```
@Controller
public class MainController {                    We auto-wire the LoggedUserManagementService
                                                 bean to find out if the user already logged in.
  private final LoggedUserManagementService loggedUserManagementService;

  public MainController(
    LoggedUserManagementService loggedUserManagementService) {
    this.loggedUserManagementService = loggedUserManagementService;
  }

  @GetMapping("/main")             We take the username value,
  public String home() {           which should be different than
    String username =              null if someone logged in.
```

```
        loggedUserManagementService.getUsername();

    if (username == null) {        ◁────┐  If the user is not logged in, we
        return "redirect:/";            │  redirect the user to the login page.
    }

    return "main.html";        ◁────┐  If the user is logged in, we return
  }                                 │  the view for the main page.
}
```

You need to add the main.html that defines the view in the "resources/templates" folder of your Spring Boot project. The following listing shows the content of the main.html page.

Listing 9.8   The content of the main.html page

```
<!DOCTYPE html>
<html lang="en" xmlns:th="http://www.thymeleaf.org">
<head>
    <meta charset="UTF-8">
    <title>Welcome</title>
</head>
<body>
    <h1>Welcome</h1>
</body>
</html>
```

To allow the user to log out is also easy. You just need to set the username in the LoggedUserManagementService session bean as null. Let's create a logout link on the page and also add the logged-in username in the welcome message. The following listing shows the changes to the main.html page that defines our view.

Listing 9.9   Adding a logout link to the main.html page

```
<!DOCTYPE html>
<html lang="en" xmlns:th="http://www.thymeleaf.org">
<head>                                                   We get the username
    <meta charset="UTF-8">                               from the controller
    <title>Login</title>                                 and display it on the
</head>                                                   page in the welcome
<body>                                                   message.
    <h1>Welcome, <span th:text="${username}"></span></h1>  ◁──┘
    <a href="/main?logout">Log out</a>   ◁──┐
</body>                                      │  We add a link on the page that sets an HTTP
</html>                                      │  request parameter named "logout." When the
                                            │  controller gets this parameter, it will erase the
                                            │  value of the username from the session.
```

These main.html page changes also assume some changes in the controller for the functionality to be complete. The next listing shows how to get the logout request parameter in the controller's action and send the username to the view where it is displayed on the page.

Listing 9.10 Logging out the user based on the logout request parameter

We get the logout request parameter if present.

```
@Controller
public class MainController {

  // Omitted code

  @GetMapping("/main")
  public String home(
      @RequestParam(required = false) String logout,
      Model model
  ) {
    if (logout != null) {
      loggedUserManagementService.setUsername(null);
    }

    String username = loggedUserManagementService.getUsername();

    if (username == null) {
      return "redirect:/";
    }

    model.addAttribute("username" , username);
    return "main.html";
  }
}
```

We add a Model parameter to send the username to the view.

If the logout parameter is present, we erase the username from the LoggedUserManagementService bean.

We send the username to the view.

To complete the app, we'd like to change the LoginController to redirect users to the main page once they authenticate. To achieve this result, we need to change the LoginController's action, as presented in the following listing.

Listing 9.11 Redirecting the user to the main page after login

```
@Controller
public class LoginController {

  // Omitted code

  @PostMapping("/")
  public String loginPost(
      @RequestParam String username,
      @RequestParam String password,
      Model model
  ) {
    loginProcessor.setUsername(username);
    loginProcessor.setPassword(password);
    boolean loggedIn = loginProcessor.login();
```

```
  if (loggedIn) {
    return "redirect:/main";
  }

  model.addAttribute("message", "Login failed!");
  return "login.html";
  }
}
```

When the user successfully authenticates, the app redirects them to the main page.

Now you can start the application and test the login. When you provide the correct credentials, the app redirects you to the main page (figure 9.13). Click the Logout link, and the app redirects you back to the login. If you try to access the main page without authenticating, the app redirects you to log in.

Figure 9.13   This flow between the two pages. When the user logs in, the app redirects them to the main page. The user can click on the logout link, and the app redirects them back to the login form.

9.3   *Using the application scope in a Spring web app*

In this section, we discuss the application scope. I want to mention its existence, make you aware of how it works, and emphasize that it's better not to use it in a production app. All client requests share an application-scoped bean (figure 9.14).

The application scope is close to how a singleton works. The difference is that you can't have more instances of the same type in the context and that we always use the HTTP requests as a reference point when discussing the life cycle of web scopes (including the application scope). We face the same concurrency problems we discussed in chapter 5 for the singleton beans for application-scoped beans: it's better to have immutable attributes for the singleton beans. The same advice is applicable to an application-scoped bean. But if you make the attributes immutable, then you can directly use a singleton bean instead.

Generally, I recommend developers avoid using application-scoped beans. It's better to directly use a persistence layer, such as a database (which you'll learn in chapter 11).

It's always best to see an example to understand the case. Let's change the application we worked on in this chapter and add a feature that counts the login attempts. You will find this example in the project "sq-ch9-ex3."

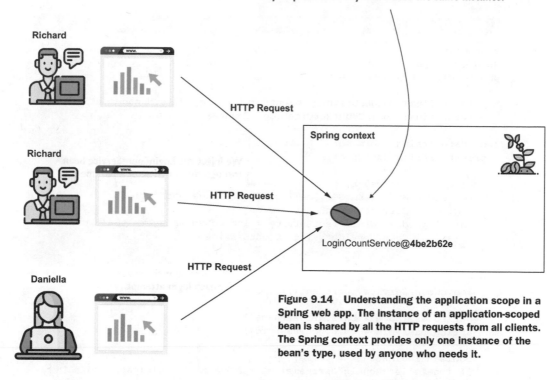

Figure 9.14 **Understanding the application scope in a Spring web app. The instance of an application-scoped bean is shared by all the HTTP requests from all clients. The Spring context provides only one instance of the bean's type, used by anyone who needs it.**

Because we have to count the login attempts from all users, we'll store the count in an application-scoped bean. Let's create a LoginCountService application-scoped bean that stores the count in an attribute. The following listing shows the definition of this class.

Listing 9.12   The LoginCountService class counts the login attempts

```
@Service
@ApplicationScope
public class LoginCountService {

  private int count;

  public void increment() {
    count++;
  }

  public int getCount() {
    return count;
  }
}
```

The @ApplicationScope annotation changes the scope of this bean to the application scope.

The LoginProcessor can then auto-wire this bean and call the increment() method for any new login attempt, as presented in the following listing.

Listing 9.13   Incrementing the login count for every login request

```
@Component
@RequestScope
public class LoginProcessor {

  private final LoggedUserManagementService loggedUserManagementService;
  private final LoginCountService loginCountService;

  private String username;
  private String password;

  public LoginProcessor(                          ◁─┐  We inject the LoginCountService bean
    LoggedUserManagementService loggedUserManagementService,   through the constructor's parameters.
    LoginCountService loginCountService) {
    this.loggedUserManagementService = loggedUserManagementService;
    this.loginCountService = loginCountService;
  }

  public boolean login() {                  ┌─ We increment the count
    loginCountService.increment();    ◁─┘   for each login attempt.

    String username = this.getUsername();
    String password = this.getPassword();

    boolean loginResult = false;
    if ("natalie".equals(username) && "password".equals(password)) {
      loginResult = true;
      loggedUserManagementService.setUsername(username);
    }

    return loginResult;
  }

  // Omitted code
}
```

The last thing you need to do is to display this value. As you've already learned in the examples we worked on, starting with chapter 7, you can use a Model parameter in the controller's action to send the count value to the view. You can then use Thymeleaf to display the value in the view. The following listing shows you how to send the value from the controller to the view.

Listing 9.14   Sending the count value from controller to be displayed on the main page

```
@Controller
public class MainController {

  // Omitted code
```

```
@GetMapping("/main")
public String home(
    @RequestParam(required = false) String logout,
    Model model
) {
  if (logout != null) {
    loggedUserManagementService.setUsername(null);
  }

  String username = loggedUserManagementService.getUsername();
  int count = loginCountService.getCount();          ◁──┐ Gets the count from the
                                                          application-scoped bean
  if (username == null) {
    return "redirect:/";
  }

  model.addAttribute("username" , username);
  model.addAttribute("loginCount", count);           ◁──┐ Sends the count
                                                          value to the view
  return "main.html";
  }
}
```

The following listing shows you how to display the count value on the page.

Listing 9.15 Displaying the count value on the main page

```
<!DOCTYPE html>
<html lang="en" xmlns:th="http://www.thymeleaf.org">
<head>
    <meta charset="UTF-8">
    <title>Login</title>
</head>
<body>
    <h1>Welcome, <span th:text="${username}"></span>!</h1>
    <h2>
    Your login number is
      <span th:text="${loginCount}"></span>       ◁──┐ Displays the count
    </h2>                                               on the page
    <a href="/main?logout">Log out</a>
</body>
</html>
```

When you run the app, you find the total number of login attempts on the main page, as presented in figure 9.15.

Welcome, natalie!

Your login number is 5

Log out

Figure 9.15   The result of the application is a web page that displays the total number of logins for all the users. This main page displays the total number of login attempts.

Summary

- Aside from the singleton and prototype bean scopes (discussed in chapters 2 through 5), you can benefit from using three more bean scopes in a Spring web app. These scopes only make sense in web apps, and that's why we call them web scopes:
  - *Request scope*—Spring creates an instance of the bean for each HTTP request.
  - *Session scope*—Spring creates an instance of the bean per HTTP session of the client. Multiple requests from the same client can share the same instance.
  - *Application scope*—There's only one instance for the whole application for that specific bean. Every request from any client can access this instance.
- Spring guarantees that a request-scoped bean instance is only accessible by one HTTP request. For this reason, you can use the instance's attributes without worrying about concurrency-related problems. Also, you don't need to worry that they might fill the app's memory. Being they are short-lived, the instances can be garbage-collected once the HTTP request ends.
- Spring creates request-scoped bean instances for every HTTP request. This is quite often. You preferably shouldn't make the instance's creation difficult by implementing logic in the constructor or a @PostConstruct method.
- Spring links a session-scoped bean instance to the HTTP session of the client. This way, a session-scoped bean instance can be used to share data among multiple HTTP requests from the same client.
- Even if from the same client, the client can send HTTP requests concurrently. If these requests change data in the session-scoped instance, they might get into race-condition scenarios. You need to consider such situations and either avoid them or synchronize your code to support the concurrency.
- I recommend avoiding the use of application-scoped bean instances. With application-scoped bean instances being shared by all the web app requests, any write operation usually needs synchronization, creating bottlenecks and dramatically

affecting the app's performance. Moreover, these beans live in your app's memory as long as the app itself, so they can't be garbage-collected. A better approach is to directly store the data in a database, as you'll learn in chapter 11.

- Both session- and application-scoped beans imply making requests less independent. We say the application manages the state the requests need (or that the app is stateful). A stateful app implies different architectural problems that are best to avoid. Of course, describing these problems is beyond the purpose of this book, but it's a good to make you aware that it's better to consider an alternative.

Implementing REST services

10

This chapter covers

- Understanding REST services
- Implementing REST endpoints
- Managing the data that the server sends to the client in the HTTP response
- Obtaining data from the client in the HTTP request body
- Managing exceptions at the endpoint level

In chapters 7 through 9, I mentioned representational state transfer (REST) services a few times concerning web applications. In this chapter, we extend the discussion on REST services, and you'll learn they are not just related to web apps.

REST services are one of the most often encountered ways to implement communication between two apps. REST offers access to functionality the server exposes through endpoints a client can call.

You use REST services to establish the communication between a client and a server in a web app. But you can also use REST services to develop the communication between a mobile app and a backend or even two backend services (figure 10.1).

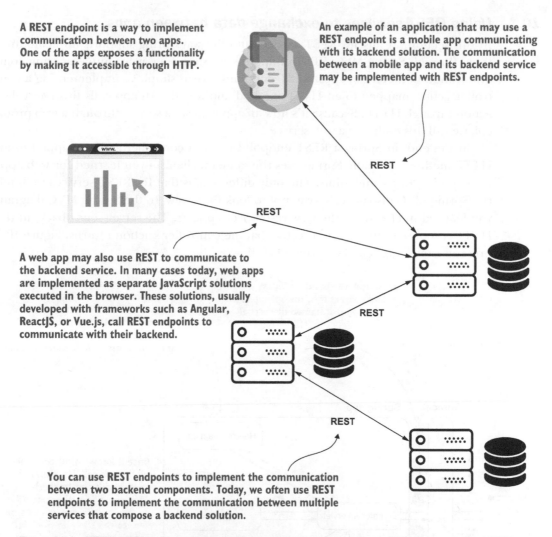

A REST endpoint is a way to implement communication between two apps. One of the apps exposes a functionality by making it accessible through HTTP.

An example of an application that may use a REST endpoint is a mobile app communicating with its backend solution. The communication between a mobile app and its backend service may be implemented with REST endpoints.

REST

REST

A web app may also use REST to communicate to the backend service. In many cases today, web apps are implemented as separate JavaScript solutions executed in the browser. These solutions, usually developed with frameworks such as Angular, ReactJS, or Vue.js, call REST endpoints to communicate with their backend.

REST

REST

You can use REST endpoints to implement the communication between two backend components. Today, we often use REST endpoints to implement the communication between multiple services that compose a backend solution.

Figure 10.1 REST services are a communication method between two apps. Today, you can find REST services in many places. A web client app or mobile app may call its backend solution through REST endpoints, but even backend services might communicate using REST web service calls.

Because in many Spring apps today you have chances to encounter and work on REST services, I consider this subject a must-learn for every Spring developer.

We'll start by discussing what exactly REST services are in section 10.1. You'll learn that Spring supports REST services with the same Spring MVC mechanism we discussed in chapters 7 through 9. In section 10.2, we discuss the essential syntaxes you need to know when working with REST endpoints. We'll work on several examples to elaborate on the critical aspects any Spring developer needs to know when implementing communication between two apps with REST services.

10.1   *Using REST services to exchange data between apps*

In this section, we discuss REST services and the way Spring supports implementing them through Spring MVC. REST endpoints are simply a way for implementing communication between two apps. REST endpoints are as simple as implementing a controller action mapped to an HTTP method and a path. An app calls this controller action through HTTP. Because it's how an app exposes a service through a web protocol, we call this endpoint a web service.

In the end, in Spring a REST endpoint is still a controller action mapped to an HTTP method and path. Spring uses the same mechanism you learned for web apps for exposing REST endpoints. The only difference is that for REST services we'll tell the Spring MVC dispatcher servlet not to look for a view. In the Spring MVC diagram you learned in chapter 7, the view resolver disappears. The server sends back, in the HTTP response to the client, directly what the controller's action returns. Figure 10.2 presents the changes in the Spring MVC flow.

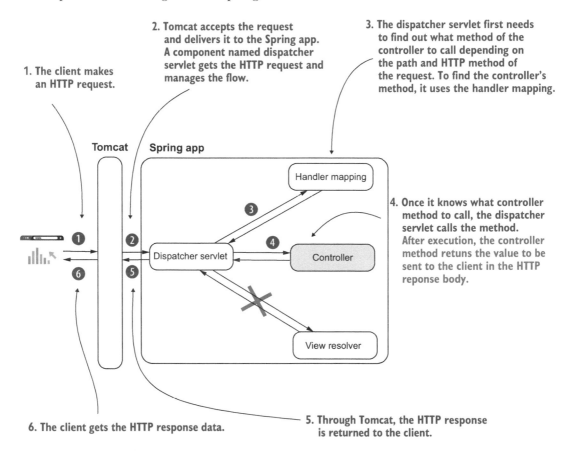

2. Tomcat accepts the request and delivers it to the Spring app. A component named dispatcher servlet gets the HTTP request and manages the flow.

3. The dispatcher servlet first needs to find out what method of the controller to call depending on the path and HTTP method of the request. To find the controller's method, it uses the handler mapping.

1. The client makes an HTTP request.

4. Once it knows what controller method to call, the dispatcher servlet calls the method. After execution, the controller method retuns the value to be sent to the client in the HTTP reponse body.

6. The client gets the HTTP response data.

5. Through Tomcat, the HTTP response is returned to the client.

Figure 10.2   When implementing REST endpoints, the Spring MVC flow changes. The app no longer needs a view resolver because the client needs the data returned by the controller's action directly. Once the controller's action completes, the dispatcher servlet returns the HTTP response without rendering any view.

You'll find REST services are comfortable to use. Their simplicity is one reason they're so often used today, and Spring makes their implementation straightforward. But before starting with our first example, I'd like to make you aware of some communication issues the REST endpoint might bring:

- If the controller's action takes a long time to complete, the HTTP call to the endpoint might time out and break the communication.
- Sending a large quantity of data in one call (through the HTTP request) might cause the call to time out and break the communication. Sending more than a few megabytes through a REST call usually isn't the right choice.
- Too many concurrent calls on an endpoint exposed by a backend component might put too much pressure on the app and cause it to fail.
- The network supports the HTTP calls, and the network is never 100% reliable. There's always a chance a REST endpoint call might fail because of the network.

When you implement the communication between two apps using REST, you always need to consider what should happen if a call fails and how it might affect the app. Ask yourself if the data could be affected in any way. Could the way you designed your app lead to data inconsistencies if an endpoint call fails? In case the app needs to display an error to the user, how would you do that? These are complex issues and require architectural knowledge outside the scope of this book, but I recommend J. J. Geewax's *API Design Patterns* (Manning, 2021), an excellent guide discussing the best practices of designing APIs.

10.2 Implementing a REST endpoint

In this section, you'll learn to implement REST endpoints with Spring. The good news is that Spring uses the same Spring MVC mechanism behind REST endpoints, so you already know a big part of how they work from chapters 7 and 8. Let's start with an example (project "sq-ch10-ex1"). I'll build my example over what we already discussed in chapters 7 and 8, and you'll learn how to transform a simple web controller into a REST controller to implement REST web services.

Listing 10.1 shows you a controller class that implements a simple action. As you learned from chapter 7, we annotate the controller class with the @Controller stereotype annotation. This way, an instance of the class becomes a bean in the Spring context, and Spring MVC knows this is a controller that maps its methods to specific HTTP paths. Also, we used the @GetMapping annotation to specify the action path and HTTP method. The only new thing you find in this listing is the use of the @ResponseBody annotation. The @ResponseBody annotation tells the dispatcher servlet that the controller's action doesn't return a view name but the data sent directly in the HTTP response.

Listing 10.1 Implementing a REST endpoint action in a controller class

```
@Controller
public class HelloController {
```
We use the @Controller annotation to mark the class as a Spring MVC controller.

```
@GetMapping("/hello")
@ResponseBody
public String hello() {
  return "Hello!";
}
}
```

We use the @GetMapping annotation to associate the GET HTTP method and a path with the controller's action.

We use the @ResponseBody annotation to inform the dispatcher servlet that this method doesn't return a view name but the HTTP response directly.

But look what happens if we add more methods to the controller, shown in the following listing. Repeating the @ResponseBody annotation on every method becomes annoying.

Listing 10.2   The @ResponseBody annotation becomes duplicated code

```
@Controller
public class HelloController {

  @GetMapping("/hello")
  @ResponseBody
  public String hello() {
    return "Hello!";
  }

  @GetMapping("/ciao")
  @ResponseBody
  public String ciao() {
    return "Ciao!";
  }
}
```

A best practice is avoiding code duplication. We want to somehow prevent repeating the @ResponseBody annotation for each method. To help us with this aspect, Spring offers the @RestController annotation, a combination of @Controller and @ResponseBody. You use @RestController to instruct Spring that all the controller's actions are REST endpoints. This way, you avoid repeating the @ResponseBody annotation. Listing 10.3 shows what you need to change in the controller to use @RestController once for the class instead of @ResponseBody for each method. To allow you to test and compare both approaches, I separated this code in the example "sq-ch10-ex2."

Listing 10.3   Using the @RestController annotation to avoid code duplication

```
@RestController
public class HelloController {

  @GetMapping("/hello")
  public String hello() {
    return "Hello!";
  }

  @GetMapping("/ciao")
  public String ciao() {
    return "Ciao!";
  }
}
```

Instead of repeating the @ResponseBody annotation for each method, we replace @Controller with @RestController.

It was indeed easy to implement a couple of endpoints. But how do we validate they work correctly? In this section, you'll learn to call your endpoints using two tools you'll often encounter in real-world scenarios:

- *Postman*—Offers a nice GUI and is comfortable to use
- *cURL*—A command-line tool useful in cases where you don't have a GUI (e.g., when you connect to a virtual machine via SSH or when you write a batch script)

Both these tools are a must-learn for any developer. In chapter 15, you'll learn a third approach for validating that an endpoint behaves as expected by writing an integration test.

First, start the application. You can use either project "sq-ch10-ex1" or "sq-ch10-ex2." They have the same behavior. The only difference is the syntax, as discussed in earlier paragraphs. As you learned in chapter 7, by default, the Spring Boot app configures a Tomcat servlet container to be accessible on port 8080.

Let's discuss Postman first. You need to install the tool on your system as presented on their official website: https://www.postman.com/. Once you have Postman installed, when you open it, you'll find it has an interface like the one presented in figure 10.3.

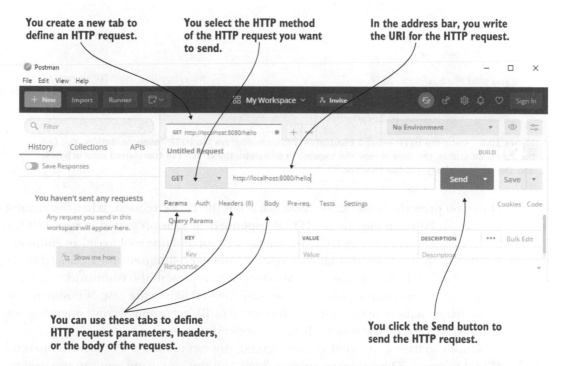

Figure 10.3 Postman offers a friendly interface to configure and send an HTTP request. You select the HTTP method, set the HTTP request URI, and then press the Send button to send an HTTP request. You can also define other configurations such as the request parameters, headers, or the request body if needed.

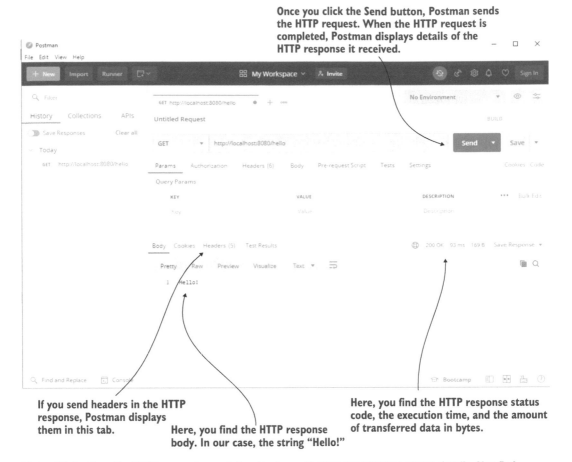

Once you click the Send button, Postman sends the HTTP request. When the HTTP request is completed, Postman displays details of the HTTP response it received.

If you send headers in the HTTP response, Postman displays them in this tab.

Here, you find the HTTP response body. In our case, the string "Hello!"

Here, you find the HTTP response status code, the execution time, and the amount of transferred data in bytes.

Figure 10.4 Once the HTTP request completes, Postman displays the HTTP response details. You find the response status, the time it took the request to complete, the amount of transferred data in bytes, and the response body and the headers.

Once you press the Send button, Postman sends the HTTP request. When the request completes, Postman displays the HTTP response details, as presented in figure 10.4.

In case you don't have a GUI, you can use a command-line tool to call an endpoint. You'll also find articles and books often use command-line tools for demonstrations rather than GUI tools because it's a shorter way to represent the command.

If you choose to use cURL as a command-line tool like in the case of Postman, you need first to make sure you install it. You install cURL according to your operating system as described on the tool's official web page: https://curl.se/

Once you have it installed and configured, you can use the `curl` command to send HTTP requests. The following snippet shows you the command you can use to send the HTTP request to test the /hello endpoint exposed by our app:

```
curl http://localhost:8080/hello
```

Upon completing the HTTP request, the console only displays the HTTP response body presented in the next snippet:

```
Hello!
```

If the HTTP method is HTTP GET, you don't need to specify it explicitly. When the method is not HTTP GET, or if you want to specify it explicitly, you can use the -X flag, as presented in the next snippet:

```
curl -X GET http://localhost:8080/hello
```

If you want to get more details of the HTTP request, you can add the -v option to the command, as presented in the next snippet:

```
curl -v http://localhost:8080/hello
```

The next snippet presents the result of this command, which is a bit more complicated. You also find details like the status, the amount of data transferred, and headers through the lengthy response:

```
  Trying ::1:8080...
* Connected to localhost (::1) port 8080 (#0)
> GET /hello HTTP/1.1
> Host: localhost:8080
> User-Agent: curl/7.73.0
> Accept: */*
>
* Mark bundle as not supporting multiuse
< HTTP/1.1 200                          ←——— The HTTP response status
< Content-Type: text/plain;charset=UTF-8
< Content-Length: 6
< Date: Fri, 25 Dec 2020 23:11:02 GMT
<
{ [6 bytes data]
100     6 100     6    0     0    857      0 --:--:-- --:--:-- --:--:--
1000                                      | The HTTP response body
Hello!                                 ←——┘
* Connection #0 to host localhost left intact
```

10.3 Managing the HTTP response

In this section, we discuss managing the HTTP response in the controller's action. The HTTP response is how the backend app sends data back to the client due to a client's request. The HTTP response holds data as the following:

- *Response headers*—Short pieces of data in the response (usually not more than a few words long)
- *The response body*—A larger amount of data the backend needs to send in the response
- *The response status*—A short representation of the request's result

Take a few minutes and review appendix C to remember the details about HTTP before going further. In section 10.3.1 and 10.3.2, we discuss the options you have for sending data in the response body. In section 10.3.3, you'll learn how to set the HTTP response status and headers if needed.

10.3.1 Sending objects as a response body

In this section, we discuss sending object instances in the response body. The only thing you need to do to send an object to the client in a response is make the controller's action return that object. In the example "sq-ch10-ex3," we define a model object named `Country` with the attributes `name` (representing the country name) and `population` (representing the number of millions of people located in that country). We implement a controller action to return an instance of type `Country`.

Listing 10.4 shows the class that defines the `Country` object. When we use an object (such as `Country`) to model the data transferred between two apps, we name this object a *data transfer object* (DTO). We can say that `Country` is our DTO, whose instances are returned by the REST endpoint we implement in the HTTP response body.

Listing 10.4 **Model of the data the server returns in the HTTP response body**

```java
public class Country {

  private String name;
  private int population;


  public static Country of(          ⟵  To make a Country instance simpler, we define a
    String name,                         static factory method that receives the name and
    int population) {                    the population. This method returns a Country
      Country country = new Country();    instance with the provided values set.
      country.setName(name);
      country.setPopulation(population);
      return country;
  }

  // Omitted getters and setters
}
```

The following listing shows the implementation of a controller's action that returns an instance of type `Country`.

Listing 10.5 **Returning an object instance from the controller's action**

```java
@RestController                        ⟵  Marking the class as a REST controller to add a bean
public class CountryController {           in the Spring context and also inform the dispatcher
                                           servlet not to look for a view when this method returns

  @GetMapping("/france")          ⟵
  public Country france() {                Mapping the controller's action to the
    Country c = Country.of("France", 67);  HTTP GET method and /france path
    return c;                       ⟵
  }                                  Returning an instance of type Country

}
```

What happens when you call this endpoint? How would the object look in the HTTP response body? By default, Spring creates a string representation of the object and formats it as JSON. JavaScript Object Notation (JSON) is a simple way to format strings as attribute-value pairs. There's a good chance you've seen JSON already, but if you haven't used it before, I prepared a discussion with everything you need to know in appendix D.

When calling the /france endpoint, the response body looks as presented in the next snippet:

```
{
    "name": "France",
    "population": 67
}
```

Figure 10.5 reminds you where you find the HTTP response body when you use Postman to call the endpoint.

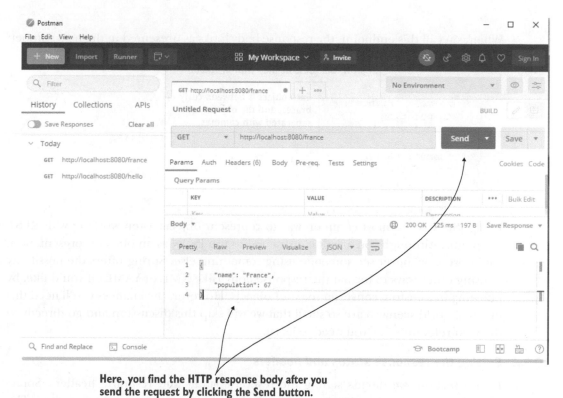

Here, you find the HTTP response body after you
send the request by clicking the Send button.

Figure 10.5 Once you press the Send button, Postman sends the request. When the request completes, Postman displays the response details, including the response body.

You could also send object collection instances in the response body. The next listing shows that we added a method that returns a `List` of `Country` objects.

Listing 10.6   Returning a collection in the response body

```
@RestController
public class CountryController {

  // Omitted code

  @GetMapping("/all")
  public List<Country> countries() {
    Country c1 = Country.of("France", 67);
    Country c2 = Country.of("Spain", 47);

    return List.of(c1,c2);        ⟵┐  Returns a collection in the
  }                                 │  HTTP response body

}
```

When you call this endpoint, the response body looks as presented in the next snippet:

```
[                    ⟵─────┐  In JSON, the list is defined with brackets.
    {
        "name": "France",        Each object is between curly
        "population": 67         braces, and the objects are
    },                           separated with commas.
    {
        "name": "Spain",
        "population": 47
    }
]
```

Using JSON is the most common way to represent objects when working with REST endpoints. Although you aren't constrained to use JSON as an object representation, you'll probably never see someone using something else. Spring offers the possibility of using other ways to format the response body (like XML or YAML) if you'd like, by plugging in a custom converter for your objects. However, the chances you'll need this in a real-world scenario are so small that we will skip this discussion and go directly to the next relevant topic you need to learn.

10.3.2 *Setting the response status and headers*

In this section, we discuss setting the response status and response headers. Sometimes it's more comfortable to send part of the data in the response headers. The response status is also an essential flag in the HTTP response you use to signal the request's result. By default, Spring sets some common HTTP statuses:

- *200 OK* if no exception was thrown on the server side while processing the request.
- *404 Not Found* if the requested resource doesn't exist.
- *400 Bad Request* if a part of the request could not be matched with the way the server expected the data.
- *500 Error on server* if an exception was thrown on the server side for any reason while processing the request. Usually, for this kind of exception, the client can't do anything, and it's expected someone should solve the problem on the backend.

However, in some cases, the requirements ask you to configure a custom status. How could you do that? The easiest and most common way to customize the HTTP response is using the `ResponseEntity` class. This class provided by Spring allows you to specify the response body, status, and headers on the HTTP response. Example "sq-ch10-ex4" demonstrates the use of the `ResponseEntity` class. In listing 10.7, a controller action returns a `ResponseEntity` instance instead of the object you want to set on the response body directly. The `ResponseEntity` class allows you to set the response body's value and the response status and headers. We set three headers and change the response status to "202 Accepted."

Listing 10.7 Adding custom headers and setting a response status

```
@RestController
public class CountryController {

  @GetMapping("/france")
  public ResponseEntity<Country> france() {
    Country c = Country.of("France", 67);
    return ResponseEntity
           .status(HttpStatus.ACCEPTED)        Changes the HTTP response
           .header("continent", "Europe")      status to 202 Accepted
           .header("capital", "Paris")
           .header("favorite_food", "cheese and wine")   Adds three custom
           .body(c);                                      headers to the response
  }
                        Sets the response body
}
```

Once you send the request using Postman, you can verify the HTTP response status changed to "202 Accepted" (figure 10.6).

In the Headers tab of the HTTP response in Postman, you also find the three custom response headers you added (figure 10.7).

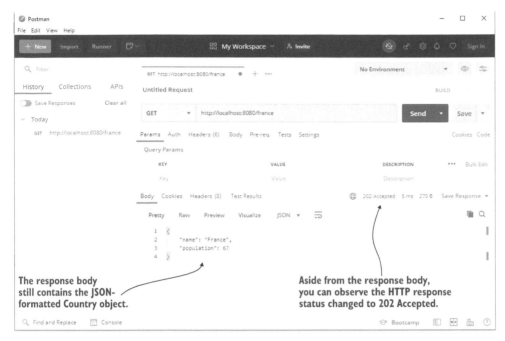

The response body still contains the JSON-formatted Country object.

Aside from the response body, you can observe the HTTP response status changed to 202 Accepted.

Figure 10.6   Once you send the HTTP request by pressing the Send button and get the HTTP response, you observe the HTTP response status is 202 Accepted. You can still see the response body as a JSON formatted string.

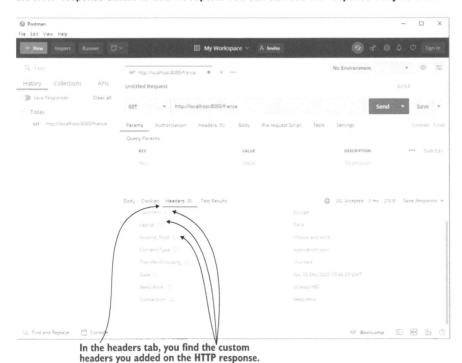

In the headers tab, you find the custom headers you added on the HTTP response.

Figure 10.7   To see the customer headers in Postman, you have to navigate to the Headers tab of the HTTP response.

10.3.3 *Managing exceptions at the endpoint level*

It's essential to consider what happens if the controller's action throws an exception. In many cases, we use exceptions to signal specific situations, some of these related to the business logic. Suppose you create an endpoint the client calls to make a payment. If the user doesn't have enough money in their account, the app might represent this situation by throwing an exception. In this case, you'll probably want to set some details on the HTTP response to inform the client of the specific situation that occurred.

One of the ways you can manage exceptions is catching them in the controller's action and using the ResponseEntity class, as you learned in section 10.3.2, to send a different configuration of the response when the exception occurs.

We'll start by demonstrating this approach with an example. I'll then show you an alternative approach I prefer by using a REST controller advice class: an aspect that intercepts an endpoint call when it throws an exception, and you can specify a custom logic to be executed for that specific exception.

Let's create a new project named "sq-ch10-ex5." For our scenario, we define an exception named NotEnoughMoneyException, and the app will throw this exception when it cannot fulfill the payment because the client doesn't have enough money in their account. The next code snippet shows the class defining the exception:

```
public class NotEnoughMoneyException extends RuntimeException {
}
```

We also implement a service class that defines the use case. For our test, we directly throw this exception. In a real-world scenario, the service would implement the complex logic for making the payment. The next code snippet shows the service class we use for our test:

```
@Service
public class PaymentService {

  public PaymentDetails processPayment() {
    throw new NotEnoughMoneyException();
  }
}
```

PaymentDetails, the returned type of the processPayment() method, is just a model class describing the response body we expect the controller's action to return for a successful payment. The next code snippet presents the PaymentDetails class:

```
public class PaymentDetails {

  private double amount;

  // Omitted getters and setters
}
```

When the app encounters an exception, it uses another model class named Error-Details to inform the client of the situation. The ErrorDetails class is also simple and only defines the error message as an attribute. The next code snippet presents the ErrorDetails model class:

```
public class ErrorDetails {

  private String message;

  // Omitted getters and setters
}
```

How could the controller decide what object to send back depending on how the flow executed? When there's no exception (the app successfully completes the payment), we want to return an HTTP response with the status "Accepted" of type PaymentDetails. Suppose the app encountered an exception during the execution flow. In that case, the controller's action returns an HTTP response with the status "400 Bad Request" and an ErrorDetails instance containing a message that describes the issue. Figure 10.8 visually presents the relationship between the components and their responsibilities.

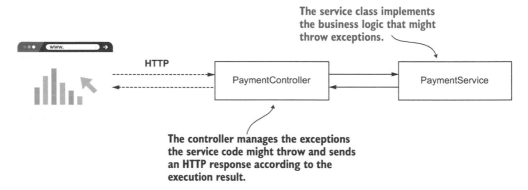

Figure 10.8   The **PaymentService** class implements the business logic that might throw exceptions. The **PaymentController** class manages the exception and sends the client an HTTP response according to the execution result.

The next listing shows this logic implemented by the controller's method.

Listing 10.8   Managing the HTTP response for exceptions in the controller's action

```
@RestController
public class PaymentController {

  private final PaymentService paymentService;

  public PaymentController(PaymentService paymentService) {
    this.paymentService = paymentService;
  }

  @PostMapping("/payment")
  public ResponseEntity<?> makePayment() {
```

```
    try {
        PaymentDetails paymentDetails =
            paymentService.processPayment();

        return ResponseEntity
                .status(HttpStatus.ACCEPTED)
                .body(paymentDetails);
    } catch (NotEnoughMoneyException e) {
        ErrorDetails errorDetails = new ErrorDetails();
        errorDetails.setMessage("Not enough money to make the payment.");
        return ResponseEntity
                .badRequest()
                .body(errorDetails);
    }
  }
}
```

We try calling the processPayment() method of the service.

If calling the service method succeeds, we return an HTTP response with status Accepted and the PaymentDetails instance as a response body.

If an exception of type NotEnoughMoneyException is thrown, we return an HTTP response with status Bad Request and an ErrorDetails instance as a body.

Start the application and call the endpoint using Postman or cURL. We know that we made the service method to always throw the NotEnoughMoneyException, so we expect to see the response status message is "400 Bad Request," and the body contains the error message. Figure 10.9 presents the result of sending a request to the /payment endpoint in Postman.

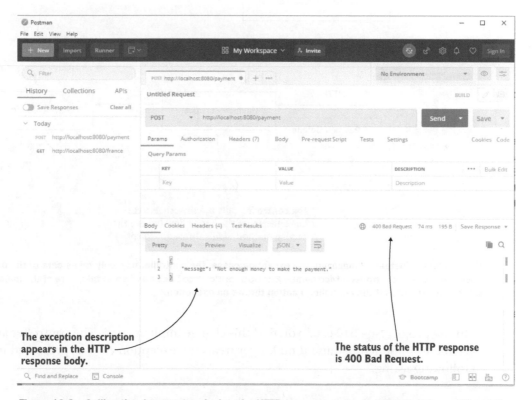

The exception description appears in the HTTP response body.

The status of the HTTP response is 400 Bad Request.

Figure 10.9   Calling the /payment endpoint, the HTTP response status is "400 Bad Request" and the exception message appears in the response body.

This approach is good, and you'll often find developers using it to manage the exception cases. However, in a more complex application, you would find it more comfortable to separate the responsibility of exception management. First, sometimes the same exception has to be managed for multiple endpoints, and, as you guessed, we don't want to introduce duplicated code. Second, it's more comfortable to know you find the exception logic all in one place when you need to understand how a specific case works. For these reasons, I prefer using a REST controller advice, an aspect that intercepts exceptions thrown by controllers' actions and applies custom logic you define according to the intercepted exception.

Figure 10.10 presents the changes we want to make in our class design. Take some time to compare this new class design with the one in figure 10.8.

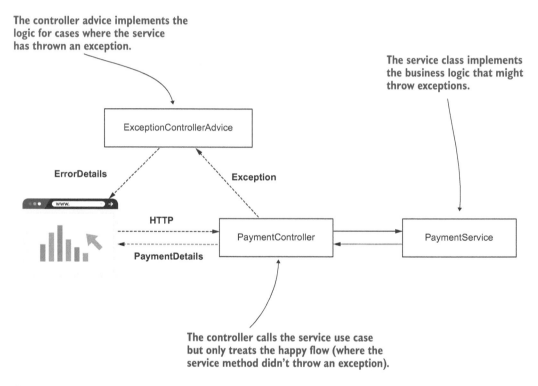

The controller advice implements the logic for cases where the service has thrown an exception.

The service class implements the business logic that might throw exceptions.

The controller calls the service use case but only treats the happy flow (where the service method didn't throw an exception).

Figure 10.10   Instead of managing the exception cases, the controller now only takes care of the happy flow. We added a controller advice named `ExceptionControllerAdvice` to take care of the logic that will be implemented if the controller's action throws an exception.

In the project "sq-ch10-ex6," you find this change implemented. The controller action is much simplified because it no longer treats the exception case, as presented in the following listing.

Listing 10.9   Controller's action that no longer treats the exception case

```
@RestController
public class PaymentController {

  private final PaymentService paymentService;

  public PaymentController(PaymentService paymentService) {
    this.paymentService = paymentService;
  }

  @PostMapping("/payment")
  public ResponseEntity<PaymentDetails> makePayment() {
      PaymentDetails paymentDetails = paymentService.processPayment();
      return ResponseEntity
            .status(HttpStatus.ACCEPTED)
            .body(paymentDetails);
  }
}
```

Instead, we created a separate class named ExceptionControllerAdvice that implements what happens if the controller's action throws a NotEnoughMoneyException. The ExceptionControllerAdvice class is a REST controller advice. To mark it as a REST controller advice, we use the @RestControllerAdvice annotation. The method the class defines is also called an exception handler. You specify what exceptions trigger a controller advice method using the @ExceptionHandler annotation over the method. The following listing shows the REST controller advice class's definition and the exception handler method that implements the logic associated with the NotEnough-MoneyException exception.

Listing 10.10   Separating the exception logic with a REST controller advice

```
@RestControllerAdvice              ◄───────────   We use the @RestControllerAdvice
public class ExceptionControllerAdvice {          annotation to mark the class as a
                                                  REST controller advice.

  @ExceptionHandler(NotEnoughMoneyException.class)                    ◄───
  public ResponseEntity<ErrorDetails> exceptionNotEnoughMoneyHandler() {
    ErrorDetails errorDetails = new ErrorDetails();
    errorDetails.setMessage("Not enough money to make the payment.");
    return ResponseEntity
        .badRequest()            We use the @ExceptionHandler method to associate
        .body(errorDetails);     an exception with the logic the method implements.
  }
}
```

NOTE   In production apps, you sometimes need to send information about the exception that occurred, from the controller's action to the advice. In this case, you can add a parameter to the advice's exception handler method of the type of the handled exception. Spring is smart enough to pass the exception reference from the controller to the advice's exception handler method. You can then use any details of the exception instance in the advice's logic.

10.4   *Using a request body to get data from the client*

In this section, we discuss getting data from the client in the HTTP request body. You learned in chapter 8 that you can send data in the HTTP request using request parameters and path variables. Because REST endpoints rely on the same Spring MVC mechanism, nothing from the syntaxes you learned in chapter 8 changes regarding sending data in request parameters and path variables. You can use the same annotations and implement the REST endpoints identically as you were implementing the controller actions for your web pages.

However, we didn't discuss one essential thing: the HTTP request has a request body, and you can use it to send data from the client to the server. The HTTP request body is often used with REST endpoints. As also mentioned in appendix C, when you need to send a larger quantity of data (my recommendation is anything that takes more than 50 to 100 characters), you use the request body.

To use the request body, you just need to annotate a parameter of the controller's action with @RequestBody. By default, Spring assumes you used JSON to represent the parameter you annotated and will try to decode the JSON string into an instance of your parameter type. In the case Spring cannot decode the JSON-formatted string into that type, the app sends back a response with the status "400 Bad Request." In the project "sq-ch10-ex7," we implement a simple example of using the request body. The controller defines an action mapped to the /payment path with HTTP POST and expects to get a request body of PaymentDetails type. The controller prints the amount of the PaymentDetails object in the server's console and sends the same object in the response body back to the client.

The next listing shows the definition of the controller in the project "sq-ch10-ex7."

Listing 10.11   Getting data from the client in the request body

```
@RestController
public class PaymentController {

  private static Logger logger =
    Logger.getLogger(PaymentController.class.getName());

  @PostMapping("/payment")
  public ResponseEntity<PaymentDetails> makePayment(          ◁──  We get the payment
    @RequestBody PaymentDetails paymentDetails) {                    details from the HTTP
                                                                      request body.
    logger.info("Received payment " +          We log the amount of the payment
    paymentDetails.getAmount());     ◁──       in the server's console.

    return ResponseEntity            ◁──
          .status(HttpStatus.ACCEPTED)           We send back the payment details object
          .body(paymentDetails);                 in the HTTP response body, and we set the
  }}                                              HTTP response status to 202 ACCEPTED.
```

Figure 10.11 shows you how to use Postman to call the /payment endpoint with a request body.

To set the request body, you select the Body tab on the HTTP request configuration. You then choose the option "raw" by clicking the radio button and then choose JSON as the formatting style.

In the text area you write the JSON-formatted request body representing the PaymentDetails object. Then you click the Send button to send the HTTP request.

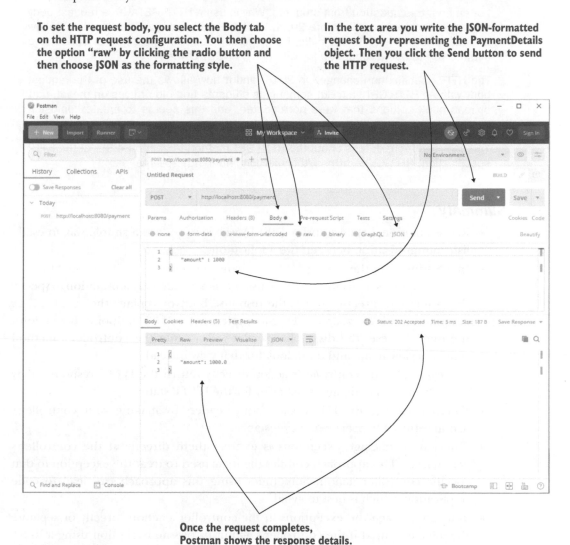

Once the request completes, Postman shows the response details.

Figure 10.11 Using Postman to call the endpoint and specify the request body. You need to fill the JSON-formatted request body in the request body text area and select the data encoding as JSON. Once the request completes, Postman displays the response details.

If you prefer using cURL, you can use the command presented by the next snippet:

```
curl -v -X POST http://127.0.0.1:8080/payment -d '{"amount": 1000}' -H
    "Content-Type: application/json"
```

Can an HTTP GET endpoint use a request body?

I often hear this question from students. Why is using HTTP GET with a request body the subject of confusion? Before 2014, the HTTP protocol specification didn't allow a request body for HTTP GET calls. No implementation for the client or server side allowed you to use a request body with an HTTP GET call.

The HTTP specification changed in 2014, and it now allows the use of the request body with an HTTP GET call. But sometimes students find old articles on the internet or read book editions that were not updated, and this seems to create confusion years later.

You can read more details about the HTTP GET method in section 4.3.1 of the HTTP specification, RFC 7231: https://tools.ietf.org/html/rfc7231#page-24.

Summary

- Representational state transfer (REST) web services are a simple way to establish communication between two applications.
- In a Spring app, the Spring MVC mechanism supports the implementation of REST endpoints. You either need to use the @ResponseBody annotation to specify that a method directly returns the response body or replace the @Controller annotation with @RestController to implement a REST endpoint. If you don't use one of these, the dispatcher servlet will assume the controller's method returns a view name and try to look for that view instead.
- You can make the controller's action directly return the HTTP response body and rely on Spring default's behavior for the HTTP status.
- You can manage the HTTP status and headers by making your controller's action return a ResponseEntity instance.
- One way to manage exceptions is to treat them directly at the controller's action level. This approach couples the logic used to treat the exception to that specific controller action. Sometimes using this approach can lead to code duplication, which is best to avoid.
- You can manage the exceptions in the controller's action directly or separate the logic executed if the controller's action throws an exception using a REST controller advice class.
- An endpoint can get data from the client through the HTTP request in request parameters, path variables, or the HTTP request body.

Consuming
REST endpoints

This chapter covers

- Calling REST endpoints using Spring Cloud OpenFeign
- Calling REST endpoints using RestTemplate
- Calling REST endpoints using WebClient

In chapter 10, we discussed implementing REST endpoints. REST services are a common way to implement the communication between two system components. The client of a web app can call the backend, and so can another backend component. In a backend solution composed of multiple services (see appendix A), these components need to "speak" to exchange data, so when you implement such a service using Spring, you need to know how to call a REST endpoint exposed by another service (figure 11.1).

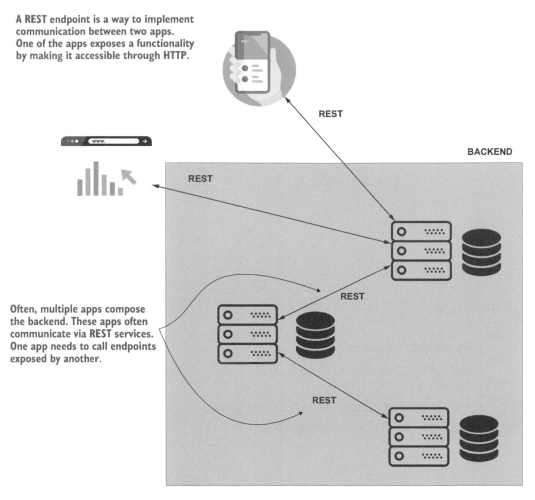

A **REST** endpoint is a way to implement communication between two apps. One of the apps exposes a functionality by making it accessible through HTTP.

Often, multiple apps compose the backend. These apps often communicate via **REST** services. One app needs to call endpoints exposed by another.

Figure 11.1   Often, a backend app needs to act as a client for another backend app, and calls exposed REST endpoints to work with specific data.

In this chapter, you'll learn three ways to call REST endpoints from a Spring app:

1 OpenFeign—A tool offered by the Spring Cloud project. I recommend developers use this feature in new apps for consuming REST endpoints.

2 RestTemplate—A well-known tool developers have used since Spring 3 to call REST endpoints. RestTemplate is often used today in Spring apps. However, as we'll discuss in this chapter, OpenFeign is a better alternative to RestTemplate, so if you work on a new app, you'll probably avoid RestTemplate and use Open-Feign instead.

3 WebClient—A Spring feature presented as an alternative to RestTemplate. This feature uses a different programming approach named *reactive programming*, which we'll discuss at the end of this chapter.

The first Spring capability we discuss, in section 11.1, is `OpenFeign`, which is part of the Spring Cloud family and a feature I recommend for all new implementations today. As you'll learn, `OpenFeign` offers a simple syntax and makes calling a REST endpoint from a Spring app straightforward.

In section 11.2, we'll use `RestTemplate`. But be careful! `RestTemplate` has been put in maintenance mode starting with Spring 5, and it will eventually be deprecated. Why am I teaching you about it, then? Most of today's Spring projects use `RestTemplate` to call REST endpoints because they started when this was the only or the best solution for implementing such a capability. For some of these apps, `RestTemplate`'s capabilities are enough and work fine, so replacing them makes no sense. Sometimes the time needed to replace `RestTemplate` with a newer solution might be too costly, so learning it is still a must for a Spring developer.

Here's an interesting fact that usually creates confusion for students. In the `RestTemplate` documentation (http://mng.bz/7lWe), `WebClient` is given as a recommendation for replacing the use of `RestTemplate`. In section 11.3, I'll explain why using `WebClient` is not always the best alternative to `RestTemplate`. We'll discuss `WebClient` and clarify when it's best to use this capability.

To teach you these three fundamental ways, we'll write an example for each. We'll first implement a project that exposes an endpoint. Our purpose is to call the endpoint in each approach we discuss in this chapter: `OpenFeign`, `RestTemplate`, and `WebClient`.

Suppose you implement an app that allows users to make payments. To make a payment, you need to call an endpoint of another system. Figure 11.2 visually presents this scenario. Figure 11.3 details the scenario showing the request and response details.

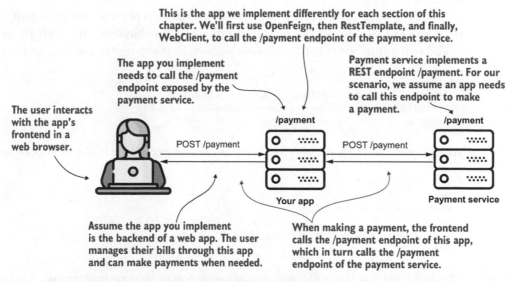

Figure 11.2   To properly teach you how to call REST endpoints, we'll implement several examples. For each example, we implement two projects. One exposes a REST endpoint. The second demonstrates the implementation for calling that REST endpoint using `OpenFeign`, `RestTemplate`, and `WebClient`.

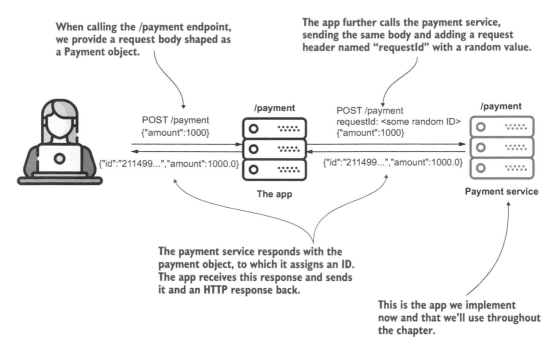

Figure 11.3   The payment service exposes an endpoint that requires an HTTP request body. The app uses `OpenFeign`, `RestTemplate`, or `WebClient` to send requests to the endpoint the payment service exposes.

With this first project, we implement the payment service app. We'll use this app in all our next examples.

Let's create the project "sq-ch11-payments," which represents the payments service. It's a web app, so, like all the projects we discussed in chapters 7 through 10, we need to add to the pom.xml file the web dependency, as presented in the next code snippet:

```
<dependency>
    <groupId>org.springframework.boot</groupId>
    <artifactId>spring-boot-starter-web</artifactId>
</dependency>
```

We'll model the payment with the `Payment` class, as presented in the next code snippet:

```
public class Payment {
  private String id;
  private double amount;

 // Omitted getters and setters
}
```

Listing 11.1 shows the endpoint's implementation in the controller class. Technically, it doesn't do much. The method receives a `Payment` instance and sets a random ID to the payment before returning it. The endpoint is simple but good enough for our demonstration. We use HTTP POST. We need to specify a request header and the request body. The endpoint returns a header in the HTTP response and the Payment object in the response body when called.

Listing 11.1 The /payment endpoint's implementation in the controller class

The app exposes the endpoint with HTTP POST at the path /payment.

```
@RestController
public class PaymentsController {

    private static Logger logger =
        Logger.getLogger(PaymentsController.class.getName());

    @PostMapping("/payment")
    public ResponseEntity<Payment> createPayment(
        @RequestHeader String requestId,
        @RequestBody Payment payment
    ) {
        logger.info("Received request with ID " + requestId +
            " ;Payment Amount: " + payment.getAmount());

        payment.setId(UUID.randomUUID().toString());

        return ResponseEntity
            .status(HttpStatus.OK)
            .header("requestId", requestId)
            .body(payment);
    }

}
```

We use a logger to prove the right controller's method gets the correct data when the endpoint is called.

The endpoint needs to get a request header and the request body from the caller. The controller method gets these two details as parameters.

The method sets a random value for the payment's ID.

The controller action returns the HTTP response. The response has a header and the response body that contains the payment with the random ID value set.

You can now run this app, and it will start Tomcat on port 8080, which is the Spring Boot default, as we discussed in chapter 7. The endpoint is accessible, and you could call it with cURL or Postman. But the purpose of this chapter is to learn how to implement an app that calls the endpoint, so this is exactly what we will do in sections 11.1, 11.2, and 11.3.

11.1   *Calling REST endpoints using Spring Cloud OpenFeign*

In this section, we discuss a modern approach for calling REST endpoints from a Spring app. In most apps, developers have used RestTemplate (that we'll discuss in section 11.2). As mentioned earlier in this chapter, RestTemplate is in maintenance mode starting with Spring 5. Moreover, RestTemplate will be deprecated soon, so I prefer to begin this chapter by discussing the alternative to RestTemplate I recommend you use: OpenFeign.

With OpenFeign, as you'll find out in the example we write in this section, you only need to write an interface, and the tool provides you with the implementation.

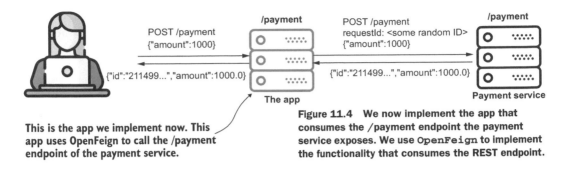

This is the app we implement now. This app uses OpenFeign to call the /payment endpoint of the payment service.

Figure 11.4   We now implement the app that consumes the /payment endpoint the payment service exposes. We use `OpenFeign` to implement the functionality that consumes the REST endpoint.

To teach you how `OpenFeign` works, we'll create the project "sq-ch11-ex1" and implement an app that uses `OpenFeign` to call the endpoint app "sq-ch11-payments" exposes (figure 11.4).

We'll define an interface where we declare the methods that consume REST endpoints. The only thing we need to do is annotate these methods to define the path, the HTTP method, and eventually parameters, headers, and the body of the request. The interesting thing is that we don't need to implement the methods ourselves. You define with the interface methods based on the annotations, and Spring knows to implement them. We rely again on the excellent magic of Spring.

Figure 11.5 shows the class design for the application we'll build that consumes a REST endpoint.

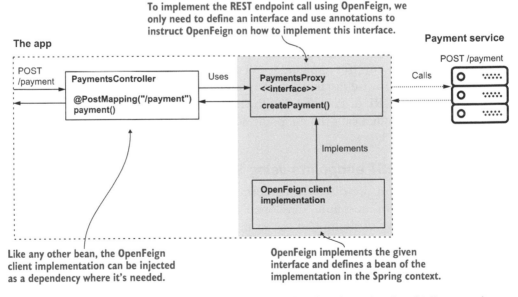

Figure 11.5   With `OpenFeign`, you only need to define an interface (a contract) and tell `OpenFeign` where to find this contract to implement it. `OpenFeign` implements the interface and provides the implementation as a bean in the Spring context based on configurations you define with annotations. You can inject the bean from the Spring context anywhere you need it in your app.

Your pom.xml file needs to define the dependency, as shown by the next code snippet:

```
<dependency>
    <groupId>org.springframework.cloud</groupId>
    <artifactId>spring-cloud-starter-openfeign</artifactId>
</dependency>
```

Once you have the dependency in place, you can create the proxy interface (as presented in figure 11.5). In OpenFeign terminology, we also name this interface the OpenFeign client. OpenFeign implements this interface, so you don't have to bother writing the code that calls the endpoint. You only need to use a few annotations to tell OpenFeign how to send the request. The following listing shows you how simple the definition of the request is with OpenFeign.

> **Listing 11.2   Declaring an OpenFeign client interface**

```
@FeignClient(name = "payments",
                url = "${name.service.url}")     ◄──┤ We use the @FeignClient annotation to configure
public interface PaymentsProxy {                     the REST client. A minimal configuration defines a
                                                     name and the endpoint base URI.

    @PostMapping("/payment")     ◄──┤ We specify the endpoint's
    Payment createPayment(            path and HTTP method.
        @RequestHeader String requestId,     ┤ We define the request
        @RequestBody Payment payment);         headers and body.

}
```

The first thing to do is annotate the interface with the @FeignClient annotation to tell OpenFeign it has to provide an implementation for this contract. We have to assign a name to the proxy using the name attribute of the @FeignClient annotation, which OpenFeign internally uses. The name uniquely identifies the client in your app. The @FeignClient annotation is also where we specify the base URI of the request. You can define the base URI as a string using the url attribute of @FeignClient.

> **NOTE**   Ensure you always store URIs and other details that might differ from one environment to another in the properties files and never hardcode them in the app.

You can define a property in the project's "application.properties" file and refer it from the source code using the following syntax: ${property_name}. Using this practice, you don't need to recompile the code when you want to run the app in different environments.

Each method you declare in the interface represents a REST endpoint call. You use the same annotations you learned in chapter 10 for the controller's actions to expose REST endpoints:

- To specify the path and HTTP method: `@GetMapping`, `@PostMapping`, `@Put-Mapping`, and so on
- To specify a request header: `@RequestHeader`
- To specify the request body: `@RequestBody`

I find this aspect of reusing the annotation beneficial. Here, by "reusing the annotation," I mean `OpenFeign` uses the same annotations we use when we define the endpoints. You don't have to learn something specific to `OpenFeign`. Just use the same annotations as for exposing the REST endpoints in the Spring MVC controller classes.

`OpenFeign` needs to know where to find the interfaces defining the client contracts. We use the `@EnableFeignClients` annotation on a configuration class to enable the `OpenFeign` functionality and tell `OpenFeign` where to search for the client contracts. In the following listing, you find the project's configuration class where we enable the `OpenFeign` clients.

Listing 11.3   Enabling the `OpenFeign` clients in the configuration class

```
@Configuration
@EnableFeignClients(
    basePackages = "com.example.proxy")          We enable the OpenFeign clients and
public class ProjectConfig {                      tell the OpenFeign dependency where
}                                                 to search for the proxy contracts.
```

You can now inject the `OpenFeign` client through the interface you defined in listing 11.2. Once you enable `OpenFeign`, it knows to implement the interfaces annotated with `@FeignClient`. In chapter 5, we discussed that Spring is smart enough to provide you with a bean instance from its context when you use an abstraction, and this is exactly what you do here. The following listing shows you the controller class that injects the `FeignClient`.

Listing 11.4   Injecting and using the `OpenFeign` client

```
@RestController
public class PaymentsController {

  private final PaymentsProxy paymentsProxy;

  public PaymentsController(PaymentsProxy paymentsProxy) {
    this.paymentsProxy = paymentsProxy;
  }

  @PostMapping("/payment")
  public Payment createPayment(
      @RequestBody Payment payment
      ) {
    String requestId = UUID.randomUUID().toString();
    return paymentsProxy.createPayment(requestId, payment);
  }
}
```

Now start both projects (the payments service and this section's app) and call the app's /payment endpoint using cURL or Postman. Using cURL, the request command looks the following snippet:

```
curl -X POST -H 'content-type:application/json' -d '{"amount":1000}'
➡ http://localhost:9090/payment
```

In the console where you executed the cURL command, you'll find a response, as presented in the next snippet:

```
{"id":"1c518ead-2477-410f-82f3-54533b4058ff","amount":1000.0}
```

In the payment service's console, you find the log proving that the app correctly sent the request to the payment service:

```
Received request with ID 1c518ead-2477-410f-82f3-54533b4058ff ;Payment
➡ Amount: 1000.0
```

11.2 *Calling REST endpoints using RestTemplate*

In this section, we again implement the app that calls the /payment endpoint of the payment service, but this time we use a different approach: RestTemplate.

I don't want you to conclude that RestTemplate has any problems. It is being put to sleep not because it's not working properly or because it's not a good tool. But as apps evolved, we started to need more capabilities. Developers wanted to be able to benefit from different things that aren't easy to implement with RestTemplate, such as the following:

- Calling the endpoints both synchronously and asynchronously
- Writing less code and treating fewer exceptions (eliminate boilerplate code)
- Retrying call executions and implementing fallback operations (logic performed when the app can't execute a specific REST call for any reason)

In other words, developers prefer to get more things out of the box rather than implement them wherever possible. Remember that reusing code and avoiding boilerplate code is one of the primary purposes of frameworks, as discussed in chapter 1. You'll get the chance to compare the examples we implement in sections 11.1 and 11.2 and observe that using OpenFeign is much easier than using RestTemplate.

> **NOTE** Here is a good lesson I learned in my experience: When something is called "deprecated" or "legacy," it doesn't necessarily mean you shouldn't learn it. Sometimes, deprecated technologies are still used in projects many years after being declared deprecated, including RestTemplate and the Spring Security OAuth project.

The steps for defining the call are as follows (figure 11.6):

1 Define the HTTP headers by creating and configuring an `HttpHeaders` instance.

2 Create an `HttpEntity` instance that represents the request data (headers and body).

3 Send the HTTP call using the `exchange()` method and get the HTTP response.

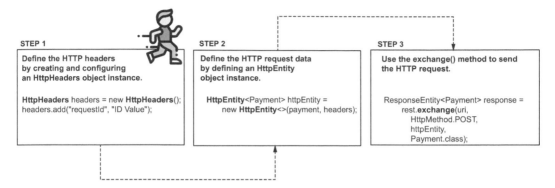

Figure 11.6 To define a more complex HTTP request, you have to use the `HttpHeaders` class to define the headers, then the `HttpEntity` class to represent the full request data. Once you defined the data on the request, you call the `exchange()` method to send it.

We start implementing this example in the project "sq-ch11-ex2." In listing 11.5, you find the definition of the proxy class. Observe how the `createPayment()` method defines the header by creating an `HttpHeaders` instance and adding the needed header "requestId" to this instance using the `add()` method. It then creates a `HttpEntity` instance based on the headers and the body (received by the method as a parameter). The method then sends the HTTP request using `RestTemplate`'s `exchange()` method. The `exchange()` method's parameters are the URI and the HTTP method, followed by the `HttpEntity` instance (that holds the request data) and the type expected for the response body.

Listing 11.5 The app's `PaymentsProxy` calling the /payment endpoint

```
@Component
public class PaymentsProxy {

    private final RestTemplate rest;

    @Value("${name.service.url}")                      We take the URL to the payment
    private String paymentsServiceUrl;      ◁┘         service from the properties file.

    public PaymentsProxy(RestTemplate rest) {   ◁┐     We inject the RestTemplate from the
        this.rest = rest;                             Spring context using constructor DI.
    }

    public Payment createPayment(Payment payment) {
```

```
        String uri = paymentsServiceUrl + "/payment";

        HttpHeaders headers = new HttpHeaders();
        headers.add("requestId",
                UUID.randomUUID().toString());

        HttpEntity<Payment> httpEntity =
            new HttpEntity<>(payment, headers);

        ResponseEntity<Payment> response =
            rest.exchange(uri,
                HttpMethod.POST,
                httpEntity,
                Payment.class);

        return response.getBody();
    }
}
```

We build the HttpHeaders object to define the HTTP request headers.

We build the HttpEntity object to define the request data.

We send the HTTP request and retrieve the data on the HTTP response.

We return the HTTP response body.

We define a simple endpoint to call this implementation, the same as we did for the small endpoint we called in section 11.1.1. The next listing shows you how to define the controller class.

Listing 11.6 Defining a controller class to test the implementation

```
@RestController
public class PaymentsController {

    private final PaymentsProxy paymentsProxy;

    public PaymentsController(PaymentsProxy paymentsProxy) {
        this.paymentsProxy = paymentsProxy;
    }

    @PostMapping("/payment")
    public Payment createPayment(
        @RequestBody Payment payment
        ) {
        return paymentsProxy.createPayment(payment);
    }
}
```

We define a controller action and map it to the /payment path.

We get the payment data as a request body.

We call the proxy method, which in turn calls the endpoint of the payments service. We get the response body and return the body to the client.

We run both apps, the payments service ("sq-ch11-payments") and this section's app ("sq-ch11-ex2"), on different ports to validate our implementation works as expected. For this example, I kept the same configuration from section 11.1.1: port 8080 for the payment service and port 9090 for this section's app.

Using cURL, you can call the app's endpoint, as presented in the next snippet:

```
curl -X POST -H 'content-type:application/json' -d '{"amount":1000}'
➥ http://localhost:9090/payment
```

In the console where you executed the cURL command, you'll find a response, as presented in the next snippet:

```
{
  "id":"21149959-d93d-41a4-a0a3-426c6fd8f9e9",
  "amount":1000.0
}
```

In the payment service's console, you find the log proving that the app correctly sent the payment service request:

```
Received request with ID e02b5c7a-c683-4a77-bd0e-38fe76c145cf ;Payment
⇒ Amount: 1000.0
```

11.3   *Calling REST endpoints using WebClient*

In this section, we discuss using `WebClient` to call REST endpoints. `WebClient` is a tool used in different apps and is built on a methodology we call a *reactive approach*. The reactive methodology is an advanced approach, and I recommend studying it once you know the basics well. A good starting point is reading chapters 12 and 13 of *Spring in Action*, 6th ed., by Craig Walls (Manning, 2021).

Spring's documentation recommends using `WebClient`, but that's only a valid recommendation for reactive apps. If you aren't writing a reactive app, use `OpenFeign` instead. Like anything else in software, it fits well for some cases, but might complicate things for others. Choosing `WebClient` to implement the REST endpoint calls is strongly coupled to making your app reactive.

> **NOTE**   If you decide not to implement a reactive app, use `OpenFeign` to implement the REST client capabilities. If you implement a reactive app, you should use a proper reactive tool: `WebClient`.

Even though reactive apps are a bit beyond the basics, I'd like to make sure you know what using `WebClient` looks like and how this tool differs from others we have discussed so that you can compare the approaches. Let me tell about reactive apps and then use `WebClient` to call the /payment endpoint we used as an example in sections 11.1 and 11.2.

In a nonreactive app, a thread executes a business flow. Multiple tasks compose a business flow, but these tasks are not independent. The same thread executes all the tasks composing a flow. Let's take an example to observe where this approach might face issues and how we can enhance it.

Suppose you implement a banking application where a bank's client has one or more credit accounts. The system component you implement calculates the total debt of a bank's client. To use this functionality, other system components make a REST call to send a unique ID to the user. To calculate this value, the flow you implement includes the following steps (figure 11.7):

1   The app receives the user ID.
2   It calls a different service of the system to find out if the user has credits with other institutions.
3   It calls a different service of the system to get the debt for internal credits.
4   If the user has external debts, it calls an external service to find out the external debt.
5   The app sums the debts and returns the value in an HTTP response.

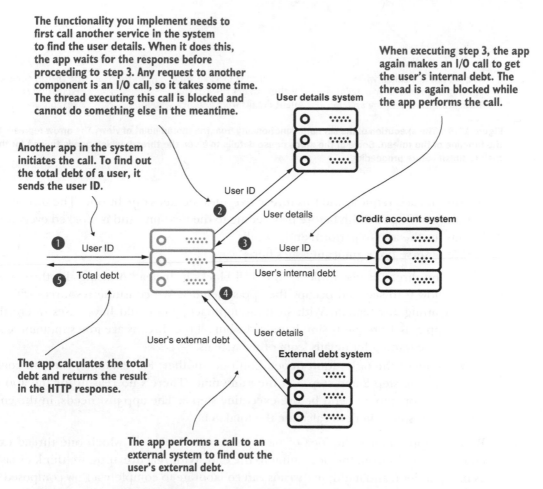

The functionality you implement needs to first call another service in the system to find the user details. When it does this, the app waits for the response before proceeding to step 3. Any request to another component is an I/O call, so it takes some time. The thread executing this call is blocked and cannot do something else in the meantime.

When executing step 3, the app again makes an I/O call to get the user's internal debt. The thread is again blocked while the app performs the call.

User details system

Another app in the system initiates the call. To find out the total debt of a user, it sends the user ID.

User ID

② User details

Credit account system

① User ID

③ User ID

⑤ Total debt

User's internal debt

④

User's external debt

User details

External debt system

The app calculates the total debt and returns the result in the HTTP response.

The app performs a call to an external system to find out the user's external debt.

Figure 11.7   A functionality scenario for demonstrating the usefulness of a reactive approach. A banking app needs to call several other apps to calculate the total debt of a user. Due to these calls, the thread executing the request is blocked several times while waiting for I/O operations to finish.

These are just fictive steps of functionality, but I designed them to prove where using a reactive app could be helpful. Let's analyze these steps deeper. Figure 11.8 presents the execution of the scenario from the thread's point of view. The app creates a new

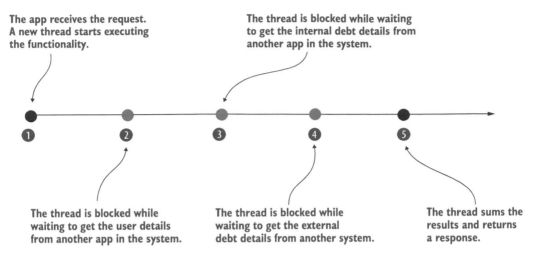

The app receives the request. A new thread starts executing the functionality.

The thread is blocked while waiting to get the internal debt details from another app in the system.

The thread is blocked while waiting to get the user details from another app in the system.

The thread is blocked while waiting to get the external debt details from another system.

The thread sums the results and returns a response.

Figure 11.8 The execution of the scenario functionality from the thread point of view. The arrow represents the timeline of the thread. Some of the steps cause details to block the thread, which needs to wait for the task to finish before proceeding.

thread for each request, and this thread executes the steps one by one. The thread has to wait for a step to finish before proceeding to the next one and is blocked every time it waits for the app to perform an I/O call.

We observe two significant issues here:

1 The thread is idle while an I/O call blocks it. Instead of using the thread, we allow it to stay and occupy the app's memory. We consume resources without gaining any benefit. With such an approach, you could have cases where the app gets 10 requests simultaneously, but all the threads are idle simultaneously while waiting for details from other systems.

2 Some of the tasks don't depend on one another. For example, the app could execute step 2 and step 3 at the same time. There's no reason for the app to wait for step 2 to end before executing step 3. The app just needs, in the end, the result of both to calculate the total debt.

Reactive apps change the idea of having one atomic flow in which one thread executes all its tasks from the beginning to the end. With reactive apps, we think of tasks as independent, and multiple threads can collaborate to complete a flow composed of multiple tasks.

Instead of imagining this functionality as steps on a timeline, imagine it as a backlog of tasks and a team of developers solving them. With this analogy, I'll help you imagine how a reactive app works: the developers are threads, and the tasks in the backlog are the steps of a functionality.

Two developers can implement two different tasks simultaneously if they don't depend on one another. If a developer gets stuck on a task because of an external

Thread 1

Come on folks! We have three simultaneous requests! Hey Ginny, I'll take **step 2 of the first request**.

The tasks that need to be performed

Thread 2

Okay George! I'll take **step 3 of the first request**. I see it doesn't depend on you!

Thread 3

Guys, I'm blocked waiting for the external credit list on **step 4 of the second request**. I'll leave it for later and start on **step 1 of the third request**.

Thread 4

Ginny, the task you left earlier because it was blocked can be solved now. I'll continue it!

Figure 11.9 An analogy of the way a reactive app works. A thread doesn't take a request's tasks in order and wait when it's blocked. Instead, all tasks from all requests are on a backlog. Any available thread can work on tasks from any request. This way, independent tasks can be solved in parallel, and the threads don't stay idle.

dependency, they can leave it temporarily and work on something else. The same developer can get back to the task once it's not blocked anymore, or another developer can finish solving it (figure 11.9).

Using this approach, you don't need one thread per each request. You can solve multiple requests with fewer threads because the threads don't have to stay idle. When blocked on a certain task, the thread leaves it and works on some other task that isn't blocked.

Technically, in a reactive app, we implement a flow by defining the tasks and the dependencies between them. The reactive app specification offers us two components: the producer and the subscriber to implement the dependencies between tasks.

A task returns a producer to allow other tasks to subscribe to it, marking the dependency they have on the task. A task uses a subscriber to attach to a producer of another task and consume that task's result once it ends.

Figure 11.10 shows the discussed scenario implemented in a reactive approach. Take a few minutes to compare this visual with figure 11.8. Instead of being steps on a

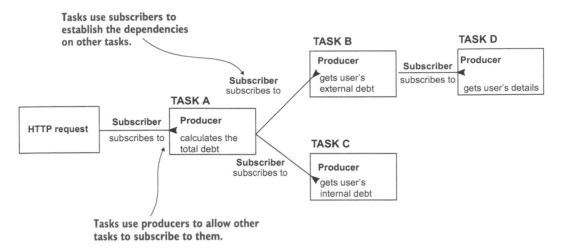

Figure 11.10 In a reactive app, the steps become tasks. Each task marks its dependencies on other tasks and allows other tasks to depend on them. Threads are free to execute any task.

timeline, the tasks are independent of any thread and declare their dependencies. Multiple threads can execute these tasks, and no thread has to wait for a task when an I/O communication blocks it. The thread can begin executing another task.

Moreover, tasks that are not dependent on one another can be simultaneously executed. In figure 11.10, tasks C and D, which were initially steps 2 and 3 in the nonreactive design, can now be executed simultaneously, which helps make the app more performant.

For this demonstration, we use the projects "sq-ch11-payments" (the payments service) and "sq-ch11-ex3" (the app). We used the payment service in sections 11.1 and 11.2, and it exposes the /payment endpoint accessible using the HTTP POST method. For this section's app, we use WebClient to send requests to the endpoint the payment service exposes.

Because WebClient imposes a reactive approach, we need to add a dependency named WebFlux instead of the standard web dependency. The next code snippet shows the WebFlux dependency, which you can add to your pom.xml file or choose where you build the project using start.spring.io:

```
<dependency>
    <groupId>org.springframework.boot</groupId>
    <artifactId>spring-boot-starter-webflux</artifactId>
</dependency>
```

To call the REST endpoint, you need to use a WebClient instance. The best way to create easy access is to put it in the Spring context using the @Bean annotation with a configuration class method, as you learned in chapter 2. The following listing shows you the app's configuration class.

Listing 11.7 Adding a `WebClient` bean to the Spring context in the configuration class

```
@Configuration
public class ProjectConfig {

  @Bean
  public WebClient webClient() {
    return WebClient
            .builder()        ⟵┐   Creates a WebClient bean and
            .build();              adds it in the Spring context
  }
}
```

Listing 11.8 shows the proxy class's implementation, which uses `WebClient` to call the endpoint the app exposes. The logic is similar to what you've learned for `Rest-Template`. You take the base URL from the properties file; specify the HTTP method, headers, and body; and execute the call. `WebClient`'s methods' names differ, but it's quite easy to understand what they're doing after reading their names.

Listing 11.8 Implementing a proxy class with `WebClient`

```
@Component
public class PaymentsProxy {

  private final WebClient webClient;
                                          We take the base URL
  @Value("${name.service.url}")    ⟵┐   from the properties file.
  private String url;

  public PaymentsProxy(WebClient webClient) {
    this.webClient = webClient;
  }
                                          We specify the HTTP method we
  public Mono<Payment> createPayment(    use when making the call.
    String requestId,
    Payment payment) {                   We specify the URI for the call.
    return webClient.post()        ⟵┐
                                          We add the HTTP header value
         .uri(url + "/payment")    ⟵    to the request. You can call the
         .header("requestId", requestId)    ⟵    header() method multiple times if
         .body(Mono.just(payment), Payment.class)    you want to add more headers.
         .retrieve()
         .bodyToMono(Payment.class);    ⟵
  }                                          We get the HTTP
}                                            response body.
```

We provide the HTTP request body.

We send the HTTP request and obtain the HTTP response.

In our demonstration, we use a class named `Mono`. This class defines a producer. In listing 11.8, you find this case, where the method performing the call doesn't get the input directly. Instead, we send a `Mono`. This way, we can create an independent task that provides the request body value. The `WebClient` subscribed to this task becomes dependent on it.

The method also doesn't return a value directly. Instead, it returns a Mono, allowing another functionality to subscribe to it. This way, the app builds the flow, not by chaining them on a thread, but by linking the dependencies between tasks through producers and consumers (figure 11.11).

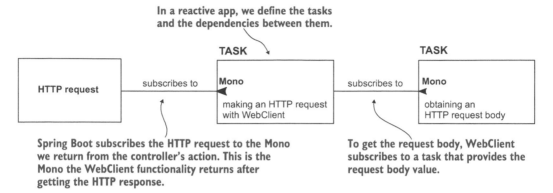

Figure 11.11   The tasks chain in a reactive app. When building a reactive web app, we define the tasks and the dependencies between them. The WebFlux functionality initiating the HTTP request subscribes to the task we create through the producer the controller's action returns. In our case, this producer is the one we get by sending the HTTP request with WebClient. For WebClient to make the request, it subscribes to another task that provides the request body.

Listing 11.8 also shows the proxy method that consumes a Mono producing the HTTP request body and returns it to what the WebFlux functionality subscribes.

To prove the call works correctly, as we did in this chapter's previous examples, we implement a controller class that uses the proxy to expose an endpoint we'll call to test our implementation's behavior. The following listing shows the implementation of the controller class.

Listing 11.9   A controller class exposing an endpoint and calling the proxy

```
@RestController
public class PaymentsController {

  private final PaymentsProxy paymentsProxy;

  public PaymentsController(PaymentsProxy paymentsProxy) {
    this.paymentsProxy = paymentsProxy;
  }

  @PostMapping("/payment")
  public Mono<Payment> createPayment(
      @RequestBody Payment payment
    ) {
    String requestId = UUID.randomUUID().toString();
    return paymentsProxy.createPayment(requestId, payment);
  }
}
```

You can test the functionality of both apps, "sq-ch11-payments" (the payments service) and "sq-ch11-ex3," by calling the /payment endpoint with cURL or Postman. Using cURL, the request command looks like the following snippet:

```
curl -X POST -H 'content-type:application/json' -d '{"amount":1000}'
➥ http://localhost:9090/payment
```

In the console where you executed the cURL command, you'll find a response like the next snippet:

```
{
  "id":"e1e63bc1-ce9c-448e-b7b6-268940ea0fcc",
  "amount":1000.0
}
```

In the payment service console, you find the log proving that this section's app correctly sends the request to the payment service:

```
Received request with ID e1e63bc1-ce9c-448e-b7b6-268940ea0fcc ;Payment
➥ Amount: 1000.0
```

Summary

- In a real-world backend solution, you often find cases when a backend app needs to call endpoints exposed by another backend app.
- Spring offers multiple solutions for implementing the client side of a REST service. Three of the most relevant solutions are as follows:
  - OpenFeign—A solution offered by the Spring Cloud project that successfully simplifies the code you need to write to call a REST endpoint and adds several features relevant to how we implement services today
  - RestTemplate—A simple tool used to call REST endpoints in Spring apps
  - WebClient—A reactive solution for calling REST endpoints in a Spring app
- You shouldn't use RestTemplate in new implementations. You can choose between OpenFeign and WebClient to call REST endpoints.
- For an app following a standard (nonreactive) approach, the best choice is using OpenFeign.
- WebClient is an excellent tool for an app designed on a reactive approach. But before using it, you should deeply understand the reactive approach and how to implement a reactive app with Spring.

Using data
sources in Spring apps

This chapter covers

- What a data source is
- Configuring a data source in a Spring app
- Using JdbcTemplate to work with a database

Almost every app today needs to store data it works with, and often apps use databases to manage the data they persist. For many years, relational databases have provided applications with a simple and elegant way to store data you can successfully apply in many scenarios. Spring apps, like other apps, often need to use databases to persist data, and for this reason, you need to learn how to implement such capabilities for your Spring apps.

In this chapter, we discuss what a data source is and the most straightforward way to make your Spring app work with a database. That straightforward way is the JdbcTemplate tool that Spring offers.

Figure 12.1 shows your progress in previous chapters on learning to use Spring to implement various fundamental capabilities in a system. We have made good

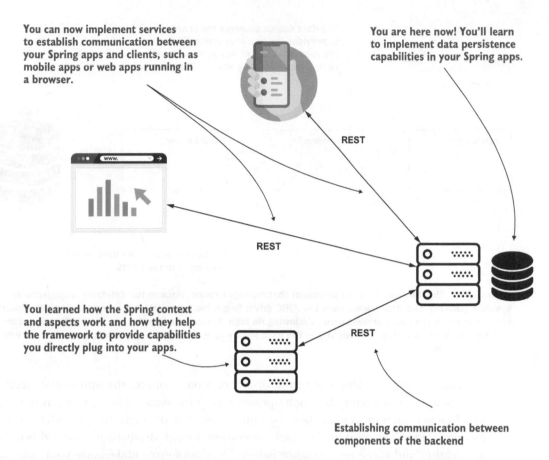

You can now implement services to establish communication between your Spring apps and clients, such as mobile apps or web apps running in a browser.

You are here now! You'll learn to implement data persistence capabilities in your Spring apps.

REST

REST

You learned how the Spring context and aspects work and how they help the framework to provide capabilities you directly plug into your apps.

REST

Establishing communication between components of the backend

Figure 12.1 You already understand the essential parts you implement with Spring in a system. In chapters 1 through 6, you learned the fundamentals and what makes Spring able to provide the capabilities you use in your apps. In chapters 7 through 11, you learned to implement web apps and REST endpoints to establish communication between the system's components. You now start your journey in learning the valuable skills of making your Spring app work with persisted data.

progress, and you can now use Spring to implement capabilities in various parts of a system.

12.1 *What a data source is*

In this section, we discuss an essential component your Spring app needs to access a database: the data source. The data source (figure 12.2) is a component that manages connections to the server handling the database (the database management system, also known as DBMS).

NOTE DBMS is software whose responsibility is to allow you to efficiently manage persisted data (add, change, retrieve) while keeping it secure. A DBMS manages the data in databases. A database is a persistent collection of data.

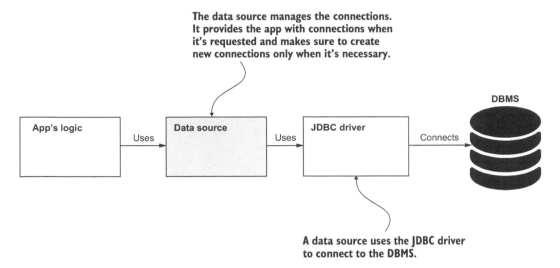

The data source manages the connections. It provides the app with connections when it's requested and makes sure to create new connections only when it's necessary.

| App's logic | Uses | Data source | Uses | JDBC driver | Connects | DBMS |

A data source uses the JDBC driver to connect to the DBMS.

Figure 12.2   The data source is a component that manages connections to the database management systems (DBMS). The data source uses the JDBC driver to get the connections it manages. The data source aims to improve the app's performance by allowing its logic to reuse connections to the DBMS and request new connections only when it needs them. The data source also makes sure to close the connections when it releases them.

Without an object taking the responsibility of a data source, the app would need to request a new connection for each operation with the data. This approach is not realistic in a production scenario because communicating through the network for establishing a new connection for each operation would dramatically slow down the application and cause performance issues. The data source makes sure your app only requests a new connection when it really needs it, improving the app's performance.

When working with any tool related to data persistence in a relational database, Spring expects you to define a data source. For this reason, it's important we first discuss where a data source fits in the app's persistence layer and then demonstrate how to implement a data persistence layer in examples.

In a Java app, the language's capabilities to connect to a relational database is named Java Database Connectivity (JDBC). JDBC offers you a way to connect to a DBMS to work with a database. However, the JDK doesn't provide a specific implementation for working with a particular technology (such as MySQL, Postgres, or Oracle). The JDK only gives you the abstractions for objects an app needs to work with a relational database. To gain the implementation of this abstraction and enable your app to connect to a certain DBMS technology, you add a runtime dependency named the JDBC driver (figure 12.3). Every technology vendor provides the JDBC driver you need to add to your app to enable it to connect to that specific technology. The JDBC driver is not something that comes either from the JDK or from a framework such as Spring.

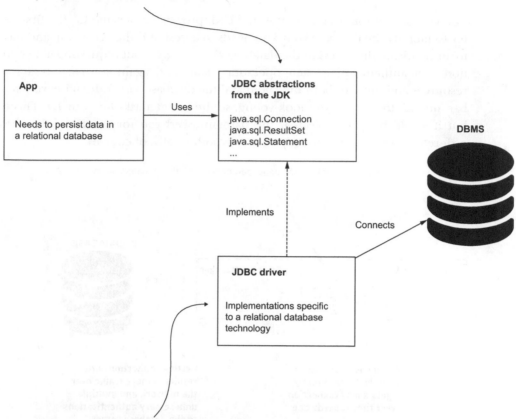

The app uses JDBC abstractions provided by the JDK. Interfaces such as Connection, Statement, and ResultSet of the java.sql package offered by the JDK are common in apps using plain JDBC to connect to a database.

However, abstractions are not enough. The app needs the implementations that enable it to connect to a specific database. A JDBC driver offers the implementations for a specific DBMS. For example, if you need your app to connect to a MySQL database server, you need to add the MySQL JDBC driver, which implements the JDBC abstractions provided by the JDK and defines a way to connect to a MySQL server.

Figure 12.3 When connecting to a database, a Java app uses JDBC. The JDK provides a set of abstractions, but the app needs a certain implementation that depends on the relational database technology the app connects to. A runtime dependency named JDBC driver offers these implementations. For each specific technology, such a driver exists, and the app needs the exact driver that offers the implementations for the server technology it needs to connect to.

The JDBC driver gives you a way to obtain a connection to the DBMS. A first option is to use the JDBC driver directly and implement your app to require a connection each time it needs to execute a new operation on the persisted data. You'll often find this approach in Java fundamentals tutorials. When you learn JDBC in a Java fundamentals tutorial, the examples generally use a class named `DriverManager` to get a connection, as presented in the following code snippet:

```
Connection con = DriverManager.getConnection(url, username, password);
```

The `getConnection()` method uses the URL provided as a value for the first parameter to identify the database your app needs to access and the username and password to authenticate the access to the database (figure 12.4). But requesting a new connection and authenticating each operation again and again for each is a waste of resources and time for both the client and the database server. Imagine you go into a bar and ask for a beer; you look young, so the barman asks for your ID. This is fine, but it would become tedious if the barman asked you for the ID again when you ordered the second and the third beer (hypothetically, of course).

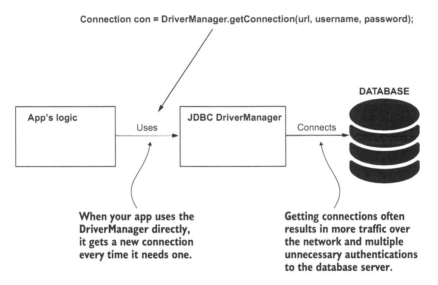

Figure 12.4 Your app can reuse connections to the database server. If it doesn't request new connections, the app becomes less performant by executing unnecessary operations. To achieve this behavior, the app needs an object responsible for managing the connections—a data source.

A data source object can efficiently manage the connections to minimize the number of unnecessary operations. Instead of using the JDBC driver manager directly, we use a data source to retrieve and manage the connections (figure 12.5).

> **NOTE** A data source is an object whose responsibility is to manage the connections to a database server for the app. It makes sure your app efficiently requests connections from the database, improving the persistence layer operations' performance.

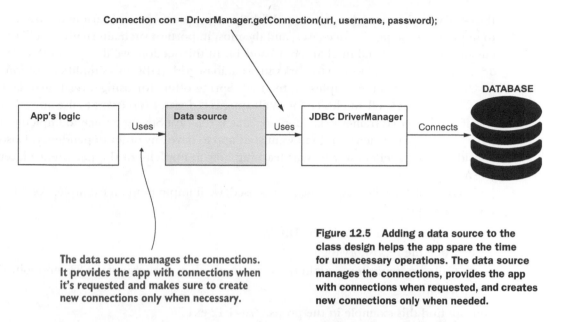

Figure 12.5 Adding a data source to the class design helps the app spare the time for unnecessary operations. The data source manages the connections, provides the app with connections when requested, and creates new connections only when needed.

For Java apps, you have multiple choices for data source implementations, but the most commonly used today is the HikariCP (Hikari connection pool) data source. The convention configuration of Spring Boot also considers HikariCP the default data source implementation too, and this is what we'll use in the examples. You can find out more about this data source here: https://github.com/brettwooldridge/HikariCP. HikariCP is open source, and you can help contribute to its development.

12.2 *Using JdbcTemplate to work with persisted data*

In this section, we implement our first Spring app that uses a database, and we discuss the advantages Spring provides for implementing the persistence layer. Your app can use a data source to obtain connections to the database server efficiently. But how easily can you write code to work with the data? Using JDBC classes provided by the JDK has not proven to be a comfortable way to work with persisted data. You have to write verbose blocks of code even for the simplest operations. In Java fundamentals examples, you might have seen code like that presented in the next snippet:

```
String sql = "INSERT INTO purchase VALUES (?,?)";
try (PreparedStatement stmt = con.prepareStatement(sql)) {
  stmt.setString(1, name);
  stmt.setDouble(2, price);
  stmt.executeUpdate();
} catch (SQLException e) {
  // do something when an exception occurs
}
```

Such a lengthy block of code for a simple operation of adding a new record to a table! And consider that I skipped the logic in the catch block. But Spring helps us minimize the code we write for such operations. With Spring apps, we can use various alternatives to implement the persistence layer, and the most important such alternatives we'll discuss in this chapter and in chapters 13 and 14. In this section, we'll use a tool named JdbcTemplate that allows you to work with a database with JDBC in a simplified fashion.

JdbcTemplate is the simplest of the tools Spring offers for using a relational database, but it's an excellent choice for small apps as it doesn't force you to use any other specific persistence framework. JdbcTemplate is the best Spring choice to implement a persistence layer when you don't want your app to have any other dependency. I also consider it an excellent way to start learning how to implement the persistence layer of Spring apps.

To demonstrate how JdbcTemplate is used, we'll implement an example. We'll follow these steps:

1 Create a connection to the DBMS.
2 Code the repository logic.
3 Call the repository methods in methods that implement REST endpoints' actions.

You can find this example in the project "sq-ch12-ex1."

For this app, we have a table "purchase" in a database. This table stores details about the products bought from an online shop and the price of the purchase. The columns of this table are as follows (figure 12.6):

- *id*—An auto-incrementing unique value that also takes the responsibility of the primary key of the table
- *product*—The name of the purchased product
- *price*—The purchase price

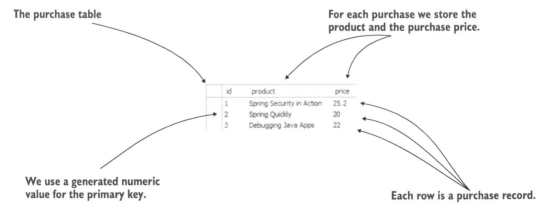

Figure 12.6   The purchase table. Each purchase is stored as a row in the table. The attributes we store for a purchase are the purchased product and the purchase price. The primary key of the table (ID) is a numeric generated value.

This book's examples don't depend on the relational database technology you choose. You can use the same code with a technology of your choice. However, I had to choose certain technology for the examples. In this book, we'll use H2 (an in-memory database, excellent for examples, and, as you'll find in chapter 15, for implementing integration tests) and MySQL (a free and light technology you can easily install locally to prove the examples work with something other than an in-memory database). You can choose to implement the examples with some other relational database technology you prefer, like Postgres, Oracle, or MS SQL. In such a case, you will have to use a proper JDBC driver for your runtime (as mentioned earlier in this chapter and as you know from Java fundamentals). Also, the SQL syntaxes might be different between two different relational-database technologies. You'll have to adapt them to the technology of your choice if you choose to use something else.

> **NOTE** Your app uses a JDBC driver for the H2 database as well. But for H2, you don't have to add it separately because it comes with the H2 database dependency you added in the pom.xml file.

For this book's examples, I assume you already know SQL basics and you understand simple SQL query syntaxes. I also assume you have worked with JDBC in at least theoretical examples because you learn this in Java fundamentals—a mandatory prerequisite for learning Spring. But you might want to refresh your knowledge in this area before going further. I recommend chapter 21 of *OCP Oracle Certified Professional Java SE 11 Developer Complete Study Guide* by Jeanne Boyarsky and Scott Selikoff (Sybex, 2020) for the JDBC part. For a refresher on SQL, I recommend *Learning SQL*, 3rd ed., by Alan Beaulieu (O'Reilly Media, 2020).

The requirements for the app we implement are simple. We'll develop a backend service that exposes two endpoints. Clients call one endpoint to add a new record in the purchase table and a second endpoint to get all the records from the purchase table.

When working with a database, we implement all the capabilities related to the persistence layer in classes we (by convention) name *repositories*. Figure 12.7 shows you the class design of the application we want to implement.

> **NOTE** A repository is a class responsible with working with a database.

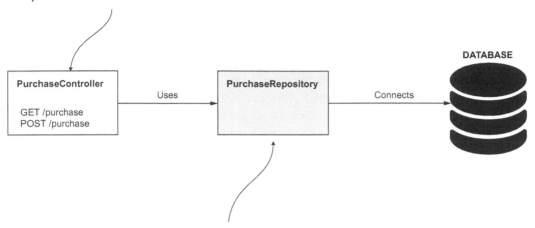

PurchaseController is a REST controller. It exposes two endpoints. The client calls the POST /purchase endpoint to add a new purchase record and the GET /purchase endpoint to get all the existing purchase records from the database.

PurchaseRepository uses the JdbcTemplate tool provided by Spring. JdbcTemplate uses a data source and connects to the database server through JDBC.

Figure 12.7   A REST controller implements two endpoints. When a client calls the endpoints, the controller delegates to a repository object to use the database.

We start the implementation as usual, by adding the necessary dependencies. The next code snippet shows you the dependencies you need to add as they appear in the project's pom.xml file:

```
<dependency>
    <groupId>org.springframework.boot</groupId>
    <artifactId>spring-boot-starter-web</artifactId>
</dependency>
<dependency>
    <groupId>org.springframework.boot</groupId>
    <artifactId>spring-boot-starter-jdbc</artifactId>
</dependency>
<dependency>
    <groupId>com.h2database</groupId>
    <artifactId>h2</artifactId>
    <scope>runtime</scope>
</dependency>
```

We use the same web dependency as we did in previous chapters to implement the REST endpoints.

We add the JDBC starter to get all the needed capabilities to work with databases using JDBC.

We add the H2 dependency to get both an in-memory database for this example and a JDBC driver to work with it.

The app only needs the database and the JDBC driver at runtime. The app doesn't need them for compilation. To instruct Maven we only want these dependencies at runtime, we add the scope tag with the value "runtime."

Even if you don't have a database server for this example, the H2 dependency simulates the database. H2 is an excellent tool we use both for examples and application tests when we want to test an app's functionality but exclude its dependency on a database (we discuss application tests in chapter 15).

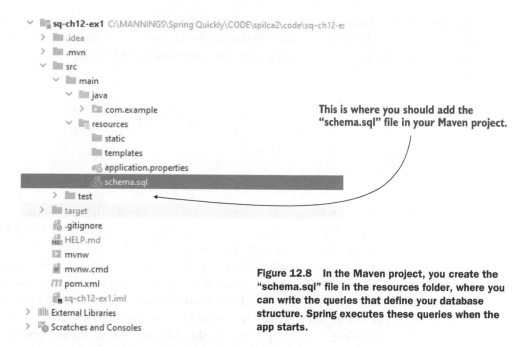

This is where you should add the "schema.sql" file in your Maven project.

Figure 12.8 In the Maven project, you create the "schema.sql" file in the resources folder, where you can write the queries that define your database structure. Spring executes these queries when the app starts.

We need to add a table that stores the purchase records. In theoretical examples, it's easy to create a database structure by adding a file named "schema.sql" to the Maven project's resources folder (figure 12.8).

In this file, you can write all the structural SQL queries you need to define the database structure. You also find developers name these queries "data description language" (DDL). We'll also add such a file in our project and add the query to create the purchase table, as presented in the next code snippet:

```
CREATE TABLE IF NOT EXISTS purchase (
    id INT AUTO_INCREMENT PRIMARY KEY,
    product varchar(50) NOT NULL,
    price double NOT NULL
);
```

NOTE Using a "schema.sql" file to define the database structure only works for theoretical examples. This approach is easy because it's fast and allows you to focus on the things you learn rather than the definition of the database structure in a tutorial. But in a real-world example, you will need to use a dependency that also allows you to version your database scripts. I recommend you look at Flyway (https://flywaydb.org/) and Liquibase (https://www.liquibase.org/). These are two highly appreciated dependencies for database schema versioning. They are beyond Spring basics, so we won't use them in examples in this book. But it's one of the things I recommend you learn right after the fundamentals.

We need a model class to define the purchase data in our app. Instances of this class map the rows of the purchase table in the database, so each instance needs an ID, the product, and the price as attributes. The next code snippet shows the `Purchase` model class:

```
public class Purchase {

  private int id;
  private String product;
  private BigDecimal price;
  // Omitted getters and setters
}
```

You might find it interesting that the `Purchase` class price attribute's type is `Big-Decimal`. Couldn't we have defined it as a `double`? Here's an important thing I want you to be aware of: in theoretical examples, you often find `double` used for decimal values, but in many real-world examples, using `double` or `float` for decimal numbers isn't the right thing to do. When operating with `double` and `float` values, you might lose precision for even simple arithmetic operations such as addition or subtraction. This effect is caused by the way Java stores such values in memory. When you work with sensitive information such as prices, you should use the `BigDecimal` type instead. Don't worry about the conversion. All the essential capabilities Spring provides know how to use `BigDecimal`.

> **NOTE** When you want to store a floating-point value accurately and make sure you don't lose decimal precision when executing various operations with the values, use `BigDecimal` and not `double` or `float`.

To easily get a `PurchaseRepository` instance when we need it in the controller, we'll also make this object a bean in the Spring context. The simplest approach is to use a stereotype annotation (such as `@Component` or `@Service`), as you learned in chapter 3. But instead of using `@Component`, Spring provides a focused annotation for repositories we can use: `@Repository`. As you learned in chapter 3 to use `@Service` for service classes, for repositories, you should use the `@Repository` stereotype annotation to instruct Spring to add a bean to its context. The following listing shows you the repository class definition.

> **Listing 12.1 Defining the `PurchaseRepository` bean**

```
@Repository                              ◁──────    We use the @Repository stereotype
public class PurchaseRepository {                   annotation to add a bean of this class
                                                    type to the Spring context.
}
```

Now that `PurchaseRepository` is a bean in the application context, we can inject an instance of `JdbcTemplate` that we'll use to work with the database. I know what you're thinking! "Where is this `JdbcTemplate` instance coming from? Who created this instance so that we can already inject it into our repository?" In this example, like in many production scenarios, we'll benefit once more from Spring Boot's magic. When Spring Boot saw you added the H2 dependency in pom.xml, it automatically configured a data source and a JdbcTemplate instance. In this example, we'll use them directly.

If you use Spring but not Spring Boot, you need to define the DataSource bean and the JdbcTemplate bean (you can add them in the Spring context using the @Bean annotation in the configuration class, as you learned in chapter 2). In section 12.3, I'll show you how to customize them and for which scenarios you need to define your own data source and JdbcTemplate instances. The following listing shows you how to inject the JdbcTemplate instance Spring Boot configured for your app.

Listing 12.2 Injecting a `JdbcTemplate` bean to work with persisted data

```
@Repository
public class PurchaseRepository {

  private final JdbcTemplate jdbc;

  public PurchaseRepository(           ◁——    We use constructor injection to get
    JdbcTemplate jdbc) {                       the JdbcTemplate instance from the
                                               application context.
    this.jdbc = jdbc;
  }

}
```

Finally, you have a JdbcTemplate instance, so you can implement the app's requirements. JdbcTemplate has an update() method you can use to execute any query for data mutation: INSERT, UPDATE or DELETE. Pass the SQL and the parameters it needs, and that's it; let JdbcTemplate take care of the rest (obtaining a connection, creating a statement, treating the SQLException, and so on). The following listing adds a storePurchase() method to the PurchaseRepository class. The storePurchase() method uses JdbcTemplate to add a new record in the purchase table.

Listing 12.3 Using `JdbcTemplate` to add a new record to a table

```
@Repository
public class PurchaseRepository {              The method takes a parameter that
                                               represents the data to be stored.
  private final JdbcTemplate jdbc;
                                               The query is written as a string,
  public PurchaseRepository(JdbcTemplate jdbc) {    and question marks (?) replace
    this.jdbc = jdbc;                               the queries' parameter values.
  }                                                  For the ID, we use NULL because
                                                     we configured the DBMS to
  public void storePurchase(Purchase purchase) { ◁—    generate the value for this
    String sql =                            ◁————       column.
```

```
    "INSERT INTO purchase VALUES (NULL, ?, ?)";

jdbc.update(sql,
        purchase.getProduct(),
        purchase.getPrice());
    }

}
```

The JdbcTemplate update() method sends the query to the database server. The first parameter the method gets is the query, and the next parameters are the values for the parameters. These values replace, in the same order, each question mark in the query.

With a couple of lines of code, you can insert, update, or delete records in tables. Retrieving data is no more difficult than this. As for the insert, you write and send a query. To retrieve data, this time, you'll write a SELECT query. And to tell JdbcTemplate how to transform the data into Purchase objects (your model class), you implement a RowMapper: an object responsible for transforming a row from the ResultSet into a specific object. For example, if you want to get the data from the database modeled as Purchase objects, you need to implement a RowMapper to define the way a row is mapped to a Purchase instance (figure 12.9).

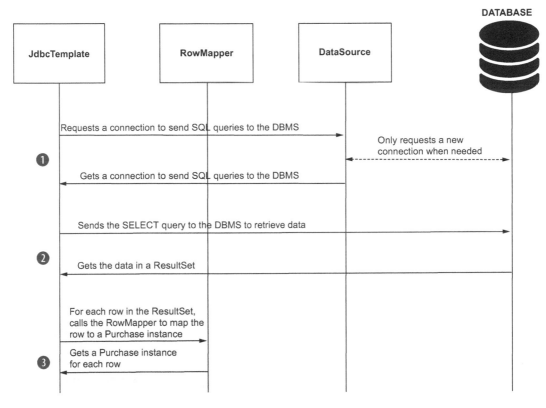

Figure 12.9 JdbcTemplate uses the RowMapper to change the ResultSet to a list of Purchase instances. For each row in the ResultSet, JdbcTemplate calls the RowMapper to map the row to a Purchase instance. The diagram presents all three steps JdbcTemplate follows to send the SELECT query: (1) get a DBMS connection, (2) send the query and retrieve the result, and (3) map the result to Purchase instances.

The following listing shows you how to implement a repository method to get all the records in the purchase table.

Listing 12.4 Using `JdbcTemplate` to select records from a database

The method returns the records it retrieves from the database in a list of Purchase objects.

We implement a RowMapper object that tells JdbcTemplate how to map a row in the result set into a Purchase object. In the lambda expression, parameter "r" is the ResultSet (the data you get from the database), while parameter "i" is an int representing the row number.

We define the SELECT query to get all the records from the purchase table.

We set the data into a Purchase instance. JdbcTemplate will use this logic for each row in the result set.

We send the SELECT query using the query method, and we provide the row mapper object for JdbcTemplate to know how to transform the data it gets in Purchase objects.

```java
@Repository
public class PurchaseRepository {

  // Omitted code

  public List<Purchase> findAllPurchases() {
    String sql = "SELECT * FROM purchase";

    RowMapper<Purchase> purchaseRowMapper = (r, i) -> {
      Purchase rowObject = new Purchase();
      rowObject.setId(r.getInt("id"));
      rowObject.setProduct(r.getString("product"));
      rowObject.setPrice(r.getBigDecimal("price"));
      return rowObject;
    };

    return jdbc.query(sql, purchaseRowMapper);
  }
}
```

Once you have the repository methods and you can store and retrieve records in the database, it's time to expose these methods through endpoints. The following listing shows you the controller implementation.

Listing 12.5 Using the repository object in the controller class

We use constructor dependency injection to get the repository object from the Spring context.

We implement an endpoint a client calls to store a purchase record in the database. We use the repository storePurchase() method to persist the data the controller's action gets from the HTTP request body.

```java
@RestController
@RequestMapping("/purchase")
public class PurchaseController {

  private final PurchaseRepository purchaseRepository;

  public PurchaseController(
      PurchaseRepository purchaseRepository) {
    this.purchaseRepository = purchaseRepository;
  }

  @PostMapping
  public void storePurchase(@RequestBody Purchase purchase) {
    purchaseRepository.storePurchase(purchase);
  }
}
```

```
@GetMapping
public List<Purchase> findPurchases() {
  return purchaseRepository.findAllPurchases();    ◁──┐
  }
}
```

> We implement an endpoint the client calls to get all the records from the purchase table. The controller's action uses the repository's method to get the data from the database and returns the data to the client in the HTTP response body.

If you run the application now, you can test the two endpoints using Postman or cURL.

To add a new record in the purchase table, call the /purchase path with HTTP POST, as presented in the next snippet:

```
curl -XPOST 'http://localhost:8080/purchase' \
-H 'Content-Type: application/json' \
-d '{
    "product" : "Spring Security in Action",
    "price" : 25.2
}'
```

You can then call the HTTP GET /purchase endpoint to prove the app stored the purchase record correctly. The next snippet shows the cURL command for the request:

```
curl 'http://localhost:8080/purchase'
```

The HTTP response body of the request is a list of all the purchase records in the database, as presented in the next snippet:

```
[
    {
        "id": 1,
        "product": "Spring Security in Action",
        "price": 25.2
    }
]
```

12.3 *Customizing the configuration of the data source*

In this section, you'll learn how to customize the data source that `JdbcTemplate` uses to work with the database. The H2 database we used in section 12.2 is excellent for examples and tutorials and to get started with implementing the persistence layer for an app. In production apps, however, you need more than an in-memory database, and often you need to configure the data source as well.

To discuss using a DBMS in real world–type scenarios, we'll change the example we implemented in section 12.2 to use a MySQL server. You'll observe the logic in the example doesn't change, and changing the data source to point to a different database isn't tricky. These are the steps we'll follow:

1   In section 12.3.1, we'll add a MySQL JDBC driver and configure a data source using the "application.properties" file to point to a MySQL database. We'll still let Spring Boot define the DataSource bean in the Spring context based on the properties we define.

2   In section 12.3.2, we'll change the project to define a custom DataSource bean and discuss when something like this is needed in real-world scenarios.

12.3.1   *Defining the data source in the application properties file*

In this section, we'll connect our application to a MySQL DBMS. Production-ready applications use external database servers, so having this skill will help you.

The project for this section's demonstration is "sq-ch12-ex2." If you want to run the example yourself (which I recommend) you'll need to install a MySQL server and create a database you'll connect to. You can also adapt the example to use an alternative database technology as well (such as Postgres or Oracle) if you wish.

We follow two simple steps for performing this transformation:

1   Change the project dependencies to exclude H2 and add the adequate JDBC driver.

2   Add the connection properties for the new database to the "application.properties" file.

For step 1, in the pom.xml file, exclude the H2 dependency. If you use MySQL you need to add the MySQL JDBC driver. The project now needs to have the dependencies, as presented in the next snippet:

```
<dependency>
    <groupId>org.springframework.boot</groupId>
    <artifactId>spring-boot-starter-jdbc</artifactId>
</dependency>
<dependency>
    <groupId>org.springframework.boot</groupId>
    <artifactId>spring-boot-starter-web</artifactId>
</dependency>
<dependency>
    <groupId>mysql</groupId>
    <artifactId>mysql-connector-java</artifactId>    ⟵⎯⎯  We add the MySQL JDBC
    <scope>runtime</scope>                                 driver as a runtime
</dependency>                                               dependency.
```

For step 2, the "application.properties" file should look like the following code snippet. We add the spring.datasource.url property to define the database location, and the spring.datasource.username and spring.datasource.password properties to define the credentials the app needs to authenticate and get connections from the DBMS. Additionally, we need to use the spring.datasource.initialization-mode property with the value "always" to instruct Spring Boot to use the "schema.sql" file and create the purchase table. You don't need to use this property with H2. For H2, Spring Boot runs by default the queries in the "schema.sql" file, if this file exists:

**We configure the URL that defines
the location to the database.**

```
spring.datasource.url=jdbc:mysql://localhost/spring_quickly?
useLegacyDatetimeCode=false&serverTimezone=UTC
spring.datasource.username=<dbms username>
spring.datasource.password=<dbms password>
spring.datasource.initialization-mode=always
```

**We configure the credentials
to authenticate and get
connections from the DBMS.**

**We set the initialization mode to
"always" to instruct Spring Boot to run
the queries in the "schema.sql" file.**

> **NOTE**   Storing secrets (such as passwords) in the properties file is not a good
> practice in production-ready applications. Such private details are stored in
> secret vaults. We won't discuss secret vaults in this book because this subject is
> way beyond fundamentals. But I want you to be aware that defining the pass-
> words in this way is only for examples and tutorials.

With these couple of changes, the application now uses the MySQL database. Spring
Boot knows to create the DataSource bean using the spring.datasource properties
you provided in the "application.properties" file. You can start the app and test the
endpoints like you did in section 12.2.

To add a new record in the purchase table, call the /purchase path with HTTP
POST, as presented in the next snippet:

```
curl -XPOST 'http://localhost:8080/purchase' \
-H 'Content-Type: application/json' \
-d '{
    "product" : "Spring Security in Action",
    "price" : 25.2
}'
```

You can then call the HTTP GET /purchase endpoint to prove the app stored the purchase record correctly. The next snippet shows the cURL command for the request:

```
curl 'http://localhost:8080/purchase'
```

The HTTP response body of the request is a list of all the purchase records in the
database, as presented in the next snippet:

```
[
    {
        "id": 1,
        "product": "Spring Security in Action",
        "price": 25.2
    }
]
```

12.3.2 *Using a custom DataSource bean*

Spring Boot knows how to use a DataSource bean if you provide the connection
details in the "application.properties" file. Sometimes this is enough, and as usual, I
recommend you go with the simplest solution that solves your problems. But in other

cases, you can't rely on Spring Boot to create your `DataSource` bean. In such a case, you need to define the bean yourself. Some scenarios in which you need to define the bean yourself are as follows:

- You need to use a specific `DataSource` implementation based on a condition you can only get at runtime.
- Your app connects to more than one database, so you have to create multiple data sources and distinguish them using qualifiers.
- You have to configure specific parameters of the `DataSource` object in certain conditions your app has only at runtime. For example, depending on the environment where you start the app, you want to have more or fewer connections in the connection pool for performance optimizations.
- Your app uses Spring framework but not Spring Boot.

Don't worry! The `DataSource` is just a bean you add to the Spring context like any other bean. Instead of letting Spring Boot choose the implementation for you and configure the `DataSource` object, you define a method annotated with `@Bean` in a configuration class (as you learned in chapter 3) and add the object to the context yourself. This way, you have full control over the object's creation.

We'll change example "sq-ch12-ex2" to define a bean for the data source instead of letting Spring Boot create it from the properties file. You find these changes in the project "sq-ch12-ex3." We'll create a configuration file and define a method annotated with `@Bean`, which returns the `DataSource` instance we add to the Spring context. The next listing shows the configuration class and the definition of the method annotated with `@Bean`.

Listing 12.6 Defining a `DataSource` bean for your project

We annotate the method with @Bean to instruct Spring to add the returned value to its context.

```
@Configuration
public class ProjectConfig {

    @Value("${custom.datasource.url}")
    private String datasourceUrl;

    @Value("${custom.datasource.username}")
    private String datasourceUsername;

    @Value("${custom.datasource.password}")
    private String datasourcePassword;

    @Bean
    public DataSource dataSource() {
        HikariDataSource dataSource =
            new HikariDataSource();
```

The connection details are configurable, so it's a good idea to continue defining them outside of the source code. In this example, we keep them in the "application.properties" file.

The method returns a DataSource object. If Spring Boot finds a DataSource already exists in the Spring context it doesn't configure one.

We'll use HikariCP as the data source implementation for this example. However, when you define the bean yourself, you can choose other implementations if your project requires something else.

```
        dataSource.setJdbcUrl(datasourceUrl);           We set the connection
        dataSource.setUsername(datasourceUsername);      parameters on the data source.
        dataSource.setPassword(datasourcePassword);
        dataSource.setConnectionTimeout(1000);  ◁───
                                                      You can configure other properties as
        return dataSource;  ◁───                      well (eventually in certain conditions). In
    }                          We return the          this case, I use the connection timeout
}                              DataSource instance,    (how much time the data source waits
                               and Spring adds it to   for a connection before considering it
                               its context.            can't get one) as an example.
```

Don't forget to configure values for the properties you inject using the @Value annotation. In the "application.properties" file these properties should look like the next code snippet. I have intentionally used the word "custom" in their name to stress that we chose these names, and they're not Spring Boot properties. You can give these properties any name:

```
custom.datasource.url=jdbc:mysql://localhost/spring_quickly?
useLegacyDatetimeCode=false&serverTimezone=UTC

custom.datasource.username=root
custom.datasource.password=
```

You can now start and test project "sq-ch12-ex3." The results should be the same as for the previous two projects in this chapter.

To add a new record in the purchase table, call the /purchase path with HTTP POST, as presented in the next snippet:

```
curl -XPOST 'http://localhost:8080/purchase' \
-H 'Content-Type: application/json' \
-d '{
    "product" : "Spring Security in Action",
    "price" : 25.2
}'
```

You can then call the HTTP GET /purchase endpoint to prove the app stored the purchase record correctly. The next snippet shows the cURL command for the request:

```
curl 'http://localhost:8080/purchase'
```

The HTTP response body of the request is a list of all the purchase records in the database, as presented in the next snippet:

```
[
    {
        "id": 1,
        "product": "Spring Security in Action",
        "price": 25.2
    }
]
```

NOTE If you didn't clean up the purchase table and use the same database as for the project "sq-ch12-ex2," the result would contain the records you added previously.

Summary

- For a Java application, the Java Development Kit (JDK) provides abstractions of the objects the app needs to connect to a relational database. The app always needs to add a runtime dependency that provides the implementations of these abstractions. We name this dependency the JDBC driver.

- A data source is an object managing the connections to a database server. Without a data source, the app would request connections too often, affecting its performance.

- By default, Spring Boot configures a data source implementation named HikariCP, which uses a connection pool to optimize the way your app uses the connection to the database. You can use a different data source implementation if it helps your app.

- JdbcTemplate is a Spring tool that simplifies the code you write to access a relational database using JDBC. The JdbcTemplate object depends on a data source to connect to the database server.

- To send a query that mutates data in a table, you use the JdbcTemplate object's update() method. To send SELECT queries to retrieve data, you use one of the JdbcTemplate's query() methods. You'll most often need to use such operations for changing or retrieving persisted data.

- To customize the data source your Spring Boot application uses, you configure a custom bean of the type java.sql.DataSource. If you declare a bean of this type in Spring's context, Spring Boot will use it instead of configuring a default one. You use the same approach if you need a custom JdbcTemplate object. We generally use the Spring Boot–provided defaults, but specific cases sometimes need custom configurations or implementations for various optimizations.

- You can create multiple data source objects, each with their own JdbcTemplate object associated if you want your app to connect to multiple databases. In such a scenario, you'd need to use the @Qualifier annotation to distinguish between objects of the same type in the application context (as you learned in chapters 4 and 5).

Using transactions in Spring apps

This chapter covers
- What a transaction is
- How Spring manages transactions
- Using transactions in a Spring app

One of the most important things we take into consideration when managing data is to keep accurate data. We don't want specific execution scenarios to end up with wrong or inconsistent data. Let me give you an example. Suppose you implement an application used to share money—an electronic wallet. In this application, a user has accounts where they store their money. You implement a functionality to allow a user to transfer money from one account to another. Considering a simplistic implementation for our example, this implies two steps (figure 13.1):

1. Withdraw money from the source account.
2. Deposit money into the destination account.

Both these steps are operations that change data (mutable data operations), and both operations need to be successful to execute the money transfer correctly. But what if the second step encounters a problem and can't complete? If the first finished, but step 2 couldn't complete, the data becomes inconsistent.

Before the money transfer operation

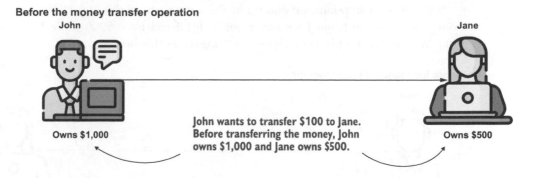

John wants to transfer $100 to Jane. Before transferring the money, John owns $1,000 and Jane owns $500.

Step 1: Withdraw $100 from John's account.

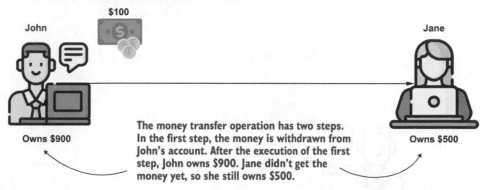

The money transfer operation has two steps. In the first step, the money is withdrawn from John's account. After the execution of the first step, John owns $900. Jane didn't get the money yet, so she still owns $500.

Step 2: Deposit $100 into Jane's account.

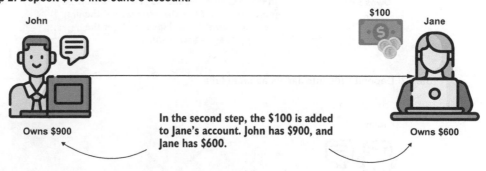

In the second step, the $100 is added to Jane's account. John has $900, and Jane has $600.

Figure 13.1 An example of a use case. When transferring money from one account to another account, the app executes two operations: it subtracts the transferred money from the first account and adds it to the second account. We'll implement this use case, and we need to make sure its execution won't generate inconsistencies in data.

Say John sends $100 to Jane. John had $1,000 in his accounts prior to making the transfer, while Jane had $500. After the transfer completes, we expect that John's account will hold $100 less (that is $1,000 − $100 = $900), while Jane will get the $100. Jane should have $500 + $100 = $600.

If the second step fails, we end up in a situation where the money has been taken from John's account, but Jane never got it. John will have $900 while Jane still has $500. Where did the $100 go? Figure 13.2 illustrates this behavior.

Before the money transfer operation

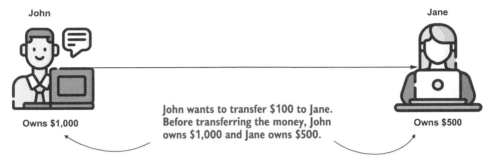

Step 1: Withdraw $100 from John's account.

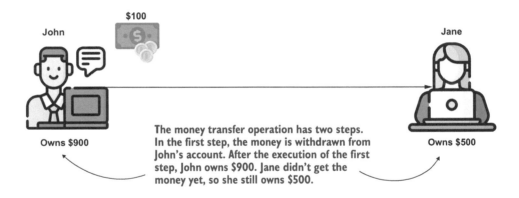

Step 2: Deposit $100 into Jane's account fails.

Figure 13.2   If one of the steps of a use case fails, data becomes inconsistent. For the money transfer example, if the operation that subtracts the money from the first accounts succeeds, but the operation that adds it to the destination account fails, money is lost.

To avoid such scenarios in which data becomes inconsistent, we need to make sure either both steps correctly execute or neither of them do. Transactions offer us the possibility to implement multiple operations that either correctly execute all or none.

13.1 *Transactions*

In this section, we discuss *transactions*. A transaction is a defined set of mutable operations (operations that change data) that can either correctly execute them altogether or not at all. We refer to this as *atomicity*. Transactions are essential in apps because they ensure the data remains consistent if any step of the use case fails when the app already changed data. Let's again consider a (simplified) transfer money functionality consisting of two steps:

1 Withdraw money from the source account.
2 Deposit money into the destination account.

We can start a transaction before step 1 and close the transaction after step 2 (figure 13.3). In such a case, if both steps successfully execute, when the transaction ends (after step 2), the app persists the changes made by both steps. We also say, in this case, that the transaction "commits." The "commit" operation happens when the transaction ends and all the steps are successfully executed, so the app persists the data changes.

COMMIT The successful end of a transaction when the app stores all the changes made by the transaction's mutable operations.

If step 1 executes without a problem, but step 2 fails for any reason, the app reverts the changes step 1 made. This operation is named *rollback*.

ROLLBACK The transaction ends with rollback when the app restores the data to the way it looked at the beginning of the transaction to avoid data inconsistencies.

Before the money transfer operation

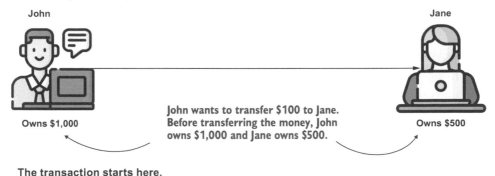

John wants to transfer $100 to Jane. Before transferring the money, John owns $1,000 and Jane owns $500.

The transaction starts here.

Step 1: Withdraw $100 from John's account.

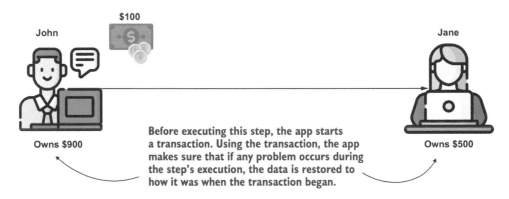

Before executing this step, the app starts a transaction. Using the transaction, the app makes sure that if any problem occurs during the step's execution, the data is restored to how it was when the transaction began.

Step 2: Deposit $100 into Jane's account fails.

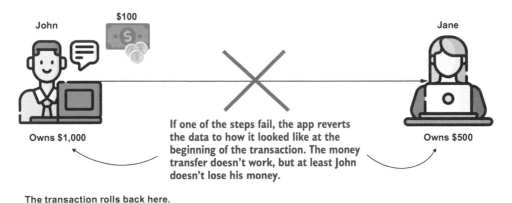

If one of the steps fail, the app reverts the data to how it looked like at the beginning of the transaction. The money transfer doesn't work, but at least John doesn't lose his money.

The transaction rolls back here.

Figure 13.3   A transaction solves possible inconsistencies that could appear if any of the steps of a use case fail. With a transaction, if any of the steps fail, the data is reverted to how it was at the transaction start.

13.2 How transactions work in Spring

Before showing you how to use transactions in your Spring app, let's discuss how transactions work in Spring and the capabilities the framework offers you for implementing transactional code. In fact, a Spring AOP aspect lies behind the scenes of a transaction. (We discussed how aspects work in chapter 6.)

An aspect is a piece of code that intercepts specific methods' execution in a way that you define. In most cases today, we use annotations to mark the methods whose execution an aspect should intercept and alter. For Spring transactions, things aren't different. To mark a method we want Spring to wrap in a transaction, we use an annotation named @Transactional. Behind the scenes, Spring configures an aspect (you don't implement this aspect yourself; Spring provides it) and applies the transaction logic for the operations executed by that method (figure 13.4).

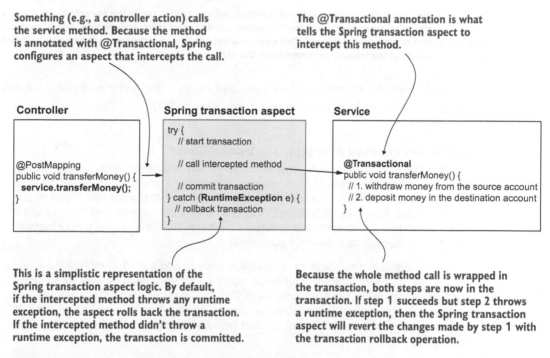

Something (e.g., a controller action) calls the service method. Because the method is annotated with @Transactional, Spring configures an aspect that intercepts the call.

The @Transactional annotation is what tells the Spring transaction aspect to intercept this method.

Controller

```
@PostMapping
public void transferMoney() {
    service.transferMoney();
}
```

Spring transaction aspect

```
try {
    // start transaction

    // call intercepted method

    // commit transaction
} catch (RuntimeException e) {
    // rollback transaction
}
```

Service

```
@Transactional
public void transferMoney() {
    // 1. withdraw money from the source account
    // 2. deposit money in the destination account
}
```

This is a simplistic representation of the Spring transaction aspect logic. By default, if the intercepted method throws any runtime exception, the aspect rolls back the transaction. If the intercepted method didn't throw a runtime exception, the transaction is committed.

Because the whole method call is wrapped in the transaction, both steps are now in the transaction. If step 1 succeeds but step 2 throws a runtime exception, then the Spring transaction aspect will revert the changes made by step 1 with the transaction rollback operation.

Figure 13.4 When you use the @Transactional annotation with a method, an aspect configured by Spring intercepts the method call and applies the transaction logic for that call. The app doesn't persist the changes the method makes if the method throws a runtime exception.

Spring knows to rollback a transaction if the method throws a runtime exception. But I'd like to emphasize the word "throws." When I teach Spring in class, students often understand that it's enough that some operation inside the transferMoney() method throws a runtime exception. But this is not enough! The transactional method should throw the exception further so that the aspect knows it should rollback the changes. If

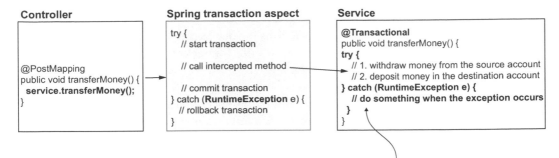

If one of the operations in the method throws a runtime
exception, but the method uses a try-catch block to treat
it, the exception never gets to the aspect. The aspect can't
know such an exception occured, so it will commit the transaction.

Figure 13.5   If a runtime exception is thrown inside the method, but the method treats the exception and doesn't
throw it back to the caller, the aspect won't get this exception and will commit the transaction. When you treat
an exception in a transactional method, such as in this case, you need to be aware the transaction won't be rolled
back, as the aspect managing the transaction cannot see the exception.

the method treats the exception in its logic and doesn't throw the exception further,
the aspect can't know the exception occurred (figure 13.5).

What about checked exceptions in transactions?

Thus far, I've only discussed runtime exceptions. But what about the checked exceptions? Checked exceptions in Java are those exceptions you have to treat or throw;
otherwise, your app won't compile. Do they also cause a transaction rollback if a
method throws them? By default, no! Spring's default behavior is only to roll back a
transaction when it encounters a runtime exception. This is how you'll find transactions used in almost all real-world scenarios.

When you work with a checked exception, you have to add the "throws" clause in the
method signature; otherwise, your code won't compile, so you always know when
your logic could throw such an exception. For this reason, a situation represented
with a checked exception is not an issue that could cause data inconsistency, but is
instead a controlled scenario that should be managed by the logic the developer
implements.

If, however, you'd like Spring to also roll back transactions for checked exceptions,
you can alter Spring's default behavior. The @Transactional annotation, which
you'll learn to use in section 13.3, has attributes for defining which exceptions you
want Spring to roll back the transactions for.

However, I recommend you always keep your application simple and, unless needed,
rely on the framework's default behavior.

13.3 Using transactions in Spring apps

Let's start with an example that teaches you how to use transactions in a Spring app. Declaring a transaction in a Spring app is as easy as using an annotation: @Transactional. You use @Transactional to mark a method you want Spring to wrap in a transaction. You don't need to do anything else. Spring configures an aspect that intercepts the methods you annotate with @Transactional. This aspect starts a transaction and either commits the method's changes if everything went fine or rolls back the changes if any runtime exception occurred.

We'll write an app that stores account details in a database table. Imagine this is the backend of an electronic wallet app you implement. We'll create the capability to transfer money from one account to another. For this use case, we'll need to use a transaction to ensure the data stays consistent if an exception occurs.

The class design of the app we implement is straightforward. We use a table in a database to store the account details (including the money amount). We implement a repository to work with the data in this table, and we implement the business logic (the money transfer use case) in a service class. The service method that implements the business logic is where we'll need to use a transaction. We expose this use case by implementing an endpoint in the controller class. To transfer money from one account to another, someone needs to call this endpoint. Figure 13.6 illustrates the app's class design.

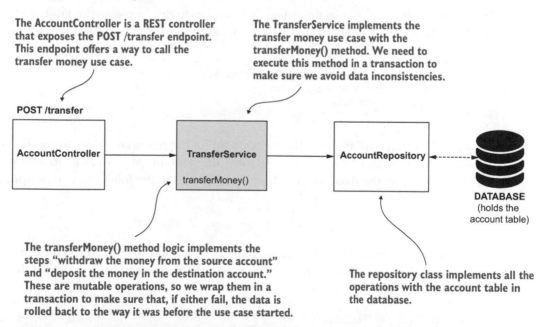

The AccountController is a REST controller that exposes the POST /transfer endpoint. This endpoint offers a way to call the transfer money use case.

The TransferService implements the transfer money use case with the transferMoney() method. We need to execute this method in a transaction to make sure we avoid data inconsistencies.

The transferMoney() method logic implements the steps "withdraw the money from the source account" and "deposit the money in the destination account." These are mutable operations, so we wrap them in a transaction to make sure that, if either fail, the data is rolled back to the way it was before the use case started.

The repository class implements all the operations with the account table in the database.

Figure 13.6 We implement the transfer money use case in a service class and expose this service method through a REST endpoint. The service method uses a repository to access the data in the database and change it. The service method (which implements the business logic) must be wrapped in a transaction to avoid data inconsistencies if problems occur during the method execution.

You find the example in the project "sq-ch13-ex1." We'll create a Spring Boot project and add the dependencies to its pom.xml file, as presented in the next code snippet. We continue using Spring JDBC (as we did in chapter 12) and an H2 in-memory database:

```
<dependency>
    <groupId>org.springframework.boot</groupId>
    <artifactId>spring-boot-starter-web</artifactId>
</dependency>
<dependency>
    <groupId>org.springframework.boot</groupId>
    <artifactId>spring-boot-starter-data-jdbc</artifactId>
</dependency>
<dependency>
    <groupId>com.h2database</groupId>
    <artifactId>h2</artifactId>
    <scope>runtime</scope>
</dependency>
```

The app works with only one table in a database. We name this table "account," and it has the following fields:

- *id*—The primary key. We define this field as an INT value that self increments.
- *name*—The name of the account's owner.
- *amount*—The amount of money the owner has in the account.

We use a "schema.sql" file in the project's resources folder to create the table. In this file, we write the SQL query to create the table, as presented in the next code snippet:

```
create table account (
    id INT NOT NULL AUTO_INCREMENT PRIMARY KEY,
    name VARCHAR(50) NOT NULL,
    amount DOUBLE NOT NULL
);
```

We also add a "data.sql" file near the "schema.sql" in the resources folder to create two records we'll use later to test. The "data.sql" file contains SQL queries to add two account records to the database. You find these queries in the following code snippet:

```
INSERT INTO account VALUES (NULL, 'Helen Down', 1000);
INSERT INTO account VALUES (NULL, 'Peter Read', 1000);
```

We need a class that models the account table to have a way to refer to the data in our app, so we create a class named Account to model the account records in the database, as shown in the following listing.

Listing 13.1   The Account class that models the account table

```
public class Account {

  private long id;
  private String name;
```

```
  private BigDecimal amount;

  // Omitted getters and setters
}
```

To implement the "transfer money" use case, we need the following capabilities in the repository layer:

1 Find the details for an account using the account ID.
2 Update the amount for a given account.

We'll implement these capabilities as discussed in chapter 10, using JdbcTemplate. For step 1, we implement the method findAccountById(long id), which gets the account ID in a parameter and uses JdbcTemplate to get the account details for the account with that ID from the database. For step 2, we implement a method named changeAmount(long id, BigDecimal amount). This method sets the amount it gets as the second parameter to the account with the ID it gets in the first parameter. The next listing shows you the implementation of these two methods.

Listing 13.2   Implementing the persistence capabilities in the repository

We add a bean of this class in the Spring context using the @Repository annotation to later inject this bean where we use it in the service class.

We use constructor dependency injection to get a JdbcTemplate object to work with the database.

```
@Repository
public class AccountRepository {

  private final JdbcTemplate jdbc;

  public AccountRepository(JdbcTemplate jdbc) {
    this.jdbc = jdbc;
  }

  public Account findAccountById(long id) {
    String sql = "SELECT * FROM account WHERE id = ?";
    return jdbc.queryForObject(sql, new AccountRowMapper(), id);
  }

  public void changeAmount(long id, BigDecimal amount) {
    String sql = "UPDATE account SET amount = ? WHERE id = ?";
    jdbc.update(sql, amount, id);
  }
}
```

We get the details of an account by sending the SELECT query to the DBMS using the JdbcTemplate queryForObject() method. We also need to provide a RowMapper to tell JdbcTemplate how to map a row in the result to our model object.

We change the amount of an account by sending an UPDATE query to the DBMS using the JdbcTemplate update() method.

As you learned in chapter 12, when you use JdbcTemplate to retrieve data from the database using a SELECT query, you need to provide a RowMapper object, which tells Jdbc-Template how to map each row of the result from the database to your specific model object. In our case, we need to tell JdbcTemplate how to map a row in the result to the Account object. The next listing shows you how to implement the RowMapper object.

Listing 13.3   Mapping the row to a model object instance with a RowMapper

We implement the RowMapper contract and provide the
model class we map the result row into as a generic type.

```
public class AccountRowMapper
   implements RowMapper<Account> {

  @Override
  public Account mapRow(ResultSet resultSet, int i)
    throws SQLException {
    Account a = new Account();
    a.setId(resultSet.getInt("id"));
    a.setName(resultSet.getString("name"));
    a.setAmount(resultSet.getBigDecimal("amount"));
    return a;
  }
}
```

We implement the mapRow()
method, which gets the query
result as a parameter (shaped
as a ResultSet object) and
returns the Account instance
we map the current row to.

We map the values on the
current result row to the
Account's attributes.

We return the account instance
after mapping the result values.

To test the app more easily, let's also add the capability to get all the account details from the database, as shown in the following listing. We'll use this capability when verifying that the app works as we expect.

Listing 13.4   Getting all the account records from the database

```
@Repository
public class AccountRepository {

  // Omitted code

  public List<Account> findAllAccounts() {
    String sql = "SELECT * FROM account";
    return jdbc.query(sql, new AccountRowMapper());
  }

}
```

In the service class, we implement the logic for the "transfer money" use case. The `TransferService` class uses the `AccountRepository` class to manage the data in the account table. The logic the method implements is as follows:

1 Get the source and destination account details to find out the amount in both accounts.

2 Withdraw the transferred amount from the first account by setting a new value, which is the account minus the amount to be withdrawn.

3 Deposit the transferred amount into the destination account by setting a new value, the current amount of the account plus the transferred amount.

Listing 13.5 shows you how the `transferMoney()` method of the service class implements this logic. Observe that points 2 and 3 define mutable operations. Both these operations change the persisted data (i.e., they update some account's amounts). If we don't wrap them in a transaction, we can get in those cases where the data becomes inconsistent because one of the steps fails.

Fortunately, we only need to use the @Transactional annotation to mark the method as transactional and tell Spring it needs to intercept this method's executions and wrap them in transactions. The following listing shows you the implementation of the money transfer use case logic in the service class.

Listing 13.5 Implementing the money transfer use case in the service class

```
@Service
public class TransferService {

  private final AccountRepository accountRepository;

  public TransferService(AccountRepository accountRepository) {
    this.accountRepository = accountRepository;
  }

  @Transactional                                    ⟵─── We use the @Transactional
  public void transferMoney(long idSender,               annotation to instruct Spring to wrap
                            long idReceiver,             the method's calls in transactions.
                            BigDecimal amount) {
    Account sender =
      accountRepository.findAccountById(idSender);       We get the accounts' details
    Account receiver =                                   to find the current amount
      accountRepository.findAccountById(idReceiver);     in each account.

    BigDecimal senderNewAmount =
      sender.getAmount().subtract(amount);
    BigDecimal receiverNewAmount =                       We calculate the new amount
      receiver.getAmount().add(amount);                  for the destination account.

    accountRepository                                    We set the new amount value
      .changeAmount(idSender, senderNewAmount);          for the sender account.

    accountRepository                                    We set the new amount value
      .changeAmount(idReceiver, receiverNewAmount);      for the destination account.
  }
}
```

We calculate the new amount for the sender account.

Figure 13.7 visually presents the transaction scope and the steps the transferMoney() method executes.

Let's also implement a method that retrieves all the accounts. We'll expose this method with an endpoint in the controller class we'll define later. We will use it to check the data was correctly changed when testing the transfer money use case.

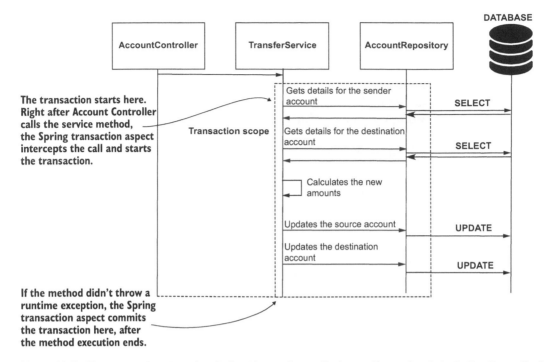

The transaction starts here. Right after Account Controller calls the service method, the Spring transaction aspect intercepts the call and starts the transaction.

If the method didn't throw a runtime exception, the Spring transaction aspect commits the transaction here, after the method execution ends.

Figure 13.7   The transaction starts just before the service method execution and ends just after the method successfully ended. If the method doesn't throw any runtime exception, the app commits the transaction. If any step causes a runtime exception, the app restores the data to how it was before the transaction started.

Using @Transactional

The @Transactional annotation can also be applied directly to the class. If used on the class (as presented in the next code snippet), the annotation applies to all the class methods. Often in real-world apps you will find the @Transactional annotation used on the class, because the methods of a service class define use cases and, in general, all the use cases need to be transactional. To avoid repeating the annotation on each method, it's easier just to mark the class once. When using @Transactional on both the class and the method, the method level's configuration overrides the one on the class:

```
@Service
@Transactional
public class TransferService {

    // Omitted code

    public void transferMoney(long idSender,
                              long idReceiver,
                              BigDecimal amount) {

        // Omitted code
    }
}
```

We often use the @Transactional annotation directly with the class. If the class has multiple methods, @Transactional applies to all of them.

The next listing shows you the implementation of the getAllAccounts() method, which returns a list of all the database's account records.

Listing 13.6   Implementing a service method that returns all the existing accounts

```
@Service
public class TransferService {

  // Omitted code

  public List<Account> getAllAccounts() {
    return accountRepository.findAllAccounts();
  }
}
```

In the following listing, you find the AccountController class's implementation that defines the endpoints that expose the service methods.

Listing 13.7   Exposing the use cases through REST endpoints in the controller class

```
@RestController
public class AccountController {

  private final TransferService transferService;

  public AccountController(TransferService transferService) {
    this.transferService = transferService;
  }

  @PostMapping("/transfer")          ◀──  We use the HTTP POST method for the
  public void transferMoney(              /transfer endpoint because it operates
      @RequestBody TransferRequest request  ◀──  changes in the database's data.
      ) {
    transferService.transferMoney(   ◀──┐  We use a request body to get the
        request.getSenderAccountId(),     │  needed values (source account ID,
        request.getReceiverAccountId(),   │  destination account ID, and amount
        request.getAmount());             │  to be transferred).
  }                                       │
                                      We call the service transferMoney()
  @GetMapping("/accounts")            method, the transactional method that
  public List<Account> getAllAccounts() {  implements the transfer money use case.
    return transferService.getAllAccounts();
  }
}
```

We use an object of type TransferRequest as the transferMoney() controller action parameter. The TransferRequest object simply models the HTTP request body. Such objects, whose responsibility is to model the data transferred between two apps, are DTOs. The following listing shows the definition of the TransferRequest DTO.

Listing 13.8   The `TransferRequest` data transfer object modeling the HTTP request body

```
public class TransferRequest {

  private long senderAccountId;
  private long receiverAccountId;
  private BigDecimal amount;

  // Omitted code
}
```

Start the application, and let's test how the transaction works. We use cURL or Postman to call the endpoint the app exposes. First, let's call the /accounts endpoint to check how the data looks before executing any transfer money operation. The next snippet shows you the cURL command to use to call the /accounts endpoint:

```
curl http://localhost:8080/accounts
```

Once you run this command, you should find an output in the console similar to the one presented in the next snippet:

```
[
 {"id":1,"name":"Helen Down","amount":1000.0},
 {"id":2,"name":"Peter Read","amount":1000.0}
]
```

We have two accounts in the database (we inserted them earlier in this section when we defined the "data.sql" file). Both Helen and Peter own $1,000 each. Let's now execute the transfer money use case to transfer $100 from Helen to Peter. In the next code snippet, you find the cURL command you need to run to call the /transfer endpoint to send $100 from Helen to Peter:

```
curl -XPOST -H "content-type:application/json" -d '{"senderAccountId":1,
➥ "receiverAccountId":2, "amount":100}' http://localhost:8080/transfer
```

If you call the /accounts endpoint again, you should observe the difference. After the money transfer operation, Helen has $900, while Peter now has $1,100:

```
curl http://localhost:8080/accounts
```

The result of calling the /accounts endpoint after the money transfer operation is presented in the next snippet:

```
[
 {"id":1,"name":"Helen Down","amount":900.0},
 {"id":2,"namc":"Peter Read","amount":1100.0}
]
```

The app is working, and the use case gives the expected result. But where do we prove the transaction really works? The app correctly persists the data when everything goes well, but how do we know the app indeed restores the data if something in the method throws a runtime exception? Should we just trust it does? Of course not!

NOTE One of the most important things I learned about apps is that you should never trust something works unless you tested it properly!

I like to say that until you test any feature of your app, it is in a Schrödinger state. It both works and doesn't work until you prove its state. Of course, this is just a personal analogy I make with an essential concept from quantum mechanics.

Let's test the transaction rolls back as expected when some runtime exception occurs. I duplicated the project "sq-ch13-ex1" in the project "sq-ch13-ex2." In this copy of the project, I add only one line of code that throws a runtime exception at the end of the transferMoney() service method, as presented in the following listing.

Listing 13.9 Simulating a problem occurs during the use case execution

```
@Service
public class TransferService {

  // Omitted code

  @Transactional
  public void transferMoney(
   long idSender,
   long idReceiver,
   BigDecimal amount) {

    Account sender = accountRepository.findAccountById(idSender);
    Account receiver = accountRepository.findAccountById(idReceiver);

    BigDecimal senderNewAmount = sender.getAmount().subtract(amount);
    BigDecimal receiverNewAmount = receiver.getAmount().add(amount);

    accountRepository.changeAmount(idSender, senderNewAmount);
    accountRepository.changeAmount(idReceiver, receiverNewAmount);

    throw new RuntimeException("Oh no! Something went wrong!");   ⟵────┐
  }                                                                    │
}       We throw a runtime exception at the end of the service method │
            to simulate a problem that occurred in the transaction.  ┘
```

Figure 13.8 illustrates the change we made in the transferMoney() service method.

We start the application and check the account records by calling the /accounts endpoint, which returns all the accounts in the database:

```
curl http://localhost:8080/accounts
```

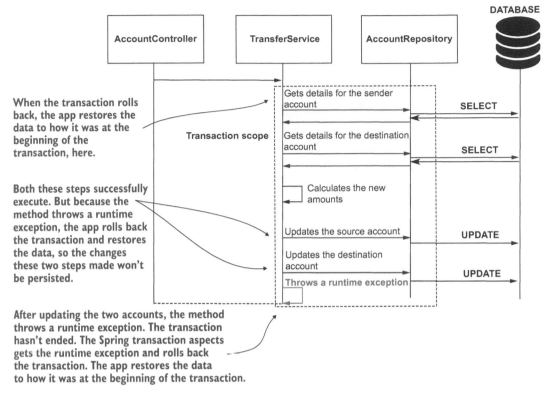

When the transaction rolls back, the app restores the data to how it was at the beginning of the transaction, here.

Both these steps successfully execute. But because the method throws a runtime exception, the app rolls back the transaction and restores the data, so the changes these two steps made won't be persisted.

After updating the two accounts, the method throws a runtime exception. The transaction hasn't ended. The Spring transaction aspects gets the runtime exception and rolls back the transaction. The app restores the data to how it was at the beginning of the transaction.

Figure 13.8   When the method throws a runtime exception, Spring rolls back the transaction. All the successful changes made on the data are not persisted. The app restores the data to how it was when the transaction started.

Once you run this command, you should find an output in the console similar to the one presented in the next snippet:

```
[
 {"id":1,"name":"Helen Down","amount":1000.0},
 {"id":2,"name":"Peter Read","amount":1000.0}
]
```

As in the previous test, we call the /transfer endpoint to transfer $100 from Helen to Peter using the cURL command, shown in the next snippet:

```
curl -XPOST -H "content-type:application/json" -d '{"senderAccountId":1,
➥ "receiverAccountId":2, "amount":100}' http://localhost:8080/transfer
```

Now, the `transferMoney()` method of the service class throws an exception, resulting in an error 500 in the response sent to the client. You should find this exception in the app's console. The exception's stack trace is similar to the one presented in the next code snippet:

```
java.lang.RuntimeException: Oh no! Something went wrong!
    at
com.example.services.TransferService.transferMoney(TransferService.java:30)
➥ ~[classes/:na]
    at
com.example.services.TransferService$$FastClassBySpringCGLIB$$338bad6b.invoke
➥ (<generated>) ~[classes/:na]
    at
org.springframework.cglib.proxy.MethodProxy.invoke(MethodProxy.java:218)
➥ ~[spring-core-5.3.3.jar:5.3.3]
```

Let's call the /accounts endpoint again and see if the app changed the accounts:

```
curl http://localhost:8080/accounts
```

Once you run this command, you should find an output in the console similar to the one presented in the next snippet:

```
[
 {"id":1,"name":"Helen Down","amount":1000.0},
 {"id":2,"name":"Peter Read","amount":1000.0}
]
```

You observe the data didn't change even if the exception happens after the two operations that change the amounts in the accounts. Helen should have had $900 and Peter $1,100, but both of them still have the same amounts in their accounts. This result is the consequence of the transaction being rolled back by the app, which causes the data to be restored to how it was at the beginning of the transaction. Even if both mutable steps were executed, when the Spring transaction aspect got the runtime exception, it rolled back the transaction.

Summary

- A transaction is a set of operations that change data, which either execute together or not at all. In a real-world scenario, almost any use case should be the subject of a transaction to avoid data inconsistencies.
- If any of the operations fail, the app restores the data to how it was at the beginning of the transaction. When that happens, we say that the transaction rolls back.
- If all the operations succeed, we say the transaction commits, which means the app persists all the changes the use case execution did.
- To implement transactional code in Spring, you use the @Transactional annotation. You use the @Transactional annotation to mark a method you expect Spring to wrap in a transaction. You can also annotate a class with @Transactional to tell Spring that any class methods need to be transactional.
- At execution, a Spring aspect intercepts the methods annotated with @Transactional. The aspect starts the transaction, and if an exception occurs the aspect rolls back the transaction. If the method doesn't throw an exception, the transaction commits, and the app persists the method's changes.

14

Implementing data persistence with Spring Data

This chapter covers

- How Spring Data works
- Defining Spring Data repositories
- Using Spring Data JDBC to implement a Spring app's persistence layer

In this chapter, you'll learn to use Spring Data, a Spring ecosystem project that gives you the possibility of implementing a Spring app's persistence layer with minimum effort. As you already know, an application framework's essential role is providing out-of-the-box capabilities that you can directly plug into apps. Frameworks help us save time and also make apps' design easier to understand.

You'll learn to create the app's repositories by declaring interfaces. You'll let the framework provide implementations for these interfaces. You'll literally enable your app to work with a database without implementing the repository yourself and with minimum effort.

We'll start the chapter by discussing how Spring Data works, and in section 14.2 you'll learn how Spring Data integrates into Spring apps. We'll then continue in section 14.3 with a practical example where you'll learn to use Spring Data JDBC to implement an application's persistence layer.

14.1 *What Spring Data is*

In this section, we discuss what Spring Data is and why we should use this project to implement a Spring app's persistence capabilities. Spring Data is a Spring ecosystem project that simplifies the persistence layer's development by providing implementations according to the persistence technology we use. This way, we only need to write a few lines of code to define the repositories of our Spring app. Figure 14.1 offers a visual representation of Spring Data's place from an app's perspective.

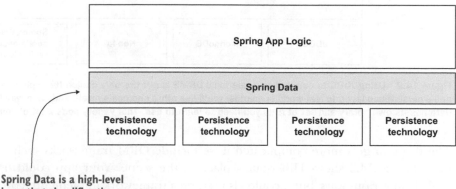

Spring Data is a high-level layer that simplifies the persistence implementation by unifying the various persistence technologies under the same abstractions.

Figure 14.1 The Java ecosystem offers a large number of various persistence technologies. You use each technology in a specific way. Each technology has its own abstractions and class design. Spring Data offers a common abstraction layer over all these persistence technologies to simplify the use of multiple persistence technologies.

Let's see where Spring Data fits in a Spring app. In an app, you have various technologies you can use to work with persisted data. In chapters 12 and 13, we used JDBC, which directly connects to a relational DBMS through a driver manager. But JDBC isn't the only approach you can use to connect to a relational database. Another common way to implement data persistence is using an ORM framework, such as Hibernate. And relational databases aren't the only kind of persisting data technologies. An app might use one of the various NoSQL technologies out there to persist data.

Figure 14.2 shows you some of Spring's alternatives to persist data. Each alternative has its own way of implementing the app's repositories. Sometimes, you even have more options to implement the app's persistence layer for one technology (such as JDBC). For example, with JDBC, you can use `JdbcTemplate`, as you learned in chapter 12, but you could work directly with the JDK interfaces (`Statement`, `PreparedStatement`, `ResultSet`, and so on). Having so many ways to implement the app's persistence capabilities adds complexity.

You have various choices for implementing the persistence layer. Your app might directly connect to a relational DBMS through JDBC, or it can choose other libraries to connect to a NoSQL implementation such as MongoDB, Neo4J, or another persistence technology.

Figure 14.2   Using JDBC to connect to a relational DBMS is not the only choice for implementing an app's persistence layer. In real-world scenarios, you'll use other choices as well, and each way to persist data has its own library and set of APIs you need to learn to use. This variety adds a lot of complexity.

The diagram gets more complicated if we include ORM frameworks such as Hibernate. Figure 14.3 shows Hibernate's place in the scene. Your app could use JDBC directly in various ways, but it could also rely on a framework implemented over JDBC.

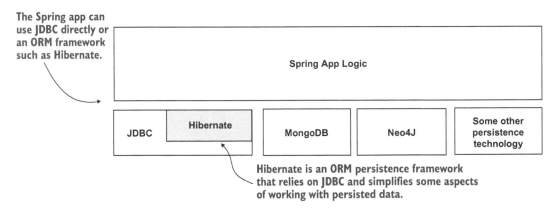

The Spring app can use JDBC directly or an ORM framework such as Hibernate.

Hibernate is an ORM persistence framework that relies on JDBC and simplifies some aspects of working with persisted data.

Figure 14.3   Sometimes apps use frameworks built on top of JDBC, such as Hibernate. The variety in choices makes implementing a persistence layer complex. We want to eliminate this complexity from our apps, and, as you'll learn, Spring Data helps us do this.

Don't be worried! You don't need to learn all these at once, and you don't need to know all of them to learn Spring Data. Fortunately, knowing what we already discussed in chapters 12 and 13 on JDBC is enough for a foundation to start learning Spring Data. The reason I made you aware of all these is to demonstrate why Spring Data is so valuable. You might have already asked yourself, "Is there a way we can implement the persistence for all these technologies instead of having to know different approaches for each?" The answer is yes, and Spring Data helps us achieve this goal.

Spring Data simplifies the implementation of the persistence layer by doing the following:

- Providing a common set of abstractions (interfaces) for various persistence technologies. This way, you use a similar approach for implementing the persistence for different technologies.
- Allowing the user to implement the persistence operations using only the abstractions, for which Spring Data provides the implementations. This way, you write less code, so you more quickly implement the app's capabilities. With less written code, the app also becomes easier to understand and maintain.

Figure 14.4 shows Spring Data's position in a Spring app. As you observe, Spring Data is a high-level layer over the various ways to implement the persistence. So, whichever is your choice to implement your app's persistence, if you use Spring Data, you'll write the persistence operations similarly.

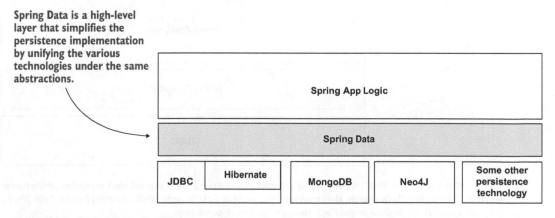

Figure 14.4 Spring Data simplifies the persistence layer implementation by offering a common set of abstractions for various technologies.

14.2 *How Spring Data works*

In this section, we discuss how Spring Data works and how you'll use it for implementing your Spring app's persistence layer. When developers use the term "Spring Data," they refer in general to all the capabilities this project provides to your Spring app to connect to one persistence technology or another. In an app, generally you use a specific technology: JDBC, Hibernate, MongoDB, or another technology.

The Spring Data project offers different modules for one technology or another. These modules are independent of one another, and you can add them to your project using different Maven dependencies. So, when you implement an app, you don't use *the* Spring Data dependency. There is no such thing as one Spring Data dependency. The Spring Data project provides one Maven dependency for each persistence fashion it supports. For example, you can use the Spring Data JDBC module to connect to the DMBS directly through JDBC, or use the Spring Data Mongo module to connect to a MongoDB database. Figure 14.5 shows what Spring Data looks like using JDBC.

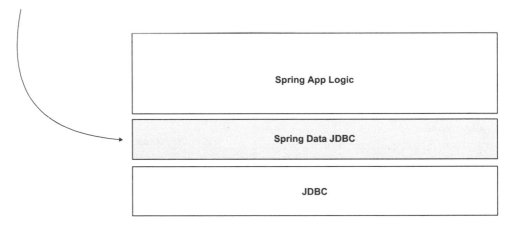

Figure 14.5   **If the app uses JDBC, it only needs the part of the Spring Data project that manages persistence through JDBC. The Spring Data module that manages the persistence through JDBC is called Spring Data JDBC. You add this Spring Data module to your app through its own dependency.**

You can find the full list of Spring Data modules on Spring Data's official page: https://spring.io/projects/spring-data.

Whichever persistence technology your app uses, Spring Data provides a common set of interfaces (contracts) you extend to define the app's persistence capabilities. Figure 14.6 presents the following interfaces:

- `Repository` is the most abstract contract. If you extend this contract, your app recognizes the interface you write as a particular Spring Data repository. Still, you won't inherit any predefined operations (such as adding a new record, retrieving all the records, or getting a record by its primary key). The `Repository` interface doesn't declare any method (it is a marker interface).
- `CrudRepository` is the simplest Spring Data contract that also provides some persistence capabilities. If you extend this contract to define your app's persistence capabilities, you get the simplest operations for creating, retrieving, updating, and deleting records.
- `PagingAndSortingRepository` extends `CrudRepository` and adds operations related to sorting the records or retrieving them in chunks of a specific number (pages).

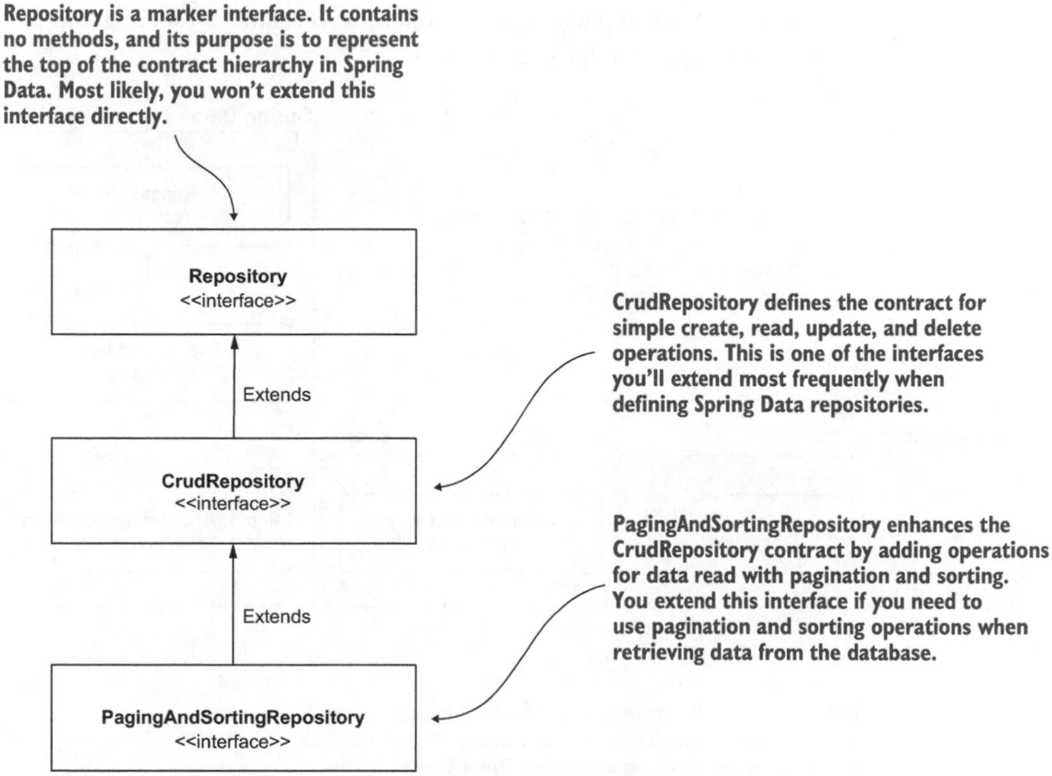

Repository is a marker interface. It contains no methods, and its purpose is to represent the top of the contract hierarchy in Spring Data. Most likely, you won't extend this interface directly.

CrudRepository defines the contract for simple create, read, update, and delete operations. This is one of the interfaces you'll extend most frequently when defining Spring Data repositories.

PagingAndSortingRepository enhances the CrudRepository contract by adding operations for data read with pagination and sorting. You extend this interface if you need to use pagination and sorting operations when retrieving data from the database.

Figure 14.6 To implement your app's repositories using Spring Data, you extend specific interfaces. The main interfaces that represent Spring Data contracts are `Repository`, `CrudRepository`, and `PagingAndSortingRepository`. You extend one of these contracts to implement your app's persistence capabilities.

NOTE Don't confuse the @Repository annotation we discussed in chapter 4 with the Spring Data Repository interface. The @Repository annotation is the stereotype annotation you use with classes to instruct Spring to add an instance of the annotated class to the application context. This Repository interface we discuss in this chapter is specific to Spring Data and, as you'll learn, you extend it or another interface that extends from it to define a Spring Data repository.

Maybe you wonder why Spring Data provides multiple interfaces that extend one another. Why not only one interface with all the operations in it? By implementing multiple contracts that extend each other instead of providing you one "fat" contract with all the operations, Spring Data gives your app the possibility to implement only the operations it needs. This approach is a known principle called *interface segregation*. For example, if your app only needs to use CRUD operations, it extends the Crud-Repository contract. Your app won't get the operations related to sorting and paging records, making your app simpler (figure 14.7).

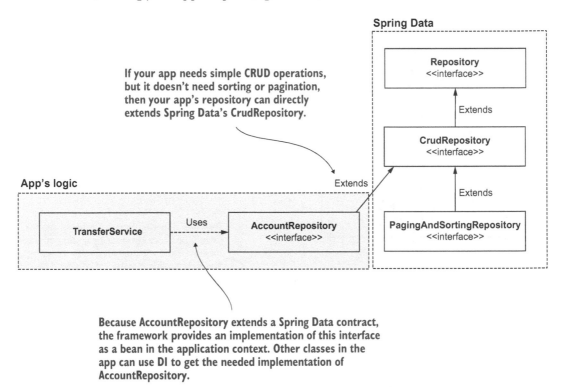

Figure 14.7   To create a Spring Data repository, you define an interface that extends one of the Spring Data contracts. For example, if your app only needs CRUD operations, the interface you define as a repository should extend the CrudRepository **interface. The app adds a bean that implements the contract you define to the Spring context, so any other app components that need to use it can simply inject it from the context.**

If your app also needs paging and sorting capabilities over simple CRUD operations, it should extend a more particular contract, the PagingAndSortingRepository interface (figure 14.8).

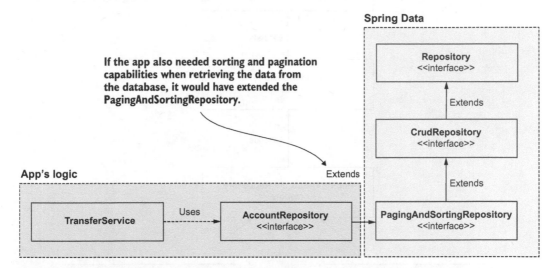

Figure 14.8 If the app needs sorting and paging capabilities, it should extend a more particular contract. The app provides a bean that implements the contract, which can then be injected from any other component that needs to use it.

Some Spring Data modules might provide specific contracts to the technology they represent. For example, using Spring Data JPA, you also can extend the JpaRepository interface directly (as presented in figure 14.9). The JpaRepository interface is a contract more particular than PagingAndSortingRepository. This contract adds operations applicable only when using specific technologies like Hibernate that implement the Jakarta Persistence API (JPA) specification.

Another example is using a NoSQL technology such as MongoDB. To use Spring Data with MongoDB, you would need to add the Spring Data Mongo module to your app, which also provides a particular contract named MongoRepository that adds operations specific to this persistence technology.

When an app uses certain technologies, it extends Spring Data contracts that provide operations particular to that technology. The app could still implement CrudRepository if it doesn't need more than the CRUD operations, but these specific contracts usually provide solutions that are more comfortable to use with the specific technology they're made for. In figure 14.10, the AccountRepository class (of the app) extends from JpaRepository (specific to the Spring Data JPA module).

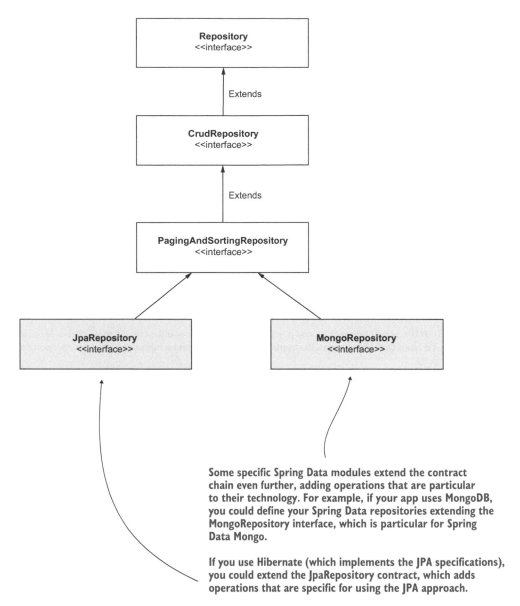

Some specific Spring Data modules extend the contract chain even further, adding operations that are particular to their technology. For example, if your app uses MongoDB, you could define your Spring Data repositories extending the MongoRepository interface, which is particular for Spring Data Mongo.

If you use Hibernate (which implements the JPA specifications), you could extend the JpaRepository contract, which adds operations that are specific for using the JPA approach.

Figure 14.9   Spring Data modules that are specific to certain technologies might provide particular contracts that define operations you can apply only with those technologies. When using such technologies, your app most likely will use these specific contracts.

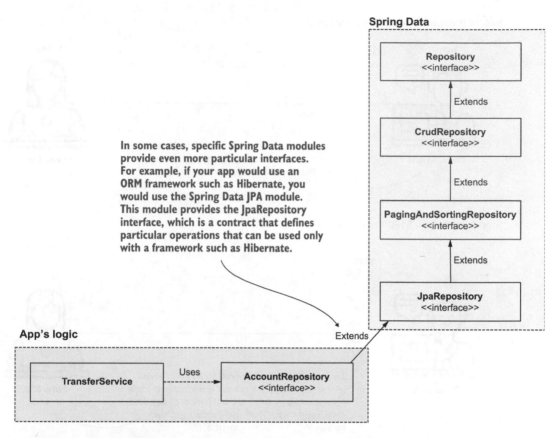

Figure 14.10 Different Spring Data modules might provide other, more particular contracts. For example, if you use an ORM framework such as Hibernate (which implements the JPA) with Spring Data, you can extend the JpaRepository interface, which is a more particular contract that provides operations applicable only when using a JPA implementation, such as Hibernate.

14.3 Using Spring Data JDBC

In this section, we use Spring Data JDBC to implement the persistence layer of a Spring app. We discussed that all you need to do is extend a Spring Data contract, but let's see it in action. In addition to implementing a plain repository, you'll also learn how to create and use custom repository operations.

We'll consider a scenario similar to the one we worked on in chapter 13. The application we build is an electronic wallet managing its users' accounts. A user can transfer money from their account to another account. In this tutorial, we implement the money transfer use case to allow the user to send money from one account to another. The money transfer operation has two steps (figure 14.11):

1 Withdraw a given amount from the sender's account.
2 Deposit the amount in the destination account.

Before the money transfer operation

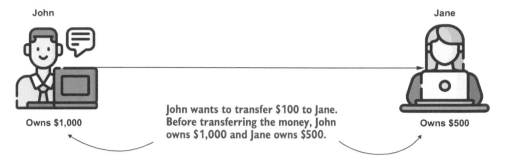

John wants to transfer $100 to Jane.
Before transferring the money, John
owns $1,000 and Jane owns $500.

Step 1: Withdraw $100 from John's account.

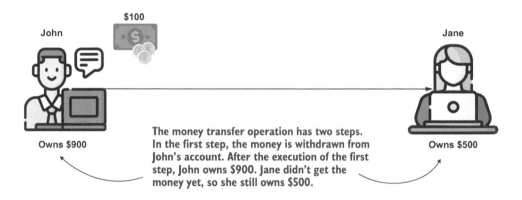

The money transfer operation has two steps.
In the first step, the money is withdrawn from
John's account. After the execution of the first
step, John owns $900. Jane didn't get the
money yet, so she still owns $500.

Step 2: Deposit $100 into Jane's account.

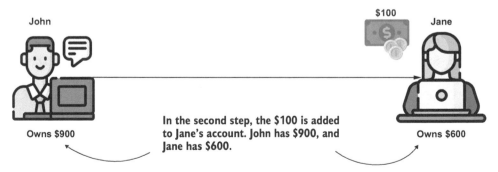

In the second step, the $100 is added
to Jane's account. John has $900, and
Jane has $600.

Figure 14.11   The money transfer use case implies two steps. First, the app withdraws the transferred
amount from the sender's (John's) account. Second, the app deposits the transferred amount into the
receiver's (Jane's) account.

We'll store the account details in a table in the database. To keep the example short and simple and allow you to focus on this section's subject, we'll use an H2 in-memory database (as discussed in chapter 12).

The account table has the following fields:

- *id*—The primary key. We define this field as an INT value that self increments.
- *name*—The name of the account's owner
- *amount*—The amount of money the owner has in the account

You can find this example in the project "sq-ch14-ex1." The dependencies we need to add to the project (in the pom.xml file) are presented in the next code snippet:

```
<dependency>
    <groupId>org.springframework.boot</groupId>
    <artifactId>spring-boot-starter-web</artifactId>
</dependency>
<dependency>
    <groupId>org.springframework.boot</groupId>
    <artifactId>spring-boot-starter-data-jdbc</artifactId>
</dependency>
    <dependency>
    <groupId>com.h2database</groupId>
    <artifactId>h2</artifactId>
    <scope>runtime</scope>
</dependency>
```

We use the Spring Data JDBC module to implement this app's persistence layer.

We add a "schema.sql" file in the Maven project's resources folder to create the account table in the app's H2 in-memory database. This file stores the DDL query needed to create the account table, as presented in the next code snippet:

```
create table account (
    id INT NOT NULL AUTO_INCREMENT PRIMARY KEY,
    name VARCHAR(50) NOT NULL,
    amount DOUBLE NOT NULL
);
```

We also need to add a couple of records to the account table. We use these records to test the application later when we finish implementing it. To instruct the app to add a couple of records, we create a "data.sql" file in the Maven project's resource folder. To add two records in the account table, we'll write a couple of INSERT statements in the "data.sql" file, as presented in the next code snippet:

```
INSERT INTO account VALUES (NULL, 'Jane Down', 1000);
INSERT INTO account VALUES (NULL, 'John Read', 1000);
```

At the end of the section, we'll demonstrate the app works by transferring $100 from Jane to John. Let's model the account table records with a class named Account. We use a field to map each column in the table with the proper type.

Remember that, for decimals, I recommend using `BigDecimal` instead of `double` or `float` to avoid potential issues with the precision in arithmetic operations.

For several operations it provides, such as retrieving data from the database, Spring Data needs to know which field maps the table's primary key. You use the `@Id` annotation, as shown in listing 14.1, to mark the primary key. The following listing shows the `Account` model class.

Listing 14.1   The `Account` class that models the account table records

```
public class Account {

    @Id                          We annotate the attribute that models the
    private long id;             primary key with the @Id annotation.

    private String name;
    private BigDecimal amount;

    // Omitted getters and setters

}
```

Now that you have a model class, we can implement the Spring Data repository (listing 14.2). We only need CRUD operations for this application, so we'll write an interface that extends the `CrudRepository` interface. All the Spring Data interfaces have two generic types you need to provide:

1. The model class (sometimes named entity) for which you write the repository
2. The primary key field type

Listing 14.2   Defining the Spring Data repository

```
public interface AccountRepository          The first generic type value is the type of
    extends CrudRepository<Account, Long> {  the model class representing the table. The
                                             second is the type of the primary key field.
}
```

When you extend the `CrudRepository` interface, Spring Data provides simple operations like getting a value by its primary key, getting all the records from the table, deleting records, and so on. But it can't give you all the possible operations you could implement with SQL queries. In a real-world app, you need custom operations, which need a written SQL query to be implemented. How do you implement a custom operation in a Spring Data repository?

Spring Data makes this aspect so easy that you sometimes don't even need to write a SQL query. Spring Data knows to interpret the method's names based on some naming definition rules and creates the SQL query behind the scenes for you. For example, say you want to write an operation to get all the accounts for a given name. In Spring Data, you can write a method with the following name: `findAccountsByName`.

When the method name starts with "find," Spring Data knows you want to SELECT something. Next, the word "Accounts" tells Spring Data what you want to SELECT. Spring Data is so smart that I could have even named the method findByName. It would still know what to select just because the method is in the AccountRepository interface. In this example, I wanted to be more specific and make the operation name clear. After the "By" in the method's name, Spring Data expects to get the query's condition (the WHERE clause). In our case, we want to select "ByName," so Spring Data translates this to WHERE name = ?.

Figure 14.12 visually represents the relationship between the method's name and the query Spring Data creates behind the scenes.

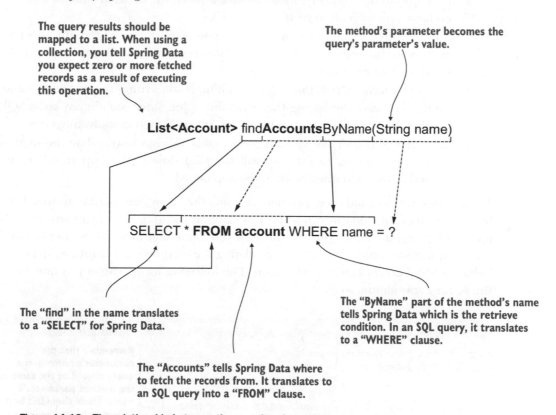

Figure 14.12 The relationship between the repository's method name and the query Spring Data creates behind the scenes

The following listing shows the definition of the method in the AccountRepository interface.

Listing 14.3 Adding a repository operation to get all the accounts with a specified name

```
public interface AccountRepository
    extends CrudRepository<Account, Long> {
```

```
  List<Account> findAccountsByName(String name);

}
```

This magic of translating a method's name into a query looks incredible at first sight. However, with experience you realize it's not a silver bullet. It has a few disadvantages, so I always recommend developers explicitly specify the query instead of relying on Spring Data to translate the method's name. The main disadvantages of relying on the method's name are as follows:

- If the operation requires a more complex query, the method's name would be too large and difficult to read.
- If a developer refactors the method's name by mistake, they might affect the app's behavior without realizing it (unfortunately, not all apps are roughly tested, and we need to consider this).
- Unless you have an IDE that offers you hints while writing the method's name, you need to learn the Spring Data's naming rules. Since you already know SQL, learning a set of rules applicable only for Spring Data is not advantageous.
- Performance is affected because Spring Data also has to translate the method name into a query, so the app will initialize slower (the app translates the method names into queries when the app boots).

The simplest way to avoid these problems is using the @Query annotation to specify the SQL query that the app will run when you call that method. When you annotate the method @Query, it's no longer relevant how you name that method. Spring Data will use the query you provide instead of translating the method's name into a query. The behavior also becomes more performant. The following listing shows you how to use the @Query annotation.

Listing 14.4   Using the @Query annotation to specify the SQL query for an operation

```
public interface AccountRepository
  extends CrudRepository<Account, Long> {


  @Query("SELECT * FROM account WHERE name = :name")
  List<Account> findAccountsByName(String name);

}
```

Remember that the parameter's name in the query should be the same as the method parameter's name. There shouldn't be any spaces between the colon (:) and the parameter's name.

You use the @Query annotation in the same way to define any query. However, when your query changes data, you also need to annotate the method with the @Modifying annotation. If you use UPDATE, INSERT, or DELETE, you also need to annotate the method with @Modifying. The following listing shows you how to use @Query to define an UPDATE query for a repository method.

Listing 14.5   Defining a modifying operation in the repository

```
public interface AccountRepository
    extends CrudRepository<Account, Long> {

    @Query("SELECT * FROM account WHERE name = :name")
    List<Account> findAccountsByName(String name);

    @Modifying
    @Query("UPDATE account SET amount = :amount WHERE id = :id")
    void changeAmount(long id, BigDecimal amount);

}
```

> We annotate the methods that define operations that change data with the @Modifying annotation.

Use DI to get a bean that implements the `AccountRepository` interface wherever you need it in the app. Don't worry that you only wrote the interface. Spring Data creates a dynamic implementation and adds a bean to your app's context. Listing 14.6 shows how the `TransferService` component of the app uses constructor injection to get a bean of type `AccountRepository`. In chapter 5 you learned that Spring is smart and knows that if you requested a DI for a field with an interface type, it needs to find a bean that implements that interface.

Listing 14.6   Injecting the repository in the service class to implement the use case

```
@Service
public class TransferService {

    private final AccountRepository accountRepository;

    public TransferService(AccountRepository accountRepository) {
        this.accountRepository = accountRepository;
    }

}
```

Listing 14.7 shows the implementation of the money transfer use case. We use the `AccountRepository` to get the account details and change the accounts' amounts. We continue to use the `@Transactional` annotation, as you learned in chapter 13, to wrap the logic in a transaction and make sure we don't mess with the data if any of the operations fail.

Listing 14.7   Implementing the transfer money use case

```
@Service
public class TransferService {

    private final AccountRepository accountRepository;

    public TransferService(AccountRepository accountRepository) {
        this.accountRepository = accountRepository;
```

```
  }

  @Transactional                      <──────
  public void transferMoney(
    long idSender,
    long idReceiver,
    BigDecimal amount) {

    Account sender =
      accountRepository.findById(idSender)
        .orElseThrow(() -> new AccountNotFoundException());

    Account receiver =
      accountRepository.findById(idReceiver)
        .orElseThrow(() -> new AccountNotFoundException());

    BigDecimal senderNewAmount =
      sender.getAmount().subtract(amount);

    BigDecimal receiverNewAmount =
      receiver.getAmount().add(amount);

    accountRepository
      .changeAmount(idSender, senderNewAmount);

    accountRepository
      .changeAmount(idReceiver, receiverNewAmount);
  }

}
```

We wrap the use case logic in a transaction to avoid data inconsistencies if any instruction fails.

We get the sender and receiver's account details.

We calculate the new account amounts by subtracting the transferred value from the sender account and adding it to the destination account.

We change the accounts' amounts in the database.

In the transfer money use case, we used a simple runtime exception class named AccountNotFoundException. The next code snippet presents the definition of this class:

```
public class AccountNotFoundException extends RuntimeException {
}
```

Let's add a service method to retrieve all the records from the database and get the account details by the owner's name. We'll use these operations when testing our app. To get all records, we didn't write the method ourselves. Our AccountRepository inherits the findAll() method from the CrudRepository contract, as shown in the following listing.

Listing 14.8 Adding service methods to retrieve account details

```
@Service
public class TransferService {

  // Omitted code

  public Iterable<Account> getAllAccounts() {
    return accountRepository.findAll();        <──────
```

AccountRepository inherits this method from the Spring Data CrudRepository interface.

```
    }

    public List<Account> findAccountsByName(String name) {
        return accountRepository.findAccountsByName(name);
    }
}
```

The following listing shows you how the `AccountController` class exposes the money transfer use case through a REST endpoint.

Listing 14.9   Exposing the transfer money use case with a REST endpoint

```
@RestController
public class AccountController {

    private final TransferService transferService;

    public AccountController(TransferService transferService) {
        this.transferService = transferService;
    }

    @PostMapping("/transfer")
    public void transferMoney(
        @RequestBody TransferRequest request
        ) {
        transferService.transferMoney(
            request.getSenderAccountId(),
            request.getReceiverAccountId(),
            request.getAmount());
    }

}
```

We get the sender and destination account IDs and the transferred amount in the HTTP request body.

We call the service to execute the money transfer use case.

The next code snippet presents the `TransferRequest` DTO implementation the `/transfer` endpoint uses to map the HTTP request body:

```
public class TransferRequest {

    private long senderAccountId;
    private long receiverAccountId;
    private BigDecimal amount;

    // Omitted getters and setters
}
```

In the next listing, we implement an endpoint to fetch the records from the database.

Listing 14.10   Implementing an endpoint to retrieve account details

```
@RestController
public class AccountController {
```

```
// Omitted code

@GetMapping("/accounts")
public Iterable<Account> getAllAccounts(
    @RequestParam(required = false) String name
) {
  if (name == null) {
    return transferService.getAllAccounts();
  } else {
    return transferService.findAccountsByName(name);
  }
}

}
```

We use an optional request parameter to get the name for which we want to return the account details.

If no name is provided in the optional request parameter, we return all the account details.

If a name is provided in the request parameter, we only return the account details for the given name.

We start the application and check the account records by calling the /accounts endpoint, which returns all accounts in the database:

```
curl http://localhost:8080/accounts
```

Once you run this command, you should find an output in the console similar to the one presented in the next snippet:

```
[
 {"id":1,"name":"Jane Down","amount":1000.0},
 {"id":2,"name":"John Read","amount":1000.0}
]
```

We call the /transfer endpoint to transfer $100 from Jane to John using the cURL command shown in the next snippet:

```
curl -XPOST -H "content-type:application/json" -d '{"senderAccountId":1,
➥ "receiverAccountId":2, "amount":100}' http://localhost:8080/transfer
```

If you call the /accounts endpoint again, you should observe the difference. After the money transfer operation, Jane has only $900, while John now has $1,100:

```
curl http://localhost:8080/accounts
```

The result of calling the /accounts endpoint after the money transfer operation is presented in the next snippet:

```
[
 {"id":1,"name":"Jane Down","amount":900.0},
 {"id":2,"name":"John Read","amount":1100.0}
]
```

You can also request to see only Jane's accounts if you use the name query parameter with the /accounts endpoint, as presented in the next snippet:

```
curl http://localhost:8080/accounts?name=Jane+Down
```

As presented in the next snippet, in the response body for this cURL command, you'll only get Jane's accounts:

```
[
    {
        "id": 1,
        "name": "Jane Down",
        "amount": 900.0
    }
]
```

Summary

- Spring Data is a Spring ecosystem project that helps us more easily implement a Spring app's persistence layer. Spring Data provides an abstraction layer over multiple persistence technologies and facilitates the implementation by providing a common set of contracts.
- With Spring Data, we implement repositories through interfaces that extend standard Spring Data contracts:
  - Repository, which doesn't provide any persistence operation
  - CrudRepository, which provides simple CREATE, READ, UPDATE, DELETE (CRUD) operations
  - PagingAndSortingRepository, which extends CrudRepository and adds operations for the pagination and sorting of the fetched records
- When using Spring Data, you choose a certain module according to the persistence technology your app uses. For example, if your app connects to the DBMS through JDBC, your app needs the Spring Data JDBC module, while if your app uses a NoSQL implementation such as MongoDB, it needs the Spring Data Mongo module.
- When extending a Spring Data contract, your app inherits and can use the operations defined by that contract. However, your app can define custom operations with methods in the repository interfaces.
- You use the @Query annotation with the Spring Data repository method to define the SQL query your app executes for that specific operation.
- If you declare a method and don't explicitly specify a query with the @Query annotation, Spring Data will translate the method's name into a SQL query. The method name needs to be defined based on Spring Data rules to understand and translate it into the correct query. If Spring Data cannot solve the method name, the application fails to start and throws an exception.
- It is preferable to use the @Query annotation and avoid relying on Spring Data to translate the method name into the query. Using the name translation approach could come with difficulties:
  - It creates long and difficult-to-read method names for more complex operations, which affect the app's maintainability.

- – It slows down the app's initialization because the app needs now to also translate the method names.
- – You need to learn the Spring Data method name convention.
- – It runs the risk of affecting the app's behavior by an incorrect refactor of the method name.
- Any operation that changes data (e.g., executes INSERT, UPDATE, or DELETE queries) must be annotated with the @Modifying annotation to instruct Spring Data that the operation changes data records.

Testing your Spring app

This chapter covers

- Why testing apps is important
- How tests work
- Implementing unit tests for Spring apps
- Implementing Spring integration tests

In this chapter, you'll learn to implement tests for your Spring apps. A test is a small piece of logic whose purpose is to validate that a specific capability your app implements works as expected. We'll classify the tests into two categories:

- *Unit tests*—Focus only on an isolated piece of logic
- *Integration tests*—Focus on validating that multiple components correctly interact with each other

But when I only use the term "test," I refer to both these categories.

Tests are essential for any application. They ensure that the changes we make during the app's development process don't break existing capabilities (or at least they make errors less likely) and also serve as documentation. Many developers (unfortunately) disregard tests because they are not directly part of the app's business logic, and, of course, it takes some time to write them. Because of this, tests seem to not have a significant impact. Indeed, their impact is not usually visible in the short term, but trust me, tests are invaluable in the long term. I can't stress enough how important it is to make sure you properly test your app's logic.

Why should you write a test instead of relying on manually testing a capability?

- Because you can run that test over and over again to validate things are working as expected with minimum effort (validates the app behaves correctly continuously)
- Because by reading the test steps you can easily understand the use-case purpose (serves as documentation)
- Because tests provide early feedback about new application issues during the development process

Why wouldn't the app's capabilities work a second time if they initially worked?

- Because we continuously change the app's source code to fix bugs or add new features. When you change the source code, you might break previously implemented capabilities.

If you write tests for those capabilities, you can run them any time you change the app to validate things are still working as expected. If you affected some existing functionality, you'd find out what happened before delivering your code to production. *Regression testing* is the approach of constantly testing existing functionality to validate it still works correctly.

A good approach is making sure you test all the relevant scenarios for any specific capability you implement. You can then run the tests any time you change something to validate the previously implemented capabilities were not affected by your changes.

Today, we don't rely only on developers running the tests manually, but we make their execution part of the app's build process. Generally, development teams use what we call a *continuous integration* (CI) approach: they configure a tool such as Jenkins or TeamCity to run a build process every time a developer makes changes. A continuous integration tool is software we use to execute the steps needed to build and sometimes install the apps we implement during the development process. This CI tool also runs the tests and notifies the developers if something has been broken (figure 15.1).

In section 15.1, we start by drawing a big picture of what a unit test is and how it works. In section 15.2, we discuss the two most encountered types of tests you'll find used with Spring apps: unit and integration tests. We'll take examples of capabilities we implemented throughout this book and implement tests for them.

Before diving deep into this chapter, I'd like to make you aware that testing is a complex subject, and we'll focus only on the essential knowledge you need to have when testing Spring apps. But testing is a subject that deserves its own bookshelf. I recommend you also read the book *JUnit in Action* (Manning, 2020) by Cătălin Tudose, which reveals more testing jams that you'll find valuable.

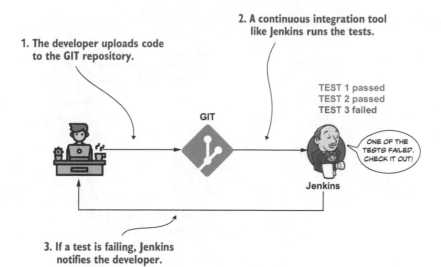

1. The developer uploads code to the GIT repository.

2. A continuous integration tool like Jenkins runs the tests.

GIT

TEST 1 passed
TEST 2 passed
TEST 3 failed

ONE OF THE TESTS FAILED. CHECK IT OUT!

Jenkins

3. If a test is failing, Jenkins notifies the developer.

Figure 15.1   A CI tool, such as Jenkins or TeamCity, runs the tests every time a developer changes the app. If any of the tests fail, the CI tool notifies the developers to check which capability doesn't work as expected and correct the problem.

15.1   *Writing correctly implemented tests*

In this section, we discuss how tests work and what a correctly implemented test is. You'll learn how to write your app's code to make it easy to test, and you'll observe that there's a strong connection between making the app testable and making it maintainable (i.e., easy to change to implement new features and correct errors). Testability and maintainability are software qualities that help one another. By designing your app to be testable, you also help to make it maintainable.

We write tests to validate the logic implemented by a specific method in the project works in the desired way. When you test a given method, usually you need to validate multiple scenarios (ways in which the app behaves depending on different inputs). For each scenario, you write a test method in a test class. In a Maven project (such as the examples we implemented throughout the book), you write the test classes in the project's test folder (figure 15.2).

A test class should focus only on a particular method whose logic you test. Even simple logic generates various scenarios. For each scenario, you'll write a method in the test class that validates that specific case.

Let's take an example. Remember the money transfer use case we discussed in chapters 13 and 14? This was our simple implementation of transferring a given amount between two different accounts. The use case had only four steps:

1 Find the source account details in the database.
2 Find the destination account details in the database.
3 Calculate the new amounts for the two accounts after the transfer.
4 Update the accounts' amount values in the database.

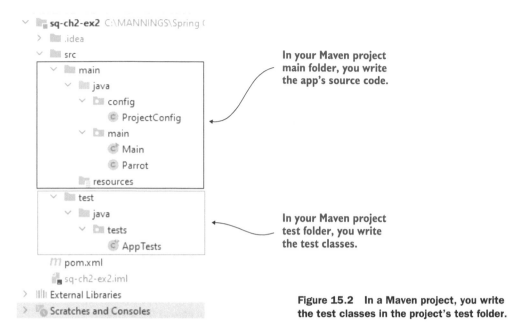

In your Maven project main folder, you write the app's source code.

In your Maven project test folder, you write the test classes.

Figure 15.2   In a Maven project, you write the test classes in the project's test folder.

Even with only these steps, we can still find multiple scenarios relevant for testing:

1 Test what happens if the app can't find the source account details.
2 Test what happens if the app can't find the destination account details.
3 Test what happens if the source account doesn't have enough money.
4 Test what happens if the amounts update fails.
5 Test what happens if all the steps work fine.

For each test scenario, you need to understand how the app should behave and write a test method to validate it works as desired. For example, if for test case 3, you don't want to allow a transfer to happen if the source account doesn't have enough money, you'll test that the app throws a specific exception and the transfer doesn't happen. But depending on the app's requirements, you could allow a defined credit limit for the source account. In such a case, your test needs to take this limit into consideration as well.

The test scenario implementation is strongly related to how the app should work, but technically, the idea is the same in any app: you identify the test scenarios, and you write a test method for each (figure 15.3).

A critical thing to observe is that we can find multiple relevant test scenarios, even for a small method—another reason to keep the methods in your application small! If you write large methods with many code lines and parameters that focus on multiple things simultaneously, identifying the relevant test scenario becomes extremely difficult. We say that the app's testability decreases when you fail to separate the different responsibilities into small and easy-to-read methods.

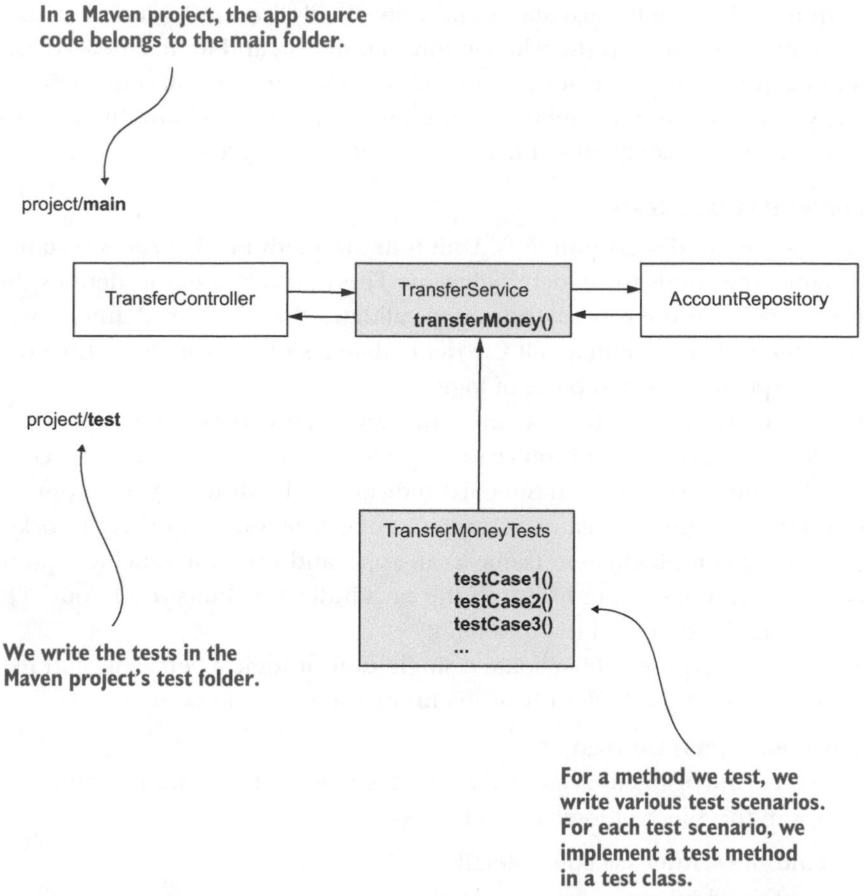

In a Maven project, the app source
code belongs to the main folder.

project/**main**

```
┌──────────────────┐        ┌──────────────────┐        ┌──────────────────┐
│                  │ ──────>│  TransferService │ ──────>│                  │
│ TransferController│       │  transferMoney() │       │ AccountRepository│
│                  │ <──────│                  │ <──────│                  │
└──────────────────┘        └──────────────────┘        └──────────────────┘
```

project/**test**

```
┌──────────────────┐
│ TransferMoneyTests│
│                  │
│   testCase1()    │
│   testCase2()    │
│   testCase3()    │
│      ...         │
└──────────────────┘
```

We write the tests in the
Maven project's test folder.

For a method we test, we
write various test scenarios.
For each test scenario, we
implement a test method
in a test class.

Figure 15.3 For any piece of logic you test, you need to find the relevant test scenarios. For each
test scenario, you write a test method in a test class. You add the test classes in the app's Maven
project test folder. In this figure, the `TransferMoneyTests` class is a test class that contains the
test scenarios for the `transferMoney()` method. `TransferMoneyTests` defines multiple test
case methods to test each relevant scenario in the `transferMoney()`'s method logic.

15.2 *Implementing tests in Spring apps*

In this section, we use two testing techniques for Spring apps you often encounter in
real-world projects. We'll demonstrate each technique by considering a use case we
implemented in the previous chapters and write the tests for it. These techniques are
(in my perspective) a must-know for any developer:

- *Writing unit tests to validate a method's logic.* The unit tests are short, fast to execute, and focus on only one flow. These tests are a way to focus on validating a
  small piece of logic by eliminating all the dependencies.
- *Writing Spring integration tests to validate a method's logic and its integration with specific capabilities the framework provides.* These tests help you make sure your app's
  capabilities still work when you upgrade dependencies.

In section 15.2.1, you'll learn about unit tests. We'll discuss why unit tests are important and the steps you consider when writing a unit test, and we'll write a couple of unit tests as examples for use cases we implemented in the previous chapters. In section 15.2.2, you'll learn to implement integration tests, how these are different from unit tests, and how they complement the unit tests in a Spring app.

15.2.1 *Implementing unit tests*

In this section, we discuss unit tests. Unit tests are methods that call a certain use case in specific conditions to validate behavior. The unit test method defines the conditions in which the use case executes and validates the behavior defined by the app's requirements. They eliminate all the dependencies of the capability they test, covering only a specific, isolated piece of logic.

Unit tests are valuable because when one fails, you know something is wrong with a particular piece of code, and you're shown exactly where you need to correct it. A unit test is like one of your car's dashboard indicators. If you try starting your car and it fails to start, it might be because you ran out of gas or your battery isn't working properly. A car is a complex system (same as an app), and you have no clue what the problem is unless you have an indicator. If the car's indicator shows you're out of gas, then you immediately identified the problem!

Unit tests' purpose is to validate a single unit of logic's behavior, and like a car's indicators, they help you identify problems in a specific component.

IMPLEMENTING A FIRST UNIT TEST

Let's look at one of the use cases we wrote in chapter 14: the money transfer use case. The steps in this piece of logic are as follows:

1 Find the sender's account details.
2 Find the destination account details.
3 Calculate the new amounts for each account.
4 Update the sender's account amount.
5 Update the destination account amount.

The following listing shows you the use case implementation as we worked it in the project "sq-ch14-ex1."

> **Listing 15.1   The implementation of the money transfer use case**

```
@Transactional
public void transferMoney(
  long idSender,
  long idReceiver,
  BigDecimal amount) {                   We find the details of
                                         the sender's account.
  Account sender = accountRepository.findById(idSender)  <──┐
    .orElseThrow(() -> new AccountNotFoundException());      │    We find the
                                                             │    details of the
  Account receiver = accountRepository.findById(idReceiver)  <──┤    destination
    .orElseThrow(() -> new AccountNotFoundException());      │    account.
```

```
BigDecimal senderNewAmount = sender.getAmount().subtract(amount);
BigDecimal receiverNewAmount = receiver.getAmount().add(amount);

accountRepository
  .changeAmount(idSender, senderNewAmount);
accountRepository
  .changeAmount(idReceiver, receiverNewAmount);
}
```

We calculate the accounts' amounts.

We update the new amount in the sender account.

We update the new amount in the destination account.

Usually, the most obvious scenarios and the first we write tests for are the *happy flows*: an execution that encountered no exceptions or errors. Figure 15.4 visually represents the happy flow of our money transfer use case.

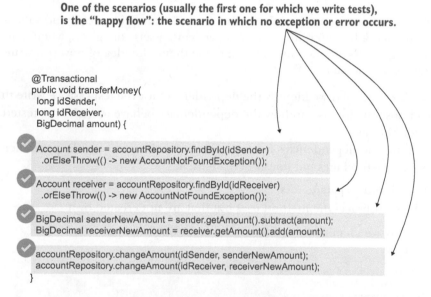

One of the scenarios (usually the first one for which we write tests), is the "happy flow": the scenario in which no exception or error occurs.

```
@Transactional
public void transferMoney(
  long idSender,
  long idReceiver,
  BigDecimal amount) {

  Account sender = accountRepository.findById(idSender)
    .orElseThrow(() -> new AccountNotFoundException());

  Account receiver = accountRepository.findById(idReceiver)
    .orElseThrow(() -> new AccountNotFoundException());

  BigDecimal senderNewAmount = sender.getAmount().subtract(amount);
  BigDecimal receiverNewAmount = receiver.getAmount().add(amount);

  accountRepository.changeAmount(idSender, senderNewAmount);
  accountRepository.changeAmount(idReceiver, receiverNewAmount);
}
```

Figure 15.4 The happy flow: an execution for which no errors or exceptions are encountered. Usually, the happy flows are the first to write tests because they are the most obvious scenarios.

Let's write a unit test for this happy flow of the money transfer use case. Any test has three main parts (figure 15.5):

1. *Assumptions*—We need to define any input and find any dependency of the logic we need to control to achieve the desired flow scenario. For this point, we'll answer the following questions: what inputs should we provide, and how should dependencies behave for the tested logic to act in the specific way we want?
2. *Call/Execution*—We need to call the logic we test to validate its behavior.
3. *Validations*—We need to define all the validations that need to be done for the given piece of logic. We'll answer this question: what should happen when this piece of logic is called in the given conditions?

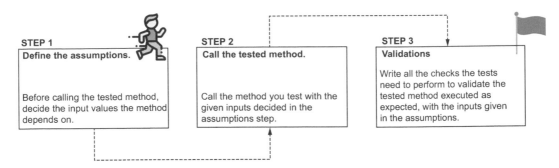

Figure 15.5   **The steps for writing a unit test. Write the assumptions by defining the method inputs. Call the method with the defined assumptions and write the checks the tests need to perform to validate the method's behavior is correct.**

> **NOTE**   Sometimes, you'll find these three steps (assumptions, call, and validations) named a bit differently: "arrange, act, and assert" or "given, when, and then." Regardless of how you prefer to name them, the idea of how you write the tests stays the same.

In the test's *assumptions*, we identify the dependencies for the test case we write the test for. We choose the inputs and how the dependencies behave to make the tested logic act in a certain way.

Which are the dependencies for the money transfer use case? Dependencies are anything the method uses but doesn't create itself:

- The method's parameters
- Object instances the method uses but that are not created by it

In figure 15.6, we identify these dependencies for our example.

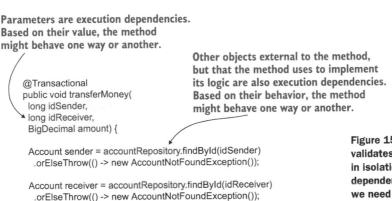

Figure 15.6   **A unit test validates a use case logic in isolation from any dependency. To write the test, we need to make sure we know the dependencies and how to control them. For our scenario, the parameters and the `AccountRepository` object are dependencies we need to control for the test.**

When we call the method to test it, we can provide any values for its three parameters to control the execution flow. But the `AccountRepository` instance is a bit more complicated. The `transferMoney()` method execution depends on how the `findById()` method of the `AccountRepository` instance behaves.

But remember, a unit test focuses on only one piece of logic, so it should not call the `findById()` method. The unit test should assume `findById()` works in a given way and assert that the tested method's execution does what's expected for the given situation.

But the tested method calls `findById()`. How could we control it? To control such a dependency, we use *mocks*: a fake object whose behavior we can control. In this case, instead of using the real `AccountRepository` object, we'll make sure the tested method uses this fake object. We'll take advantage of controlling how this fake object behaves to induce all the different executions of the `transferMoney()` method that we want to test.

Figure 15.7 shows you what we want to do. We replace the `AccountRepository` object with a mock to eliminate the tested object's dependency.

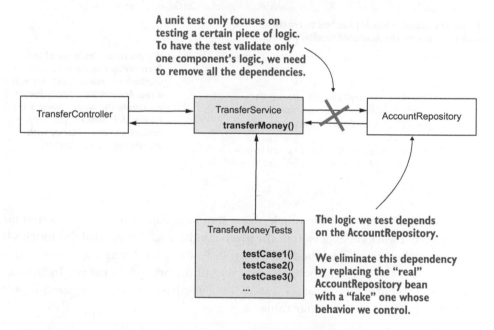

Figure 15.7 To allow the unit test to focus only on the `transferMoney()` method's logic, we eliminate the dependency to the `AccountRepository` object. We use a mock object to replace the real `AccountRepository` instance, and we control this fake instance to test how the `transferMoney()` method behaves in different situations.

In listing 15.2, we start implementing the unit test. After creating a new class in the Maven's project test folder, we start implementing the first test scenario by writing a new method we annotate with the @Test annotation.

> **NOTE** For the examples in this book, we use JUnit 5 Jupiter, the latest JUnit version, to implement the unit and integration tests. However, in real-world apps, you might also find JUnit 4 used often. This is one more reason I recommend you also read books that focus on testing. Chapter 4 of *JUnit in Action* (Manning, 2020) by Cătălin Tudose focuses on the differences between JUnit 4 and JUnit 5.

We create a TransferService instance to call the transferMoney() method that we want to test. Instead of using a real AccountRepository instance, we create a mock object that we can control. To create such a mock object, we use a method named mock(). This mock() method is provided by a dependency named Mockito (often used with JUnit to implement tests).

Listing 15.2   Creating the object whose method we want to unit test

We use the Mockito mock() method to create a mock instance for the AccountRepository object.

```
public class TransferServiceUnitTests {

  @Test
  public void moneyTransferHappyFlow() {
    AccountRepository accountRepository =
      mock(AccountRepository.class);

    TransferService transferService =
      new TransferService(accountRepository);
  }
}
```

We create an instance of the TransferService object whose method we want to test. Instead of a real AccountRepository instance, we create the object using a mock AccountRepository. This way, we replace the dependency with something we can control.

We can now specify how the mock object should behave, then call the tested method and prove it works as expected in the given conditions. You control the mock's behavior using the given() method, as shown in listing 15.3. Using the given() method, you tell the mock how to behave when one of its methods is called. In our case, we want the AccountRepository's findById() method to return a specific Account instance for a given parameter value.

> **NOTE** In a real-world app, a good practice is using the @DisplayName annotation to describe the test scenario (as you see in the next listing). In our examples, I took out the @DisplayName annotation to save space and allow you focus on the test logic. However, using it in a real-world app can help you, but also other developers on the team, better understand the implemented test scenario.

> **Listing 15.3 A unit test validating the happy flow**

We control the mock's findById() method to return the sender account instance when it gets the sender account ID. You can read this line as "If one calls the findById() method with the sender ID parameter, then return the sender account instance."

```
public class TransferServiceUnitTests {

  @Test
  @DisplayName("Test the amount is transferred " +
    "from one account to another if no exception occurs.")
  public void moneyTransferHappyFlow() {
    AccountRepository accountRepository =
      mock(AccountRepository.class);
    TransferService transferService =
      new TransferService(accountRepository);

    Account sender = new Account();
    sender.setId(1);
    sender.setAmount(new BigDecimal(1000));

    Account destination = new Account();
    destination.setId(2);
    destination.setAmount(new BigDecimal(1000));

    given(accountRepository.findById(sender.getId()))
      .willReturn(Optional.of(sender));

    given(accountRepository.findById(destination.getId()))
      .willReturn(Optional.of(destination));

    transferService.transferMoney(
        sender.getId(),
        destination.getId(),
        new BigDecimal(100)
      );

  }

}
```

We create the sender and the destination Account instances, which hold the Account details, which we assume the app would find in the database.

We call the method we want to test with the sender ID, destination ID, and the value to be transferred.

We control the mock's findById() method to return the destination account instance when it gets the destination account ID. You can read this line as "If one calls the findById() method with the destination ID parameter, then return the destination account instance."

The only thing we still need to do is tell the test what should happen when the tested method executes. What do we expect? We know this method's purpose is to transfer the money from one given account to another. So, we expect that it calls the repository instance to change the amounts with the right values. In listing 15.4, we add the test instructions that verify the method correctly called the repository instance's methods to change the amounts.

To verify a mock's object's method has been called, you use the verify() method, as presented in the following listing.

Listing 15.4   A unit test validating the happy flow

```
public class TransferServiceUnitTests {

  @Test
  public void moneyTransferHappyFlow() {
    AccountRepository accountRepository =
      mock(AccountRepository.class);
    TransferService transferService =
      new TransferService(accountRepository);

    Account sender = new Account();
    sender.setId(1);
    sender.setAmount(new BigDecimal(1000));

    Account destination = new Account();
    destination.setId(2);
    destination.setAmount(new BigDecimal(1000));

    given(accountRepository.findById(sender.getId()))
      .willReturn(Optional.of(sender));

    given(accountRepository.findById(destination.getId()))
      .willReturn(Optional.of(destination));

    transferService.transferMoney(
                    sender.getId(),
                    destination.getId(),
                    new BigDecimal(100)
                );

    verify(accountRepository)
      .changeAmount(1, new BigDecimal(900));

    verify(accountRepository)
      .changeAmount(2, new BigDecimal(1100));


  }


}
```

> **Verify that the changeAmount() method in the AccountRepository was called with the expected parameters.**

If you run the test now (usually in an IDE by right-clicking on the test class and select-ing the "Run tests" option), you should observe the tests succeed. When a test suc-ceeds, the IDE displays them in green, and the console doesn't show any exception message. If a test fails, it's usually displayed in either red or yellow in an IDE (fig-ure 15.8).

Even if you find, in many cases, the mock() method being declared inside the method, as presented in listings 15.2 through 15.4, I usually prefer a different approach to create the mock object. It's not necessarily better or more often used, but I consider it a cleaner way to use annotations to create the mock and the tested object, as presented in listing 15.5.

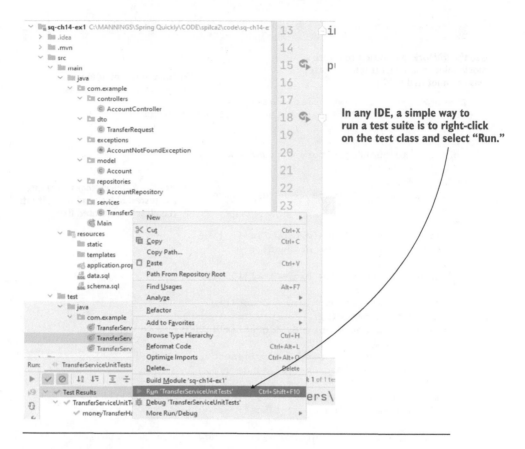

In any IDE, a simple way to run a test suite is to right-click on the test class and select "Run."

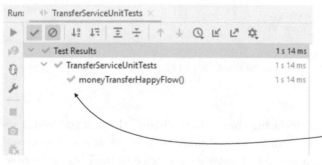

The IDE displays the results as shown in this image. A green check means the test passed. If the IDE displayed a red or yellow X, it means the tests failed. When a test fails, you can check the app's console to find out more about the reason it failed.

Figure 15.8 Running a test. An IDE usually offers several ways you can run a test. One of them is to right-click on the test class and select "Run." You can also run all the project tests by right-clicking on the project name and select "Run tests." Different IDEs might have slightly different graphical interfaces, but they all look similar to what you see in this figure. After running the tests, the IDE shows the status for each test.

Listing 15.5 Using annotations for mock dependencies

Use the @Mock annotation to create a
mock object and inject it into the test
class's annotated field.

Enable the use of @Mock and
@InjectMocks annotations.

```
@ExtendWith(MockitoExtension.class)
public class TransferServiceWithAnnotationsUnitTests {

    @Mock
    private AccountRepository accountRepository;

    @InjectMocks
    private TransferService transferService;

    @Test
    public void moneyTransferHappyFlow() {
        Account sender = new Account();
        sender.setId(1);
        sender.setAmount(new BigDecimal(1000));

        Account destination = new Account();
        destination.setId(2);
        destination.setAmount(new BigDecimal(1000));

        given(accountRepository.findById(sender.getId()))
            .willReturn(Optional.of(sender));

        given(accountRepository.findById(destination.getId()))
            .willReturn(Optional.of(destination));

        transferService.transferMoney(1, 2, new BigDecimal(100));

        verify(accountRepository)
          .changeAmount(1, new BigDecimal(900));

        verify(accountRepository)
          .changeAmount(2, new BigDecimal(1100));
    }
}
```

Use the @InjectMocks to create
the tested object and inject it into
the class's annotated field.

Observe how, instead of declaring these objects inside the test method, I took them out as the class parameters and annotated them with @Mock and @InjectMocks. When you use the @Mock annotation, the framework creates and injects a mock object in the annotated attribute. With @InjectMocks annotation, you create the object to test and instruct the framework to inject all the mocks (created with @Mock) in its parameters.

For the @Mock and @InjectMocks annotations to work, you also need to annotate the test class with the @ExtendWith(MockitoExtension.class) annotation. When annotating the class this way, you enable an extension that allows the framework to read the @Mock and @InjectMocks annotations and control the annotated fields.

Figure 15.9 summarizes the test we built. In this visual, you find the steps and code we wrote to solve each of the steps we enumerated when we started writing the test:

1 *Assumptions*—Enumerate and control the dependencies.
2 *Call*—Execute the tested method.
3 *Validations*—Verify the executed method had the expected behavior.

```
@ExtendWith(MockitoExtension.class)
public class TransferServiceWithAnnotationsUnitTests {

  @Mock
  private AccountRepository accountRepository;

  @InjectMocks
  private TransferService transferService;

  @Test
  public void moneyTransferHappyFlow() {
    Account sender = new Account();
    sender.setId(1);
    sender.setAmount(new BigDecimal(1000));

    Account destination = new Account();
    destination.setId(2);
    destination.setAmount(new BigDecimal(1000));

    given(accountRepository.findById(sender.getId()))
      .willReturn(Optional.of(sender));

    given(accountRepository.findById(destination.getId()))
      .willReturn(Optional.of(destination));

    transferService.transferMoney(1, 2, new BigDecimal(100));

    verify(accountRepository).changeAmount(1, new BigDecimal(900));
    verify(accountRepository).changeAmount(2, new BigDecimal(1100));
  }
}
```

Figure 15.9   The main parts of the test implementation. (1) Define and control the dependencies, (2) execute the tested method, and (3) verify the method behaved as expected.

WRITING A TEST FOR AN EXCEPTION FLOW

Remember that happy flows are not the only ones you need to test. You also want to know that the method executes in the desired way when it encounters an exception. Such a flow is called an *exception flow*. In our example, an exception flow could happen if either the sender or the destination account details are not found for the given ID, as presented in figure 15.10.

Listing 15.6 shows you how to write the unit test for an exception flow. If you want to check that the method throws an exception, you use assertThrows(). You specify the exception you expect the method will throw and specify the tested method. The

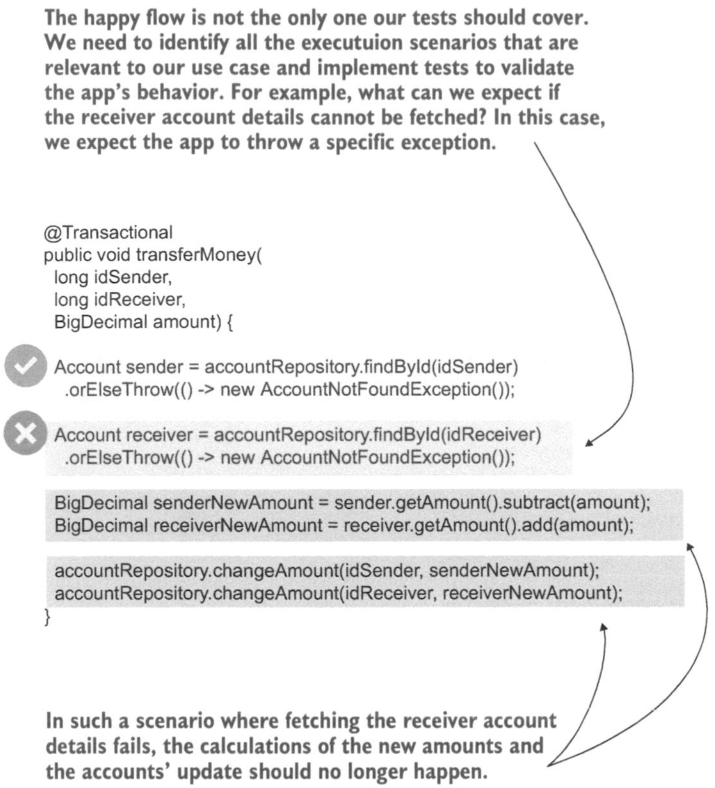

The happy flow is not the only one our tests should cover. We need to identify all the executuion scenarios that are relevant to our use case and implement tests to validate the app's behavior. For example, what can we expect if the receiver account details cannot be fetched? In this case, we expect the app to throw a specific exception.

```
@Transactional
public void transferMoney(
  long idSender,
  long idReceiver,
  BigDecimal amount) {

  Account sender = accountRepository.findById(idSender)
    .orElseThrow(() -> new AccountNotFoundException());

  Account receiver = accountRepository.findById(idReceiver)
    .orElseThrow(() -> new AccountNotFoundException());

  BigDecimal senderNewAmount = sender.getAmount().subtract(amount);
  BigDecimal receiverNewAmount = receiver.getAmount().add(amount);

  accountRepository.changeAmount(idSender, senderNewAmount);
  accountRepository.changeAmount(idReceiver, receiverNewAmount);
}
```

In such a scenario where fetching the receiver account details fails, the calculations of the new amounts and the accounts' update should no longer happen.

Figure 15.10 An exception flow is an execution that encountered an error or an exception. For example, if the receiver account details were not found, the app should throw an **AccountNotFoundException**, and the **changeAmount()** method should not be called. Exception flows are important as well, and we need to implement tests for these scenarios the same as we do for happy flows.

assertThrows() method calls the tested method and validates that it throws the expected exception.

Listing 15.6 Testing an exception flow

```
@ExtendWith(MockitoExtension.class)
public class TransferServiceWithAnnotationsUnitTests {

  @Mock
  private AccountRepository accountRepository;

  @InjectMocks
  private TransferService transferService;

  @Test
  public void moneyTransferDestinationAccountNotFoundFlow() {
    Account sender = new Account();
```

```
sender.setId(1);
sender.setAmount(new BigDecimal(1000));

given(accountRepository.findById(1L))
    .willReturn(Optional.of(sender));

given(accountRepository.findById(2L))
    .willReturn(Optional.empty());   ◄──

assertThrows(
    AccountNotFoundException.class,   ◄──
    () -> transferService.transferMoney(1, 2, new BigDecimal(100))
);

verify(accountRepository, never())   ◄──
    .changeAmount(anyLong(), any());
    }
}
```

> **We control the mock AccountRepository to return an empty Optional when the findById() method is called for the destination account.**

> **We assert that the method throws an AccountNotFoundException in the given scenario.**

> **We use the verify() method with the never() conditional to assert that the changeAmount() method hasn't been called.**

TESTING THE VALUE A METHOD RETURNS

An often encountered case is needing to check the value a method returns. The next listing shows a method we implemented in chapter 9, in the project "sq-ch9-ex1." How would you implement a unit test for this method, considering you need to test the scenario where the user provides the correct credentials to log in?

> **Listing 15.7 The implementation of the login controller action we want to unit test**

```
@PostMapping("/")
  public String loginPost(
      @RequestParam String username,
      @RequestParam String password,
      Model model
  ) {
    loginProcessor.setUsername(username);
    loginProcessor.setPassword(password);
    boolean loggedIn = loginProcessor.login();

    if (loggedIn) {
      model.addAttribute("message", "You are now logged in.");
    } else {
      model.addAttribute("message", "Login failed!");
    }

    return "login.html";
  }
```

You follow the same steps you learned in this section:

1 Identify and control the dependencies.
2 Call the tested method.
3 Verify the tested method execution behaved as expected.

Listing 15.8 shows the unit test implementation. Observe that we mocked the dependencies whose behavior we want to control or verify: the Model and the LoginProcessor objects. We instruct the LoginProcessor mock object to return true (which is equivalent to assuming the user provided the correct credentials), and we call the method we want to test.

We verify the following:

- That the method returned the string "login.html." We use an assert method to validate the method returned a value. As shown in listing 15.8, we can use the assertEquals() method, which compares an expected value with the value the method returned.
- The Model instance contains the valid message "You are now logged in." We use the verify() method to validate the addAttribute() method of the Model instance has been called with the correct value as a parameter.

Listing 15.8   Testing the returned value in a unit test

```
@ExtendWith(MockitoExtension.class)
class LoginControllerUnitTests {

    @Mock
    private Model model;                              ⟵┐
                                                        │  We define the mock
    @Mock                                               │  objects and inject them
    private LoginProcessor loginProcessor;           ⟵┤  into the instance whose
                                                        │  behavior we test.
    @InjectMocks                                        │
    private LoginController loginController;          ⟵┘

    @Test
    public void loginPostLoginSucceedsTest() {
        given(loginProcessor.login())                ⟵┐  We control the LoginProcessor mock
            .willReturn(true);                          │  instance, telling it to return true
                                                        │  when its method login() is called.
        String result =
            loginController.loginPost("username", "password", model);

        assertEquals("login.html", result);          ⟵┐  We verify the tested
                                                        │  method returned value.
        verify(model)                                ⟵┐  We verify the message
            .addAttribute("message", "You are now logged in.");   │  attribute was added
    }                                                   │  with the correct value
}                                                       │  on the model object.
```

We call the tested method with the given assumptions.

By controlling the inputs (the parameter values and how the mock objects behave), you can also test what happens in different scenarios. In the next listing, we make the LoginProcessor mock object's login() method return false to test what would happen if the login fails.

Listing 15.9   Adding the test to validate the failed login scenario

```
@ExtendWith(MockitoExtension.class)
class LoginControllerUnitTests {

  // Omitted code

  @Test
  public void loginPostLoginFailsTest() {
    given(loginProcessor.login())
      .willReturn(false);

    String result =
      loginController.loginPost("username", "password", model);

    assertEquals("login.html", result);

    verify(model)
      .addAttribute("message", "Login failed!");
  }
}
```

15.2.2 *Implementing integration tests*

In this section, we discuss integration tests. An integration test is very similar to a unit test. We'll even continue writing them with JUnit. But instead of focusing on how a particular component works, an integration test focuses on how two or more components interact.

Remember the analogy with the car's dashboard indicators? If the car's tank is full, but something breaks in the gas distribution between the tank and the engine, the car still won't start. Unfortunately, this time the gas indicator won't show you something is wrong because the tank has enough gas, and as an isolated component, it works correctly. In such a case, we don't know why the car doesn't work. The same problem might happen to an app. Even if some components work correctly when they are isolated one from another, they don't correctly "talk" to each other. Writing integration tests helps us mitigate problems that could happen when components work correctly independently but don't communicate correctly.

We'll take the same example we used for the unit tests for this example: the money transfer use case we implemented in chapter 14 (project "sq-ch14-ex1").

What kind of integrations can we test? We have a few possibilities:

- *Integration between two (or more) objects of your app.* Testing that the objects interact correctly helps you identify problems in how they collaborate if you change one of them.
- *Integration of an object of your app with some capability the framework enhances it with.* Testing how an object interacts with some capability the framework provides helps you identify issues that can occur when you upgrade the framework to a new version. The integration test helps you immediately identify if something changed in the framework and the capability the object relies on doesn't work the same way.

- *Integration of the app with its persistence layer (the database).* Testing how the repository works with the database ensures you quickly identify problems that might occur when upgrading or changing a dependency that helps your app work with persisted data (such as the JDBC driver).

An integration test looks very similar to a unit test. You still follow the same steps of identifying the assumptions, calling the tested method, and validating the results. The difference is that now the test doesn't focus on an isolated piece of logic, so you don't necessarily have to mock all the dependencies. You might allow a method you test to call another's real object's (not a mock's) method because you want to test the two objects communicate correctly. So, if for a unit test it was mandatory to mock the repository, for an integration test that is no longer mandatory. You can still mock it if the test you write doesn't care about how the service interacts with that repository, but if you want to test how these two objects communicate, you can let the real object be called (figure 15.11).

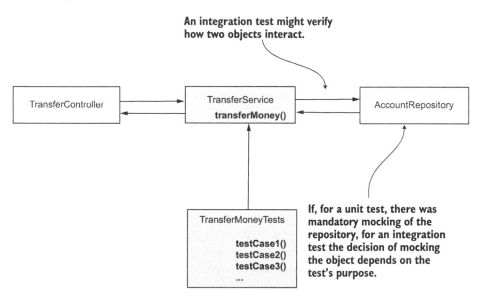

Figure 15.11   In a unit test's case, all the dependencies needed to be mocked. If the integration test's purpose is to verify how the TestService and AccountRepository interact, the repository can be the real object. An integration test can still mock an object if its purpose doesn't verify the integration with a specific component.

NOTE   If you decide not to mock the repository in an integration test, you should use an in-memory database such as H2 instead of the real database. This will help you keep your tests independent of the infrastructure that runs the app. Using the real database could cause latencies in test executions and even make tests fail in case of infrastructure or networking problems. Since you test the application and not the infrastructure, you should avoid all this trouble by using a mock in-memory database.

With a Spring app, you'll generally use integration tests to verify that your app's behavior correctly interacts with the capabilities Spring provides. We name such a test a "Spring integration test." Unlike a unit test, an integration test enables Spring to create the beans and configure the context (just as it does when running the app).

Listing 15.10 shows you how simple it is to transform a unit test into a Spring integration test. Observe that we can use the @MockBean annotation to create a mock object in our Spring Boot application. This annotation is quite similar to the @Mock annotation we used for unit tests, but it also makes sure the mock object is added to the application context. This way, you can simply use @Autowired (as you learned in chapter 3) to inject the object whose behavior you test.

Listing 15.10 Implementing a Spring integration test

```
@SpringBootTest
class TransferServiceSpringIntegrationTests {

  @MockBean                                          ◁——————  Create a mock object that is also
  private AccountRepository accountRepository;                part of the Spring context.

  @Autowired                      ◁—
  private TransferService transferService;           Inject the real object from the Spring
                                                     context whose behavior you'll test.
  @Test
  void transferServiceTransferAmountTest() {
    Account sender = new Account();
    sender.setId(1);
    sender.setAmount(new BigDecimal(1000));

    Account receiver = new Account();                Define all the
    receiver.setId(2);                               assumptions
    receiver.setAmount(new BigDecimal(1000));        for the test.

    when(accountRepository.findById(1L))
      .thenReturn(Optional.of(sender));
    when(accountRepository.findById(2L))
      .thenReturn(Optional.of(receiver));

    transferService
      .transferMoney(1, 2, new BigDecimal(100));  ◁————— Call the tested method.

    verify(accountRepository)                          Validate the tested
      .changeAmount(1, new BigDecimal(900));           method call has the
    verify(accountRepository)                          expected behavior.
      .changeAmount(2, new BigDecimal(1100));
  }

}
```

NOTE The @MockBean annotation is a Spring Boot annotation. If you have a plain Spring app and not a Spring Boot one as presented here, you won't be able to use @MockBean. However, you can still use the same approach by annotating the configuration class with @ExtendsWith(SpringExtension.class). An example using this annotation is in the project "sq-ch3-ex1."

You run the test the same way you do for any other test. However, even if it looks very similar to a unit test, Spring now knows the tested object and manages it as it would in a running app. For example, if we upgraded the Spring version and, for some reason, the dependency injection no longer worked, the test would fail even if we didn't change anything in the tested object. The same applies to any capability Spring offers to the tested method: transactionality, security, caching, and so on. You would be able to test your method's integration to any of these capabilities the method uses in your app.

NOTE In a real-world app, use unit tests to validate components' behavior and the Spring integration tests to validate the necessary integration scenarios. Even if a Spring integration test could be used to validate the component's behavior (implement all the test scenarios for the method's logic), it's not a good idea to use integration tests for this purpose. Integration tests take a longer time to execute because they have to configure the Spring context. Every method call also triggers several Spring mechanisms Spring needs, depending on what capabilities it offers to that specific method. It doesn't make sense to spend time and resources to execute these for every scenario of your app's logic. To save time, the best approach is to rely on unit tests to validate your apps' components' logic and use the integration tests only to validate how they integrate with the framework.

Summary

- A test is a small piece of code you write to validate the behavior of certain logic implemented in your app. Tests are necessary because they help you ensure that future app developments don't break existing capabilities. Tests also help as documentation.
- Tests fall into two categories: unit tests and integration tests. Each has its purposes.
  - A unit test only focuses on an isolated piece of logic and validates how one simple component works without checking how it integrates with other features. Unit tests are helpful because they execute fast and point us directly to the problem a specific component might face.
  - An integration test focuses on validating the interaction between two or more components. They are essential because sometimes two components might work correctly in isolation but don't communicate well. Integration tests help us mitigate problems generated by such cases.
- Sometimes in tests you want to eliminate dependencies to some components to allow the test to focus on how some but not all parts interact. In such cases, we replace the components we don't want to test with "mocks": fake objects you

control to eliminate dependencies you don't want to test and allow the test to focus only on specific interactions.

- Any test has three main parts:
  - *Assumptions*—Define the input values and the way the mock objects behave.
  - *Call/Execution*—Call the method you want to test.
  - *Validations*—Verify the way the tested method behaved.

appendix A
Architectural approaches

In this appendix, we discuss a few architectural concepts you encounter. To fully understand everything we discuss in this book, you need to at least be aware and have a high-level overview of these concepts. I'll take you through the concepts of monolith, service-oriented architecture, and microservices. I'll also refer you to other resources you can use to learn the subjects further.

These subjects are complex; many books and dozens of presentations have been delivered on these topics, so I can't say I'll make you an expert in just a few pages, but reading this will help you understand why you use Spring in specific scenarios we discuss in the book. We'll take an app scenario as an example and discuss the change in architectural approaches from the early ages of software development to today.

A.1 The monolithic approach

In this section, we discuss what a monolith is. You'll understand why in the early days developers designed apps monolithically, and then, in the next sections, this will help you understand why other architectural styles appeared.

When developers refer to an app as being "monolithic" or "a monolith," it means that it consists of just one component you deploy and execute. This component implements all its functionalities. For example, consider an app for managing a bookstore. The users manage the products the shop sells, the invoices, the deliveries, and the customers. In figure A.1, the presented system is a monolith, because all these functionalities are part of the same process.

> **NOTE** A business flow is something the user expects to do in the application. For example, when the shop owner sells books, the flow could be as follows: The products functionality reserves some books from the stock, the billing functionality creates an invoice for those books, and the deliveries plan when to deliver the books and notifies the customers. Figure A.2 presents a visual representation of the "sell books" business flow.

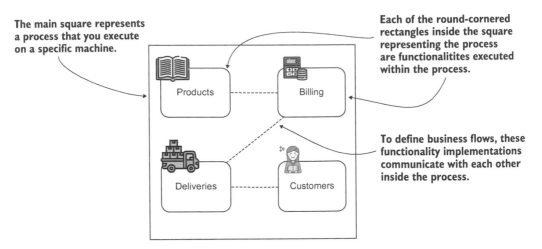

The main square represents a process that you execute on a specific machine.

Each of the round-cornered rectangles inside the square representing the process are functionalitites executed within the process.

To define business flows, these functionality implementations communicate with each other inside the process.

Figure A.1   A monolithic application. The application implements all the functionalities in just one process. The implementations interact with one another inside the process to develop the business flow.

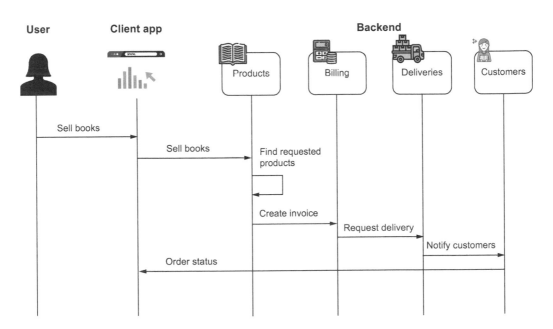

Figure A.2   An example of business flow. The user wants to sell books. The client app sends the request to the backend. Each responsibility of the backend has a role in the entire flow. The functionalities communicate with each other to complete the business flow. In the end, the client app receives the status of the order

NOTE   In figure A.2, I simplified the communication between the components to allow you to focus on the discussed subject. The class design, which results in how the components communicate with one another, may be different.

Initially, all applications were developed in a monolithic fashion, and this approach worked great in the early days of application development. In the 1990s, the internet was only a network of a few computers, but in a few years, it became a network of billions of devices. Today, technology is no longer for techies; it's for everybody. And this change implied a significant growth in the number of users and data processed for many systems. Thirty years ago, being able to call a cab anywhere you are or even sending a message from the street while waiting to cross the road wasn't something we could have imagined possible.

To deal with this change in the number of users and the growth of data, the apps needed more resources, and using only one process makes the management of the resources more difficult. The number of users and the quantity of data aren't the only things that changed with time; people started to use apps for almost anything they wanted to do remotely. For example, today you can manage your bank accounts while drinking a cappuccino at your favorite café. While this seems easy, it implies more security risks. The systems offering you these services need to be well-secured and reliable.

Of course, all these changes also brought changes in the way the apps are created and developed. Let's consider just the increase in the number of users to simplify our discussion. What's one thing you can do to enable your app to serve more requests? Well, we could run the same app on multiple systems. This way, several instances of running applications will split the requests among them so that the system can deal with a more significant load (figure A.3.). We name this approach *horizontal scaling.* Assuming a linear growth for simplicity; if one running app instance was able to deal

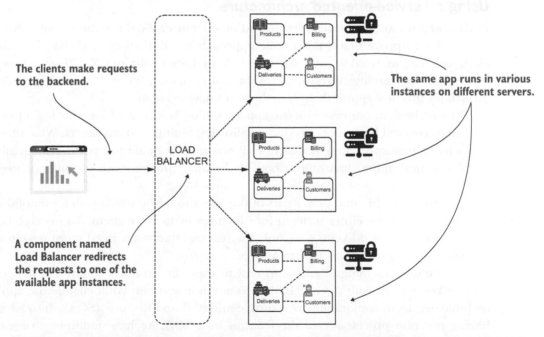

Figure A.3   Horizontal scaling. Running the same instance multiple times enables us to use more resources and serve more client requests.

with 50,000 simultaneous requests, three running app instances should be able to respond to 150,000 concurrent requests.

One other aspect we take into consideration is that, in general, an app is continuously evolving. When you make even a small change in a monolithic app, you need to redeploy everything. At the same time, with a microservices architecture, you benefit from redeploying the service only where you made the change. This simplification is a benefit for the system as well.

Is there a problem with continuing to use a monolithic approach to design an app? There might not be a problem at all. Like with any other technology or technique, designing your app as a monolith could be the best approach for your scenario. We discuss cases in which a monolith isn't the right choice, but I don't want you to get the impression that using a monolithic architecture is wrong or that the approaches I present represent a better way to develop your apps.

In many cases, people judge the use of a monolith wrongly. I always hear developers complaining that their monolithic apps are challenging to maintain. The truth is that the problem is probably not the app being a monolith. Messy code is likely the main cause of making the app difficult to maintain. Or the fact that developers mixed responsibilities and didn't use abstractions properly could be why the app become difficult to maintain. But a monolithic app doesn't necessarily need to be messy. With software evolution, there are situations in which a monolithic approach no longer works, so we need to find alternatives.

A.2   *Using a service-oriented architecture*

In this section, we discuss service-oriented architecture. We'll use the example from section 1.1 to prove that a monolithic approach has limitations and that, in some circumstances, we need to use a different style to design your app. You'll learn how a service-oriented architecture solves the presented issues, but we'll also discuss the difficulties this new approach adds to the app's development.

Let's go back to our case with the app for selling books. We have four main functionalities covered by the app: products, deliveries, billing, and customers. What often happens in real-world apps is that not all features consume the resources equally. Some consume more than others, possibly because they're more complex or used more often.

We cannot decide that only a part of the app should be scaled with a monolithic app. In our case, we either scale all four features or none of them. To manage the resources better, we'd like to scale only the features that really need more resources and avoid scaling the others (figure A.4).

Can we do something to enable us only to scale the products feature but not the others? Yes, we can split the monolith into multiple services. We'll change the app's architecture from a monolith to a service-oriented architecture (SOA). Instead of having just one process for all the features in a SOA, we have multiple processes

The products functionality consumes most of the resources. It needs to be scaled.

The billing and deliveries functionalities don't consume that many resources. They don't need to be scaled.

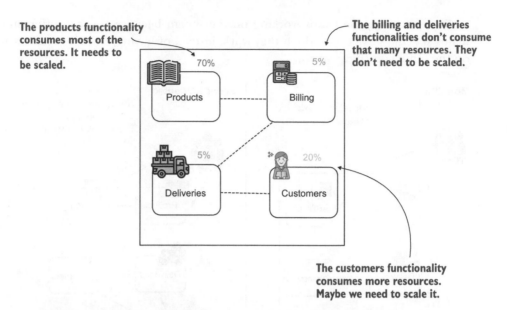

The customers functionality consumes more resources. Maybe we need to scale it.

Figure A.4 Some features are more intensively used than others. For this reason, these features consume more resources and need to be scaled.

implementing the features. We can then decide to scale only the service implementing the feature that needs more resources (figure A.5).

In a service-oriented architecture, we design each feature as a separate process. This way, you can decide to scale only the features that need more resources.

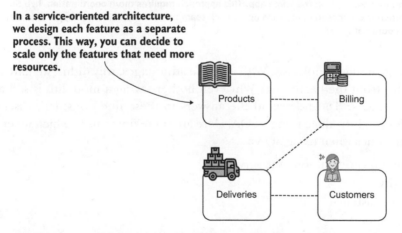

Figure A.5 In a SOA, each feature is an independent process. This way, you can decide to scale just the features that need more resources.

A SOA also has the advantage of having the responsibilities better isolated: now you know you have a dedicated app for the billing and a dedicated app for the deliveries, and so on, and it's easier to keep the implementations decoupled and more cohesive. This is beneficial for the maintainability of the system. As a consequence, it's also easier to manage the teams working on the system because you can offer different teams specific services on which they work, instead of having multiple teams working on the same app (figure A.6).

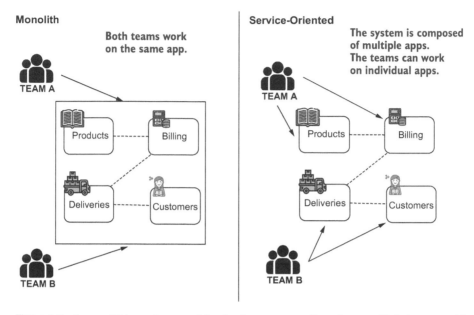

Figure A.6   A monolithic system consists of only one app, so if you have multiple teams working on the system, they all work on the same app. This approach requires more coordination. In a SOA where the system is composed of multiple apps, each team can work on different apps. This way, they need to coordinate less.

At first glance, it might look easy. With all these advantages, why didn't we have all the apps like this from the beginning? Why even bother saying a monolith is still a solution in some cases? To understand the answers to these questions, let's discuss the complexities you introduce using a SOA. Here are some domains in which we encounter different issues when using SOAs:

1 Communication among the services
2 Security
3 Data persistence
4 Deployment

Let's look at some examples.

A.2.1   *Complexity caused by communication among services*

The functionalities still need to communicate to implement the business logic flow. Earlier, with a monolithic approach, they were part of the same app, which made linking two features easy with a method call. But now that we have different processes, this is more complex.

Features now need to communicate via the network. One of the essential principles you need to remember is that the network isn't entirely reliable. Many fall into the trap of forgetting to consider what happens if, at some point, the communication between two components breaks. Unfortunately, unlike a monolithic approach, any call between two components can fail at some point in a SOA. Depending on the app, developers use different techniques or patterns to solve this issue, like repeating calls, circuit breakers, or caches.

A second aspect to consider is that there are many options to establish communication among the services (figure A.7). You could use REST services, GraphQL, SOAP, gRPC, JMS message brokers, Kafka, and so on. Which is the best approach? Of course, in any situation one or more of these approaches is fine. You'll find long debates and discussions in many books on how to choose the right fit for typical scenarios.

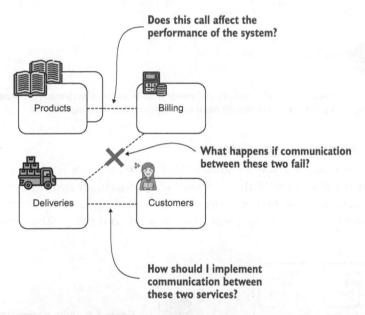

Figure A.7   Communication between services adds complexity to the system. We need to decide how to implement the communication between two services. We also need to understand what could happen if the communication fails and how to solve potential problems caused by malfunctioning communication.

A.2.2   *Complexity added to the security of the system*

By splitting our functionalities into separate services, we also introduce complexity in security configurations. These services exchange messages via the network, which might expose information. Sometimes we want pieces of the data exchanged not to be seen at all (like passwords, banking card details, or other personal data). We now need to encrypt these details before sending them. Even if we don't care if someone can see the exchanged details, in most cases we don't want anyone to be able to change them while they flow from one component to another (figure A.8).

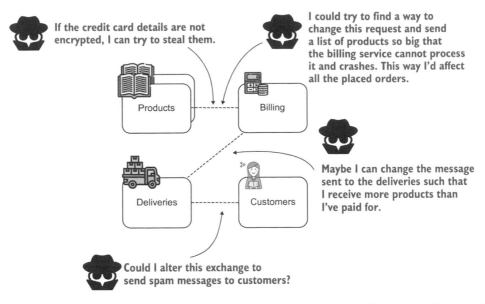

Figure A.8   In a SOA, features are separate services and communicate over the network. This aspect introduces many vulnerable points that developers need to consider when building the app.

A.2.3   *Complexity added for the data persistence*

In most cases, an app needs a way to store data. Databases are a popular way persistence is implemented in apps. With a monolithic approach, an app had one database to store the data, as presented in figure A.9. We called this a *three-tier architecture* because it consists of three tiers: the client, the backend, and the database used for persistence.

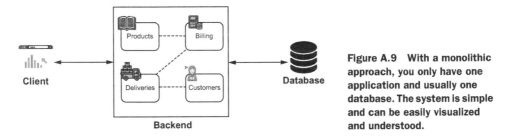

Figure A.9   With a monolithic approach, you only have one application and usually one database. The system is simple and can be easily visualized and understood.

With SOA, you now have multiple services that need to store data. And with more services, you also have more design options. Should you use just one database shared by all the services? Should you have one database for each service? Figure A.10 visualizes these options.

Most believe that sharing a database is bad practice. From my own experience with splitting a monolith into multiple services, I can tell you that having a shared database can become a deployment nightmare. But having individual databases per service also

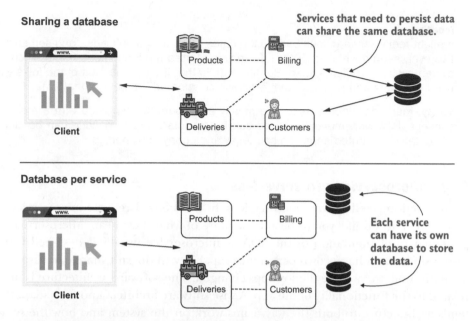

Figure A.10 In a SOA, you can decide that more services share the same database or have an individual database per service. Having various alternatives, each with its benefits and drawbacks, makes the persistence layer's design in SOA more difficult.

implies difficulties. As you'll see when we discuss transactions, it's much easier to assure data consistency with one database. When having more independent databases, it's challenging to make sure the data remains consistent among all.

A.2.4 *Complexity added in the deployment of the system*

Maybe the easiest challenge to observe is that we add a lot of complexity to the system's deployment. We also have more services now, but as you learned from the previous paragraphs, you might have multiple databases as well. When you also consider that securing the system will add even more configurations, you see how much more complex the deployment of the system becomes.

Why does a monolith have a negative connotation?

You can see that the SOAs aren't necessarily easy, so you might wonder why monolithic architecture tends to be associated with something negative. The reality is that for some systems, a monolith makes more sense than SOA.

My opinion is that the negative connotation of monolithic architecture comes from the fact that it represents old systems. In most cases, old systems were implemented before anyone was concerned about clean coding and design principles. We now consider all these principles to make sure we write maintainable code.

(continued)
It might feel strange to look back to the times when they didn't exist, and sometimes I've even seen developers blame those who started the implementation of such old systems when problems arise. But the truth is that it's not the fault of the folks who used the tools and practices that everyone considered the best at that time.

Today, many developers associate messy and poorly written code with a monolith concept. However, monolithic apps can be modular, and their code can be clean, while service-oriented apps can be messy and poorly designed.

A.3   *From microservices to serverless*

In this section, we'll discuss microservices. In this book, I refer to microservices here and there, and I'd like you to be at least aware of what they mean. Microservices are a particular implementation of the SOA. A microservice usually is designed with one responsibility and has its own persistence capability (it doesn't share databases).

With time, the way we deploy apps changed. The software architecture is not only related to the functionality of the app. A wise software architect knows to adapt the system's architecture to both the way teams work on the system and how the system is deployed. You might have heard about what we call the DevOps movement, which implies both how we deploy software as well as how we work on software development. Today, we deploy the apps in the cloud using virtual machines or containerized environments, and these approaches generally implied the need for making apps smaller. Of course, evolution came with another incertitude: how small should a service be? Many debated this question in books, articles, and discussions.

The minimization of services went so far that today we can implement a short functionality with only a few lines of code and deploy it in an environment. An event like an HTTP request, a timer, or a message triggers this functionality and makes it execute. We call these small implementations *serverless* functions. The term "serverless" doesn't imply that the function doesn't execute on a server. But because everything regarding the development is hidden and we only case for the code that implements its logic and the events that trigger it, it merely looks like no server exists.

A.4   *Further reading*

Software architecture and its evolution is such a fantastic and complex subject. I don't think there'll ever be too many books to cover this subject thoroughly. I've added this discussion to the book to help you understand the references I'll make to these notions. Still, you might want to go deeper into the subjects, so here's a list of books from my shelf. The books are in the order I recommend you read them.

1   *Microservices in Action*, by Morgan Bruce and Paulo A. Pereira (Manning, 2018), is an excellent book you can start with when learning microservices. In the book, you'll find all the microservices fundamentals subjects discussed with useful examples.

2 *Microservices Patterns*, by Chris Richardson (Manning, 2018), is a book I recommend you continue with after thoroughly reading *Microservices in Action*. The author presents a pragmatic approach on how to develop production-ready apps using microservices.

3 *Spring Microservices in Action*, by John Carnell and Illary Huaylupo Sánchez (Manning, 2020), helps you better understand how to apply Spring to build microservices.

4 *Microservices Security in Action*, by Prabath Siriwardena and Nuwan Dias (Manning 2020), goes into detail with what applying security with a microservice architecture means. Security is a crucial aspect of any system, and you always need to consider it from the development process's early stages. The book explains security from the ground up, and reading it will give you a better understanding the aspects you need to be aware of in regards to security for microservices.

5 *Monolith to Microservices*, by Sam Newman (O'Reilly Media, 2020), treats patterns for transforming a monolithic architecture into microservices. The book also discusses whether you need to use microservices and how to decide this.

appendix B
Using XML for
the context configuration

A long time ago, when I started using Spring, the developers used XML to configure the context and the Spring framework in general. Today, you can only find XML configurations in older applications that are still supported. The developers quit using XML configurations years ago and replaced them with using annotations because of the difficulty of reading the configuration code. While it's true XML has its good points, it's much easier to use annotations for reading and enhancing the app's maintainability. For this reason, I decided not to include XML configurations in this book.

If you're just now starting with Spring, my advice is to learn XML configurations only if you need to maintain an older project and have no other choice. Start by learning the approaches presented in this book. You can apply these skills with any configuration, even XML. The only thing that differs is that you use a different syntax. But it makes no sense to learn these configurations if you'll never see this approach in practice.

To give you a taste of what using XML for configuration means, I'll show you how to add a bean to the Spring context using this old-fashioned way. You can find the example in the project "sq-app2-ex1."

One difference is that with XML, you need to have a separate file in which you'll define the configurations (in fact, they can be multiple files, but I won't get into unnecessary details). I'll name this file "config.xml," and add it to my Maven project's resources folder. The context of this file is presented in the next code snippet:

```xml
<?xml version="1.0" encoding="UTF-8"?>

<beans xmlns="http://www.springframework.org/schema/beans"
  xmlns:xsi="http://www.w3.org/2001/XMLSchema-instance"
  xsi:schemaLocation="http://www.springframework.org/schema/beans
  http://www.springframework.org/schema/beans/spring-beans.xsd">

  <bean id="parrot1" class="main.Parrot">        ◄─── Creates a bean of type Parrot
    <property name="name" value="Kiki" />   ◄─┐    with the identifier parrot1
  </bean>                                       │
</beans>                          Sets the value of the │
                                  parrot's name to Kiki │
```

The <beans> tag is the root of this XML file. Inside the root tag, you find the definition of a bean of type Parrot. As in the previous snippet, to define a bean you can use another XML tag, <bean>, and to give a name to the parrot instance we use the <property> XML tag. This is the idea of XML configurations: you use different XML tags to configure specific features. Whatever we'd do using annotations, now you need to use an XML tag.

In the main class, we create an instance representing the Spring context, and we can test that Spring added the bean successfully by referring to the parrot and printing its name in the console. The next code snippet presents the implementation of the main method. I need to use another class to create the instance of the Spring context.

When creating the Spring context instance using the class ClassPathXmlApplicationContext, I also need to provide the "config.xml" file's location containing the XML configuration:

```java
public class Main {

  public static void main(String[] args) {
    var context = new ClassPathXmlApplicationContext("config.xml");
    Parrot p = context.getBean(Parrot.class);

    System.out.println(p.getName());
  }
}
```

When you run the app, the name you gave to the parrot instance (Kiki in my case) in the XML configuration will be printed in the console.

appendix C
A quick
introduction to HTTP

In this appendix, we discuss the essential aspects of HTTP any developer needs to know. Fortunately, you don't have to be an expert in HTTP and know its reference by heart to implement excellent web apps. On your journey as a software developer, you'll also learn other HTTP aspects, but I want to make sure you have all the needed information to understand the examples we work on in this book, starting with chapter 7.

Why learn about HTTP in a book about Spring? Because today most of the apps we implement with an application framework (such as Spring) are web apps—and web apps use HTTP.

We'll begin with what HTTP is, and we'll analyze its definition in a visual. We'll then discuss the details you need to know about HTTP requests a client makes and how the server responds.

C.1   What is HTTP?

In this section, we discuss what HTTP is. I prefer simple definitions, so I describe it as how a client communicates with the server in a web app. Applications prefer to have rigid ways to "speak," and the protocols offer the rules they need to exchange information. Let's analyze the HTTP definition with a visual (figure C.1).

> **HTTP**   Stateless, text-based, request-response protocol that uses the client-server computing model.

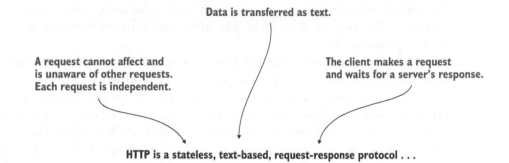

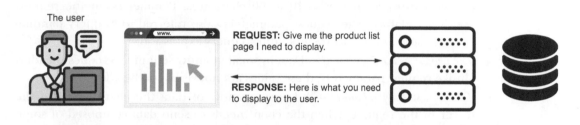

Figure C.1 HTTP is a protocol that describes how a client and a server talk. HTTP assumes a client makes a request, and the server responds. The protocol describes what the client's request and the server's response look like. HTTP is stateless, meaning the requests are independent of one another, and text-based, which means the information is exchanged as plain text.

C.2 The HTTP request as a language between client and server

In this section, we discuss the HTTP request. In the apps you implement with Spring, you'll need to use the HTTP request to send data from client to server. If you implement the client, you'll need to add data on the HTTP request. If you implement the server, you'll need to get data from the request. Either way, you need to understand the HTTP request.

The HTTP request has a simple format. The things you have to take into consideration are the following:

1 *The request URI*—The client uses the path to tell the server what resource it requests. The request URI looks like this one: http://www.manning.com/books/spring-start-here

2 *The request method*—A verb that the client uses to indicate what action it will do with the requested resource. For example, when you write an address in a web browser's address bar, the browser always uses an HTTP method named GET. In other circumstances, you'll find in the next paragraphs, the client can issue an HTTP request with a different method such as POST, PUT, or DELETE.

3 *The request parameters (optional)*—Data in small quantity the client sends to the server with the request. When I say "small quantity," I refer to something that can be expressed in maybe 10 to 50 characters. Parameters on the request aren't mandatory. The request parameters (also referred to as query parameters) are sent in the URI by appending a query expression.

4 *The request headers (optional)*—Data in small quantity sent in the request header. Unlike request parameters, these values are not visible in the URI.

5 *The request body (optional)*—A larger quantity of data the client sends to the server in the request. When the client needs to send data composed of some hundreds of characters, it can use the HTTP body. A body on the request is not mandatory.

The following snippet these details in an HTTP request:

```
POST /servlet/default.jsp HTTP/1.1    ⟵──── The request specifies the method and the path.

Accept: text/plain; text/html
Accept-Language: en-gb
Connection: Keep-Alive
Host: localhost
Referer: http://localhost/ch8/SendDetails.html       Different headers with
User-Agent: Mozilla/4.0 (MSIE 4.01;Windows 98)       values can be added
Content-Length: 33                                    as request data.
Content-Type: application/x-www-form-urlencoded
Accept-Encoding: gzip, deflate
                                                      Request parameters can
                                                      also be used to transfer
lastName=Einstein&firstName=Albert    ⟵─────────┘    request data.
```

The request URI identifies a resource on the server side the client wants to work with. The URI is the part of the HTTP request most people know about because we have to write a URI in our browser's address bar each time we access a web site. The URI has a format like that in the next snippet. In the snippet, <server_location> is the network address of the system where the server app runs, <application_port> is the port number identifying the server app instance running, and <resource_path> is a path the developer associated with a specific resource. The client needs to request a specific path to work with a particular resource:

```
http://<server_location>:<application_port>/<resource_path>
```

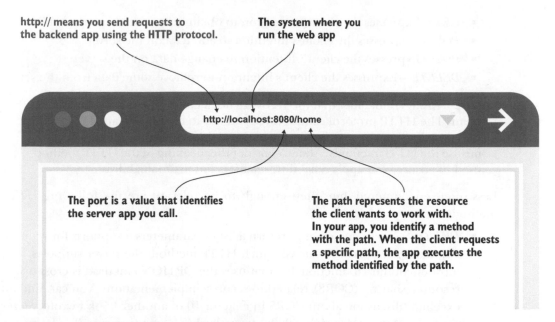

http:// means you send requests to the backend app using the HTTP protocol.

The system where you run the web app

http://localhost:8080/home

The port is a value that identifies the server app you call.

The path represents the resource the client wants to work with. In your app, you identify a method with the path. When the client requests a specific path, the app executes the method identified by the path.

Figure C.2 The HTTP request URI identifies the resource the client requests to work with. The first part of the URI identifies the protocol and the server that runs the server app. The path identifies a resource exposed by the server.

Figure C.2 analyzes the format of an HTTP request URI.

NOTE A uniform resource identifier (URI) includes a uniform resource locator (URL) and a path. We can say the formula is URI = URL + path. But in many cases, you'll find people confusing the URI with the URL or considering them to be the same thing. You need to remember that the URL identifies the server and the application. When you add a path to a specific resource of that application, it becomes a URI.

Once the client identifies the resource in the request, it uses a verb named *HTTP request method* to specify what it will do with the resource. The way the client specifies the method depends on how it sends the call to the server. For example, if the call is made directly by the browser, when you write an address in the address bar, the browser will send a GET request. In most cases, when you click a submit button on a form on a web page, the browser uses POST. The developer of the web page decides what method the browser should use when sending a request that originated as a result of submitting a form. You'll learn more about this aspect in chapter 8. An HTTP request can also be sent by a script written in a client-side language such as JavaScript. In this case, the developer of the script decides what HTTP method the request will use.

The HTTP methods you'll find most often in web apps are as follows:

- *GET*—Expresses the client's intention to obtain some data from the server
- *POST*—Expresses the client's intention to add data on the server
- *PUT*—Expresses the client's intention to change data on the server
- *DELETE*—Expresses the client's intention to remove some data from the server

> **NOTE**   Always remember that the verbs are not a constraint to what you implement. The HTTP protocol cannot force you not to implement an HTTP GET functionality that changes data on the backend side. However, you should never misuse the HTTP methods! Always consider the meaning of the HTTP method used to ensure your app's reliability, security, and maintainability.

Less often encountered, but often enough to be relevant are the following HTTP methods:

- *OPTIONS*—Tells the server to return a list of parameters it supports for request. For example, the client can ask which HTTP methods the server supports. The most encountered functionality that uses the OPTIONS method is cross-origin resource sharing (CORS) related to security implementations. You can find an excellent discussion about CORS in chapter 10 of another book I wrote, *Spring Security in Action* (Manning, 2020; https://livebook.manning.com/book/spring-security-in-action/chapter-10/).
- *PATCH*—May be used if only part of the data representing a specific resource on the backed is changed. HTTP PUT is used only when the client's action completely replaces a specific resource or even adds it where the data to be updated doesn't exist. In my experience, developers still tend to use HTTP PUT in most cases—even where the action represents only a PATCH.

The URI and the HTTP method are mandatory. The client needs to mention the resource it works with (through URI) and what it does with that resource (the method) when making an HTTP request.

For example, the request represented in the next snippet could be a way to instruct the server to return all the products it manages. We consider here that the product is a resource the server manages:

```
GET http://example.com/products
```

The request represented in the next snippet could mean that the client wants to remove all the products from the server:

```
DELETE http://example.com/products
```

But sometimes the client also needs to send data with the request. The server needs this data to complete the request. Say the client doesn't want to delete all the products, just a specific one. Then the client needs to tell the server what product to delete and send this detail in the request. The HTTP request could look like the one presented in the next snippet, where the client uses a parameter to tell the server they want to delete the product "Beer":

```
DELETE http://example.com/products?product=Beer
```

A client uses either the *request parameters, request headers,* or the *request body* to send data to the server. The request parameters and the request body are optional for the HTTP request. A client needs to add them only if they want to send specific data to the server.

The request parameters are key-value pairs the client can attach to the HTTP request to send specific information to the server. We use the request parameters to send small, individual quantities of data. If more data needs to be exchanged, the best way to send the data is through the HTTP request body. In chapters 7 through 10, we use both these approaches to send data from client to server in the HTTP request.

C.3   *The HTTP response: The way the server responds*

In this section, we discuss the HTTP response. HTTP is the protocol that allows the client to communicate with the server in a web app. Once you take care of the client's request in an app, it's time to implement the server's response. In response to a client's request, the server sends the following:

- *The response status*—An integer between 100 and 599 that defines a short representation of the request's result.
- *Response headers (optional)*—Similar to request parameters, they represent key-value pair data. They are designed for sending a small amount of data (10 to 50 characters) from server to client in response to a client's request.
- *The response body (optional)*—A way for the server to send a larger quantity (e.g., the server needs to send some hundreds of characters or entire files) of data back to the client.

The next snippet helps you visualize the HTTP response.

```
                                        The HTTP response specifies the HTTP
HTTP/1.1 200 OK   ⟵───   version and the response code and message.

Server: Microsoft-IIS/4.0
Date: Mon, 14 May 2012 13:13:33 GMT              The HTTP response can
Content-Type: text/html                          send data through the
Last-Modified: Mon, 14 May 2012 13:03:42 GMT     response headers.
Content-Length: 112

<html>
<head><title>HTTP Response</title></head>        The HTTP response
<body>Hello Albert!</body>                        can send data in
</html>                                           the response body.
```

The response status is the only mandatory detail a server delivers in response to a client's request. The status tells the client if the server understood the request and everything worked fine, or if the server encountered issues while processing the client's request. For example, the server returns a status value starting with 2 to tell the client that everything was fine. The HTTP status is a short representation of the result of the full request (including if the server was able to manage the business logic of the request). You don't need to learn all the statuses in detail. I'll enumerate and describe the ones you'll find more often in real-world implementations:

- Starting with 2, meaning the server correctly processed the request. The request processing is okay, and the server executed what the client asked.
- Starting with 4, where the server tells the client something is wrong with its request (it's a problem on the client side). For example, the client requested a resource that doesn't exist, or the client sent some request parameters that the server didn't expect.
- Starting with 5, where the server communicates that something went wrong on its side. For example, the server needed to connect to a database but the it was not accessible. In this case, the server sends back a status telling the client that it couldn't complete the request but not because of something the client didn't do well.

NOTE   I will skip the values starting with 1 and 3, which you'll encounter less often in apps, so that you can focus on the other three essential categories.

Different values starting with 2 are variations of messages saying that the server correctly processed the client's request. A few examples are as follows:

- *200—OK* is the most known and most straightforward of the response statuses. It just tells the client the server didn't encounter any issue when processing its request.
- *201—Created* might be used, for example, in response to a POST request to tell the client that the server managed to add the requested resource. It's not always mandatory to add such detail to the response status, and that's why 200—OK is, in general, the most used response status to identify that everything's okay.
- *204—No Content* could tell the client it shouldn't expect a response body for this response.

When an HTTP response status value starts with 4, the server tells the client something was wrong with the request. The client did something wrong when requesting a specific resource. It could be that the resource doesn't exist (the well-known 404—Not Found), or maybe some validation of the data didn't go well. Some of the most often encountered client error response statuses are as follows:

- *400—Bad Request*—A generic status often used to represent any kind of problem with the HTTP request (e.g., validation of the data or problem with reading a specific value in the request body or a request parameter).

- *401—Unauthorized*—A status value generally used to communicate to the client that the request needs authentication.
- *403—Forbidden*—A status value generally sent by the server to tell the client it's not authorized to execute its request.
- *404—Not Found*—A status value sent by the server to inform the client the requested resource doesn't exist.

When the response status starts with 5, it means something went wrong on the server side, but it's the server's issue. The client sent a valid request, but the server could not complete it for some reason. The most often used status from this category is 500—Internal Server Error. This response status is a generic error value the server sends to inform the client that an issue occurred while the backend was processing its request.

If you want to go more in-depth and learn about more status codes, this page is nice to read: https://datatracker.ietf.org/doc/html/rfc7231

Optionally, the server sends back data to the client in response through either the response headers or the response body.

C.4 The HTTP session

In this section, we discuss the HTTP session, a mechanism that allows a server to store data between multiple request-response interactions with the same client. Remember that for HTTP every request is independent of another. In other words, a request doesn't know anything about other previous, next, or simultaneous requests. A request cannot share data with order requests or access the details the backend responds for them.

However, you'll find scenarios where the server needs to correlate some requests. A good example is the cart functionality of an online shop. A user adds multiple items to their cart. To add an item to the cart, the client makes a request. To add a second item, the client makes another request. The server needs a way to know that the same client previously added an item to the same cart (figure C.3).

One way to implement such behavior is using the HTTP session. The backend assigns a unique identifier named "session ID" to a client and then associates it with a place in the app's memory. Each request the client sends after being assigned the session ID needs to contain the session ID in a request header. This way, the backend app knows to associate the specific session requests (figure C.4).

The HTTP session usually ends after a time if the client doesn't send more requests. You can configure this time, usually both in the servlet container and the app. It shouldn't be more than maybe a few hours. If the session lives too long, the server will spend a lot of memory. For most apps, a session ends after less than one hour if the client doesn't send more requests.

If the client sends another request after the session ended, the server will start a new session for that client.

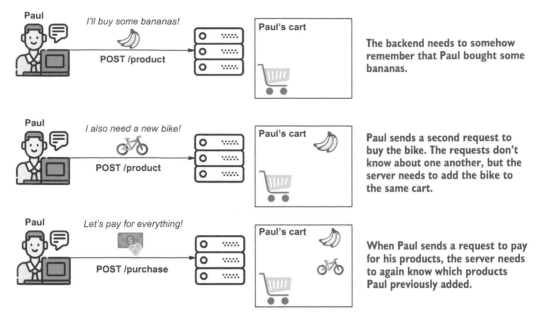

Figure C.3 For an online shop, the backend needs to identify the clients and remember the products they added to their carts. The HTTP requests are independent one from another, so the backend needs to find another way to remember the products added by each client.

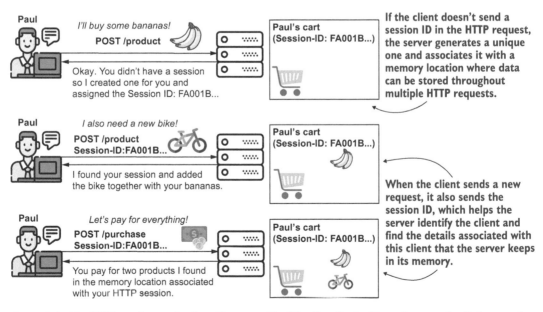

Figure C.4 The HTTP session mechanism. The server identifies the client with a unique session ID it generates. The client sends the session ID in the next requests, so the backend app knows which memory location it reserved earlier for the client.

appendix D
Using JSON formatting

In this appendix, we discuss JavaScript Object Notation (JSON). JSON is an often-used way to format the data exchanged by apps in the HTTP request and response when using REST endpoints to communicate (figure D.1). Because REST endpoints are one of the most encountered ways to establish communication between apps, and JSON is the main way to format the data exchanged, understanding and knowing how to use JSON formatting is essential.

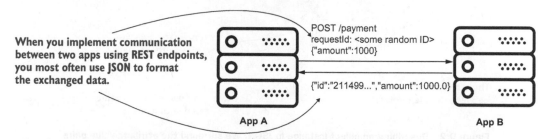

When you implement communication between two apps using REST endpoints, you most often use JSON to format the exchanged data.

POST /payment
requestId: <some random ID>
{"amount":1000}

{"id":"211499...","amount":1000.0}

App A   App B

Figure D.1   When you implement business logic, it sometimes implies establishing communication between multiple apps. Most often, you use JSON to format the data the apps exchange. To implement and test your REST endpoints, you need to understand JSON.

Fortunately, JSON is easy to understand, and it only follows a few rules. First, you need to know that what you represent with JSON are object instances using their attributes. Like in the case of a Java class, the attributes are identified with names and hold values. You may say the object Product has an attribute name and an attribute price. An instance of the Product class assigns values to the attributes. For example, the name is "chocolate" and the price is 5. If you want to represent this in JSON, you need to consider the following rules:

369

- To define an object instance in JSON, we use curly braces.
- Between the curly braces, we enumerate the attribute-value pairs, separating them with commas.
- The attribute names are written between double quotes.
- The string values are written between double quotes. (Any double quote the string contains needs to have a backslash "\" in front of it.)
- The numerical values are written without quotes.
- The attribute name and its value are separated by a colon.

Figure D.2 presents the JSON-formatted product instance with the attribute name "chocolate" and the price "5."

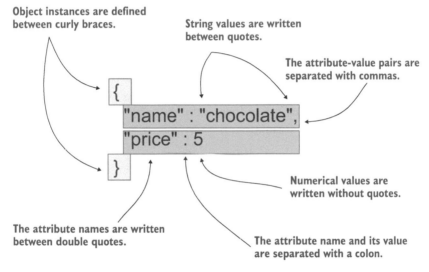

Object instances are defined between curly braces.

String values are written between quotes.

The attribute-value pairs are separated with commas.

```
{
    "name" : "chocolate",
    "price" : 5
}
```

Numerical values are written without quotes.

The attribute names are written between double quotes.

The attribute name and its value are separated with a colon.

Figure D.2   Describing an object instance in JSON. We surround the attribute-value pairs with curly braces. A colon separates the attribute name and its value. The attribute-value pairs are separated with commas.

In JSON, the object itself doesn't have a name or a type. Nowhere does it say the snippet describes a product. The object's only relevant items are its attributes. Figure D.2 details the JSON rules for describing an object.

An object might contain another object instance as the value of one of its attributes. If the `Product` has a `Pack` and the `Pack` is an object described by its attribute `color`, then a representation of a `Product` instance looks like the next snippet:

```
{
    "name" : "chocolate",
    "price" : 5,
    "pack" : {
        "color" : "blue"
    }
}
```

The value of the attribute pack is an object instance.

The same rules repeat. You can have many attributes representing other objects and nest them as many times as you need.

If you want to define a collection of objects in JSON, you use brackets, and you separate the entries with commas. The next code snippet shows you how to define a collection that contains two `Product` instances:

```
[
  {
    "name" : "chocolate",
    "price" : 5
  },
  {
    "name" : "candy",
    "price" : 3
  }
]
```

We use brackets to surround the object instances in a collection.

The instances are separated with commas.

appendix E
Installing MySQL
and creating a database

In this appendix, I will show you how to create a MySQL database. In some of the examples we implement in chapters 12 through 14, we use an external database management system (DBMS). For these examples, you'll need to create a database for your app to use prior to implementing the project.

For the database technology, you have plenty of options to choose from, like MySQL, Postgres, Oracle, MS SQL server, and so on. I encourage you to select the technology you like if you already have a preferred one. For the examples in the book, I had to choose a certain database technology, and I decided to use MySQL, which is free, lite, and easy to install on any operating system. You'll find MySQL used in general for tutorials and examples.

For learning Java and Spring, it's irrelevant which DBMS technology you use. The Java and Spring classes and methods are the same, whether you choose MySQL, Oracle, Postgres, or any other relational database technology.

The steps for creating a database for use in the examples are the following:

1 Install the DBMS on your local system; we will use MySQL.
2 Install a client application for the DBMS; we will use MySQL Workbench, which is one of the most known client apps for MySQL.
3 In the client app, connect to the local DBMS installation.
4 Create the database you want to use in the example.

Step 1: Install a DBMS on your local system

The first step is to make sure you have a DBMS to work with. The examples in this book use MySQL, but you can choose to install another DBMS if you prefer using another technology. If you choose to install MySQL, you can find the installer for download here: https://dev.mysql.com/downloads/mysql/.

Download the installer according to your operating system and follow the steps as presented in the installation guide here: https://dev.mysql.com/doc/refman/8.0/en/installing.html.

Note that during the installation of the DBMS you might be required to create an account. Remember these credentials because you'll need them in step 3.

Step 2: Install a client application for your DBMS

To work with the DBMS, you need a client app, which is used to create the database and sometimes alter its structure and validate your app. You need to install a client app according to the DBMS technology of your choice. If you work with MySQL, you can use MySQL Workbench, one of the most used MySQL clients.

Download MySQL Workbench installer according to your operating system (https://dev.mysql.com/downloads/workbench/) and install it as described in the installation manual: https://dev.mysql.com/doc/workbench/en/wb-installing.html.

Step 3: Connecting to the local DBMS

Once you install the DBMS on your local system and a client for your DBMS, you need to connect the client to the DBMS. To set up the connection, you need the credentials you configured in step 1. If the DBMS installation didn't request you set up a username and password, you could use the username "root" with an empty password.

I show you how to add the connection in MySQL Workbench. As presented in figure E.1, once you open MySQL Workbench, click the plus icon near "MySQL Connections."

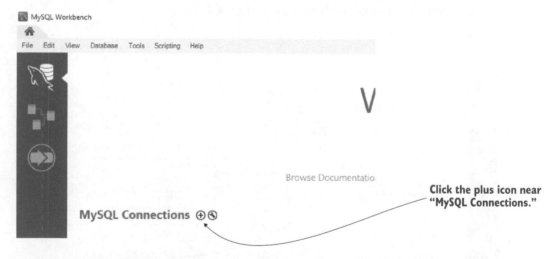

Figure E.1 Once you open MySQL Workbench, click on the plus icon near the label "MySQL Connections" to add a new connection.

A popup window appears once you click the plus button, and you have to give the connection a name and use the credentials you configured during the DMBS installation. MySQL Workbench uses these credentials to authenticate at the DBMS (figure E.2).

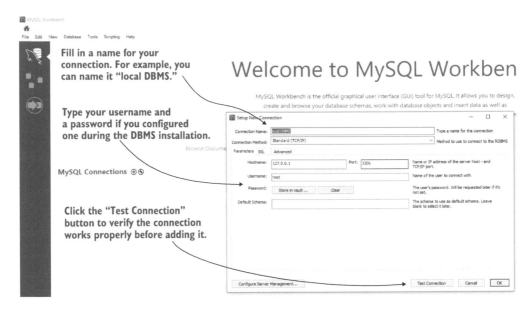

Figure E.2   Give the connection a name and fill in the credentials you configured when installing the DBMS. Then, click on the "Test Connection" button to verify that MySQL Workbench can connect to the database.

For some MySQL versions, MySQL Workbench might display a warning message. For implementing the examples in this book, this won't affect you, so click the "Continue Anyway" button if you get such a message (figure E.3).

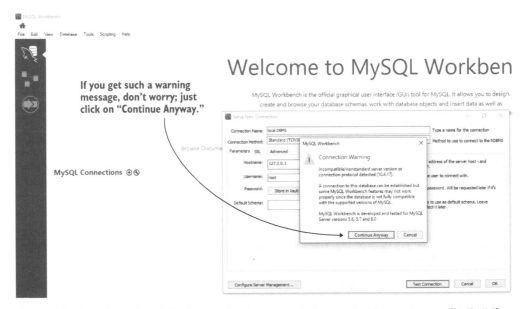

Figure E.3   Sometimes MySQL Workbench displays a warning message. This warning won't affect the way you implement the examples in the book. You can click on the "Continue Anyway" button if such a message is displayed.

If the connection details are correct and MySQL Workbench managed to connect to your local DBMS, you will see a popup like the one in figure E.4.

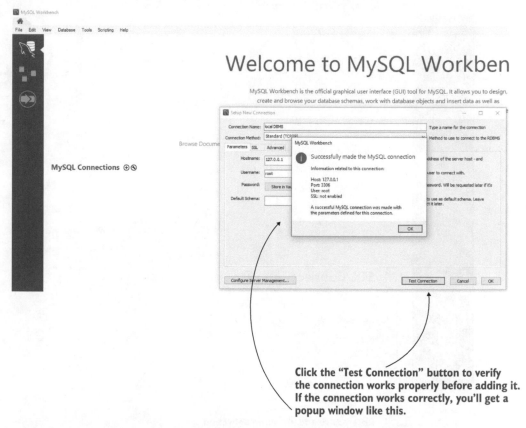

Click the "Test Connection" button to verify the connection works properly before adding it. If the connection works correctly, you'll get a popup window like this.

Figure E.4   If MySQL Workbench connected to the local DBMS, it displays a "Successfully made the MySQL connection" message in a popup dialog.

Once you click the OK button, the new connection is added, and in the MySQL Workbench home screen, you can now see it as a rectangle with the name you gave it (figure E.5).

Once you've added a new connection,
double-click on the rectangle representing it
in the home screen of MySQL Workbench.

Figure E.5   In the MySQL Workbench main screen, you can now see the connection you added. The connection is displayed as a gray rectangle, and it has the connection's name.

Step 4: Add a new database

Now that you've added a connection, it's time to use it and create a database. The examples we implement in chapters 12 through 14 use databases. You need to add a database before developing an app that uses it.

After you double click on the rectangle in the MySQL Workbench home screen that represents the connection to the local DBMS, you will see a screen like the one in figure E.6. Click on the small cylinder icon in the toolbar to add a new database.

You have to give the database a name, then click on the Apply button, as presented in figure E.7.

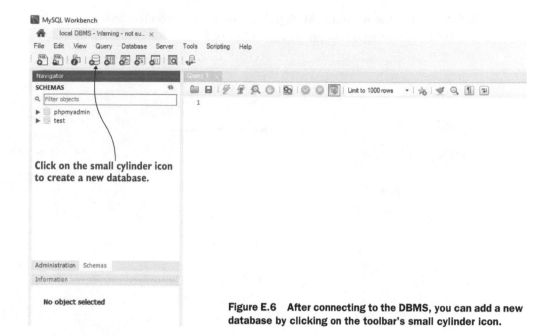

Figure E.6   After connecting to the DBMS, you can add a new database by clicking on the toolbar's small cylinder icon.

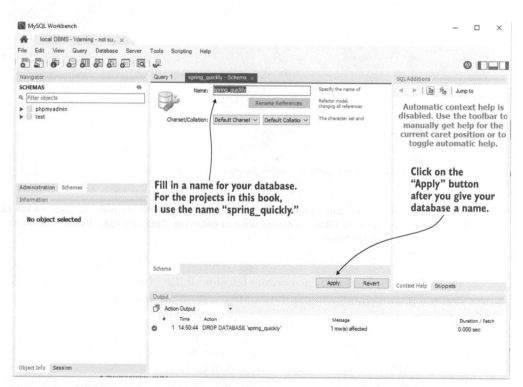

Figure E.7   Give the database a name. Our examples use "spring_quickly." Click on the Apply button to create the database.

Before adding the database, MySQL Workbench asks you to confirm once more. Click the Apply button again, as presented in figure E.8.

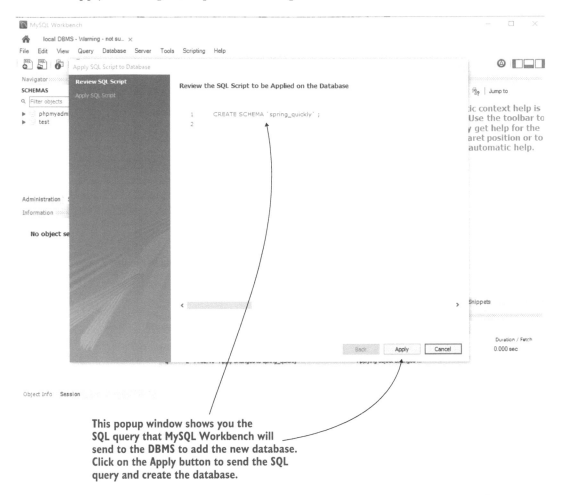

This popup window shows you the SQL query that MySQL Workbench will send to the DBMS to add the new database. Click on the Apply button to send the SQL query and create the database.

Figure E.8   You need to again confirm the creation of the database. In this screen, you also see the query MySQL Workbench sends to the DBMS to create the new database. Click the Apply button to execute the query and create the new database.

If you find your new database on the left side of the window, it means you successfully created it, and your Spring app should be able to use it as well (figure E.9).

If everything went fine, the new database
appears on the left side of the window.

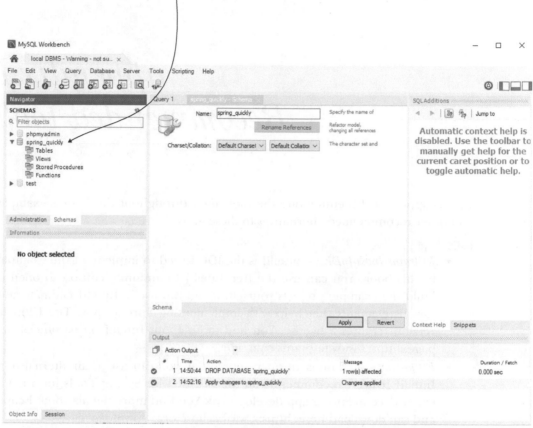

Figure E.9   The new database appears on the left side of the window. If you can see it there, it means you successfully created a new database.

appendix F
Recommended tools

In this appendix, I'll enumerate the tools used throughout the book's examples and other recommended alternatives to these tools.

IDEs

- *JetBrains IntelliJ IDEA*—IntelliJ is the IDE I used to implement the examples in this book. You can use the free IntelliJ Community edition to open or build the example projects yourself. If you can use it, IntelliJ Ultimate adds various elements that help with implementing Spring apps. The Ultimate version requires a license. You find more about IntelliJ on its official web page: https://www.jetbrains.com/idea/.
- *Eclipse IDE*—Eclipse is an open source IDE you can use as an alternative to IntelliJ IDEA. I recommend you use Eclipse with Spring Tools for a better experience in Spring app development. You find more details about Eclipse and can download here: https://www.eclipse.org/downloads/.
- *Spring Tools*—Spring Tools is a set of tools you can integrate with known open source IDEs such as Eclipse to ease the Spring app implementation. You find more about Spring Tools on its official page: https://spring.io/tools.

REST TOOLS

- *Postman*—Postman is an easy-to-use tool to test REST endpoints. You can use it to test the book's examples with apps that expose REST endpoints. However, Postman is more complex and has various other capabilities that include automation scripts and app documentation. Find out more about Postman on its web page: https://www.postman.com/.
- *cURL*—cURL is a simple command-line tool you can use to call REST endpoints. You can use it as a light alternative to Postman for testing the REST examples provided with the book. You can download cURL and find more details on how to install it here: https://curl.se/download.html.

MYSQL

- *MySQL Server*—MySQL Server is a DBMS you can easily install on your local system to test the book's examples that require a local database. You can download and find more details about MySQL Server on its web page: https://dev.mysql .com/downloads/mysql/.

- *MySQL Workbench*—MySQL Workbench is a client tool for the MySQL Server. You can use this tool to access the databases managed by the MySQL server to validate that your app works correctly with the persisted data. You can download and find more details about MySQL Workbench on the following page: https://www .mysql.com/products/workbench/.

- *SQLYog*—An alternative to MySQL Workbench is SQLYog. You can download the tool here: https://webyog.com/product/sqlyog/.

POSTGRESQL

- *PostgreSQL*—PostgreSQL is an alternative DBMS to MySQL that you can use to test the examples in the book or implement similar apps that require a database. You find more details about PostgreSQL on its web page: https://www .postgresql.org/download/.

- *pgAdmin*—pgAdmin is a tool you can use to administrate a PostgreSQL DBMS. If you chose to use PostgreSQL instead of MySQL to run an example that requires a database, you would also need pgAdmin to manage the DBMS. Discover more details about pgAdmin on the following page: https://www.pgadmin.org/.

appendix G
Recommended learning materials for further study

This appendix enumerates some excellent learning material I recommend you continue with after reading this book.

- *Spring in Action*, 6th ed., by Craig Walls (Manning, 2021). I recommend continuing your reading on Spring with this book. You will start with a refresher on what you learned in *Spring Start Here* and continue learning a variety of projects that are part of the Spring ecosystem. You'll find excellent discussions on Spring Security, asynchronous communication, Project Reactor, RSocket, and using Spring Boot's actuator.

- *Spring Security in Action* by Laurenţiu Spilcă (Manning, 2020). Securing apps is a paramount subject you need to learn right after you finish with the basics. You find a detailed discussion on using Spring Security to protect your app from different kinds of attacks by properly implementing authentication and authorization in this book.

- *Spring Boot Up and Running* by Mark Heckler (O'Reilly Media, 2021). Spring Boot is one of the most important projects in the Spring ecosystem. Most teams today use Spring Boot to ease the implementation of their Spring apps. This is also why we used Spring Boot in more than half the chapters of this book. Once you finish with the basics, I recommend you to take a deep dive into the details of Spring Boot. I found this book to be an excellent resource for a developer learning Spring.

- *Reactive Spring* by Josh Long (self-published, 2020). In my projects, using a reactive approach for implementing web apps comes with great advantages. Long discusses these advantages and demonstrates how to properly implement Spring reactive apps in this book. I recommend you read this book after reading *Spring in Action* by Craig Walls.

- *JUnit in Action* by Cătălin Tudose (Manning, 2020). As we discussed in chapter 15, it's important to test your application. In this book, we discuss the basics of testing Spring apps. But as this subject is so complex, it deserves its own book. Catalin discusses testing Java apps in detail in this book. I recommend you read this book to strengthen your knowledge of writing tests.

- *Learning SQL*, 3rd ed., by Alan Beaulieu (O'Reilly Media, 2020). In chapters 12 through 14, we discuss implementing the Spring app's persistence layer. In these chapters, I use SQL queries, assuming you already know the SQL basics. If you need a refresher on SQL, I recommend you read this book, which details all the essential SQL techniques you need to use in most apps.

- *OCP Oracle Certified Professional Java SE 11 Developer Complete Study Guide* by Jeanne Boyarsky and Scott Selikoff (Sybex, 2020). To start learning Spring, you need to apply most of the basics. But we sometimes need to refresh our knowledge even on the most fundamental syntaxes and techniques. Jeanne and Scott's book for the OCP exam preparation is the first one I use to remember the basic syntaxes, and I always read the latest edition when I prepare to upgrade my OCP certification.

- *Spring Framework playlist on my YouTube channel.* If you enjoy video tutorials and live events, you can find me on my YouTube channel (youtube.com/c/laurentiuspilca) discussing Java subjects. You find a full playlist on Spring here: http://mng.bz/yJQE. Subscribe to the channel to get notified when I post new videos or schedule new live events.

- *My blog* (laurspilca.com/blog). Aside from my YouTube channel, you'll find me writing articles on my blog. I recommend you follow the blog, where you can read different articles on Java topics.

index

385